**Provides a new narrative history of the ancient
civilization in the ancient Near East and Egypt t**

Written by an expert in the field, this book presents a narrative history of Babylon
from the time of its First Dynasty (1880–1595) until the last centuries of the
city's existence during the Hellenistic and Parthian periods (ca. 331–75 AD).
Unlike other texts on Ancient Near Eastern and Mesopotamian history, it offers
a unique focus on Babylon and Babylonia, while still providing readers with an
awareness of the interaction with other states and peoples. Organized chronologically, it places the various socio-economic and cultural developments and institutions in their historical context. The book also gives religious and intellectual
developments more respectable coverage than books that have come before it.

   A History of Babylon, 2200 BC–AD 75 teaches readers about the most important
phase in the development of Mesopotamian culture. The book offers in-depth
chapter coverage on the Sumero-Addadian Background, the rise of Babylon,
the decline of the first dynasty, Kassite ascendancy, the second dynasty of Isin,
Arameans and Chaldeans, the Assyrian century, the imperial heyday, and Babylon
under foreign rule.

- Focuses on Babylon and Babylonia
- Written by a highly regarded Assyriologist
- Part of the very successful Histories of the Ancient World series
- An excellent resource for students, instructors, and scholars

A History of Babylon, 2200 BC–AD 75 is a profound text that will be ideal for
upper-level undergraduate and graduate courses on Ancient Near Eastern and
Mesopotamian history and scholars of the subject.

Paul-Alain Beaulieu, PhD, is Professor of Assyriology at the University of
Toronto. He is the author of several articles and books on the history and culture
of Babylonia, as well as the greater spectrum of Mesopotamian history. He has
been teaching Assyriology and Ancient Near Eastern History for more than
twenty years.

Blackwell History of the Ancient World

This series provides a new narrative history of the ancient world, from the beginnings of civilization in the ancient Near East and Egypt to the fall of Constantinople. Written by experts in their fields, the books in the series offer authoritative accessible surveys for students and general readers alike.

Published

A History of Babylon

2200 BC–AD 75

Paul-Alain Beaulieu

WILEY Blackwell

This edition first published 2018
© 2018 John Wiley & Sons Ltd

The right of Paul-Alain Beaulieu to be identified as the author of this work has been asserted in accordance with law.

Registered Office(s)
John Wiley & Sons Ltd, The Atrium, Southern Gate, Chichester, West Sussex, PO19 8SQ, UK
Wiley-VCH Verlag GmbH & Co. KGaA, Boschstr. 12, 69469 Weinheim, Germany
John Wiley & Sons Singapore Pte. Ltd, 1 Fusionopolis Walk, #07-01 Solaris South Tower, Singapore 138628

Editorial Office
101 Station Landing, Medford, MA 02155, USA

For details of our global editorial offices, customer services, and more information about Wiley products visit us at www.wiley.com.

Wiley also publishes its books in a variety of electronic formats and by print-on-demand. Some content that appears in standard print versions of this book may not be available in other formats.

Library of Congress Cataloging-in-Publication Data

Names: Beaulieu, Paul-Alain, author.
Title: A history of Babylon, 2200 BC–AD 75 / by Paul-Alain Beaulieu.
Description: Hoboken, NJ : John Wiley & Sons Ltd, [2018] | Series: Blackwell history of the ancient world | Includes bibliographical references and index.
Identifiers: LCCN 2017037670 (print) | LCCN 2017052840 (ebook) | ISBN 9781119459071 (pdf) | ISBN 9781119459118 (epub) | ISBN 9781405188999 (cloth) | ISBN 9781405188982 (pbk.)
Subjects: LCSH: Babylon (Extinct city)—History.
Classification: LCC DS70.5.B3 (ebook) | LCC DS70.5.B3 B43 2018 (print) | DDC 935/.5–dc23
LC record available at https://lccn.loc.gov/2017037670

Cover Images: (Front cover) www.BibleLandPictures.com / Alamy Stock Photo; (Back cover) © OnstOn/iStockphoto
Cover Design: Wiley

Set in 10.5/12.5pt Plantin by SPi Global, Pondicherry, India

10 9 8 7 6 5 4 3 2 1

In memory of William W. Hallo (1928–2015)

Contents

List of Illustrations

List of Tables

List of Maps

Preface

The rediscovery of the civilizations of the Ancient Near East ranks as one of the greatest achievements of modern humanistic scholarship. Among these Babylon stands out like a magical name, even if only for its Biblical resonance. Numerous books have been dedicated to the Ancient Near East, investigating its literature, culture, science, history, religion, archaeology, art, material culture, and even technology, and the interested reader can easily find excellent surveys of its history and civilization, including Marc Van de Mieroop's *A History of the Ancient Near East* in the present series. And yet, histories devoted specifically to Babylon remain a rarity. One may learn with some surprise that the only book in the English language titled *A History of Babylon* was written more than a century ago: Leonard W. King, *A History of Babylon from the Foundation of the Monarchy to the Persian Conquest* (London: Chatto and Windus, 1915). It is now hopelessly outdated, although one can still read it with profit and marvel at its surprising insights. Much more recent and up-to-date is Joan Oates, *Babylon* (London: Thames and Hudson, 1979). In many respects this is an outstanding book. It pays attention to all aspects of Babylonian civilization and its legacy, with special attention to archaeology, and weaves them together in a flowing, elegant prose. In 2016 Trevor Bryce authored *Babylonia* for the Oxford Series Very Short Introductions, and the title reminds one that writing the history of Babylon is not limited to the history of a city, but encompasses that of an ancient polity, indeed, an entire civilization which flourished in southern and central Iraq in ancient times. Brief introductions similar to Bryce's have also appeared in French and German. Nevertheless, there is ample room for a new, comprehensive, and analytical approach to the history of Babylon which takes into account all the evidence and tackles the vexing problem of reconstructing the political history of an ancient, vanished civilization on the basis of written sources which, although surprisingly abundant at times, remain overall quite fragmentary. This being said, I believe that enough has survived to enable one to write a continuous narrative, a history in the very traditional use of the term, and this is the purpose of this book, which is both a general introduction and a manual, of interest as much to the lay reader as to college and graduate students, and one which brings to the forefront all the progress made in recent decades.

This book has been very long in the making and acknowledgments are in order. First and foremost my warmest thanks go to Odette Boivin, who carefully read the final draft of the manuscript, pointing out many inconsistencies and saving me at times from factual errors. She accomplished this task with remarkable stoicism while writing her doctoral dissertation on the First Dynasty of the Sealand at the University of Toronto. I am likewise indebted to my colleague Clemens Reichel who commented at length on the second chapter, and to Piotr Steinkeller who commented also on the second and on the third chapters. Many of their suggestions have been incorporated in the final version. I also thank another doctoral student of mine, Jean-Philippe Delorme, who read through the entire manuscript with his keen interest in historical issues. I am grateful to the staff of Wiley-Blackwell for their patience during the long period of gestation of this book, and for their efficiency producing it. Finally a note of gratitude goes to Stephen Batiuk who freely gave his time to draw the maps without which some of the historical narrative would be hard to follow. I have dedicated this book to the memory of William W. Hallo (1928–2015), my teacher at Yale, knowing that he would have been very proud to see his vision as historian carried on by another one of his students, and my only regret is that he did not live long enough to see it come to fruition.

List of Abbreviations

AD	Anno Domini
Babylon I	First Dynasty of Babylon
BC	Before Christ
BM	British Museum, London
CE	Common Era
ED	Early Dynastic (I, II, III, IIIa, IIIb)
IM	Iraq Museum, Baghdad
Isin I	First Dynasty of Isin
Isin II	Second Dynasty of Isin
PN	Personal Name
Sealand I	First Dynasty of the Sealand
Sealand II	Second Dynasty of the Sealand
SKL	Sumerian King List
SKL-Ur III	Sumerian King List, Ur III Version
Ur III	Third Dynasty of Ur

Author's Note

The timespan covered by this book is almost entirely before our era. Therefore, for the sake of convenience, the acronyms BC and BCE are not used unless absolutely necessary. By contrast, years in our era are marked as AD except when it is obvious. Ancient dates are abbreviated in the following order: month (Roman numeral), day (Arabic numeral), and year (e.g. V-17 means fifth month, seventeenth day, in a given year). Names in ancient languages are spelled with conventional English transliteration rather than with diacritics: thus the name of the sun-god is Shamash rather than Šamaš. Long vowels are not indicated: Nabu instead of Nabû. Names of peoples and places appear with their common English form if there is one: thus Nebuchadnezzar instead of the more accurate Nabu-kudurru-usur, Nineveh and not Ninua, and of course Babylon rather than Babilu or Babili. Words in ancient languages are in italics. When ancient textual sources are translated, passages and words that are entirely or partly illegible are given between square brackets, although these are used sparingly in order to increase legibility.

1

Introductory Concerns

The name Babylon still evokes ambivalent images. Symbol of corruption and depravity in the Judeo-Christian tradition, depicted in the Bible as arrogant imperial city, home to ruthless despots and doomed to destruction by the prophets of Israel, Babylon never fully reclaimed in the modern perception her legitimate status as one of the longest lived, and intellectually most creative civilizations of the ancient world. Indeed, if Babylon still casts its long shadow over our lives, it is not solely as epitome of moral decadence. Fundamental elements of time reckoning, such as the division of the hour into sixty minutes and the minute into sixty seconds, ultimately originate in the Babylonian sexagesimal system which used a base sixty rather than the base ten of our decimal system. The same Babylonian methods still survive in the division of the circle into 360 degrees. Many essential features of astrology, such as the practice of casting horoscopes and the division of the zodiac into twelve signs, began with the scientific and religious speculations of Babylonian astronomers. One must count as the most enduring contribution of Babylon to world civilization the development of an elaborate predictive mathematical astronomy which ranks as the earliest documented science in history. And indeed, the achievements of Babylonian scientists received ample recognition in antiquity, especially from the Greeks.

Beyond this legacy, the civilization of Babylon has emerged in a far more complex light since historians began more than a century and a half ago to study the rich epigraphic and material remains discovered in the soil of Iraq. Excavations have uncovered cities crowded with houses, temples, military compounds, and palaces. Many buildings have yielded spectacular textual finds amounting to tens of thousands of clay tablets inscribed in cuneiform, the writing system invented by the Sumerians five thousand years ago and inherited by the Babylonians. These are the sources on which we rely to reconstruct the history of Babylon. Before

A History of Babylon: 2200 BC–AD 75, First Edition. Paul-Alain Beaulieu.
© 2018 John Wiley & Sons Ltd. Published 2018 by John Wiley & Sons Ltd.

modern excavations began little information was available on the civilizations of the ancient Near East. Those civilizations had vanished almost without a trace, obliterated from the collective memory of humankind. Babylon, for instance, was known mainly from the Bible. However, if the Bible contains some genuine historical material, such as the capture of Jerusalem by Nebuchadnezzar at the beginning of the sixth century and the deportation of Judeans to Babylonia, much that it preserves ranks either as historical romance, exemplified by the saga of Babylon's fall in the Book of Daniel, or as legend, first and foremost the tale of the Tower of Babel in Genesis. Some ancient Greek writers gave accounts of Babylonian history, but these must also be handled with caution. Herodotus probably never visited Babylon, as almost everything he writes on the city has been contradicted by cuneiform sources and archaeological excavations. The material found in the writings of Ctesias, a Greek physician who spent part of his life at the Persian court, ranks even lower. Ctesias became the most influential propagator of the legend of Semiramis, the Assyrian queen whom he credits with the foundation of Babylon (Figure 1.1). There is no basis for this tale, as for almost every alleged historical fact reported by Ctesias concerning Assyria and Babylon.

Among the Greeks, however, Ptolemy stands out as an exception. Hailed as the greatest scientist of the ancient world, Ptolemy lived in Alexandria in the second century of our era. His *Almagest* summed up ancient astronomical knowledge and remained the ultimate reference on astral science and cosmology until the Renaissance. Remarkably, Ptolemy quotes in detail a number of Babylonian astronomical observations, the earliest one being an eclipse of the moon which occurred in the first year of the Babylonian king Marduk-apla-iddina II, on March 19/20, 721. He also used for astronomical dating a list of kings who reigned in Babylon from the accession of Nabonassar. Known as the Ptolemaic Canon (Canon of Ptolemy), this list formed the essential chronological backbone for ancient Near Eastern history until the modern era. Other material was preserved in the writings of Berossus, a Babylonian priest who lived at the beginning of the third century at a time when Babylonia had become a province of the Seleucid Empire. Berossus wrote in Greek a compendium on Babylonian history and culture and dedicated it to the Seleucid ruler Antiochus I (281–261). The work, entitled *Babyloniaka*, has not survived in its original form and is known from quotations found in the writings of ancient authors. Berossus recorded little information that we can consider reliable as historical facts except for the period of the Babylonian empire in the sixth century.

Thus, very little of the history of Babylon was known until the rediscovery and decipherment of cuneiform texts: a chronology from the mid-eighth century onwards with names of rulers, and scattered historical facts about the Babylonian Empire and the fate of Babylon under Persian and Greek rule. This is not much if we consider that Babylon is already mentioned in cuneiform documents from the last centuries of the third millennium and rose to prominence as dominant political and cultural center of ancient Iraq under Hammu-rabi (1792–1750). To write a history of Babylon one therefore depends almost entirely on cuneiform texts, and this is the subject to which we must now turn our attention.

Figure 1.1   Semiramis. This imaginary portrait of the Assyrian queen who allegedly built Babylon was executed about 1639–40 for a portfolio of "World Marvels" (Les Merveilles du Monde) published by the French engraver Pierre Mariette. The Semiramis legend enjoyed wide currency as fact until the decipherment of cuneiform in the modern era revealed its shaky historical foundations. *Source*: The Metropolitan Museum of Art, NYC (MMA 53.601.112), Public Domain.

1.1   Assyriology and the Writing of History

Assyriology is the academic discipline devoted to the study of the ancient civilizations of Iraq. It emerged a century and a half ago in the wake of the decipherment of cuneiform. The word originally referred to the study of Assyria, where excavations first started and initial discoveries of cuneiform texts occurred. Soon, however, digs began in the south of Iraq, revealing to the world the civilizations of Babylon and its predecessors, the Sumerians and Akkadians, but by then the term Assyriology had already become entrenched. From its inception Assyriology developed the strong philological orientation that still characterizes it today. The study of the Sumerian and Akkadian languages can absorb the energies of apprentice Assyriologists for many years, not to mention the added onus of mastering the writing system. Basically this does not seem so different from learning any other set of languages, but Assyriologists must also penetrate the world of a very distant and vanished civilization, entirely depending on the point of view of ancient scribes to do so. Therefore, Assyriology has defined itself primarily as the study of an ancient textual and intellectual tradition.

Historians rely on textual sources, but Assyriologists do not study archives neatly filed in a monastery, state ministry, or national library, accumulated through uninterrupted tradition until now. The recovery of textual sources from ancient Iraq is the direct outcome of the rise of archaeology in modern times. Cuneiform texts represent material remains of ancient human activity like every other artifact unearthed in an excavation, be it a piece of pottery, of jewelry, remnants of textiles, animal bones, or architectural structures. Analysis of the context in which cuneiform tablets are discovered provides crucial information bearing on their interpretation. It is therefore all the more deplorable that so many cuneiform tablets have come to light without proper recording of their find spots, often as the result of illicit digs. The contribution of archaeology is evidently not limited to recording the find spots of cuneiform tablets. Archaeology has long developed into an autonomous discipline which draws on a wide range of technical and scientific fields and is informed by a variety of theoretical approaches. Ancient Iraq has also left a rich visual record which tells us a story that often seems very different from the textual evidence. The interpretation of this record falls within the purview of art history. Archaeology and art history constitute separate humanistic fields but they also belong, like philology, to the auxiliary sciences of history, and all three disciplines must necessarily be integrated into historical research although no one can hope nowadays to master all of them. The present book is written from the point of view of an Assyriologist and relies mainly on the philological interpretation of cuneiform sources, but also integrates some of the findings of archaeology and art history.

1.1.1 Cuneiform Texts as Historical Sources

Interpreting cuneiform documents presents a number of challenges. The sources discussed in the present book are written for the most part in Babylonian, a branch of Akkadian, the ancient Semitic language spoken in Iraq. As the result of more than a century of philological and linguistic research, Babylonian is now surprisingly well known for an extinct language, but many uncertainties remain. Problems of vocabulary, for instance, can sometimes impede historical research. What is the precise meaning of this one word describing a technical term for irrigation? And how about that other word which refers to an institution that appears in several documents, but none of which gives us enough background information to determine its nature? Babylonian belongs to the Semitic language family, and often cognates in other Semitic languages such as Arabic, Aramaic, and Hebrew have helped determine the basic meaning of an Akkadian word. Indeed, this information played a crucial role in the decipherment of Babylonian cuneiform. But the limitations of this method are obvious. Words change meaning throughout their history, and therefore, in the absence of ancient native explanations, the semantic range of a word must ultimately be determined from the multiple contexts in which it occurs. Also, we must always remember that in Babylonia, as in all ancient civilizations, the sphere of writing was limited. Only certain people acquired literacy, mostly professional scribes, and few things were recorded in writing. Babylon, like all ancient societies, functioned mostly as an oral society, which means that knowledge and information circulated preferably in oral form rather than in writing. Texts fulfilled a basic function as aids to memory. One of the dominant characteristics of the Babylonian written legacy is the near complete absence of explanatory and analytical contents. These belonged to the oral sphere. To be sure, Babylonian scholars created a rich lexical corpus listing thousands of words with entries detailing basic facts such as spellings, synonyms, translation in Sumerian and other languages, but without providing definitions such as we find in our dictionaries and encyclopedias.

Even when words are clear, however, the information gleaned from cuneiform texts can still prove difficult to contextualize. For instance, an exchange of official letters may contain essential data, but as is always the case in epistolary exchanges, there is a considerable amount of information that is not expressed in the body of the letters because it was assumed to be common knowledge by the correspondents. To us, however, such knowledge is no matter of course and we often wish letter writers had detailed the entire context of their exchange. Other problems stem from the complexity of the cuneiform script. Cuneiform belongs typologically to logo-syllabic writing systems. Such systems still flourish today, notably Chinese and its derived scripts of East Asia. In a logo-syllabic system, each sign has multiple values and can express an entire word, a syllable, or a determinative. For example, the cuneiform sign we conventionally call GIŠ can be used either for the word *iṣu* "wood, tree," or for its syllabic values (*giš, iṣ, eṣ, is, es, iz, ez*), in which cases the values are purely phonetic and do not carry the meaning "wood" or "tree." In addition, GIŠ belongs to a restricted group of signs which can also serve as determinatives, signs which precede or follow a word to indicate its semantic class. When it fulfills this role, GIŠ precedes names of trees and wooden objects. The cuneiform script includes hundreds of signs with multiple values, and requires several years of study before one can confidently read a cuneiform text.

The cuneiform script displays a highly abstract appearance; each sign being composed of a number of wedges with horizontal, vertical, and diagonal orientation, with the addition of a small triangular sign impressed with the top of the stylus and conventionally called the *Winkelhaken*. The name cuneiform means "wedge-shaped, nail-shaped" and derives from Latin *cuneus* "wedge." Clay tablets were molded into shape probably by an assistant, and while the clay was still wet the scribe impressed the signs on the tablet with a sharpened reed stylus. A cuneiform tablet characteristically displays the outward appearance of a piece of terracotta covered with a network of short strokes and small triangles, with many signs having a similar look. On the whole the cuneiform writing system, except for the earlier periods of its development, poses no major quandary for Assyriologists. However, some difficulties may arise if the document is sloppily written or not well preserved. Indeed, many clay tablets have come to us in a damaged state, with erosion of the surface or chunks missing. In such cases the script can be hard to read, and sometimes Assyriologists scrutinizing the same damaged surface will come up with different results. Missing pieces present a particular challenge because part of the text is lost and must be restored from parallels or plausible guesses as to what should have been present in the gap. If the damaged or missing portion belongs to the crucial section of a text that has great historical relevance, such as a list of kings, a chronicle, or a royal letter addressed to an official, this can lead to repeated collations of the text and the publication of conflicting theories about the lost passage.

While clay tablets make up our main documentary source for the history of Babylon, we must not lose sight of the fact that they did not constitute the sole medium for cuneiform writing. Cuneiform is found on other clay artifacts such as cylinders and barrel-shaped objects which were generally preferred for building inscriptions. Stone monuments of various shapes also bear cuneiform inscriptions, notably the famous Law Code of Hammu-rabi inscribed on a black basalt stele preserved in the Louvre. We know that small wooden or ivory boards filled with wax were widely used for writing as well. Wooden boards have nearly all perished but one damaged set dating from the eighth century and inscribed with astrological omens has survived; it was found in a well in the Assyrian city of Nimrud (ancient Kalhu). The use of writing boards for scholarly texts is amply documented; we know they made up a substantial portion of the library amassed by the Assyrian king Ashurbanipal in his capital Nineveh in the seventh century. Writing boards were also used in the administration of large compounds such as temples. Clay tablets had to be inscribed relatively fast before they dried out and became unusable as writing surface. Wax, on the other hand, could be softened again at will, making writing boards an ideal support for texts which needed periodical update such as inventories and running accounts. Unfortunately, all this documentation has vanished.

1.1.1.1   Archival texts

Cuneiform texts from ancient Babylonia are mostly of a practical nature. These may be categorized as archival, in that they record the day to day running of an administration, private business, or household unit, and were filed temporarily to be discarded later, when their relevance to the conduct of affairs had ceased. Among these archives we find a broad typological distribution of administrative texts (accounts, memoranda, inventories, receipts, disbursements, lists of expenditures), legal documents (bills of sale, exchange, real estate transactions, marriage contracts, wills, promissory notes, loans, business partnership agreements, court decisions), as well as private and official letters. Except letters, archival documents are usually dated, which considerably enhances their value as historical source. The quantity of archival documents from the ancient Near East is unparalleled in the ancient world. A rough estimate of cuneiform tablets and fragments discovered in the past two centuries may easily reach half a million, of which the archival documentation from Babylonia forms the larger part. Archives are particularly rich during the time of Babylon's rise to political leadership under its First Dynasty (1880–1595), and for the era covering the century of Assyrian hegemony (731–626), the Babylonian empire (625–539), and the first decades of Persian rule (538–485).

Cuneiform archives that have survived to this day owe it to exceptional circumstances. Archives sometimes survived because the building which housed them suffered sudden destruction, with no immediate reoccupation. The tablets lay in the destruction level under accumulations of debris until their rediscovery in modern times. In a situation involving violent destruction, the fire could bake the tablets into ceramic, enhancing their durability. In other cases documents have come down to us because their owners saved them in containers or storage rooms where their existence was forgotten. Parts of archives also survived because they were recycled as fill in the foundations of buildings. However, most archival documents are lost to us; they were simply destroyed in ancient times during periodic clean-ups of storage rooms. The term archive is therefore misleading, because ancient Near Eastern societies rarely maintained archives over long periods of time, carefully filed for later reference.

In order to use archival documents as historical source, we must evaluate the contents of the entire archive and what it represents in relation to the administration or private household that generated it. Often the absence of specific documents will be as revealing as their presence. A family archive that would include only loans, promissory notes, a few letters, and a handful of business partnership agreements, all spread over a period of thirty years, would immediately be recognized as a group of documents discarded by its owners, not as the main archive. Indeed, we would normally expect the main archive not only to cover a longer period of time, but also to include perennial documents such as sales, gifts, real estate transactions, and marriage contracts. Such family archives do exist, notably the archive of the Egibi from Babylon, spread over five generations between 606 and 484. Archives that are found more or less in the form they were left in before a sudden interruption of activities are called "living archives," while collections of documents that were discarded in ancient times receive the label "dead archives."

The royal archives of Mari constitute one of the most spectacular archaeological discoveries from the ancient Near East. The powerful city of Mari, located in Syria on the Euphrates near the border with Iraq, was captured by the armies of the Babylonian king Hammu-rabi in 1761 and its royal palace sacked and later destroyed. French excavators discovered in the palace more than 20,000 cuneiform tablets, including a few thousand letters belonging to the official and private correspondence of the kings of Mari. The texts cover about fifty years, but the bulk of them dates to a period of twenty years corresponding to the last part of the reign of Yasmah-Addu and the whole reign of Zimri-Lim, the last king of Mari. The documents which cover these last twenty years, up to the conquest by Hammu-rabi, make up the living archive. A clean-up of the storage rooms probably occurred under Zimri-Lim, when they disposed of most documents except records of the current reign and part of the preceding reign. Whatever earlier documents survived belonged to smaller batches that had become dead archives, used as fill under the floors or forgotten in storage. Initially, the contents of the diplomatic correspondence of Zimri-Lim perplexed researchers because it contained mostly letters back and forth with unimportant kingdoms north of Mari, whereas almost nothing seemed to have survived of the epistolary exchanges between Mari and such important cities as Babylon and Aleppo, the two leading powers of the Near East at that time. However, it was realized later that all such correspondence must have been removed from the palace after its capture and taken to Babylon. Indeed, we know that Babylonian scribes sorted through the archive after the fall of Mari, because clay tags originally attached to tablet containers were found in the palace inscribed with the formulas "tablets of the servants of Zimri-Lim" and "tablets of the servants of Samsi-Addu" (the father of Yasmah-Addu). One tag was found at the gate of the palace where it had probably fallen when Babylonian soldiers left with the containers. Thus, while historians may lament the loss of a crucial source, having identified the reason for the absence of these letters also constitutes an important historical fact. It demonstrates the care with which ancient chanceries handled critical diplomatic information. This work of sorting documents and reflecting on the configuration of an ancient archive may seem painstaking, yet it is essential. Archival texts constitute an exceptional source, providing a wealth of first hand information on the history, society, law, economy, and material culture of the ancient Near East.

1.1.1.2   Royal inscriptions

Royal inscriptions form the second type of historical source. These inscriptions were sometimes carved on larger monuments such as stone steles, and therefore the label "monumental texts" has also been applied to them. Most royal inscriptions belong to the genre of building inscriptions, official texts commemorating the construction or repair of various buildings and public works, temples being by far the most frequent recipients of royal benefactions. In Assyria building inscriptions developed into the genre of Annals in which the king, taking as pretext the dedication of a building, detailed his personal achievements in chronological sequence, chiefly in the military sphere. This specifically Assyrian genre provides the historian with crucial information in spite of the bias inherent to such kind of self-generated and self-centered narration. The Assyrians became a major factor in the history of Babylon in the late second and first millennia, and their royal Annals constitute an important source for those periods.

Babylonian royal inscriptions also exhibit a high level of egocentric boasting. However, cultural and religious reasons dictated a far greater restraint in the report of military achievements and a more pronounced emphasis on the moral qualities of the ruler, his piety, humility in the presence of the gods, care for his subjects, and ritual scrupulousness. The result seems more disappointing for the historian. On the other hand, the inscriptions of Babylonian kings constitute a valuable source for the study of religion and culture. The corpus is particularly rich for the reigns of Hammu-rabi (1792–1750) and Samsu-iluna (1749–1712), which correspond to the apex of Babylonian power under the First Dynasty. In the ensuing period of Kassite rule (1595–1155) royal inscriptions revert to a terse style recalling Sumerian inscriptions of the third millennium. After the end of Kassite rule sources become very sparse until the mid-eighth century, and from this long period only a handful of royal inscriptions have survived. The century of Assyrian hegemony (744–626) saw a major increase in the building activities of the monarchy, reflected in a number of very elaborate inscriptions often commissioned by the Assyrian kings themselves.

The genre of building inscriptions reached its zenith at the time of the Babylonian empire (625–539), a period of intense architectural activity. The inscriptions of Nebuchadnezzar II (604–562) represent the largest corpus in that genre for the entire history of Babylon. Building inscriptions of this era emulate earlier models but also innovate in some areas; sometimes they also mention the discovery of inscribed foundation deposits of earlier rulers. They report, for instance, on the discovery of inscriptions of the Old Akkadian rulers Sargon and Naram-Sin, of the Neo-Sumerian kings Ur-Namma and Shulgi, of Hammu-rabi, and of the Kassite kings Burna-Buriash and Shagarakti-Shuriash. The last king of Babylon, Nabonidus (555–539), even provides chronological estimates for these rulers, sometimes with errors in the range of several centuries. He claims that Hammu-rabi reigned 700 years before Burna-Buriash, and that the distance between his own reign and that of Shagarakti-Shuriash was 800 years, and as many as 3,200 years back to the time of Naram-Sin (Figure 9.4). Such statements, though usually incorrect, testify to a greater interest in historical and chronological data in the later phases of the history of Babylon, even as the city lost its political power with the Persian conquest of 539. Afterwards foreign rulers abandoned the practice of royal inscriptions for Babylonia, the only two exceptions being Cyrus the Great (reigned 538–530 as king of Babylon) and the Seleucid ruler Antiochus I (281–261).

1.1.1.3 Scholarly texts

The third category of cuneiform source with historical data are scholarly texts. Under this label we include all texts other than royal inscriptions that were meant for transmission to later generations, such as literature, science, divination, lexicography, rituals, magic, religious and theological texts. Because of its apparent perennial nature this corpus is often labeled as the "stream of tradition," and the invariability of certain compositions through time has also earned it the brand "canonical." Such designations certainly reflect important facets of the corpus, but may at the same time create the misleading impression of a monotonous flow of static works endowed with an eternal life of its own, almost impervious to the influence of the surrounding society. In fact, scribes and scholars never ceased to create new texts and even entirely new genres. Regional variations also often prevailed in the configuration of an accepted corpus. In certain periods many texts ceased to be copied and disappeared from the official cultural memory, while others were modified, abridged, expanded, or edited.

A number of scholarly texts can be considered strictly historical because they consist essentially of narratives about the past. As all ancient societies, the Babylonians produced historical epics and literary narratives portraying their rulers as heroes and paragons of wisdom. Such texts must be approached critically, all the more so when a composition is attested in a period that is very distant from the events it reports. We will return to this important question below. In the course of time Babylonian scribes also produced a substantial corpus of chronographic documents which include King Lists, Astronomical Diaries, Chronicles, and Lists of Year Names.

1.1.1.3.1   King lists

King lists supply the basic chronographic scheme. It is therefore important to discuss them in some detail. In addition to the Ptolemaic Canon, which is preserved in Greek, several cuneiform king lists contain data that are relevant and for the most part reliable. For the history of Babylon, the most important such documents are:

King List A: this text is known from a single Neo-Babylonian manuscript preserved in the British Museum (BM 33332). In its complete form, King List A contained the names of all the kings of Babylon from the beginning of the First Dynasty in the early nineteenth century until at least the rise of the Babylonian empire at the end of the seventh century. The beginning and end of the text are lost and the surface is worn. The list groups the kings into dynasties, called *palû* in Babylonian, and provides the length of each reign. It remains to this day the most important chronographic document for the history of Babylon.

King List B: this smaller list, also in the British Museum (BM 38122), records the names of the kings of the first two Babylonian dynasties (1894–1475), adding lengths of reigns only for the First Dynasty. The document dates from the Neo-Babylonian period and labels the two dynasties as *palû*.

King List C: this document lists the first seven rulers of the Second Dynasty of Isin (1153–1065) with the lengths of their reigns. The manuscript is Neo-Babylonian, although probably a copy of an original dating shortly after the last king mentioned in the list.

Synchronistic King List: this list is so named because it runs parallel lists of kings who reigned in Assyria and Babylonia, proposing synchronisms between them. The list comes from Assur and dates to the seventh century, ending with Ashurbanipal and Kandalanu. The synchronisms it proposes are often erroneous, especially for the earlier parts of the list. Nevertheless each of the two lists taken independently generally agrees with other chronographic material as to the names of rulers and their order of succession.

King List 14: this is a fragment of a synchronistic list quite different in format from the previous one. It is important because it preserves the names of some poorly attested Babylonian rulers of the first millennium.

Uruk King List: this list came to light during the German excavations at Uruk and is now in the Iraq Museum (IM 65066). The top and bottom parts of the tablet are lost. The preserved section includes kings with lengths of their reigns from Kandalanu (647–627) to the Persian king Darius I (522–486), and after a gap continues from Darius III (335–331) down to the Seleucid ruler Seleucus II Callinicus (246–226). There is no division into dynasties.

King List of the Hellenistic Period: this tablet is preserved in the British Museum (BM 35603) and almost certainly comes from Babylon. It mentions kings with the lengths of their reigns beginning with Alexander the Great and going at least as late as the Seleucid ruler Antiochus IV Epiphanes (175–164). The text also supplies the filiations of kings and short notes concerning their deaths, but does not arrange them into dynasties.

King List A expresses a key concept of Babylonian historiography; this concept is denoted by the Babylonian word *palû*, loosely translated as "dynasty." The term came into Babylonian as loanword from Sumerian *bala*, which means "to rotate, to turn over" and in third millennium Sumerian texts also denotes "term of duty" and "turn of office." From example, the kings of the Third Dynasty of Ur, who ruled Babylonia from 2112 to 2004, enforced a redistributive system called the *bala*, by which a select number of provincial cities were obligated in turn to provide goods and services to the state. As we will see later, Babylon belonged to that group of cities. More important, the term *bala* also acquired the meaning "reign" (of an individual king or a ruling house) and eventually entered the sphere of chronographic writing. The Lamentation over the Destruction of Sumer and Ur, a Sumerian literary composition which bemoans the collapse of the Third Dynasty of Ur and the sack of its capital at the end of the third millennium, reflects on the conclusion of the city's hegemony in the following terms:

> Ur was granted kingship, but it was not granted an eternal reign (*bala*); from time immemorial, since the land was founded, until the population multiplied, who has ever seen a reign (*bala*) of kingship that would forever take precedence?[1]

The same philosophy is reflected in the Sumerian King List (SKL), in which every city in turn exerts hegemony over Sumer and Akkad (i.e. Babylonia). Some manuscripts of the List refer to these periods of hegemonies as the *bala* of a city. The later Babylonian historiography borrowed the concept and applied it to the succession of kings and royal houses recognized in Babylon.

The Sumerian term *bala* and its Babylonian form *palû* mirror a concept of time and history that is cyclical rather than linear. All ancient civilizations share this rotating view of historical time which appears to deny the possibility of change and progress. New kings and dynasties merely repeat patterns established

Table 1.1   The Ten Babylonian Dynasties

I	First Dynasty of Babylon	1880–1595
II	First Dynasty of the Sealand	1732–1475
III	Kassite Dynasty	1594–1155
IV	Second Dynasty of Isin	1153–1022
V	Second Dynasty of the Sealand	1025–1005
VI	Dynasty of Bazi	1004–985
VII	Elamite Dynasty	984–979
VIII	Dynasty of E	978–732
IX	Ninth Dynasty of Babylon	731–626
X	Neo-Babylonian Dynasty	625–539

in primeval times by gods and civilizing heroes. Indeed, their political ideal is to emulate them. The periodization of Babylonian history into *palûs* appears to have been largely abandoned after the seventh century. The later king lists, such as the Uruk King List and the King List from the Hellenistic Period, proceed from the basic assumption of a continuous succession of rulers. The change must probably be attributed to the rise of linear concepts of time during the second half of the first millennium, culminating in the adoption of dating according to the Seleucid Era at the end of the third century.

If we take King Lists A and B as matrix and fill their textual gaps with the data culled from other king lists and chronographic texts, we arrive at the division of the history of Babylon into ten dynasties (Table 1.1).

These names derive partly from modern conventions and do not always reflect ancient usage. For example, the First Dynasty of Babylon is never called by this name in ancient sources; King List B simply calls it *palê Babili* "Dynasty of Babylon." The name for the First Dynasty of the Sealand in King Lists A and B is *palê Urukug* "Dynasty of Urukug," presumably after its place of origin, but other sources refer to some of its individual rulers as "king of the Sealand" and therefore the term has been applied to the entire dynasty. The label "First" was added by modern historians to differentiate it from the Second Dynasty of the Sealand, called *palê tamti* in King List A. The entry naming the third dynasty in King List A is lost. However, another source refers to that historical era as *palê Kasshi* "Dynasty of the Kassites." King List A lists the Second Dynasty of Isin as *palê Ishin* "Dynasty of Isin," probably its city of origin, but it is necessary to number it as "Second" in order to differentiate it from the First Dynasty of Isin, which ruled Babylonia for about a century between the collapse of the Third Dynasty of Ur in 2004 and the beginnings of Babylon as independent polity after 1880.

The eighth and ninth dynasties form the most problematic groups. The era of the Dynasty of E (*palê* E) emerges from contemporary sources as one of relative political instability. The term "E" itself seems obscure. The most likely hypothesis views it as a reference to Babylon, as the sign E followed by the determinative KI for geographic names is a frequent designation of the city in cuneiform texts of the first millennium. The Dynasty of E included in fact several separate groups of rulers, a fact which is recognized in another important work of Babylonian historiography, the Dynastic Chronicle, which breaks it up into smaller dynasties. The Ninth Dynasty also formed a grab bag of independent rulers since King List A attaches separate labels for dynasties to many of its rulers. Most historians have in fact dropped the designations Dynasty of E and Ninth Dynasty of Babylon altogether. It still seems preferable, however, to adhere to the tradition of King List A because the manuscript of the list clearly separates the two groups by the same horizontal rulings dividing the previous rulers into dynasties. Finally, the designation *palû* for the Neo-Babylonian Dynasty never occurs in our sources. This is because these rulers appear in king lists created during the Hellenistic period, when that chronographic genre abandoned the concept of *palû*. Historians often refer to this dynasty as the Chaldean Dynasty, after its presumed ethnic origin. The term Neo-Babylonian Dynasty is also a modern creation and never occurs in ancient sources.

Although ancient scribes assumed that these dynasties all ruled in succession in Babylon, we know that the First Dynasty of the Sealand overlapped partly with the First Dynasty of Babylon and the Kassite Dynasty. Indeed, southern Babylonia seceded at the end of the eighteenth century to form a separate polity ruled by the First Dynasty of the Sealand (Sealand is an ancient name for the southernmost part of Iraq, bordering on the Persian Gulf). After the end of the First Dynasty our sources become very sparse for a period of uncertain length during which the rulers of the Sealand and the Kassites competed for power. The contest ended in the fifteenth century when the Kassites eliminated the Sealand dynasts and reunified Babylonia under their rule. The dates given here for the First Dynasty of the Sealand and the beginning of the Kassite Dynasty are uncertain.

It would be erroneous to view Babylonian dynasties as ancient equivalents of the Valois and Bourbon dynasties of France, or the Tudor in England. Agnatic succession was not the sole legitimate means of acceding to the throne in Babylon. While the First Dynasty fits the traditional understanding of a dynasty, our sources record numerous usurpations and changes of ruling families within each *palû*. The *palû*s of the first millennium do not even form dynasties at all, even in the loosest understanding of the term. We must understand the term dynasty more as a cycle, or as an era characterized by the hegemony of an ethnic or tribal group (the Kassites), a city (Babylon, Isin), or a region (Sealand). However, regardless of the origin of a *palû*, it is probable, yet not assured, that all the kings recorded in the Babylonian King Lists were believed in ancient times to have ruled in Babylon, forming a continuous line of rulers.

Babylonian King Lists are not free of the usual errors that pepper ancient manuscript traditions. The data from King Lists A and B are sometimes at variance with more dependable sources; the names of some kings are misspelled, and the lengths of reigns at times slightly incorrect. On the main points, however, the data from king lists are substantiated by external sources, and we must therefore take their view of Babylonian history seriously. A recent epigraphic discovery has in fact enhanced their status. Until a few years ago the First Dynasty of the Sealand was documented by only a couple of oblique references outside king lists,

Table 1.2 Babylon under Foreign Rule

XI	Achaemenid (Persian) Dynasty	538–331
XII	Argead (Macedonian) Dynasty	330–307
XIII	Seleucid (Macedonian) Dynasty	305–141
XIV	Arsacid (Parthian) Dynasty	141 BC–AD 224

to the point that some historians even questioned the existence of some of its rulers whose names ring like artificial Sumerian expressions, typical of philological speculations of later Babylonian scholars and unlikely to have been borne by real people. A few years ago, however, such doubts evaporated subsequent to the publication of archival texts bearing dating formulas of two of these rulers with abstruse names, Peshgaldaramesh and Ayadaragalamma. Thus, a dynasty known almost exclusively from later king lists has now emerged as truly historical. This should remind us that, if ancient traditions should always be handled critically, they must never be dismissed lightly.

The history of Babylon did not conclude with the loss of political independence. Later king lists, such as the Uruk King List, the King List of the Hellenistic Period, and also the first portion of the Ptolemaic Canon, simply record in succession all rulers recognized in Babylon, native or foreign, acknowledging no particular break in the Persian conquest of 539. Persian rulers from Cyrus the Great (538–530) to Xerxes (485–465) still claimed the title of "king of Babylon." The Seleucid monarchs of the Hellenistic period considered Babylonia a core area of their empire, and one with which they often interacted even on a personal level. We can therefore supplement the ten Babylonian *palûs* with the four dynasties that ruled Babylon as a regional center of their empire. The list must end with the Arsacid Dynasty, as Babylonian civilization became extinct in the first two centuries of our era, with the cuneiform writing system falling into disuse and Babylonian temples being destroyed or abandoned (Table 1.2).

Another periodization of the history of Babylon which is often encountered is the division into three cultural eras: Old Babylonian (2004–1595), Middle Babylonian (1595–1000), and Neo-Babylonian (after 1000). The same division also applies to the three stages of the Babylonian language, with another phase called Late Babylonian after 626. Babylonian historiographers did not recognize this periodization.

As Babylon did not end abruptly in 539, it did not come into existence suddenly in 1880. Textual evidence shows that Babylon existed long before that date as provincial town under successive lines of Sumerian and Akkadian rulers. The history of Iraq in the third millennium is not well known because of the scarcity of contemporary sources and the vagueness of later, native traditions. The situation is particularly acute when we reach the remotest periods, before the rise of the Sargonic dynasty in the twenty-fourth century. Table 1.3 provides a general chronology for this formative period when Babylon evolved within the framework of Sumero-Akkadian civilization.

Table 1.3 Babylon under Sumerian and Akkadian rule

Early Dynastic III Period	2600–2335
Sargonic (Old Akkadian) Dynasty	2334–2154
Third Dynasty of Ur	2112–2004
First Dynasty of Isin	2017–1794

1.1.1.3.2 Astronomical Diaries

The so-called Astronomical Diaries are also useful to the historian. They compile daily astronomical observations, mainly eclipses and the position of the moon and planets as well as meteorological phenomena. They also record market prices for basic commodities such as barley, dates, sesame, and wool; and contain occasional notes on political and historical events as well as occurrences of omens. For example, the Diaries for the year 331 report on the triumphal entrance of Alexander the Great into Babylon one month after his decisive victory at Gaugamela against Darius III. The Diaries come from Babylon and most of the information they record is centered on the capital. The two earliest preserved Diaries date to the years 652 and 568, and a handful cover the early Persian period. However, the majority dates between the fourth and second centuries, and a smaller number to the early part of the first century down to the year 60–59. Most scholars agree that the Diaries began with the reign of Nabonassar in 747. In a sense they represent the ancient historian's dream come true, recording data that are reliable and securely anchored in an absolute chronology, even if the sum of really crucial information preserved in the extant Diaries is not extensive. Some entries are introduced by the verb *alteme* "I heard that," reminding us that in the ancient world almost all information circulated orally.

1.1.1.3.3 Chronicles

Chronicles form the third genre of chronographic source for the history of Babylon. A chronicle can be defined as a chronologically ordered account of history written from the perspective of an observer rather than participant. In this respect chronicles differ fundamentally from royal inscriptions and annals which highlight the monarchical ego as maker of history. These are composed usually in the first person, chronicles in the third. Many cuneiform chronicles have been recovered, and they vary widely in terms of historical reliability. Although some chronicles were produced in Assyria, the genre is more typical of Babylonia. Most Babylonian chronicles were produced in two specific periods and places: Borsippa in the middle of the sixth century and Babylon during the Hellenistic period. The systematic compiling of chronicles in Babylonia was in fact a late phenomenon, a conclusion which seems inescapable if we look at the Borsippa production. Chronicles of the Babylonian empire of the sixth century are roughly contemporary with the scribes who compiled them; they record continuous, year by year information with specific dates for events. Chronicles which deal with the seventh century still give precise chronological data, with years of reign, months and even days when events occurred. However, these events can be separated by gaps of several years. On the other hand, chronicles dealing with events prior to the seventh century tend to record information that is increasingly patchy as we recede back in time; precise chronological data are usually lacking and events are recorded as having occurred "in the time" of a given king. Therefore it seems unlikely that the Borsippa Chronicles are copies of older manuscripts. Rather, they were mostly created in the sixth century using whatever sources at hand. This explains why recent events are better documented. The chronicles of the Hellenistic period form a distinct group which is close in formulation and thematic interest to the Astronomical Diaries. In this book chronicles will be referenced mostly by numbers according to the recent edition by J.-J. Glassner, *Mesopotamian Chronicles* (Atlanta, GA: 2004). A table of chronicles is provided in the Appendix.

One chronicle deserves particular attention: the Dynastic Chronicle. This chronicle, preserved in a fragmentary state, ranks as one of the most ambitious chronographic document produced in Babylon. In its complete state, it probably offered nothing less than a survey of Babylonian history from the creation of the world until the heyday of imperial Babylon in the seventh and six centuries. It is known from two seventh-century manuscripts from the Library of Ashurbanipal and two more from Neo-Babylonian libraries. The two Neo-Babylonian manuscripts are intra-linear bilinguals, with one line in the Sumerian language followed by another line giving the translation in Babylonian. The Sumerian language lent an aura of great antiquity to the composition, which in fact largely borrows its material from SKL for the third millennium, and also from the Eridu Genesis (another Sumerian literary composition) for the opening section dealing with primeval history. Indeed, the narrative begins when the gods ordained the plans of heaven and earth and bestowed on humankind the institution of kingship. For the part dealing specifically with Babylon the Dynastic Chronicle appears to agree with King Lists A and B, except that it breaks the Dynasty of E into smaller dynasties. The Dynastic Chronicle entirely revolves around the concept of *palû*, which it applies retroactively even to the antediluvian period, when mythical rulers reigned for tens of thousands of years. Berossus may have drawn some of his inspiration and source material from the Dynastic Chronicle for the composition of his *Babyloniaka*.

1.1.1.3.4   Year names and date lists

In the second half of the third millennium a new method of dating appeared in Iraq: year names. Until the end of the Early Dynastic III period, scribes dated documents computing the years of a ruler with numbers. The method is well documented in the kingdom of Lagash, where we find such dates as "Lugalanda, prince of Lagash, (year) 2" and "Urukagina, king of Lagash, (year) 1." The Old Akkadian (Sargonic) dynasty generalized the system of year names, which consisted of christening new years with a formula referring to a recent or ongoing event. For example, we find in archival documents from the reign of Sargon of Agade (2334–2279) and his grandson Naram-Sin (2254–2218) such year names as "the year Sargon went to Shimurrum," "the year Naram-Sin laid the foundations of the temple of the god Enlil in Nippur and of the temple of the goddess Ishtar in Zabalam," and "the year Naram-Sin was victorious over Shimurrum at Kirasheniwe and captured Baba, governor of Shimurrum, and Dubul, governor of Arame."Year names contain no indication of their placement within a reign, so ancient scribes compiled lists of year names (date lists) to classify dated documents in chronological order. Many such date lists have been recovered and they constitute the fourth class of chronographic document from Babylonia. They represent a priceless source for the historian, especially in cases where year names record events of particular historical significance. One must be careful of course not to confuse the year name with the year of the event, which in most cases took place in the preceding year. Thus, the thirty-third year of Hammu-rabi, which corresponds to the year 1760, is named after the conquest of Mari. That event, however, occurred in the year 1761, during the thirty-second year of Hammu-rabi. The practice of year names was abandoned during the Kassite Dynasty, when dating by year numbers of the current ruler came back into fashion. From that period on, year numbers remained in use until the institution of the Seleucid Era at the end of the fourth century. Date lists may have provided the basic chronological material for king lists. Unlike other chronographic documents, however, their status as scholarly texts is open to debate. Many date lists continued to be copied after they had lost any practical value, but transmission of these lists stopped after the middle of the second millennium.

1.2 Historical Science and the Handling of Sources

Historical science recognizes a broad division of sources into primary and secondary. Because all cuneiform tablets were discovered in excavations and provide first hand information on the ancient Near East, Assyriologists tend to treat them all as primary sources, but this creates a lot of confusion. A primary source is a source that was created during the period that is being studied by the historian. A secondary source is a later interpretation of the events of a period, often on the basis of primary sources which may no longer be available to us. Historical research relies preferably on primary sources. Secondary sources belong to the study of historiography, namely the writing of history and how perceptions of the past evolved within a given society. This must not create the impression that primary sources necessarily reflect the objective truth. Even the most trite and dispassionate archival document mirrors the point of view of the administration that produced it. What counts is that the point of view reflected in primary sources is at least contemporary with the period under study and not a later understanding by individuals with no immediate knowledge and experience of it. The greatest pitfall of historical research is presentism, the anachronistic rewriting of the past in accordance with the ideas and sensibilities of the present time. Presentism has flourished in all ages. Ancient secondary sources abound in reinventions of history, some deliberate, others more accidental but no less misleading.

Archival cuneiform texts fall squarely within the category of primary sources. Royal inscriptions, for all their bias, also rank as primary sources. Problems arise mainly with the third category, scholarly texts. Some literary compositions give accounts of history which appear entirely fictional and thus can claim no value as primary sources. One such composition is the Letter of Samsu-iluna studied by apprentice scribes in Neo-Babylonian schools. Allegedly addressed by the Babylonian king Samsu-iluna to an official named Enlil-nadin-shumi, the letter accuses the priesthood of Babylonia of sacrilegious behavior and threatens them with the direst punishment, including roasting in an oven; the text even contains instructions to inscribe the encyclical admonition on steles. Basic common sense suggests the letter is apocryphal, and it would be naive to search through primary sources from the reign of Samsu-iluna hoping to find corroboration of this imaginary episode, evidently created for the edification of junior scribes and instilling in them obedience to the monarchy. In typical presentist fashion, the depiction of the royal figure in the text fits the political climate of the Babylonian empire in the sixth century, not that of the First Dynasty of Babylon one millennium earlier. Not all literary texts with historical content can be so easily dismissed, however, especially if they were composed not long after the events they describe. A case in point is the Verse Account of Nabonidus, a pamphlet written to vilify the rule of the last king of Babylon. Even though the text is highly tendentious and the single manuscript of it we have dates from much later, it clearly contains first hand information probably recorded by the author from personal experience. Indeed, correlations can be established between the claims of the Verse Account and sources contemporary with Nabonidus, including details which would have been almost impossible for a later compiler to retrieve. Still, however, the manuscript we have might represent a later, embellished edition, yet one preserving substantial original information.

Even genres that seem to record absolutely secure data can be questioned, for instance chronicles of the Neo-Babylonian and Hellenistic periods. Should we consider them as primary or secondary sources? Historians tend to treat them as primary, and indeed their apparent objective and dispassionate recording of events, advancing no interpretation of history or value judgment has reinforced the notion that they simply concatenate basic facts. However, manuscripts of these chronicles are rarely contemporary with the events they describe, and sometimes the time distance can be significant. For instance, the chronicle of the reign of Nabonidus (Chronicle 26) probably dates to the third century (Figure 1.2). Was it composed at that time, or is it an exact copy of an earlier manuscript contemporary with the events it describes? In the first instance the chronicle would qualify as a secondary source and we would have to address the issue of the sources used by its author, the Astronomical Diaries being the most likely candidate. However, if we posit that the author just compiled entries from the Diaries, Chronicle 26 still represents an original composition, if only because it would have endowed disconnected notices in the Diaries with fresh meaning by taking them out of context and framing them within a narrative; the compiler might also have inserted elements of his own to adapt his narrative to the outlook

Figure 1.2   Nabonidus Chronicle (Chronicle 26). This fragment of a larger tablet preserves parts of a chronicle about the reign of Nabonidus. Such chronicles provide crucial information on political events, but not all can be considered absolutely reliable. In this particular case the chronicle may have been written long after the events it reports, raising the questions of the sources used in its composition. *Source*: © The Trustees of the British Museum.

of his time. Unfortunately we cannot verify this hypothesis because no Diary covering the time of Nabonidus has survived. From a strictly methodological point of view, most historians would classify Chronicle 26 as a secondary rather than primary source.

These remarks should not instill irrational doubts as to the value of all ancient sources. The information contained in the Neo-Babylonian and Hellenistic chronicles is generally considered reliable. The point should only be stressed that historians must be circumspect in handling the textual production of ancient scribal cultures. The ideal scenario for the historian of Babylon is a combination of all three categories of cuneiform sources: archives from the palace (state archives), from temples, and from private families, in addition to royal inscriptions and well-preserved scholarly texts (chronicles and literary compositions). The possibility of correlating the claims of a chronicle or royal inscription with the information gleaned from archival texts instills more confidence that we thread on solid grounds in our effort to resurrect the past. This ideal scenario does not occur very often, and many centuries still bathe in relative obscurity. On the other hand, some crucial periods, such as the reign of Hammu-rabi (1792–1750) and the time of the Babylonian empire (625–539) have emerged into fuller light because of the relative abundance of primary and secondary sources.

1.3 Chronology

There is no history without chronology, and accordingly we take for granted that historical discourse proceeds from a secure chronological framework. When we read that the storming of the Bastille, conventionally understood as the start of the French Revolution, took place on the fourteenth of July AD 1789, we can precisely estimate the time distance which separates us from that event. The reason is simple: we use the same calendar as they did in France in 1789, the Gregorian calendar, and the same era for the count of years, the Christian Era (AD is from Latin *Anno Domini* "the year of the Lord"), also called the Common Era (CE). The Gregorian calendar originates in a decree by Pope Gregory XIII in AD 1582 to reform the Julian calendar, instituted by Julius Caesar in 46 BC. The two calendars are basically the same except that over centuries a discrepancy of a few days accumulates between them (three days every four centuries) because of their different calculation of the length of the equinoctial year. We refer to dates after the reform as Gregorian dates, and before as Julian dates. When we date events before our era, we use Julian dates and the BC negative year count ("Before Christ;" alternatively BCE "Before the Common Era"). However, Babylon had different year counts and calendars. How can we relate our chronology to theirs? In other terms, when a cuneiform document is dated to the fifth day of the seventh month in the forty-second year of Nebuchadnezzar II, how can we translate that date into a Julian date? First we must find a synchronism between our own year count and the ones used in Babylon, and then take into account the fact that the Babylonian calendar was lunisolar.

The first task is relatively easy back to the year 747, thanks to the Ptolemaic Canon and the Seleucid Era. The Seleucid Era began when Seleucus I, one of the generals of Alexander the Great, seized power in Babylon in 305 and calculated retroactively the beginning of his reign to the year 311. However, the Era began effectively only when Antiochus I, upon the death of Seleucus I in 281, continued with the regnal count of his father instead of starting anew with his own. Cuneiform documents from the Hellenistic period are always dated to the Seleucid Era. The Era survived the demise of the Seleucid kingdom at the hands of the Romans and continues to be used even to this day among Near Eastern Christians. In late antiquity, it was used concurrently with the Christian era and also with the Roman dating system by consular years. These eras overlap as interlocking year counts; they are synchronic. We can therefore recede back in time and translate all Seleucid Era years into AD and BC years. For the period before the institution of the Seleucid Era back to 747, we use mainly the Ptolemaic Canon. The Canon lists all kings recognized in Babylon from Nabonassar (747–734) until Alexander IV, son of Alexander the Great (316–305), and then switches to rulers recognized in Alexandria in Egypt starting with Ptolemy I (305–285) until the Roman emperor Antoninus Pius (AD 138–160). Since the Canon overlaps with the count of the Seleucid Era after 311, we can project our count of BC years back to 747, the first year of Nabonassar. The data from the Canon are supplemented by cuneiform chronographic documents such as King List A, the Uruk King List, and the King List of the Hellenistic Period, Neo-Babylonian, and Hellenistic chronicles, the Astronomical Diaries and other cuneiform astronomical texts, and also with the Babylonian observational data preserved in Ptolemy's Almagest. Ptolemy facilitates our task by dating astronomical phenomena according to an era starting with the accession of Nabonassar. The chronology back to 747 is thus basically secure.

The next step is the calendar. The Julian calendar is purely solar and based on the equinoctial year, the time elapsing between two vernal equinoxes. The equinoctial year includes approximately 365.25 days. The Babylonian calendar was lunisolar, based on lunar months with periodic intercalations ordered by state authorities. Months coincided with lunar cycles and began with the reappearance of the lunar crescent on the horizon. Since lunar months last on average either twenty-nine or thirty days, a year based on twelve lunar months included about 354 days. This means that after three years the calendar accumulated a discrepancy of about thirty days with the equinoctial year. This was solved by inserting an intercalary month on average every three years. In Babylon this month was added either after the sixth or the twelfth month. With the combined data from the Astronomical Diaries and dated documents, scholars have compiled tables reconstructing the Babylonian calendar between 626 BC and AD 75 and synchronized it with the Julian calendar. With the help of these conversion tables, we can translate all Babylonian dates starting in 626 into Julian dates. Thus, when Chronicle 26 tells us that the capture of Babylon by the Persians took place on the sixteenth day of the seventh month in the seventeenth year of Nabonidus, we can easily convert that date into a Julian date: October 12, 539. We must also keep in mind that the Babylonian year began in the spring (March or April), and therefore one Babylonian year overlapped with two Julian years. Thus the third year of Nebuchadnezzar II must be reckoned as 602–601, since it began on April 10, 602 and ended on March 29, 601. To simplify matters, most histories reckon that year simply as 602.

Before 747 the chronology becomes more uncertain. Babylonian documentation is astonishingly poor for the early part of the first millennium. At that point Assyrian sources supply most data. In Assyria dating was by eponyms; an official gave his name to the year, like the consuls in Rome. The Neo-Assyrian Canon of Eponyms is a year-by-year list of eponyms with notes on various events of importance. It extends from 910 until 649 and can be synchronized with the Ptolemaic Canon and Babylonian chronographic sources after 747. The Canon records an eclipse of the sun in the ninth regnal year of the Assyrian king Ashur-dan III (772–755): "Eponymy of Bur-Saggile from Guzana; revolt in the citadel; in the month of Simanu the sun had an eclipse." The entry almost certainly refers to the near total solar eclipse which occurred on June 15, 763. This allows us to establish a secure chronology for Assyria back to 910. As we move into the second millennium chronographic sources become much less dependable. King List A and the Assyrian King List supply the basic chronology, but they are known from later manuscripts and not free of errors. Between ca. 1400 until 910, our chronological placement of reigns and events accumulates an error of a few years by the turn of the century, and possibly more as we reach the first half of the fourteenth century.

The main chronological issue concerns the middle of the second millennium. King List A is not entirely preserved at this point; it also assumes that the first three Babylonian Dynasties reigned in succession, whereas they overlapped for an unknown period of time. Therefore our only source for Babylonia becomes useless. Considerable amounts of data have been marshaled to settle the issue: astronomical dating, archaeological and art historical evidence, synchronisms with other parts of the Near East, dendrochronology, but to this day the puzzle remains unsolved. By and large four chronologies have been proposed: high (Hammu-rabi reigned 1848–1806), middle (1792–1750), low (1728–1686), and ultra-low (1696–1654). This book adheres to the middle chronology, conventionally used by almost everybody, although the evidence now speaks increasingly in favor of a slightly lower chronology.

The relative chronology from the beginning of the Third Dynasty of Ur until the end of the First Dynasty of Babylon seems more or less established thanks to the survival of king lists and lists of year names, as well as vast numbers of dated archival texts, although there are still many issues awaiting solutions, in particular synchronisms between competing dynasties before the unification of Babylonia by Hammu-rabi. According to the middle chronology this period covers the years 2112 to 1595, and it would move together as a unit if another chronology was adopted (e.g. 2048 to 1531 in the low chronology). For the third millennium the chronology becomes very uncertain. We cannot estimate the time gap between the end of the Sargonic Dynasty and the beginning of the Third Dynasty of Ur, and the length of Sargonic reigns is provided by SKL, which contains unreliable numbers. Before the Sargonic Dynasty, archaeological periods supply the basic chronological scheme.

NOTE

1. After Michalowski 1989: 59, lines 366–8.

FURTHER READING

For a general introduction to the cuneiform script see Finkel and Taylor 2015 and Walker 1990. On the use of cuneiform texts as historical sources see Van de Mieroop 1999 and Grayson 1980, and for ancient archives in general Brosius 2003. Charpin 2011 offers an excellent survey of the place of cuneiform texts, literary and archival, in the daily life of Babylonia. A list of chronicles and king lists, with editions of the latter, can be found in Grayson 1980–1983, and a convenient list of Mesopotamian rulers with their dates is compiled by Walker 1995. For editions of the chronicles see Grayson 2000 and Glassner 2004 (see also the Appendix in this book), and for recent discussion of their origins Waerzeggers 2012 and 2015. Translations and editions of chronicles are also found on the Livius Web Site. Year names are compiled by Sigrist and Damerow CDLI. An excellent introduction to ancient chronology in general is Bickerman 1980, to be complemented by Parker and Dubberstein 1956 for late Babylonian chronology; the Livius Web site has a useful introduction to Mesopotamian chronology.

Bickerman, Elias. 1980. *Chronology of the Ancient World* (2nd ed). Ithaca, NY: Cornell University Press.

Brosius, Maria (ed). 2003. *Ancient Archives and Archival Traditions: Concepts of Record-Keeping in the Ancient World*. Oxford: Oxford University Press.

Charpin, Dominique. 2011. *Reading and Writing in Babylon*. Cambridge, MA: Harvard University Press.

Finkel, Irving, and Taylor, Jonathan. 2015. *Cuneiform: Ancient Scripts*. London: British Museum Press.

Glassner, Jean-Jacques. 2004. *Mesopotamian Chronicles*. Atlanta, GA: Society for Biblical Literature.

Grayson, Albert Kirk. 1980. "Histories and Historians of the Ancient Near East: Assyria and Babylonia." *Orientalia* 49: 140–94.

Grayson, Albert Kirk. 1980–1983. "Königslisten und Chroniken. B. Akkadisch." *Reallexikon der Assyriologie und vorderasiatischen Archäologie* 6: 86–135.

Grayson, Albert Kirk. 2000. *Assyrian and Babylonian Chronicles*. Winona Lake, IN: Eisenbrauns.

Livius Web Site on Chronicles: http://www.livius.org/sources/about/mesopotamian-chronicles/?

Livius Web Site on Chronology: http://www.livius.org/articles/misc/mesopotamian-chronology/.

Michalowski, Piotr. 1989. *The Lamentation over the Destruction of Sumer and Ur*. Mesopotamian Civilizations 1. Winona Lake, IN: Eisenbrauns.

Parker, Richard, and Dubberstein, Waldo. 1956. *Babylonian Chronology 626 B.C.–A.D. 75* Providence, RI: Brown University Press.

Sigrist, Marcel, and Damerow, Peter. CDLI. Mesopotamian Year Names: http://cdli.ucla.edu/tools/yearnames/yn_index.html.

Van de Mieroop, Marc. 1999. *Cuneiform Texts and the Writing of History*. London: Routledge.

Waerzeggers, Caroline. 2012. "The Babylonian Chronicles: Classification and Provenance." *Journal of Near Eastern Studies* 71: 285–98.

Waerzeggers, Caroline. 2015. "Facts, Propaganda, or History? Shaping Political Memory in the Nabonidus Chronicle." In Silverman, Jason M., and Waerzeggers, Caroline (eds), *Political Memory in and after the Persian Empire*. SBLANEM 13. Atlanta: SBL Press: 95–124.

Walker, Christopher. 1990. "Cuneiform." In Hooker, J. T. (ed.), *Reading the Past: Ancient Writing from Cuneiform to the Alphabet*. Berkeley and Los Angeles: University of California Press and British Museum: 14–73.

Walker, Christopher. 1995. "Mesopotamian Chronology." In Collon, Dominique. *Ancient Near Eastern Art*. Berkeley and Los Angeles: University of California Press. 230–8.

2
The Sumero-Akkadian Background

The subject of the history of Babylon cannot be studied without first considering the context of the rise of civilization in that part of the world. By the end of the fourth millennium southern Iraq had acquired most of the distinctive traits that would make it one of the first great civilizations in history, notably the development of irrigation technology which provided the foundations for a prosperous agrarian society, the invention of writing and the emergence of bookkeeping and bureaucracy, and a communal life focused on the city and its temples. However, Babylon played no leading role in these developments. Throughout the third millennium it remained a town of no particular political significance, at least one about which we know very little. Nevertheless it participated in the political and cultural growth of Mesopotamian civilization, of which it will become one of the two dominant manifestations in the second and first millennia, the other one being Assyria.

2.1 Babylonia as Geographic Unit

The region we call Babylonia corresponds by and large to the southern half of the modern Republic of Iraq, beginning north of its present capital Baghdad and extending all the way to the shores of the Persian Gulf. This region acquired the designation "Babylonia" quite late. For most of its history Babylonia was known as "Sumer and Akkad" and the dividing line between these two entities ran near the city of Nippur. By the end of the third and the beginning of the second millennia the kings of Ur, Isin, and Babylon often claimed and effectively exercised kingship over Sumer and Akkad. The rulers of the Babylonian empire in the sixth century still bore the title "king of Sumer and Akkad" in their inscriptions, although it had by then become an archaism. In the second and first millennia

A History of Babylon: 2200 BC–AD 75, First Edition. Paul-Alain Beaulieu.
© 2018 John Wiley & Sons Ltd. Published 2018 by John Wiley & Sons Ltd.

the name Akkad often substituted for "Sumer and Akkad." In the Babylonian language the word Babylonian always referred to an inhabitant of Babylon exclusively, and therefore "Akkadian" became the accepted designation for all native people of Babylonia. The Kassites introduced the toponym Karduniash, which might be an early equivalent for Babylonia, although its precise geographic referents remain unclear. The Assyrian sometimes referred to Babylonia as the "land of Babylon," on the model of their own country which they called the "land of Assur," Assur being the capital. This Assyrian usage appears to be the earliest word for Babylonia that derives from the name of the city Babylon, but it is the Greeks who coined a separate term for the land: "Babylonia." Thus, ironically, the words Babylonia for the land, and Babylonians for its people did not originate in Babylon, but instead reflect the perception of other peoples. History abounds in similar cases. We now use the term Babylonia simply as geographic term and often anachronistically, that is, even for periods when Babylon did not play any political role or may not even have yet come into existence (see Map 2.1).

Another geographic term which requires defining is Mesopotamia. The term was also coined by the Greeks and means "between the rivers." Greek historians and geographers used it mostly in reference to the area of northern Iraq and Syria that lay between the Tigris and the Euphrates, but sometimes also to the entire region between the two rivers from eastern Turkey to the Persian Gulf. Historians have adopted the term Mesopotamia as a name for the civilization which flourished in ancient Iraq and neighboring areas in northeastern Syria and southeastern Turkey. The term has no specific equivalent in the ancient Near East and reflects a modern construct, functioning as an umbrella term under which we include such diverse peoples and cultures as the Sumerian city states of the third millennium; the kingdom of Mari of the third and early second millennia, which belonged to both the east Semitic world of Iraq and the west Semitic world of the Levant; the highly centralized Assyrian empire of the first millennium; and of course Babylon. Several common traits nevertheless unify Mesopotamia, among which the cuneiform writing system with its scholarly tradition, and the religion, both susceptible to regional variation, figure prominently. The word Iraq did not appear until Late Antiquity and became common usage only in the Arab-Islamic period.

2.2   The Natural Environment

If Herodotus coined the famous phrase that Egypt was a gift of the Nile, one could echo the Greek historian by declaring Babylonia a gift of the Tigris and Euphrates. The two rivers take their source in eastern Turkey but meander through different paths before they reach central Iraq. The Tigris follows an eastern course, crossing the ancient heartland of Assyria and entering Babylonia in the region of Baghdad, where it meets the Diyala before continuing its path towards the Persian Gulf. The Euphrates veers off westward, enters northern Syria where it defines the boundary between the Levantine and Mesopotamian

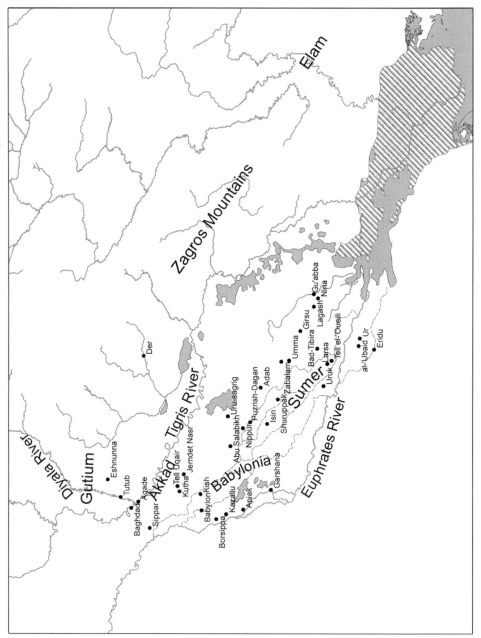

Map 2.1 Early Babylonia. Map Design: Stephen Batiuk, University of Toronto.

worlds, and then turns southeast, entering Babylonia near the modern city of Fallujah, and then follows a southern course to reach the Persian Gulf. The Tigris and Euphrates come very close to one another when they enter Babylonia, but flow at an increasing distance in the south before coming near one another again when they approach the Persian Gulf. The two rivers have deep beds in the north, but shallow and therefore unstable and shifting beds in northern Babylonia, creating a flood plain which has caused the two rivers to alter their course several times throughout history. This happened during the flooding season in the spring, when melting snow and abundant rain in the north swelled the two rivers which came rushing to northern Babylonia, causing them to leave their bed and find a new course. It is therefore important to realize that in ancient times the path of the Tigris and Euphrates in Babylonia did not look at all what it is today. They stayed much closer to one another, flowing along parallel paths. This explains why most Babylonian cities that were important in Antiquity are not located on the present course of the two rivers.

The Tigris and Euphrates played in the ecology of Babylonia a role comparable to the Nile in Egypt, sustaining life as well as imposing constraints on its development. Ancient Near Eastern civilizations were essentially agrarian. The term Fertile Crescent has often been applied to the large, roughly crescent-shaped zone in which they developed, comprising Egypt, the Levant, southern Anatolia and Mesopotamia. However, natural conditions in this vast zone varied greatly. Some regions could sustain dry farming, agriculture that depends mainly on rainfall. The minimal requirement for dry farming is generally set at about 200 millimeters of mean annual rainfall, but optimal conditions begin only at 300 mm. Since Babylonia (and Egypt as well) lay below the 200 mm line, it could sustain agriculture only by a combination of artificial irrigation and natural rain. The absolute necessity of irrigation played a major role in its history and became an overall concern of the state, especially in the early periods. The royal inscriptions and year names of the First Dynasty of Babylon often commemorate the building and repair of the irrigation network. Irrigation, however, could also lead to environmental depletion with salinization of arable soil, caused by inadequate drainage of the fields after they received excess salt and silt deposits from irrigation water. Salinization brought about periodic collapses of the agricultural system in ancient times and has affected agricultural output in the region to this day. Although contemporary Iraq has two agricultural cycles a year, one in summer and one in winter for grain, ancient Babylonia knew only one winter cycle, with seeding season in October and November and harvest season between April and June. The spring flood represented a threat almost as important as salinization since it coincided with the harvest season. In order to prevent flooding of the fields and destruction of the harvest, an elaborate system of dams and dikes had to be built along the banks of the rivers, another major concern of early rulers.

Babylonia has a subtropical climate with two seasons: a dry, hot summer lasting from May to October, and a relatively cold, damp winter from December to March. The heat in the summer can be extreme (95° to 120° Fahrenheit in midday), with sandstorms because of the proximity of the desert. The region possesses few natural resources besides agriculture and farm products. To be sure, clay, reed, limestone, and bitumen abound, but Babylonia lacked most metals and stones. These had to be imported, sometimes from distant regions (copper from Anatolia; lapis lazuli from Afghanistan). Merchants, working either independently or for the state, played the key role in these commercial networks. The most important resource Babylonia lacked was wood. Some forests existed, especially in the region of Umma in the third millennium, but most wood came from mountain areas, the best quality being provided by cedars from Lebanon. Rulers of ancient Mesopotamian states took great pride in campaigning to that region, often in reality, sometimes in their imagination, to fell cedar trees and bring them back to their homeland, where they served to roof palaces and temples. The topos endured, as well as the need, and still in the sixth century Nebuchadnezzar II left monumental rock inscriptions at Wadi Brissa and other sites in Lebanon in which he claims to have cut tall cedars and taken them to Babylon.

2.3   The Neolithic Revolution

Urban civilization traces its roots back to the Neolithic revolution. The long process leading to the emergence of cities began with the development of agriculture, which favored in turn the specialization of human tasks and the earliest technological advances. Although Babylonia eventually took the lead in the growth of large scale cities at the end of the fourth millennium, it did not provide the initial impetus. Indeed, as we have just seen, the particular ecological conditions of the region hampered the development of rain fed agriculture. During the Proto-Neolithic period (12,000–9000/8500) agriculture developed initially in the dry farming zone of the Near East, more precisely in an arc that extended from Palestine to northern Syria and then reached eastwards to northern Iraq. This period witnessed the discovery of some basic crops, and the domestication of the dog around 10,500. Expansion of human settlement seems to have occurred by duplication of communities, with some people leaving a community to create another one on the same model. This favored the maintenance of an egalitarian social structure. The largest Near Eastern site during that period was Jericho in Palestine, which by 9000 had been surrounded by a stone wall and included about 1,500 inhabitants living in round huts.

During the next period, the Pre-Pottery Neolithic (9000–7000), agriculture spread to the Zagros Mountains east of Iraq and to southern Anatolia. The size and number of settlements increased markedly and round huts were replaced by rectangular structures. By the end of this period several plants were already cultivated (barley, einkorn wheat, emmer wheat, bread wheat, flax, and spelt) and basic farm animals had been domesticated: goats (8,500), sheep (8,000), pigs (7,500), cattle (7,000), as well as the cat (7,000). During the Pottery Neolithic (7000–4000) agriculture spread to southeastern and central Europe, to Iran and further eastwards, and also to Egypt and from there to northern and eastern

Africa. Pottery developed during this period and becomes the most ubiquitous artifact found on archaeological sites. Pottery manufacture follows constant and consistent patterns of change, and therefore the distribution and variation of pottery types constitute an important clue for the classification and periodization of cultures. Chatal Hoyuk (7400–6200) in southern Anatolia ranks as the most complex site of the transition from the Pre-Pottery to the Pottery Neolithic, with more than 1000 households (ca. 5000 inhabitants) and possible evidence for organized religion. In Iraq, the most prominent cultures of that period are the Hassuna and Samarra cultures in the north until about 6000, followed by the Halaf culture (6000–5400) in the dry-farming zone extending from northern Syria and southeastern Anatolia to the Zagros mountains, with developments in the Levantine coast as well. The Halaf gave way to the Ubaid culture expanding from the south after 5400. The end of this period saw the domestication of the donkey (4000).

2.4   The Ubaid Period (6500–4000)

The Ubaid represents the earliest culture of Babylonia, and it is so named because archaeologists first identified its characteristic pottery at the site of al-Ubaid near Ur. Other Ubaid sites have been discovered since, such as Tell el-Oueili near Larsa, the oldest Ubaid site to date, Hajji Muhammad near Uruk, and Eridu along the Persian Gulf. The Ubaid period has traditionally been divided into a sequence numbered I to IV (IV being the most recent), but the discovery at Tell el-Oueili of material earlier than Ubaid I has prompted the introduction of a fifth phase called Ubaid 0. Surveys indicate that population density in Babylonia during the Ubaid period remained low and human agglomerations small. The Ubaid culture shares certain affinities with other cultures of the Near East, most prominently the Samarra culture in the north, and some have argued that the initial impetus for its development came from that region, perhaps as the result of migrations. Archaeologists have unearthed sixteen levels at Eridu, which forms the largest and best known Ubaid site and the one with the longest history. Levels XVI (the earliest) to VI belong to the Ubaid period; the later ones correspond to the Uruk and Jemdet Nasr periods. The site covers an area of more than ten hectares and must have included a few thousand people. The most impressive archaeological remains unearthed at Eridu consist of a sequence of ever larger structures built on top of one another. The earliest one in level XVI covers a very small area (ca. twelve by fifteen feet), but the later buildings contemporary with the Uruk period show characteristic aspects of the large-scale sacral architecture of Mesopotamia. Most, but not all scholars assume that these superimposed buildings functioned as temples from the beginning.

The Babylonians later viewed Eridu as their oldest city, the earliest one in their canonical list of antediluvian cities, and archaeology has confirmed this ancient belief in the city's temporal priority. The Sumerian god Enki, named Ea in Akkadian, resided in Eridu and ranked as one of the highest gods in the pantheon.

In the early second millennium the theologians of Babylon identified his son Asaluhi with their god Marduk in order to enhance the latter's pedigree. Some have speculated that the earliest remains found in the building sequence at Eridu already attest to a cult of Enki, with altar, offering table, cultic niches, as well as remains of fish bones and small animals, which suggest the presentation of offerings. However, even if we accept the cultic function of the earliest levels of the Eridu sequence, we have no proof that the posited cult revolved around Enki. On the other hand, we can single out traits of the Ubaid culture that herald emblematic aspects of the later Babylonian civilization. First and foremost, the Ubaid culture witnessed the development of the tripartite building characterized by a central rectangular space flanked by two rows of auxiliary or storage rooms, which became later the distinctive plan for Babylonian temples. Ubaid Babylonia may also have been the earliest area in the Near East to practice irrigation farming on a significant scale, although recent climatological data suggest that before the third millennium southern Mesopotamia may have also benefited from northern monsoonal rainfall. Last but not least, the Ubaid material culture began to spread all over the Near East during the last phase of its development, including sites in Iran and the Arabian Peninsula. The Ubaid Expansion thus represents the first of several cultural waves radiating from Babylonia to other regions of the Near East in prehistoric and historical times.

2.5   The Uruk Period (4000–3100)

The Ubaid was followed by the Uruk period (4000–3100), which saw the emergence of urban civilization in Babylonia. This process was accompanied by a number of important technological innovations, including the invention of writing and the development of metallurgy with copper smelting. The replacement of polished stone with copper as main material for the manufacture of tools signaled the passage of the Neolithic to the Chalcolithic (4000–3000). The new culture that developed in Babylonia during the Chalcolithic derives its name from the site of Uruk (modern Warka) in the south, which seems to have spearheaded its development and was continuously occupied from the late Ubaid period until the first century of our era. The Uruk archaeological sequence includes eighteen levels; the most ancient ones, Uruk XVIII to XIII, being contemporary with Ubaid IV; Uruk XII to VI corresponding to the Early and Middle Uruk Period (4000–3400); Uruk V and IV to the Late Uruk Period (3400–3100); Uruk III to the Jemdet Nasr Period (3100–2900); and finally Uruk II and I to the historical periods (2900–100 AD). The Uruk period witnessed a significant demographic explosion; archaeological surveys have shown that by the middle of the fourth millennium the density and size of settlements correspond to a population at least ten times larger than the Ubaid period. At that point Uruk replaced Eridu as main center of urban civilization. This important shift appears to be reflected in the later Sumerian myth "Inanna and Enki" which describes how Inanna, the goddess of Uruk, stole all the arts of civilization from Enki, the god of Eridu.

By the middle of the fourth millennium the Uruk civilization began to expand outside Babylonia. During this phase called the Uruk Expansion, which lasted until about 3100, the artifacts typical of the Uruk material culture appear in numerous sites of the Near East, replicating the earlier wave of Ubaid Expansion. This Middle and Late Uruk assemblage includes innovations such as: cylinder seals with the same repertory of motifs at all sites; coarsely manufactured and mass produced bevelled-rim bowls of standardized shape and size which may have been used to dole out rations; numerical tokens, clay balls and tablets, which bear evidence of an early accounting system; and in architecture the tripartite building which had already begun to develop in the late Ubaid period. Archaeologists have proposed models to explain the Uruk Expansion; the most likely hypothesis views it as commercial expansion by means of trading emporiums where the material culture of the center, Uruk, was reproduced on a smaller scale. However, the possibility that these trading posts represent colonies and that Uruk exerted actual political control over vast areas cannot be excluded. At the same time, the early emergence of large urban centers, a phenomenon once thought to be exclusive to Babylonia, can now be evidenced at other sites in the north such as Habuba Kabira and Hamoukar, and also at Susa in southwestern Iran. There is no doubt that these centers would have vied with Uruk for political power and perhaps kept its expansionist energies in check. At any rate, Uruk became so dominant in Babylonia that no other site there approached it in term of size; by the end of the Uruk period it had extended over 250 hectares. The city then displayed large scale monumental architecture, and at the very end of the Uruk period, in level Uruk IVa, writing appeared, in all probability a local invention.

2.6 The Jemdet Nasr Period (3100–2900)

Around 3100 the Uruk Expansion came to an end, when all sites outside Babylonia which previously displayed Uruk assemblages replaced them with local artifacts. The Uruk civilization retreated to its homeland during the Jemdet Nasr period (3100–2900), named after the site of Jemdet Nasr (ancient name unknown) halfway between Babylon and Baghdad where this cultural phase was first identified. The Jemdet Nasr does not represent a radical departure from what preceded; the main tendencies of the Uruk culture continued to govern the development of Babylonia. The site of Uruk escalated its growth to huge proportions, reaching a size of about 400 hectares, which is larger than Athens in the fifth century and about half the size of Rome during the early imperial period. It may have become the largest human agglomeration in the world at that time with a population estimated at about 40,000 inhabitants by some scholars. However, such high estimates may be viewed with skepticism since not a single dwelling from that era has been excavated. The Uruk III level, which corresponds to the Jemdet Nasr phase, has produced spectacular epigraphic and artistic evidence for the elaboration of a centralized bureaucratic state ruled by a charismatic figure, the Priest-King of Uruk (Figure 2.1).

Figure 2.1   Archaic tablet from Uruk. This account of barley distribution bears a cylinder seal impression of a male figure, hunting dogs, and boars. The male figure, partly visible on the right, is probably the Priest King of Uruk. The clay tablet belongs to the Uruk III (Jemdet Nasr) period, ca. 3100–2900. The signs can be classified as proto-cuneiform as many still have a clear pictographic aspect. Measurements: 2.17 × 2.36 × 1.63 in. (5.5 × 6 × 4.15 cm).
Source: The Metropolitan Museum of Art, NYC (MMA 1988.433.1), Public Domain.

Writing, which had begun during the Uruk IVa phase, is now documented by a few thousand clay tablets known as the Archaic Texts from Uruk. Most of them date to the middle of the Uruk III level (Uruk III/2) and were found in secondary context; they constitute the earliest example of archival material discarded as fill. About 85 percent of the texts consist of administrative transactions (Figure 2.1), while another 15 percent can be classified as lexical, basically lists of signs arranged semantically (fishes, birds, trees and woods, occupations, vessels, geographic names, and so on). Some of these lists continued to be copied down to the early second millennium, when they were provided with additional columns translating each Sumerian entry into Akkadian. These have provided considerable help in deciphering the archaic script. Few scholars doubt that the invention of writing in the Uruk period was stimulated by the needs of a complex administration, but the presence of lexical lists at this initial stage seems significant. Although scribes certainly used these lists as learning tools for writing administrative accounts, their content is not wholly dependent on the latter. Many signs found in the lists do not occur in the accounts, and conversely many signs that are common in the accounts, for instance its complex numerical and metrological systems, did not find their way into the lists. This suggests that the invention of writing, albeit motivated principally by practical needs, was also accompanied by a reflection on its nature and on its potential for ordering and classifying society, realia, and the world. In other terms, the lists attest to the elaboration, already at an early date, of an autonomous intellectual tradition nurtured by the scribal elite and independent of other activities. This trend will leave an indelible imprint on later intellectual developments in Babylonia.

The texts still prove hard to read because the script does not denote syntactic relations and the signs do not follow a fixed order. Nevertheless, there is no doubt that the script is the direct ancestor of the later cuneiform system. Some scholars have questioned the assumption that the language of the texts is Sumerian, even proposing that the Sumerians came to Babylonia only around the end of the Jemdet Nasr period. Others, however, have pointed to a few cases where the early script makes use of phonetic indicators which can be explained only if we assume that it denotes Sumerian. Culturally, we seem to be in a Sumerian world already. The administrative accounts mention offerings to only one deity, written with the sign later used for the Sumerian goddess Inanna, the anthropomorphic projection of the planet Venus. Four distinct forms of the deity appear in the texts: Inanna-HUD, Inanna-SIG, Inanna-NUN, and Inanna-KUR, the latter being the only one not attested as recipient of offerings. The first two Inannas can be translated as Inanna-of-the-morning and Inanna-of-the-evening, representing the two appearances of the planet Venus as morning and evening star. The goddess Inanna-KUR probably represents Inanna-of-the-netherworld, and embodies the periodic disappearance of the planet Venus, which was explained in mythology as a voyage of Inanna to the netherworld. Finally Inanna-NUN, often translated as Princely-Inanna (NUN is the sign for "prince"), could also represent Inanna-of-Eridu (NUN followed by the determinative KI appears later as the sign for the city of Eridu), possibly reflecting the principal motif of the later myth "Inanna and Enki," Inanna's theft of the attributes of civilization from Eridu and their transfer to Uruk. Later syncretism assimilated the Sumerian Inanna to her Semitic equivalent Ishtar, who became one of the most important deities of the Babylonian pantheon and perpetuated the same mythological motifs associated with the Inanna goddesses of the Uruk and Jemdet Nasr period. The division of the functions of Ishtar between a goddess of war symbolized by the morning star and a goddess of love symbolized by the evening star, and the motif of the descent of Ishtar to the netherworld, became distinctive properties of the Babylonian Ishtar, who was still worshiped in the Neo-Babylonian period as chief goddess of Uruk.

The archaic texts disclose far fewer details on the political organization of the city than on its religion. The lexical list for occupations begins with a figure called the *nameshda* (*nam-shita*); later copies of the list equate this word with Akkadian *sharru* "king," probably erroneously since the scribes no longer understood the contents of the list very well. Although the title *nameshda* rarely appears in administrative accounts, some scholars have claimed that the word designates the Priest-King of Uruk who is depicted on such artifacts as cylinders seals, stone monuments, on the famous Uruk Vase, where he is portrayed meeting a female figure who might be Inanna or a female impersonator of the goddess, and even on ivory knife-handles from Egypt, testifying to the widespread influence of

Babylonia during the late Uruk and Jemdet Nasr phases. Other scholars have maintained that the word designating the Priest-King is *en*, which frequently appears in the archaic administrative texts and is known later as one of the designations of the ruler of the Early Dynastic city-states, especially at Uruk. The Priest-King is depicted in the iconography as master of animals, as hunter, and as leading officiating figure in religious ceremonies. He appears earlier on a cylinder seal impression which has been dated to the Uruk V level where he presides over the beating of naked and bound prisoners. All these represent emblematic activities of later Mesopotamian rulers, and even the outward appearance of the Priest-King, who wears a long tunic and is coiffed with a round cap with curled rim, as well as his long trimmed beard, recall features of later Mesopotamian royal portraiture. In the absence of more explicit data in the archaic texts on the social and political structure of the city, the iconography of the Priest-King leaves little doubt as to the despotic nature of the regime in place at Uruk during the Jemdet Nasr period.

The Priest-King possibly ruled most, if not all of Babylonia at that time. The main evidence for Babylonian political unity comes from a small number of archaic texts discovered at the sites of Jemdet Nasr and Tell Uqair (possibly ancient Urum) and jars found at Ur which all bear similar seals with symbols for Babylonian cities; a few of them also occur as signs for the same cities in the script. Several texts appear to record offerings for the three deities of Uruk, also designated as the three Inannas of Uruk. Some scholars claim that this evidence supports the notion of a centralized Babylonian polity ruled from Uruk, or a kind of league that could be named the Kengir League, Kengir being the native Sumerian term for Sumer, and that the texts and seals attest to the existence of a centralized offering system involving all members of the league. This claim seems cogent but still needs to be supported by more explicit evidence. Archaeologically the Jemdet Nasr period already shows traits of the Early Dynastic Period, where the political landscape was dominated by several large cities. Babylon, if it existed at all in that period, must have been a rather small community in the shadow of larger regional centers such as Jemdet Nasr and Tell Uqair, and probably looked insignificant from the perspective of the large metropolis of Uruk.

2.7 The Early Dynastic Period (2900–2350)

Babylonia enters history during the Early Dynastic (ED) period. This is true insofar as history begins with the production of documents reflecting some form of historical consciousness, for which the writings produced during the Late Uruk and Jemdet Nasr periods clearly do not qualify. However the scribes expanded the sphere of writing only slowly to genres other than lexical lists and accounts (Figure 2.2), which is still what we mostly find in the archaic texts from Ur (ca. 2700). The earliest royal inscription dates from around 2600, and literary texts appear at about the same time at Shuruppak (modern Fara)

Figure 2.2   Stele of Ushumgal. This monument of gypsum alabaster dating to the ED I
(2900–2750/2700) and probably from Umma records a transaction on land, houses, and
livestock, involving a priest of the god Shara named Ushumgal, depicted here, and his
daughter, who appears on the other side. These monuments are often named "early *kudurrus*"
to distinguish them from those that appeared during the Kassite period. Measurements:
H. 22.4 × W. 14.7 × D. 9.5 cm (8 7/8 × 5 3/4 × 3 3/4 in.). *Source*: The Metropolitan Museum
of Art, NYC (MMA 58.29), Public Domain.

and Abu-Salabikh (ancient name unknown). Only the last century of the ED
period (2450–2350) produced written documentation that is varied and abundant enough to enable us to write some form of history, and still most of the
evidence concerns only the state of Lagash in southeastern Babylonia, leaving
much of the rest in the mist. Later works of literature and historiography about
the ED became part of the curriculum of schools during the Ur III and Old
Babylonian periods, notably SKL, the Tummal Chronicle, and the epic cycle
about the legendary ancient rulers of Uruk: Enmerkar, Lugalbanda, and
Gilgamesh. These compositions contain little historical information that can be
trusted without corroboration from primary sources. The ED can be further
subdivided into three units: ED I (2900–2750/2700), ED II (2750/2700–2600),
and ED III (2600–2350), the latter comprising two phases, ED IIIa (2600–2450)
and ED IIIb (2450–2350). These divisions reflect archaeological periods based
on the results of the excavations conducted in the Diyala region by the University of Chicago in the 1930s. However, that area displays a distinctive material
culture not necessarily shared by other regions of Babylonia, and in spite of the

fact that the current subdivision into sub-periods should be revised historians still keep it for the sake of convenience.

The dominant trait of the ED is the expansion of cities. Archaeological surveys and excavations have shown that the former prominence of Uruk gave way to a more complex urban network along the Tigris and Euphrates as well as major canals connected to them (Adab, Zabalam, Umma, Girsu, Lagash, Bad-Tibira along the Tigris; Nippur, Shuruppak, Larsa, Ur, and Uruk along the Euphrates). It is during the ED that Babylonia acquired its characteristically dense urbanization, and this will remain true until the partial collapse of agriculture in the south during the late Old Babylonian period. Although nearly nothing of the political history of the ED can be recovered, our sources suggest that the region generally lacked unity except in the form of leagues or temporary hegemonies. According to SKL, which divides history mythically between antediluvian and postdiluvian eras, the institution of kingship first resided in Kish after the flood. Excavations at Kish have indeed uncovered the earliest building that can be classified as a palace, dating to the late ED II or the beginning of ED IIIa. Enmebaragesi, the tenth king of the first dynasty of Kish in SKL, is also the first ruler of Babylonia that we can identify from a contemporary source since his name appears on a fragment of an alabaster vase with unknown provenience: "Me-bara(ge)-si, king of Kish." This is the second earliest royal inscription of ancient Mesopotamia, datable to around 2600. The name of Enmebaragesi also appears on another fragment of an alabaster vase from Tutub (modern Khafaje) in the Diyala, perhaps suggesting Kishite hegemony over that region. He is further mentioned in a section of the short Sumerian epic tale Gilgamesh and Aga, which recounts an episode in the military conflict opposing Gilgamesh, ruler of Uruk, to Aga, ruler of Kish. The tale identifies Enmebaragesi as father of Aga. SKL and the Tummal Chronicle also both contain the sequence Enmebaragesi-Aga at Kish. The fact that Enmebaragesi appears in primary sources as historical figure has prompted some scholars to assume the historicity of Gilgamesh as well. However, should new evidence one day prove that Gilgamesh was indeed a real person, the epic tales retelling his life and exploits would still hold no more factual basis than the Homeric Epics. They embodied the memory of a heroic age for Babylonia, one that gave rise in the second millennium to the longest and richest monument of Babylonian literature: the Epic of Gilgamesh, known in Akkadian as *Shutur eli sharri* in its earliest, Old Babylonian version, and *Sha nagba imuru* in the later, standard version composed in the Middle Babylonian period.

The recent publication of an archaic inscribed plaque, probably from the ED II or, less likely, ED I period, appears to confirm that Kish held a hegemonic position quite early. The plaque contains a tally of prisoners taken during military campaigns against various cities and regions. The toponyms that can be identified are located in northern Babylonia, but also in the Diyala (e.g. Warum) and northern Mesopotamia (Assur, Nineveh and Shubur). The captives were assigned to date orchards, presumably as forced labor. All evidence points to Kish as the victorious city and place of origin of the plaque. Although it is not dated and the name of the ruler is not preserved, the plaque probably represents the earliest historical text from Mesopotamia. The number of captives is quite high, adding up to 28,970 in the preserved parts, confirming that Kish exercised considerable power over a large area. Remarkably the plaque from Kish mentions only three sites in Sumer: Nippur, Isin, and Eresh, all on the border with northern Babylonia.

In the south lay the city of Ur, revealed by the excavations led by Sir Leonard Woolley in the 1920s and which for a while competed for world attention with the discovery of the burial chambers of the pharaoh Tutankhamen. The expedition uncovered spectacular royal tombs from the ED IIIa which yielded splendid artifacts and jewelry, as well as material evidence illustrating the despotic nature of power in Sumerian city-states, with an entire retinue of servants buried with their master after having probably been ritually slaughtered. Excavations at Mari in the Middle Euphrates region and at Kish brought similar tombs to light but without the rich remains and explicit evidence found at Ur. Royal inscriptions from all three cities give the same title to their respective rulers: *lugal*, rendered as *sharru* in Akkadian, the word we translate as "king." Sumerian *lugal* originates as a compound: *lu* means "man" and *gal* means "big," therefore the *lugal* is the "big man," a frank articulation of the charismatic nature of these early forms of kingship. Another frequent title for the ruler was *ensi*, later borrowed in Akkadian as *isshiakkum* with the meaning "territorial ruler, intendant, farmer." The title *ensi* embodies a notion of leadership quite at home in Sumerian city-states, where gods and goddesses reigned over the land conceptualized as their private domain, with the population to serve them as subjects and the ruler to administer the domain on their behalf. Later Babylonian kingship will inherit these two aspects of political rule, with the *sharru* appearing to his subjects as a charismatic, dictator-like figure with vast discretionary powers, yet at the same time answerable to the gods in his function of humble caretaker, preoccupied with social justice and the maintenance of temples and canals constituting the gods' domains.

During the ED III the choice of title for rulers seems at times a matter of regional inclination. At Lagash the usual title is *ensi*, although *lugal* is attested on occasions and sometimes concurrently. Lugal-kisalsi of Uruk claims the titles of "king of Uruk" (*lugal Unug*) and "king of Ur" (*lugal Urim*). Yet other rulers of Uruk refer to their office as *nam-en* "lordship" (*nam* is a Sumerian prefix for abstract nouns), and the title *en* "lord" appears indeed in the epic cycle of Uruk as an epithet of Enmerkar, Lugalbanda and Gilgamesh. Lugal-kigene-dudu, in a votive inscription in honor of the god Enlil found at Nippur, claims that he exercised lordship (*nam-en*) in Uruk and kingship (*nam-lugal*) in Ur. He makes the same claim in a votive inscription for the goddess Inanna also found at Nippur but adds that he also held the title of "king of Kish" (*lugal Kish*), which must express his hegemonic pretensions over all Babylonia, perhaps following a military victory against the northern city. Another ruler of Uruk, En-shakush-Ana, adopted the title of "lord of Sumer" (*en kengir*) and "king of the land" (*lugal kalamma*) after his victory over the king of Kish Enbi-Ishtar, reflecting the resilience of the notion of political unity in spite of the prevailing political fragmentation.

None of these rulers can be inserted in any kind of historical narrative: we know their names and the claims they made in their inscriptions, but only their chronological placement somewhere in the ED III seems reasonably secure on archaeological and paleographic grounds. Many years ago it was proposed that the cities of southern Babylonia joined in a "league of Sumer" (the Kengir League) to counteract the actions of Kish. This theory finds support in a group of administrative texts from Shuruppak datable to the ED IIIa which provide evidence for a common militia levied from the cities of Uruk, Adab, Nippur, Lagash, Umma (Gishag), and of course Shuruppak. Uruk heads these lists and may still have been the leader of the league as in the Jemdet Nasr period, but the city of Nippur also played a federative role because of its central geographic position, its relative lack of political importance which made it neutral ground between competing cities, and especially its role as home of the god Enlil, who became the leading god of the official pantheon of Sumer and Akkad in the course of the third millennium. Nippur will retain her supremacy as religious and intellectual center until the second millennium, to see it eventually challenged by Babylon.

2.7.1   The State of Lagash

French excavations at Girsu (modern Tello) a century and a half ago revealed to the world the existence of Sumerian civilization. Girsu was the capital of the ancient state of Lagash, which included the three cities of Girsu, Lagash proper (modern al-Hiba), and Nina (modern Zurghul), as well as the important seaport of Gu'abba (Ninmarki). Among the numerous finds at Girsu one must mention a sequence of elaborate royal inscriptions (Figure 2.3) documenting the complete sequence of rulers of Lagash for a period of about two hundred years (ca. 2550–2350), and an archive of some 1700 administrative texts from the internal accounting of the temple of the goddess Ba'u (or Baba). These constitute the richest inscriptional material from the ED period. The royal inscriptions allow us to sketch a political history of the state, largely dominated – amidst numerous other conflicts – by an endless border dispute with the neighboring city of Umma. This quarrel of limited impact in the overall history of Babylonia nevertheless necessitated at some point the arbitration of Mesilim, the king of Kish, an indication of the influential position still held by this city. The dispute between Lagash and Umma also points to the specific economic and political conditions prevailing in Babylonia in the ED III, characterized by compact networks of settlements where states competed for every strip of arable land and every vital source of water, no matter how small.

The archives of the temple of Ba'u cover a period of about fifteen years corresponding to the end of the reign of En-entarzi, the entire six years of the reign of Lugalanda, and the seven years of the reign of Urukagina (or Uru'inimgina; the sign KA "mouth" also has the reading INIM "word"), after which the state of Lagash was conquered by Lugal-zagesi of Umma. As is the case with most cuneiform archives, this accumulation of documents over a rather short period corresponds to the time span between the last clean-up of

Figure 2.3   Plaque of Ur-Nanshe. This limestone plaque in the Louvre Museum bears an inscription of Ur-Nanshe, the first of a long line of well-documented rulers of Lagash during the ED III. Ur-Nanshe is depicted twice and in larger size, a common artistic convention for the ruler. In the upper register he carries the work-basket, symbolizing his role as temple builder, a motif which was revived in the first millennium (Figure 8.3). Other figures are identified with captions and include the crown prince Akurgal and six other sons of Ur-Nanshe. Measurements: W 47 × H 40 cm (18 1/4 × 15 ¼ in.). *Source*: Photo © RMN-Grand Palais (musée du Louvre) / Philipp Bernard.

the archive rooms (towards the end of the reign of En-entarzi) and the violent disruptions to which we owe the preservation of the documents (in this case the conquest of Girsu). Much of what we know about Sumerian society in the ED period rests on the data from this archive, but its interpretation remains contentious. For a long time there prevailed the theory of the "Sumerian temple state (or city)," based on the perception that the temples controlled all the land and resources, and that the ruling and priestly classes derived their authority from managing the gods' domains into a vast redistributive system. Critics of this theory have questioned the representativeness of our sources: can we extend to all of Sumer the data obtained from one archive, especially in a city which contained several more temples of equal importance, not to mention the possibility of undocumented royal, communal and private ownership of land? Yet the importance of temples cannot be denied. Based on the data from the archive, the temple of Ba'u alone possessed about 4,500 hectares of land, which represents an enormous area. One fourth of the land was allocated to the high-priest (the *en*) for the maintenance of the cult and his household, and the rest allocated to the staff of the temple as salary, with a portion leased out to tenant farmers. The temple was also an important economic center, employing craftsmen and workers in addition to the staff devoted to cultic functions, estimates for the temple of Ba'u being about 1,200 employees. In and of itself, however, this type of economic organization does not seem to warrant the elaboration of a particular theory of the Sumerian state, since it is also quite typical of large institutional landowners – whether state or temples – in second and first millennium Babylonia, and indeed of a number of ancient agrarian societies.

2.7.1.1 The reforms of Urukagina

The originality of the Sumerian city-state lies more in the elaboration of specific religious ideas, notably the role of the ruler as conscientious steward of the gods' domains. These notions came to the forefront of political discourse during the reign of Urukagina, the last ED IIIb ruler of Lagash. Urukagina is best known for his Reform Texts, preserved in several of his inscriptions. He claims to have reduced the economic and administrative power of the *ensi* and to have restored land to their previous owners, the gods Ningirsu, Ba'u and Shulshaga. What that rhetoric conceals remains uncertain, but the assertion that he returned land to the gods seems supported by a change of terminology in the archives of the temple of Ba'u. Before his reign, allocated land is often described as "property of Lugalanda" (Urukagina's predecessor) and "property of Baranamtarra" (Lugalanda's wife), while after his reform the texts refer to allocated land as "property of the goddess Ba'u." The change may have been purely cosmetic, resulting in no significant adjustment in the socio-economic fabric of the state. However, Urukagina also corrected a number of abuses (or so he claims), and, more importantly he decreed a cancellation of debts and other penalties, providing the earliest evidence for a practice that will become a cornerstone of the legislative activities of the First Dynasty of Babylon in the form of the Edicts of Redress (*mesharum*). His Reform Texts conclude with a statement that he would not abandon the orphan and the widow to the powerful, a claim that will also become a topos of royal legislative literature. Hammu-rabi makes exactly the same assertion in the prologue of his Code. The Reform Texts of Urukagina prove that this important aspect of Babylonian political thought had already crystallized by the end of the ED period.

2.7.2 Babylon in the Early Dynastic Period

Historical surveys of the ED routinely ignore Babylon. However, there is potential evidence for the existence of the city during the ED in an inscription on a limestone plaque preserved in the Babylonian Collection, Yale University. The paleography of the inscription speaks in favor of a dating to the ED IIIa period, although there is no agreement on this. The text, written in what seems to be an early form of Akkadian, reads as follows: "[o o o], ruler of Babbir, son of Ahu-ilum, man of Ilum-beli, man of Ur-Kubi, builder of the temple of Marduk, the one who set up [this votive o o o]." While the name of the author of the dedication cannot be recovered, his title has elicited some discussion: "ruler of Babbir" translates a sequence of logograms which reads ENSI BAR.KI.BAR. The term ENSI must be read in Akkadian in this case, not as Sumerian *ensi*, therefore presumably as its Akkadian equivalent *isshiakkum*. The interpretation of BAR.KI.BAR presents no major difficulty if we keep in mind that the sequential order of logograms retained some freedom in monumental inscriptions until the end of the ED. Therefore we can reorder the sequence as BAR.BAR.KI, where KI is the determinative for geographic locations, leaving the name of the toponym as BAR.BAR. Reduplication of logograms normally conceals a slightly different phonetic realization, hence Babbar or Babra/Babbara seem likely names for this place. The fact that the ruler of Babbar styles himself as builder of the temple of Marduk (ᵈAMAR.UTU), known later as the patron god of Babylon, suggests very strongly that Babbar is in fact an early form of the name of Babylon and should perhaps be rendered as Babbir, which would have become later Babbil with interchange of the liquid phonemes /r/ and /l/. The later form of the name Babylon in Akkadian is Bab(b)ilu.

The identification BAR.KI.BAR = Babylon has not met with general agreement. Yet rejecting it presupposes the existence of another city with a name similar to Babylon and also dedicated to the cult of Marduk. Only excavations in the early levels of Babylon could resolve the issue. However, this seems unlikely ever to happen; these levels lie mostly under the water table and cannot be excavated. The city is known largely from its appearance in the first millennium, with limited forays into the Kassite and Old Babylonian levels. However, archaeological surveys of Babylon did yield surface finds dating to the ED. One area with such finds is the mound of Babil north of the site, where lies a Neo-Babylonian structure with a Parthian fortress built over it. Pottery shards dating from the ED to the Old Babylonian period were found there, presumably as part of the Parthian fill, but they may point to an earlier occupation of the area unless intrusive (i.e. taken from another site as fill). Shards which date as early as the ED III and are less likely to be intrusive have also been found on the surface of Amran and in the area west of Homera. These finds seem to confirm the presence of ED settlements on the site of Babylon. These settlements, whether or not we identify them as BAR.KI.BAR, must have grown under the shadow of the powerful city of Kish, located only about fifteen kilometers east.

2.8   The Sargonic (Old Akkadian) and Gutian Periods (ca. 2334–2113)

Lugal-zagesi's conquest of Lagash heralds the end of the Early Dynastic period. He transferred his capital from Umma to Uruk and embarked on a series of military campaigns aimed at uniting Babylonia under his rule, a goal reflected in his adoption of the title "king of the land" (*lugal kalama*). Soon, however, Lugal-zagesi clashed with another dynast who had established his power base in northern Babylonia in the city of Agade (or Akkade). Agade has not yet been identified but probably lay in the lower Diyala valley or along the Tigris near the Diyala. History remembers this dynast as Sargon, going back to the Akkadian original Sharru-kin "the king is legitimate," a programmatic utterance that may well be a throne name. The rise of Sargon ushers in the Sargonic (or Old Akkadian) period, an era that witnessed many cultural and political developments in Babylonia and the rise of the first empire centered on Mesopotamia (see Map 2.2). Sources become more copious and varied than for the ED. An important corpus of Old Akkadian royal inscriptions has survived, although a significant number of them are extant only in copies made later during the Old Babylonian period, mostly from monuments then in view at Nippur. Old Akkadian archives can be found at several sites in Babylonia and even in northern Mesopotamia. The generalized use of year names in archival documents provides us with welcome tidbits of historical information, although their chronological order is not known since date lists have not been preserved for that period. The deeds of the Sargonic kings, especially Sargon and his grandson Naram-Sin, gave rise to a prolific epic and wisdom literature which has little value to reconstruct the history of the period, even though isolated elements, the so-called "historical core," are sometimes corroborated by contemporary sources.

2.8.1   Akkadian and Sumerian Linguistic Areas

An important development of the Sargonic period is the introduction of Old Akkadian as the main language of royal inscriptions and administration. It did not completely displace Sumerian, which remained entrenched in the archival documentation from southern Babylonia as native language of the scribes and the majority of the population. A number of Sargon's inscriptions are known in Sumerian and Akkadian versions, a practice largely abandoned by his successors who favored inscriptions in Akkadian only. According to recent research, Old Akkadian in its standardized form reflects the language spoken in the Diyala valley. For a long time Assyriologists viewed Old Akkadian as the oldest form of a unified Akkadian language, before the split between northern (Assyrian) and southern (Babylonian) dialects at the beginning of the second millennium. A number of arguments have now been advanced to reclassify Old Akkadian either as direct ancestor of Babylonian, or as an isolated dialect closely related to Babylonian. According to these views, Assyrian would descend from another branch of Akkadian spoken in northern Iraq. The division of Babylonia into Sumerian and Akkadian speaking areas, with a linguistic border running somewhere north of Nippur, is already evident in the ED, and the predominance of Sumerian in sources from that period may simply result from the fact that ED archives have been discovered mostly in southern Babylonia (Ur, Shuruppak and Girsu). In fact, a number of clues point to the importance of the Semitic element at an early date. For instance, the site of Abu Salabikh near Nippur has yielded an important collection of literary texts in Sumerian datable to the ED IIIa, with about half of the scribes bearing Semitic names. At Kish a few rulers also bear Semitic names (e.g. Enbi-Ishtar), while the inscription of the ENSI of BAR. KI.BAR is written in an early form of Akkadian, and two of the three individuals it mentions have Semitic names (Ahu-ilum, Ilum-beli).

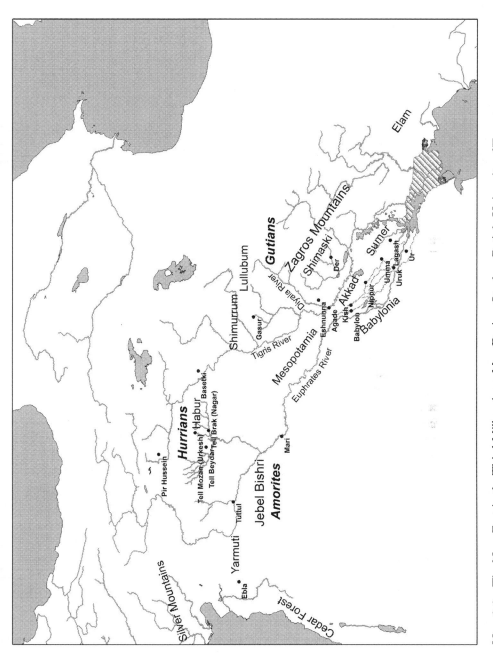

Map 2.2 The Near East in the Third Millennium. Map Design: Stephen Batiuk, University of Toronto.

As we move into northern Mesopotamia and Syria, the Semitic element becomes completely predominant. At Mari, the powerful city on the Middle Euphrates, local rulers during the ED III bore Semitic names and wrote their inscriptions and administrative texts in a form of Akkadian. The same is true of a group of over 230 tablets found in houses and administrative buildings at Tell Beydar (ancient Nabada) in the Habur region. The texts date roughly between 2450–2400 (beginning of ED IIIb). The most spectacular find occurred at Ebla (modern Tell Mardikh) in northern Syria where an archaeological expedition discovered a palace archive dating to the end of ED IIIb and the beginning of the Sargonic period. The language spoken at Ebla appears clearly Semitic, but because of the geographic location of the city Eblaite was initially classified as West Semitic. Further study has shown, however, that Eblaite shares more affinities with Akkadian and must belong to the East Semitic branch, while a number of scholars now simply consider Eblaite a Western form of Akkadian. The finds at Mari, Ebla, and Tell Beydar indicate that well before the rise of Sargon, cuneiform writing had been successfully adapted to Semitic. The sudden emergence of Old Akkadian as official language now appears less singular, rather like a step in the larger process of the diffusion of writing. The spread of the cuneiform writing technology increased in turn the influence of Sumerian. Texts from Ebla, Mari, and Tell Beydar make abundant use of Sumerian words and logograms, to the extent that it is sometimes difficult to find elements written phonetically in the local language, although the syntax of the texts is clearly Semitic. The scholastic tradition which had developed in Sumer, especially the growing corpus of lexical lists, now enjoyed even greater dissemination, carried along the roads travelled by cuneiform.

2.8.2   The Early Sargonic Period (ca. 2334–2255)

The internal chronology of the Sargonic period holds numerous uncertainties. SKL, our main source for the order of succession, filiations and length of reigns of the Sargonic rulers, credits Sargon with a reign of fifty-six years, reduced to forty years in SKL-Ur-III (a different version of SKL extant in an Ur III manuscript). However, very few of his year names have been recovered from contemporary documents. His royal inscriptions contain no secure chronological data, yet they constitute our main source for his reign. Obscurity surrounds the circumstances of his rise to power in northern Babylonia. After defeating his southern rival Lugal-zagesi, Sargon apparently brought all of Sumer (including separate campaigns against Gu'abba, Lagash, and Umma) under his rule. In another inscription he boasts of broader conquests in Syria and Lebanon as a gift from the god Dagan: "Sargon, the king, bowed down to Dagan in Tuttul. He (Dagan) gave to him (Sargon) the Upper Land: Mari, Yarmuti, and Ebla as far as the Cedar Forest and the Silver Mountains," and a year name probably to be attributed to Sargon reads "the year when Mari was destroyed." Archaeologists have uncovered important destruction levels at both Mari and Ebla datable to the early Sargonic period. However, since Naram-Sin, the grandson of Sargon, also claims to have destroyed Ebla, the question cannot be resolved on the basis of sources from Babylonia alone.

The answer may come from Ebla itself. The state archives discovered there cover roughly the last thirty-five years of the kingdom of Ebla before the destruction occurred, another typical case of ancient archival accumulation and survival; the accumulation corresponds to the entire reign of the Eblaite ruler Ishar-Damu, implying that an archival clean-up took place at the time of his accession. Remarkably, not a single reference to Sargon or even to Agade can be found in the texts from Ebla. On the other hand, one finds several references to Mari which intimate that the two cities competed with one another, and one tablet, the Enna-Dagan letter, records that in the past the city of Mari had established its hegemony over Ebla. On the basis of this evidence there is now growing consensus that Ebla's destruction came from an attack by Mari. Afterwards Mari probably ruled for some fifteen years over Ebla, to be in turn destroyed by Sargon during the reign of Ishgi-Mari. An inscribed votive statue of this ruler with its nose mutilated was found in the ED palace at Mari. Then Ebla fell in Sargon's hands as a side result of this campaign. The evidence from Ebla, still largely unknown a generation ago, reveals the existence at that time of interregional dynamics that bear a close resemblance to those of the age of Hammu-rabi. In both cases a state centered in northern Babylonia (Agade, later Babylon) emerged victorious from a struggle between competing territorial states spread over a large area from Sumer to the Levant (Ebla, Mari, and Uruk; later Aleppo, Mari, Eshnunna, and Larsa). How much effective control Sargon gained over his more remote conquests cannot be ascertained. He also claimed victories against the lands of Shimurrum in northeastern Mesopotamia and Elam in southwestern Iran.

After Sargon's death his sons Rimush (ca. 2278–2270) and Manishtushu (ca. 2269–2255) reigned successively, although SKL-Ur-III places Rimush after Manishtushu. Rimush faced opposition in Sumer and most of his inscriptions record a string of victorious battles against Adab, Zabalam, Umma, Lagash, Ur, and other places, but he also engaged in military operations against eastern powers, including Elam. Manishtushu's reign is even less known, except for brief mentions of an eastern campaign. One of the most important sources for his reign, a black diorite monument known as the Obelisk of Manishtushu, records his purchase, perhaps compulsory, of large domains in northern Babylonia which he then granted to favorites. By and large Sargon and his two sons left preexisting structures in place, content with imposing only a loose hegemony not unlike the one that Kish probably exercised earlier. Indeed, they considered themselves very much in continuity with Kish. Sargon claimed to be "king of Kish" in addition to "king of Agade," while Rimush and Manishtushu dropped "king of Agade" altogether in favor of "king of Kish" as their sole title. During the ED III "king of Kish" had gradually become detached from actual rulership in Kish to symbolize the hegemonic position gained by any ruler of Babylonia in imitation of the supremacy once exercised by Kish. The title is often translated as "king of the totality". Its later Akkadian equivalent, *shar kisshati*, in fact very much means that and carries no association with the city of Kish. However, the Kishite connection of the Sargonic rulers probably ran deeper. A tradition about Sargon which is preserved in SKL and later literature makes him an official at the court of Ur-Zababa of Kish before he revolted against his master to found Agade. This tradition, while almost certainly apocryphal, mirrors cultural and political ties between Kish and Agade that were probably very real and extended to all northern Babylonia, ties of language, religion, and probably social organization as well which remain poorly understood because of the scarcity of sources from northern Babylonia before Naram-Sin. Yet continuity between Kish and Agade makes up the cornerstone of SKL-Ur-III, which views "kingship" (*nam-lugal*) as a central- ized institution first at home in Kish, then in Agade, and then in Ur (III). In the political realm the Sargonic rulers definitively imposed the title of "king" *lugal* (*sharrum* in Akkadian), initiating the demotion of the *ensi* to the status of governor, at best vassal prince. Afterwards "kingship" (*sharrutu*) will remain the focal institution of Babylonian political life.

2.8.3   The Classical Sargonic Period (ca. 2254–2193)

The reigns of Naram-Sin (ca. 2254–2218) and Shar-kali-sharri (ca. 2217–2193) correspond to a new era that witnessed the creation of a more centralized state and impressive achievements in the visual arts. According to SKL, Naram-Sin was the son of Manishtushu and Shar-kali-sharri the son of Naram-Sin. Archival sources increase considerably during that period. About half the year names of Naram-Sin and most of Shar-kali-sharri's have been recovered from archival documents, but the chronology of events still remains elusive. SKL ascribes a reign of fifty-six years to Naram-Sin (fifty-four years in SKL-Ur-III), a figure which seems too high and probably repeats the one given for Sargon. By and large the events of his reign can be organized into two groups, those which took place before his assumption of divine status, and those after. His divinity is expressed in his inscriptions and year names by the prefixing of the determinative for gods to his name. The name Naram-Sin means "beloved of the god Sin" and it is normally written *na-ra-am-*^dEN.ZU, where the first three signs spell the word *naram* "beloved of" and the last three form the name of the moon-god Sin, writ- ten with the logogram EN.ZU (read ZU.EN > Su'en > Sin) and preceded by the divine determinative DINGIR "god" (in Sumerian), indicated in transcription by a small < d > in superscript: ^dEN.ZU. After Naram-Sin's deification this deter- minative precedes his entire name: ^d*na-ra-am-*^dEN.ZU "the divine Naram-Sin." Events which occurred before his deification include a string of campaigns against localities situated mostly in the northeast, and the suppression of the great rebellion of Babylonia. The latter event constituted the defining event of his reign and significantly altered the course of Sargonic history.

2.8.3.1   The great rebellion against Naram-Sin

The main primary source for the great rebellion is an inscription of Naram-Sin extant in a later copy from Nippur. The rebellion apparently started in northern

Babylonia, where a certain Iphur-Kish was elevated to the kingship of Kish. Then it spread to Sumer where one Amar-girid seized power at Uruk. The inscription mentions other rebels, among whom Enlil-nizu from Nippur may have been a third leader of the insurrection. It also says that Naram-Sin fought "nine battles in one year" to crush his opponents, a claim repeated in other inscriptions. The actual occurrence of the great rebellion does not appear so singular in light of the intermittent state of warfare and unrest since the ED III – Rimush faced a revolt of seemingly equal importance in Sumer earlier – but like other events in history it made an impact that seems disproportionate with its substance. Not only did it prompt Naram-Sin to initiate administrative reforms aimed at strengthening the empire's loose structure, but also it soon became memorialized in literary compositions which gradually embellished the facts in epic fashion and moved increasingly distant from the historical reality of the event. As it entered the realm of myth the great rebellion became a topos, and many subsequent rulers (starting with his own son Shar-kali-sharri) who faced similar insurgencies at the onset of their reigns left inscriptions commemorating their victories in terms borrowed directly or obliquely from the scribal tradition about Naram-Sin, the last adherent to this convention being the Persian king Darius I, who recorded his defeat of the eleven rival pretenders to the throne on the famous rock relief at Bisitun almost two thousand years later (see Figure 10.1). The topos of the great rebellion peaked during the Old Babylonian period. Samsu-iluna, Hammu-rabi's son and successor on the throne of Babylon, faced a series of rebellions in Sumer and recorded his victory over the insurrectionists in inscriptions that mimics those of Naram-Sin, thus also establishing, so to speak, his "Great Rebellion" credentials.

2.8.3.2   Deification and centralization

Naram-Sin's reaction to the great rebellion led to a number of innovations that left a distinct mark on Babylonia. The most immediate one was his own deification, recorded in an inscription on a bronze doorpost discovered at Basetki in the northern confines of Iraq. The inscription claims that the inhabitants of the capital requested from the gods of Babylonia that Naram-Sin be proclaimed god of Agade:

> Naram-Sin, the mighty, king of Agade, when the four quarters rebelled against him, by the love which the goddess Ishtar showed him, he won nine battles in one year, and he captured the kings who rose against him. Because he protected the foundations of his city from danger, (the denizens of) his city requested from (the deities) Ishtar in Ayakkum (i.e. Uruk), Enlil in Nippur, Dagan in Tuttul, Nin-hursag in Kesh, Ea in Eridu, Sin in Ur, Shamash in Sippar, (and) Nergal in Kutha, that he (Naram-Sin) be (made) god of their city, Agade, and they built in Agade a temple for him.[1]

Claims of divine parentage for the ruler occurred earlier in ED III Lagash, but they fell short of proclaiming the ruler himself a god. By attaining divine status Naram-Sin broke definitely with the Sumerian view of the *ensi* as humble servant, giving a new impetus to the *lugal* as a figure larger than life, a superhero of sorts. Some have claimed that Egyptian influence may have shaped his decision. This seems possible, but deification of the ruler in Babylonia carried fewer implications than in Egypt, where the pharaoh's position as living and immortal god constituted one of the cornerstones of the theological system. A more convincing parallel is the divinization and apotheosis of Roman emperors, a hyperbolic act recognizing their personal achievements as well as the uniqueness and transcendence of their status. Deification of the ruler never took deep roots in Babylonia and faded away under the First Dynasty of Babylon.

Naram-Sin made a number of innovations to royal titles, retaining from his predecessors only "king of Agade" and definitively abandoning "king of Kish." A rarer title which came as direct consequence of his deification is "god of Agade." The titles "mighty" (*dannum*) and "king of the four quarters" also constitute innovations which apparently followed the great rebellion, the latter replacing "king of Kish" as hegemonic title. It became a favorite expression of the universal power of the king until the first millennium, the four quarters reflecting the four points of the compass.

The rebellion had highlighted the problems of maintaining a vast realm united, calling not only for political but also administrative solutions. The study of archival texts has shown that several improvements in this area took place under Naram-Sin, notably the imposition of a normalized form of Akkadian with uniform orthographic conventions, a reform of the script which then lost many of the archaic aspects it still retained from the ED period, and rationalization of accounting techniques with the standardization of the metrological system, notably the establishment of new capacity measures such as the *gur* of 300 *silas* (ca. 300 liters), which remained in use until the first millennium. Naram-Sin also encouraged the creation of a system of provinces ruled directly by royal appointees and strengthened the defense of the empire with a network of roads and border garrisons. The site of Gasur (modern Yorghan Tepe, about fifteen kilometers southwest of Kirkuk) in the northeast, later known as Nuzi, has yielded an archive from the Sargonic period which documents such a garrison. The list would be incomplete without mentioning dramatic innovations in the realm of the figurative arts. Art expresses the mood of an era, its *Zeitgeist*, often in better ways that any other medium. In its most achieved productions, the art of the Classical Sargonic period displays fluid and graceful aesthetics which contrast with the generally austere hieratic style of ED art. The new Sargonic aesthetics pervade such masterpieces as the Stele of Naram-Sin (Figure 2.4) and a number of remarkable cylinders seals carved at the time of Shar-kali-sharri, with sexually alluring depictions of males in heroic posture propagating the notion of the invincibility and even desirability of the monarch and its symbolic surrogates. Some scholars have again detected Egyptian influence in the elaboration of this new imperial art, yet the Egyptian artistic canons of that period seem stiff and rigid in comparison. The art of the Ur III and Old Babylonian periods will retain some of the elegance of Sargonic art, but without its dynamics and naturalism.

Figure 2.4   Victory Stele of Naram-Sin (Detail). This limestone stele in the Louvre
Museum celebrates Naram-Sin's victory over Lullubum, a mountain people from the Zagros.
The deified Naram-Sin is depicted wearing the horned tiara of gods. The inscription on
the mountain peak was added by the Elamite king Shutruk-Nahhunte, who carried off the
stele to Susa in the twelfth century (section 5.9). Measurements: H 2 × W 1.05 m. *Source*:
Photo © RMN-Grand Palais (musée du Louvre) / Franck Raux.

A year name of Naram-Sin claims that his armies penetrated quite far north,
seeking the source of the Tigris and Euphrates: "The year when the divine
Naram-Sin reached the sources of the Tigris and the Euphrates rivers and was
victorious in battle over Shenaminda." A fragment of a stele inscribed in his
name was found at Pir Hussein not very far from the source of the Tigris in
eastern Turkey. Other year names and inscriptions mention campaigns in the
west (e.g. Ebla; the Cedar Forest of Lebanon) and the east (e.g. Lullubum,
Shimurrum), but the extent of permanent imperial control cannot easily be
assessed without actual proof from the areas in question. The most conclusive
evidence comes from Tell Brak (ancient Nagar) in the Habur, where Old Akkadian buildings have been identified, as well as bricks stamped with the name of
Naram-Sin and two votive inscriptions of Rimush. Local Hurrian dynasts
established their seat at the nearby site of Tell Mozan (ancient Urkesh); impres-
sions of cylinder seals discovered at Mozan bear evidence for a matrimonial
alliance between them and the ruling house in Agade. Such evidence, albeit
meager, suggests a mixed pattern of imperial control, with select strongholds
amidst a network of client states.

2.8.3.3   The reign of Shar-kali-sharri

Shar-kali-sharri records a number of military campaigns in his inscriptions and year names, but with the exception of an expedition in imitation of his father to the source of the Tigris and Euphrates they all seem to have been defensive in nature, involving attacks by the Elamites, the Gutians, and also the Amorite West Semitic tribes, who are mentioned for the first time as a threat. These attacks reduced Sargonic territory considerably and may account for Shar-kali-sharri's abandonment of the title "king of the four quarters." However, he still claimed to be "mighty" and "king of Agade," and continued to assert the ruler's divine status with such epithets as "divine hero of Agade" and "god of the land of Akkad." In his lifetime Naram-Sin had appointed him to a vice-regal position at Nippur. Shar-kali-sharri's devotion to the god Enlil probably originated in those years and blossomed after his accession to the throne, expressed in such epithets as "favorite son of the god Enlil" and "king of the creatures of the god Enlil," the latter providing plain evidence that Enlil had now become head of the pantheon and lord of the human race. The rise of the god Enlil, which began during the ED period, continued unabated under the Sargonic kings, who often claim to have received rulership from him. Several year names of Shar-kali-sharri commemorate construction work on the temple of Enlil, initiated by Naram-Sin, and an archive from Nippur dated mostly to his reign records expenditures for the final stages of its construction and decoration. They make it clear that Shar-kali-sharri rebuilt the temple in grandiose proportions, as the gold, silver, and bronze required for the construction is measured in hundreds of kilos, and the copper in tons. By the end of Shar-kali-sharri's reign, however, the Sargonic empire had practically disappeared and his death ushered in a time of chaos described by SKL as "who was king, who was not king?"

2.8.4   Babylon in the Sargonic Period

The later tradition attributed the fall of Agade to the Gutians, a mountain people from the Zagros mentioned as migrant workers and sometimes troublemakers or military opponents in Sargonic sources. A year name of Shar-kali-sharri celebrates his defeat of the Gutian king Sharlak and also mentions work on two temples in Babylon: "The year when Shar-kali-sharri laid the foundations of the temple of Anunitum and of the temple of Ilaba in Babylon, and defeated Sharlak, king of Gutium." This year name is recognized as the earliest secure mention of Babylon, written in this case KÁ.DINGIR^{ki}, one of the most common orthographies of the city's name in later sources. The logogram KÁ means "gate" in Sumerian and translates as *babu* in Akkadian, DINGIR means "god" and translates as *ilu* (as we have seen this sign also serves as determinative for divine beings), and KI is the post-posed determinative for geographic names. Therefore the compound KÁ.DINGIR^{ki} reads as *Bab-ili* "gate of the god(s)" as place name, rendering the

Akkadian form of the name Babylon: *Babilu* or *Babili*. The original name of Baby-lon, however, does not mean "gate of the gods," which represents a popular or learned pun on the city's name. The ancients relished such puns, often branded as "folk etymologies." As we have seen, *Babbar* or *Babbir* seems the most probable original form of Babylon's name and bears no relation to gates or gods, but might more plausibly be related to the Sumerian word *babbar* "white, pale, shining."

2.8.5   The Late Sargonic (ca. 2193–2154) and Gutian Periods (ca. 2153–2113)

The era extending from the death of Shar-kali-sharri to the advent of Ur-Namma, founder of the Third Dynasty of Ur, presents intractable chronological issues. After the brief period of chaos which followed Shar-kali-sharri's demise, SKL continues the dynastic list of Agade with four kings (Irgigi, Nanum, Imi and Elulu) who ruled three years (ca. 2193–2190), and concludes by attributing a reign of twenty-one years to Dudu (ca. 2190–2169) and fifteen years to Shu-Turul (ca. 2169–2154). Dudu and Shu-Turul have left a few brief inscriptions in which they still claim the titles "mighty" and "king of Agade," but very little is known about their rule, limited to the region around Agade, the Diyala river (Turul is the ancient name of the Diyala river and the name Shu-Turul means "He of the Diyala"), and a few cities of northern Babylonia. A seal inscription of a servant of Shu-Turul found at Eshnunna (Tell Asmar) indicates that the city remained under Old Akkadian control until the end of the dynasty. SKL then continues its fictional linear narrative with a fourth Dynasty of Uruk, a Dynasty of Gutium, and then a fifth Dynasty of Uruk made up of only one representative, Utu-hegal, after whom power passed to the Third Dynasty of Ur. In reality, during the late Sargonic period Babylonia returned to the political fragmentation of the ED period. A new dynasty arose at Lagash-Girsu whose most illustrious representative, the *ensi* Gudea, presided over a brilliant flowering of Sumerian art and literature, epitomized by the remarkable collection of inscribed diorite statues portraying him in standing and sitting postures (Figure 2.5). Gudea's dynasty may have been partly coeval with the Third Dynasty of Ur but the evidence remains ambiguous. The Gutians too appear to have ruled parts of Babylonia since a handful of inscriptions of Gutian kings are known. However, given the unreliability of SKL and because all the epigraphic evidence remains local in scope and cannot be readily synchronized with material from other sites, even the length of this period is unknown. Some have estimated at no more than forty years the interval from the death of Shar-kali-sharri to the advent of Ur-Namma, which would make the latter's reign begin almost immediately after the death of Shu-Turul and the end of Agade. The same view is propagated by SKL-Ur-III, which assumes a direct transition between Agade and Ur III. The chronology adopted here posits a period of about eighty years between the death of Shar-kali-sharri and the advent of Ur-Namma.

Figure 2.5   Gudea, Prince of Lagash. Gudea ruled Lagash before the rise of Ur III and is known from numerous inscriptions and statues, many of them in the Louvre Museum. This diorite statue (Gudea Statue P), probably from Girsu, depicts him in the seated pose of a ruler with his hands folded in a traditional gesture of prayer. The inscription details his building works on temples. Measurements: 17 3/8 × 8 1/2 × 11 5/8 in. (44 × 21.5 × 29.5 cm). *Source*: The Metropolitan Museum of Art, NYC (MMA 59.2), Public Domain.

2.9   The Third Dynasty of Ur (2112–2004)

Utu-hegal, the sole ruler of the Fifth Dynasty of Uruk according to SKL, left a few inscriptions including a lengthy one written in epic style and preserved only in Old Babylonian copies. He claims to have expelled the Gutians from Babylonia and captured their king Tiriqan. In addition to "king of Uruk" Utu-hegal took the typical Sargonic titles of "mighty" and "king of the four quarters." Power soon relocated to Ur, however, where Ur-Namma founded a royal line known as the Third Dynasty of Ur following the count of dynasties in SKL. Ur-Namma may have been the brother or son of Utu-hegal, who appears in an Ur III document from the reign of Shu-Sin as recipient of offerings, possibly in his quality as deceased family ancestor. The Ur III period, as it is generally known, produced an abundant archival documentation estimated conservatively at more than 100,000 tablets and which keeps increasing with new discoveries. The bulk of these texts cover a period of about forty years (2065–2025), from

Shulgi year 30 until Ibbi-Sin years 4–6, at which point state-run administrative centers were suddenly abandoned with their archival accumulation left in situ. With the exception of Ur-Namma's, the year names of Ur III are all preserved, and their order is known from date lists. Because hegemonic power had shifted back to the south the Ur III period signals a return of the Sumerian language in the administrative and legal sphere, although a number of sources still use Akkadian. Ur III royal inscriptions, also redacted mostly in Sumerian, disclose few details of political and military history except those of Shu-Sin. Some Assyriologists maintain that the official Ur III sponsorship of Sumerian conceals rampant Akkadianization of the society and that Sumerian may already have died out as spoken language. Indeed, the names of the last two rulers of the dynasty, Shu-Sin and Ibbi-Sin, are Akkadian. Others disagree, adhering to the traditional view which places the demise of Sumerian in the Isin-Larsa period (early second millennium).

2.9.1   King of Sumer and Akkad

Ur-Namma (2112–2095) initiated a return to stability in Babylonia. His inscriptions detail his reorganization of irrigation with new canals in the region of Ur and towards the south. He also claims to have reopened traffic with the Persian Gulf, bringing the "ships of Magan (Oman)" back to Ur. Renewed prosperity is evident from the intensity of Ur-Namma's building activities in Sumer, especially in the capital Ur where the cultic complex of the moon-god Nanna-Su'en (Sin) reached monumental proportions that can still be appraised nowadays from the remains of the ziggurat, whose lower levels were very successfully restored by the Iraqi Government. Ur-Namma took the title "king of Ur" from the beginning of his reign, and occasionally "lord (en) of Uruk" as a reminder of his connection to Uruk where his relative Utu-hegal had reigned. Soon he claimed the Sargonic epithet of "mighty" and, more significant, created the political concept of "king of Sumer and Akkad." After the demise of Shu-Turul, the last king of Agade, the Elamite ruler Puzur-Inshushinak occupied the Diyala and northern Babylonia. Ur-Namma claims to have liberated the region and clashed against the Gutians as well, but how much effective control he exercised over Akkad seems doubtful. He lays an assertive claim to rule much of Akkad in an inscription known as the "Ur III cadaster," which defines the landed areas ascribed to cities of northern Babylonia, including Kish, Kazallu and Apiak. Yet, we have no texts dated to his reign from northern Babylonia and his building activities are not attested there. The most important source that sheds light on Ur-Namma's activities as statesman is his Law Code, now known from an almost complete version preserved in the Schøyen Collection (Oslo and London). Written in Sumerian, the laws of Ur-Namma were copied in schools as model legislation for more than three hundred years and provided the main inspiration for those of Hammu-rabi. The question as to whether the Code of Ur-Namma and other collections of laws from the ancient Near East formed actual legislation continues to be debated. Still, the promulgation of such laws by Ur-Namma, regardless of their actual reach and applicability, signals his intention to provide Babylonia with unified institutions, a program that will be carried much further by his son and successor Shulgi.

2.9.2   Shulgi's Babylonia

The first seventeen year names of Shulgi's long reign (2094–2047) commemorate mostly pious foundations. During that period Shulgi must have consolidated Ur's hegemony over Sumer and Akkad. His eleventh year name celebrates the installation of the god Ishtaran of Der in his temple, suggesting that Shulgi now held this important center east of the Tigris which controlled access to the Diyala and to northern Babylonia from Elam. However, Der soon became contested territory again. Shulgi's twentieth year name mentions conscription at Ur, probably in preparation for the campaign against Der commemorated in his twenty-first year name. This campaign, preceded by the marriage of one of Shulgi's daughters to the ruler of Marhashi southeast of Elam (year name 18), signals a turn in Shulgi's foreign policy. The balance of his year names record a series of military expeditions targeting a large conglomeration of territories in northern Mesopotamia and east of the Tigris all the way down to southwestern Iran. Shulgi's titles now begin to express ambitions recalling Sargonic imperialism. The titles inherited from his father: "the mighty, king of Ur, king of Sumer and Akkad," often give way to "the mighty, king of Ur, king of the four quarters." The latter epithet appears more in line with the political tradition shaped by Naram-Sin, whom he also emulated by assuming divine status. Like Naram-Sin he prefixed the divine determinative to his name, a practice retained by the remaining three kings of the Ur III dynasty, added the epithet "god of his land" to his royal titles, and some state bureaucrats changed their names, adopting new ones such as Shulgi-ili ("the divine Shulgi is my personal god"). Contrary to the Sargonic kings, however, Shulgi and his successors showed little or no interest in western expansion, and for the most part their relations with the powerful kingdom of Mari remained cordial, cemented by Shulgi's marriage with the daughter of its ruler Apil-kin. Economic factors have been advanced to explain Shulgi's fixation on the east. These regions abounded in stones, metals, and wood, materials largely absent in Babylonia. Other imports such as lapis lazuli and especially tin, a strategic resource essential for the manufacture of bronze, came from further east in central Asia (Afghanistan, Tajikistan, and Uzbekistan), and in the latter part of the third millennium they began to reach Iraq through the Iranian Plateau instead of the Persian Gulf due to the introduction of the Bactrian camel as pack animal, inaugurating the famous trade route known later as the Silk Road. The desire to control these networks may easily have oriented Ur III policy towards eastern expansion.

In the middle of his reign Shulgi also launched a series of reforms that reorganized Babylonia into a homogenized polity, a process already initiated by

Ur-Namma. This aspect of Shulgi's statesmanship deserves recognition more than all his military actions because of their long term influence on Babylonia. He divided Sumer and Akkad into more than twenty provinces each headed by an *ensi*, a title which no longer denoted independent rulership of a city-state but more the position of a governor, although Ur III *ensi*s appear to have originated mostly from local elites. Military affairs in each province were entrusted to a royal deputy, the *shagina*. All provinces contributed to the *bala*, a system of taxation and redistribution of resources, including manpower. State-run centers for the administration of the *bala* were created; the best known is Puzrish-Dagan (modern Drehem) near Nippur, devoted mostly to the redistribution of livestock and animal products. Year name 38 of Shulgi commemorates its foundation, although it probably began to operate a few years earlier. In order to administer the system efficiently a number of measures were taken to harmonize bureaucratic practices, for example: a single metrological system with new weights and measurements; a common calendar based on the local calendar of Nippur and which remained in use until the first millennium, when it was eventually borrowed by the Judean exiles in Babylonia to form the standard Jewish calendar to this day; a reform of the script and bureaucratic practices (format of tablets, accounting style); a system of roads with inns at regular intervals and a service of official messengers known from hundreds of very small tablets called the "messenger texts," which record the rations to which a messenger was entitled at various stops on his trip. Land policy also makes up an important aspect of Shulgi's reforms. Traditionally, three types of land existed in Babylonia: temple land, crown land, and privately or communally owned land, the last category being the one that is the less well documented by our sources. Shulgi strengthened royal control over the temples by placing their estates directly under the control of the *ensi*s, turning them more or less into state property. Crown land probably already existed in the ED period, especially in northern Babylonia, but only under Naram-Sin do we have evidence for the creation of a systematic policy of allotments of parcels of crown land to state administrators and members of the military as salary for their services. Shulgi systematized this practice (or perhaps we just have more evidence for it because of the increase in textual evidence), laying the foundations for the *ilkum* service of the first and second millennium, especially well documented at the time of the First Dynasty of Babylon. In fact, it is almost certain that all arable land became state property during the reign of Shulgi.

Thus, the reforms of Shulgi created an authoritarian bureaucratic structure which controlled the movement of all resources. The state apparatus was run mostly by the *sukkalmah*, a kind of prime minister who exercised wide authority over the *ensi*s and also played a substantial role in foreign affairs and the military. Outside Babylonia, which formed the core of the empire, an aggregate of newly conquered provinces in the north and east became subject to a different kind of taxation called *gun-mada* "tribute of the land," which did not entitle them to *bala* redistribution. Beyond this periphery Shulgi favored the elaboration of a network of client states through matrimonial alliances that apparently often failed to produce reliable allies. Nevertheless Shulgi may have been one of the first cosmopolitan rulers in world history if we believe one of the numerous hymns composed in his honor which celebrates him as a polyglot, vaunting his ability to speak Sumerian, Akkadian, Elamite, Amorite, and Subarian (i.e. Hurrian, a language spoken in the northern confines of Mesopotamia). Shulgi is also one of the few rulers of ancient Mesopotamia with Ashurbanipal and Nabonidus who claimed to be literate. His foundation of scribal academies at Ur and Nippur testifies to his interest in literature, which he harnessed as a powerful means of legitimation among the learned and administrative classes.

2.9.3 Failure of the Ur III State

Documentation begins to increase exponentially in the middle of Shulgi's reign, with the richest archives located at Puzrish-Dagan and Umma, although Ur, Nippur, and Lagash-Girsu have also produced a significant number of texts. To these we must now add the remarkable finds of Garshana and Uru-Sagrig (Al-Sharraki), both the result of illicit digs. In their overwhelming majority these texts illuminate the operations of the state bureaucracy. Their complicated system of planning, budgeting, and accountability, recording the minutest details of the administration and transfer of resources, reaches at times a level of mathematical abstraction that would not pale in comparison with modern accounting techniques. This system has no parallel in the ancient Near East and confers on the Ur III state an exceptional place in the history of Babylonia and indeed of the ancient world. The Ur III bureaucratic experiment represents the culmination of a process which began with the invention of writing in the Uruk period and eventually endowed texts, including accounts, with a veracity of their own, encouraging belief in their supremacy and an over-reliance on the hegemonic intellectual authority of the scribes. Shulgi sponsored the elaboration of a planned economy whose primary objective was not economic growth and development (although such aims certainly existed at times), but the extraction and allocation of available resources in the most efficient manner. Given the problems raised even in modern times by all-embracing economic planning, it seems hardly surprising that the inevitable happened: collapse of the entire structure. The overextension of the state's logistical capabilities due to the incessant state of warfare in the eastern periphery compounded the problem to immeasurable proportions. During the reigns of Amar-Suen (2046–2038) and Shu-Sin (2037–2029) military engagements turned largely defensive. The inscriptions of Shu-Sin relate campaigns against two opponents that will play a significant role in the demise of the Ur III state: the Amorites and the Shimashkians. In Iran, the land known as Shimashki became united under the leadership of Yabrat and his successor Kindattu. They gradually detached the vassals of the eastern periphery from the orbit of the Ur III state, eventually discontinuing their *gun-mada* contribution. At the same time the semi-nomadic Amorite pastoralists exercised increasing pressure on the northern and eastern border of Babylonia, to the point where Shu-Sin resolved to erect a defensive wall in northern Babylonia to contain them (year names 4 to 6 of Shu-Sin). The breaking point occurred at the beginning of the reign of Ibbi-Sin (2028–2004). The last *gun-mada* contribution dates to his second year. Between his fourth and sixth years the *bala* centers were dismantled and the documentation stopped completely at Umma, Puzrish-Dagan, and Girsu, followed by Nippur in his eighth year. Local *ensi*s became virtually independent and a state of political confusion set in. The capital Ur fell to the combined attacks of the Shimashkians, Elamites, and Amorites in the twenty-fourth year of Ibbi-Sin.

2.9.4 Babylon during the Ur III Period

During the Ur III period Babylon emerged from obscurity and became a provincial center of some consequence, the capital of one of the provinces forming the core of the Ur III state, governed by an *ensi* and participating fully in the *bala* system. Babylon is now mentioned in more than forty texts, most of them from Puzrish-Dagan plus a small number from Umma and one recently published from Uru-sagrig (Al-sharraki). This seems paltry in view of the masses of records produced by the Ur III bureaucracy, but for the first time we are able to say something substantial about the city, and especially about its *ensi*s. The office seems to have been partly hereditary given that the *ensi* Itur-ilum was succeeded by his two sons Issur-ilum and Abba. This conforms to the observation that Ur III *ensi*s often came from local elites. The following *ensi*s appear in our documentation (Table 2.1).

It is notable that the names of these *ensi*s are all Akkadian, and this is also the case for a few other individuals connected with Babylon in Ur III documents: the overseers Amur-Ea and Ikum-Mishar, as well as a man in the service of the *ensi* of Babylon named Puzur-Erra. Only the scribe Lugal-dalla, who has a Sumerian name, constitutes an exception. The *ensi*s Issur-ilum and Abba both also appear as scribes during the tenure of their father Itur-ilum. The last governor Puzur-Tutu "(Under the) protection of the god Tutu" should probably be identified with a Puzur-Tutu who turns up as governor of Borsippa (Badziabba) in a literary letter from Puzur-Shulgi to the last Ur III king Ibbi-Sin. The god Tutu was a form of Marduk worshiped at Borsippa until the Old Babylonian period. Afterwards

Table 2.1 The Governors (*ensi*s) of Babylon during the Ur III Period

Governor	King
Itur-ilum,	Shulgi
Issur-ilum, son of Itur-ilum	Shulgi
Abba, son of Itur-ilum	Shulgi
Arshi-ah	Shulgi and Amar-Su'en
Shiteli	Amar-Su'en
Puzur-Tutu	Ibbi-Sin

Nabu became the god of Borsippa and Tutu was reexplained as an aspect of Nabu, who rose to a prominent position in the pantheon as son of Marduk to become even equal to his father in the first millennium. Borsippa was located only eighteen kilometers southwest of Babylon and this datum suggests that the two cities were already closely associated in the Ur III period.

Several texts mention Babylon's participation in the *bala* system. Although in the past it has been stated that Babylon contributed sheep, goats, and cattle to the *bala*, it is now clear that Puzrish-Dagan functioned as a distribution center for livestock and that Babylon, like other cities of the empire's core, withdrew animals from the state's stockyard as part of its entitlement in the *bala* system. The numbers seem respectable; the highest figures are fifty-two for cattle, 134 for sheep, and seventy-five for goats. We do not know the destination of these animals, but some must have been intended for the sacrificial cult. Babylon's contribution to the *bala* system included wood (pinewood and tamarisk) and manpower; one text refers to a cohort of about 600 workers to harvest the domains of the god Enlil. One document mentions a quantity of over 7,000 liters of beer, but does not make it clear whether the beer is delivered by the governor of Babylon or received by him. The name Babylon appears in these texts with the spellings KÁ.DINGIR^{ki} (as in the year name of Shar-kali-sharri), KÁ.DINGIR.RA^{ki} (where RA is a phonetic complement indicating the Sumerian genitive case), and also KÁ.DINGIR-*ma*^{ki}, which closely corresponds to a phonetic spelling attested in a recently published Ur III text preserved in the State Hermitage Museum: *ba-ab-bí-lum*^{ki}. The latter spelling confirms that the original form of the name (*babbar* > *babbir* > *babbil* > *babbilum*) had not been forgotten in spite of the prevalence gained by the folk etymology *bab-ili*.

NOTE

1. After Frayne 1993: 113–14.

FURTHER READING

On the prehistory of Babylonia see Nissen 1988. Detailed historical surveys with extensive discussion of sources can be found in Bauer 1998 (ED period), Foster 2015 (Old Akkadian period), and Sallaberger 1999 (Ur III). Editions and studies of royal inscriptions: Frayne 2008 (ED period), Cooper 1986 (ED, translations only), Frayne 1993 (Old Akkadian), Edzard 1997 (Gudea), and Frayne 1997 (Ur III). The historical literature on the Old Akkadian kings is edited by Westenholz 1996, the Code of Ur-Namma by Civil 2011, and SKL-Ur III by Steinkeller 2003. Specific historical issues are addressed by Hallo 1957 (royal titles in the ED), Steinkeller 1999 (development of ED kingship), Steinkeller 2013 (new ED victory inscription from Kish), Archi and Biga 2003 (Ebla, Mari and Agade at the end of the ED), Liverani 1993 (the Old Akkadian empire), Hallo 1957–1971 (chronology of the Gutian period), and Steinkeller 1987 (Ur III administration).

Archi, Alfonso, and Biga, Maria Giovanna. 2003. "A Victory over Mari and the Fall of Ebla." *Journal of Cuneiform Studies* 55: 1–44.

Bauer, Josef, 1998. "Der vorsargonische Abschnitt der Mesopotamischen Geschichte." In Bauer, J., Englund R.K., and Krebernik, M., *Mesopotamien. Späturuk-Zeit und frühdynastische Zeit*. Orbis Biblicus et Orientalis 160/1; Freiburg: Universitätsverlag, and Göttingen: Vandenhoeck & Ruprecht, 1998: 429–585.

Civil, Miguel. 2011. "The Law Collection of Ur-Namma." In George, Andrew (ed.), *Cuneiform Royal Inscriptions and Related Texts in the Schøyen Collection*. Bethesda, MD: CDL Press. 220–86.

Cooper, Jerrold. 1986. *Sumerian and Akkadian Royal Inscriptions. Vol. 1: Presargonic Inscriptions*. New Haven, CT: American Oriental Society.

Edzard, Dietz Otto. 1997. *Gudea and his Dynasty*: The Royal Inscriptions of Mesopotamia, Early Periods 3/I. Toronto: University of Toronto Press.

Foster, Benjamin R. 2015. *The Age of Agade: Inventing Empire in Ancient Mesopotamia*. London: Routledge.

Frayne, Douglas. 1993. *Sargonic and Gutian Periods (2334–2113 BC)*: The Royal Inscriptions of Mesopotamia, Early Periods 2. Toronto: University of Toronto Press.

Frayne, Douglas. 1997. *Ur III Period (2112–2004 B.C.)*: The Royal Inscriptions of Mesopotamia, Early Periods 3/II. Toronto: University of Toronto Press.

Frayne, Douglas. 2008. *Presargonic Period (2700–2350 BC)*: The Royal Inscriptions of Mesopotamia, Early Periods 1. Toronto, University of Toronto Press.

Hallo, William W. 1957. *Early Mesopotamian Royal Titles: A Philologic and Historical Analysis*. American Oriental Series vol. 43. New Haven: American Oriental Society.

Hallo, William W. 1957–1971. "Gutium." *Reallexikon der Assyriologie und vorderasiatischen Archäologie* 3: 708–20.

Liverani, Mario (ed). 1993. *Akkad: The First World Empire*. Padua: Sargon Editrice e Libreria.

Nissen, Hans. 1988. *The Early History of the Ancient Near East: 9000–2000 B.C.* Chicago: University of Chicago Press.

Sallaberger, Walther. 1999. "Ur III-Zeit." In Sallaberger, W., and Westenholz, A. *Mesopotamien: Akkade-Zeit und Ur III-Zeit*. Orbis Biblicus et Orientalis 160/3. Freiburg: Universitätsverlag, and Göttingen: Vandenhoeck & Ruprecht, 1999. 119–390.

Steinkeller, Piotr. 1987. "The Administrative and Economic Organization of the Ur III State." In Gibson, McGuire, and Biggs, Robert (eds.), *The Organization of Power: Aspects of Bureaucracy in the Ancient Near East*. Chicago: The Oriental Institute: 19–41.

Steinkeller, Piotr. 1999. "On Rulers, Priests and Sacred Marriage: Tracing the Evolution of Early Sumerian Kingship." In Watanabe, Kazuko (ed.), *Priests and Officials in the Ancient Near East*. Heidelberg: C. Winter Verlag: 103–37.

Steinkeller, Piotr. 2003. "An Ur III Manuscript of the Sumerian King List." In Sallaberger, Walter, et al. (eds.), *Literatur, Politik und Recht in Mesopotamien, Festschrift für Claus Wilcke*. Wiesbaden: Harrassowitz Verlag: 267–92.

Steinkeller, Piotr. 2013. "An Archaic 'Prisoner Plaque' from Kiš." *Revue d'assyriologie et d'archéologie orientale* 107: 131–57.

Westenholz, Joan Goodnik. 1996. *The Legends of the Kings of Akkade*. Winona Lake, IN: Eisenbrauns.

3

The Rise of Babylon

In the first half of the second millennium Babylon rose in status from provincial center to political capital of Sumer and Akkad. For a brief period in the middle of the eighteenth century Babylon's hegemony even extended over the larger part of Iraq. Scholars generally refer to the era of four centuries between the fall of Ur III and the end of Babylon I as the Old Babylonian period (2004–1595). Its first half is often labeled the Isin-Larsa period after the name of the two cities which claimed authority over Sumer and Akkad following the demise of Ur. These two centuries are also known as the Early Old Babylonian period, while the appellation Late Old Babylonian period is reserved for the last century of Babylon I (1711–1595) which followed Babylon's first imperial age under Hammu-rabi and Samsu-iluna (1792–1712), although some also include these two reigns under that label. The major unifying trait of that era is the intrusion of West Semitic Amorites in the urbanized areas of the Near East, from the Levant to Sumer, and their gradual takeover of political power (see Map 3.1).

The study of the Old Babylonian period presents the historian with an intricate puzzle. Babylon emerged as hegemonic power in a politically unstable world, where alliances between competing dynasts shifted constantly and cities could change hands several times within one generation. Sources, while sparse for certain reigns or cities can be abundant and varied for others. No fewer than 32,500 archival documents and letters dating between 2003 and 1595 have been compiled by the Archibab Project in Paris, and countless others await publication. Historical reconstruction relies largely on the year names of local dynasts and the data collected from private, temple, and state archives. The study of political history often depends on establishing which dynast enjoyed official recognition in a given place and time on the basis of year names used in local archives and also of royal inscriptions discovered in situ. Fortunately, we know the order

A History of Babylon: 2200 BC–AD 75, First Edition. Paul-Alain Beaulieu.
© 2018 John Wiley & Sons Ltd. Published 2018 by John Wiley & Sons Ltd.

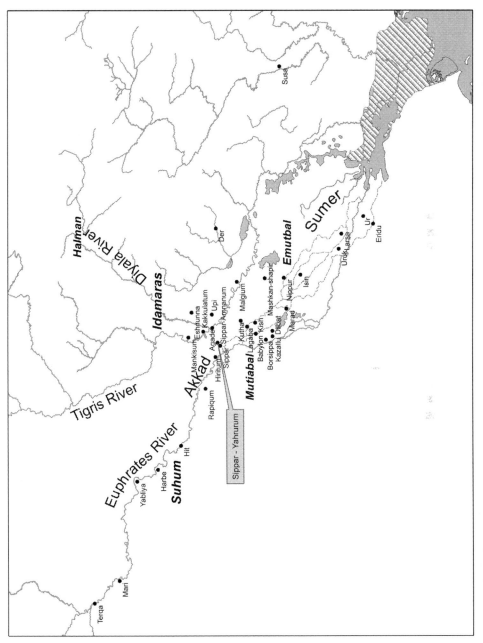

Map 3.1 Babylonia in the Amorite period. Map Design: Stephen Batiuk, University of Toronto.

of year names for most rulers of Isin, Larsa and Babylon, but chronologically ordered lists of year names (Date Lists) are lacking for many ephemeral or less well documented ruling houses. Establishing exact synchronisms between contemporary kings can also be problematic because of the absence of a common system of time reckoning. Local calendars differed from each other, with distinctive names for the months; intercalations to rectify the lunar calendar could be highly irregular, and the year began in some places in the fall rather than in the spring. Archives with archaeologically recorded provenience provide the most valuable information. The best documented epoch are the middle years of the reign of Hammu-rabi (1775–1760, years 18 to 32 of his reign), mainly because of the thousands of letters from the state archives of Mari. These letters have allowed historians to reconstruct in detail the intricate political history of the Near East for a period of about fifteen crucial years which saw Hammu-rabi impose Babylon as hegemonic power. The miraculous survival and discovery of this archive has also highlighted how little we really know about the periods not documented by comparable sources.

3.1   The First Dynasty of Isin (2017–1794)

The First Dynasty of Isin originated in the closing decade of Ur III, when the administrative structure elaborated under Shulgi fell apart under the combined assault of the Amorites, Elamites, and Shimashkians. A high official named Ishbi-Erra (2017–1985) established his power base in the city of Isin, close to Nippur in central Babylonia, gradually extended it as the Ur III state disintegrated, and eventually stood poised to claim its inheritance. He had already started using his own year names in the eighth year of Ibbi-Sin (2019), and his ambition to replace him materialized upon the capture and sack of Ur in 2004, followed by the exile of Ibbi-Sin and the statue of Nanna-Su'en, the god of Ur, to Anshan. Eager to show continuity with Ur III, Ishbi-Erra took over the hegemonic titles of "king of the four quarters" and even of "god of the land," which had been staples of the Ur III titulature since Shulgi.

By and large the kings of Isin sought to maintain and further the political, administrative, and cultural heritage of Ur III. Sumerian remained the language of administration, year names, royal inscriptions, schooling, and literature. Lipit-Ishtar (1936–1926), the fifth Isin ruler, promulgated his law code in the Sumerian language, as Ur-Namma had done in the previous century. New hymns composed in honor of the kings of Isin not only adhere to Sumerian, but they also closely emulate those of the Ur III kings, even plagiarizing in some cases hymns written for Shulgi. The kings of Isin retained Sumerian as official language even though most of them bore Akkadian names. Administrative continuity can be appraised from the Isin craft archive, which extends from the fourth year of Ishbi-Erra (2016) until the third year of Shu-ilishu (1984); the archive documents a leather workshop which maintained aspects of the Ur III state-sponsored micro-management. The archives of the temple of Inanna at Nippur show even greater continuity, with little apparent change in administrative practices between Ur III and Isin I.

The will to perpetuate Ur III explains why Isin I rulers adopted the title of "king of Isin" only gradually. Ishbi-Erra expelled the Elamites and Shimashkians from Ur eight years after the demise of Ibbi-Sin, allowing his successor Shu-ilishu to reclaim the old title of "king of Ur." Shu-ilishu also alleges to have retrieved the statue of Nanna-Su'en from Anshan. Significantly, administrative texts reappear at Ur in the fifth year of his reign. The title "king of Isin" makes a first, yet isolated appearance under his successor Iddin-Dagan (1976–1956). Only with the next king, Ishme-Dagan (1955–1937), do we see a regular use of "king of Isin," while "king of Ur" begins to recede in the background, especially after the city fell under the control of the rival king Gungunum of Larsa in 1926. Ishme-Dagan also reintroduced the Ur III title of "king of Sumer and Akkad" expressing hegemony over Babylonia and added "provider of Nippur," the religious capital of the country. Control of Nippur became in the Isin-Larsa period a powerful symbol of a ruler's hegemonic pretensions. The official scriptoria controlled by the kings of Isin bolstered their claims with the standard version of SKL, which propagates a view of history in which only one city is destined to exert hegemonic power at any given time, Isin being the latest one as successor of Ur III. The Lamentation on the Fall of Sumer and Ur justifies the fall of Ur in philosophical terms, stressing that no city had ever seen its reign (*bala*) last forever, thus indirectly justifying the rise of Isin. A joint list of Ur III and Isin I kings began to circulate, showing no break between the two ruling houses.

By the end of his reign Ishbi-Erra probably exercised his power as far as Uruk, Larsa, Ur, and Eridu in the south and as far north as Marad, Borsippa and Kazallu. What about Babylon, located very close to these northern cities? It seems probable that Babylon also acknowledged, at least nominally, the authority of Isin in the twentieth century, but there is no mention of the city during that period. The Diyala region, on the other hand, seceded quite early from Isin's control. Eshnunna, also an *ensi*-ship under Ur III, recognized the authority of Ishbi-Erra for a certain time, but soon the city became independent from Isin. Some rulers of Eshnunna entered matrimonial alliances with the Amorite chieftains, a telling sign of their growing influence only two generations after the fall of Ur. Later Eshnunna and Babylon will become rivals for the control of Akkad, the northern part of Babylonia.

As the twentieth century progressed, Isin's claim to continue the Sumero-Akkadian heritage, as redefined by the statesmanship of Shulgi, appeared increasingly hollow in the face of mounting challenges to their authority. Iddin-Dagan clashed with the Amorites and temporarily lost control of Nippur and Uruk. Historians have interpreted as a sign of waning political control Ishme-Dagan's claim to have freed Nippur from tax and military service and cancelled the obligations of its temples, and to have abolished the tithe in Sumer and Akkad. Lipit-Ishtar's promulgation of a law code may signal social unrest. After him the inscriptions of the kings of Isin are attested only at Isin and Nippur, and after Enlil-bani (1862–1839) even Nippur fell under the control of the kings of Larsa, the emerging power in the south. Larsa was controlled by an Amorite ruling house which traced its ancestry back to Naplanum. The rise of Larsa began with Zabaya (1941–1933), who claims the title of *rabian Amurrim* "chief of the Amorites" in his inscriptions, the earliest ones of his dynasty. His successor Gungunum (1932–1906) captured Ur in the seventh year of his reign and started using his own year names. From that point on, Larsa rose as the power of Isin faltered. By the beginning of the nineteenth century the fragmentation of power became extreme, with many other Amorite rulers now laying claim to political authority.

3.2   The Amorites

The term Amorite derives from the Akkadian word Amurru, which designates the West as a point of the compass. The Sumerian equivalent of Amurru is Martu, which already appears in Sumer during the Early Dynastic period and in northern Syria at Ebla. The people designated as Amurru or Martu were therefore perceived as westerners from the Mesopotamian point of view, and indeed some of the earliest evidence on the Amorites places their homeland in the Jebel Bishri, west of the middle Euphrates in Syria. An inscription of Naram-Sin recording his defeat of the coalition led by Amar-girid of Uruk already names the Jebel Bishri "the mountain of the Amorites." A year name of his son Shar-kali-sharri also records an armed encounter with the Amorites in that area. During the last two centuries of the third millennium individuals designated as Amorites appear in increasing number in cuneiform archives from the south. Shu-Sin erected a defensive wall to contain them, but to no avail. Their presence proved so disruptive that they became a significant factor in the fall of Ur III. From that time dates their settlement in Sumer and Akkad.

The Amorite language is recorded only in personal names and isolated words appearing in Akkadian context. There is no doubt that Amorite was recognized as a distinct language and must have been widely spoken in areas with a heavy Amorite presence. Yasmah-Addu, king of Mari in the early eighteenth century, was scolded by his father Samsi-Addu for having expressed the desire to learn Sumerian while being unable to speak Amorite, a language which a ruler of Mari could hardly afford to ignore. The fact that Yasmah-Addu came from an Amorite family and bore an Amorite name but spoke apparently only Akkadian, illustrates the speed with which the Amorites, once they achieved political power, assimilated to the dominant urban culture and language. Some have claimed that in Sumer, the Amorite dominance that began after the fall of Ur accelerated the demise of spoken Sumerian. Amorite and Akkadian share numerous lexical and structural features since they both belong to the Semitic language family, albeit to different branches. Amorite belongs to the West Semitic branch, which includes Aramaic, Hebrew, Phoenician, and Ugaritic.

Amorites can be characterized as semi-nomadic pastoralists. This is how the people of Babylonia perceived them. Indeed, they even created a god named Amurru to whom they gave many attributes of pastoralists. A Sumerian literary text called "The Marriage of Martu" paints a rather derogatory portrait of him, one that reflects the bias of urban dwellers. And yet, the god rose in importance throughout the Old Babylonian period, in the same measure as the Amorites gained political influence (Figure 3.1). Pastoral nomadism probably existed in the Near East since the domestication of herd animals during the Neolithic period, but nomads leave few archaeological traces, and texts fail to mention them unless their presence becomes significant enough to warrant recording by state administrations. Pastoralists migrated seasonally between two areas to tend their herds. During the winter season they grazed their animals in semi-arid areas. During the summer they moved to wet areas propitious to agriculture and the urban lifestyle; there they interacted with sedentary populations. The border between the nomad

Figure 3.1   Dedication to the god Amurru. This copper figurine preserved in the Louvre (AO 15704) is probably from Larsa. It is inscribed in Sumerian with a dedication to the god Amurru (Martu) by one Lu-Nanna for the life of Hammu-rabi, king of Babylon. The figurine depicts Lu-Nanna and not Hammu-rabi as has been claimed in the past. It bears witness to the growing importance of the god Amurru during the Old Babylonian period. *Source:* Photo © RMN-Grand Palais (musée du Louvre) / Franck Raux.

and sedentary lifestyles was porous and we must not essentialize Amorites and other pastoralists as perennially attached to a semi-nomadic life. The Mari archives provide ample evidence for Amorites dwelling in villages and practicing agriculture. The same must have happened in Babylonia. Conversely, during periods of agricultural crisis, sedentary people could opt for a pastoralist life. There is much evidence that state administrations viewed pastoralists with suspicion, as states generally seek to exert control over their populations, a much easier task when dealing with sedentary agriculturists. Yet, pastoralists and agriculturists needed each other's resources and often lived in symbiosis.

The migratory patterns of Near Eastern pastoralists cannot always be followed easily. Generally speaking, Amorites seem to have moved inside an arc extending along the Fertile Crescent that has been described as the dimorphic zone. The dimorphic zone (i.e. with two forms) includes territories propitious to both pastoralist and agriculturalist economies, and constituted the easiest area in which pastoralists could follow their seasonal migratory patterns. This zone started in northern Transjordan, extended northwards to reach inland Syria and the area west of the Middle Euphrates, right where the Jebel Bishri lies, crossed the Jezireh to join the Tigris, moved to the Diyala and the Zagros, and finally bent southwards to end in Elam and southwestern Iran. The most heavily urbanized area of Babylonia, along the Euphrates, lay outside the dimorphic zone. The portion of eastern Babylonia lying east of the present course of the Tigris, however, squarely belonged to it. This probably explains why Ur III archival texts from Babylonia often locate the Martu in the east in spite of their origin as westerners; these Amorites were wandering east of the Tigris inside the dimorphic zone. In that zone also arose new types of polities which have been called "dimorphic kingdoms," with an urban core embedded within a territory claimed by a pastoralist tribe or confederacy. Mari under the Amorite rulers is the best documented example of a dimorphic kingdom.

3.2.1   Amorite Genealogies and Histories

Scholars have pointed out that the terms Martu and Amurru do not always refer to people we would recognize as Amorites on linguistic grounds. They also became general designations for anyone with similar lifestyle or migratory patterns. Conversely, people we classify linguistically as Amorites did not necessarily, nor even habitually refer to themselves as Amorites, nor did other people always identify them with this term. In fact, several other designations existed. Lexical texts, for instance, explain Tidnu as a synonym for Amurru. This is the same demonym variously spelled Tidanum, Tidnum, Tidan, Ditan, Ditanu, and Ditana in cuneiform sources. Gudea, the prince of Lagash, claims to have imported alabaster from Tidanum, which he qualifies as an Amorite homeland. Shu-Sin named the wall he built to contain the Amorites Muriq-Tidnim: "that which keeps Tidnum at a distance." The same word turns up in personal names, notably those of the ninth and eleventh kings of the First Dynasty of Babylon,

Ammi-ditana and Samsu-ditana. A broad range of names referred to tribal subdivisions among the Amorites. The state archives of Mari mention two large groupings in Upper Mesopotamia and Syria: the Benjaminites (Bene Yamina "sons of the right," i.e. the southern tribes), and the Bensim'alites (Bene Sim'al "sons of the left," i.e. the northern tribes). Another term frequently appearing at Mari is Hana, which refers both to a land and a people, the Haneans. Yahdun-Lim (ca. 1815–1798), the Amorite leader who took control of the city of Mari, and his last successor Zimri-Lim (1776–1762), both claim the title of "King of Mari and the Land of Hana." A seal inscription refers to Yahdun-Lim as "King of Mari and the land of the (Ben)sim'alites." Such titles reflect the dimorphic nature of that kingdom, where the ruler headed a tribal confederacy or territory (Hana, the Bensim'alites) and assumed at the same time the kingship of an ancient Mesopotamian city state (Mari).

The Mari archives mention five Benjaminite tribes: the Ubrabum, the Yari-hum, the Rababum, the Amnanum and the Yahrurum. Members of these last two tribes settled further south around Sippar, northwest of Babylon, where they gave their names to the twin agglomerations of Sippar-Amnanum (also known as Sippar-rabum, Sippar-Anunitum and Sippar-durim; modern Tell ed-Der) and Sippar-Yahrurum (also Sippar-serim and Sippar-sha-Shamash; modern Abu Habba). Amnanum and Yahrurum also appear as ancestors of the First Dynasty of Babylon in a very important administrative tablet from the reign of Ammi-saduqa (1646–1626) which records provisions for the *kispum* ritual, the sacrificial banquet for the dead. The document begins by listing the ancestors of the First Dynasty. Some of the same names occur with different orthographies and order in the Assyrian King List, in which they were probably integrated as ancestors of Samsi-Addu, the Amorite chieftain who built a large empire in Upper Mesopotamia in the late nineteenth and early eighteenth centuries and reigned also in Assur. Further down the list we find the eponymous ancestor Ditanu, and then Amnanum and Yahrurum. The inclusion of these last two names provides a precious clue as to the Benjaminite affiliation of the First Dynasty. This is followed by the royal forebears of Ammi-saduqa, by three "dynasties" (*bala*) labeled as Amorite, Hanean, and Gutium, provisions for other, forgotten dynasties "not recorded on this tablet," and finally by an invitation to unknown soldiers who died on the battlefield, members of the royal family, and even to all the dead that have no caretaker, to partake in a meal:

Aram-Madara, Tubti-Yamuta, Yamquz-Zuhalamma, Heana, Namzu, **Ditanu**, Zummabu, Namhu, **Amnanu**, **Yahrurum**, Ipti-Yamuta, Buhazum, Sumalika, Ashmadu, Abi-Yamuta, **Abi-ditan**, Mam[o o], Shu[o o], Dad[o o], Sum[u-abum], Sumu-la-[el], Sabium, Apil-Sin, Sin-muballi[t], Hammu-rab[i], Samsu-ilun[a], Abi-eshu[h], Ammi-dita[na], the dynasty of the Amor[ites], the dynasty of the Hane[ans], the dynasty of Gutium, (even) the dynasty which is not recorded on this tablet, and the soldiers who fell on a military campaign for their lord, the princes, the princesses, all persons from sunrise to sunset who have neither caretaker nor intercessor, come hither, eat this, drink this (and) bless Ammi-saduqa, son of Ammi-ditana, king of Babylon!

The *kispum* list is an archival document, but it also reflects a dynastic historiography. Mention of the three "dynasties" of the Amorites, Haneans, and Gutium hints at reminiscences, based on oral tradition, about eras during which the tribal ancestors of the dynasty lived, going back as far as the Gutian period in the twenty-second century. Of great interest also is the mention of one Abi-ditan among the ancestors of the dynasty, a name in which we recognize a variant of the demonym Tidnum/Ditana. This Abi-ditan might be identical with the Abi-ditanu mentioned in an Ur III receipt of cattle from Drehem (Puzrish-Dagan) dated to the ninth year of Amar-Su'en. There he appears alongside Naplanum, who is probably the same Naplanum known as the ancestor of the Amorite dynasty of Larsa, and his nephew Ibi-ishkil. The document designates all three men as Amorites (Martu). Later the Amorite kings of Larsa created the Larsa King List which claimed implicitly that their ancestors all ruled at Larsa since Naplanum, whereas the earliest evidence for anyone claiming the title of "king of Larsa" does not antedate Gungunum. Naplanum was a contemporary of Ishbi-Erra, and the purpose of the Larsa king list may have been to create a royal line with credentials that could rival Isin's. The First Dynasty of Babylon, on the other hand, did not generate a retrospective king list propelling its ancestors to the status of actual rulers. King lists begin the count of Babylonian dynasties either with Sumu-abum or Sumu-la-el. The *kispum* list of Ammi-saduqa reflects an Amorite tribal memory at variance with the historiography propagated by the scribal schools of Sumer and Akkad, and one which was never integrated in the corpus transmitted by the scholarly tradition.

3.3   Date Lists and King Lists of Babylon I

Date lists and king lists supply our chronology for Babylon's First Dynasty. King List B provides the essential data, with all the names of the kings preserved, their family relation to their predecessor and the lengths of their reigns. Many date lists of the First Dynasty have been recovered. Some record the year names of one king or even sometimes only a segment of his reign, while others include longer periods. The most comprehensive such document is Date List A, compiled in the sixteenth year of Ammi-saduqa. It runs from Sumu-abum to the end of the reign of Samsu-iluna, covering almost two centuries (1894–1712). Date List F covers a slightly shorter period, from Hammu-rabi until Ammi-saduqa year 17, and Date List B from Hammu-rabi to Ammi-saduqa year 10. These compilations often abbreviate the year names. Their main purpose was the accurate placement of archival documents in chronological sequence. The combined evidence from Date Lists and archival documents indicates that the lengths of reigns provided by King List B are not always accurate. For example, King List B gives fifty-five years for the reign of Hammu-rabi, while according to Date Lists and all other evidence his reign lasted forty-three years. One must remember, however, that this king list dates from the Neo-Babylonian period, and that errors must have

Table 3.1 The First Dynasty of Babylon

(Sumu-abum	1894–1881)
Sumu-la-el	1880–1845
Sabium	1844–1831
Apil–Sin	1830–1813
Sin–muballit	1812–1793
Hammu–rabi	1792–1750
Samsu–iluna	1749–1712
Abi–eshuh	1711–1684
Ammi–ditana	1683–1647
Ammi–saduqa	1646–1626
Samsu–ditana	1625–1595

occurred in the transmission of manuscripts. Study of all the data allows us to establish the following list for the First Dynasty, in accordance with the Middle Chronology (Table 3.1).

Linguistically, all these names can be analyzed as Amorite with the exception of Apil-Sin and Sin-muballit (in italics), which are clearly Akkadian. Much progress has been made in recent years in our knowledge of Amorite. However, if the etymologies of such names as Sumu-la-el ("Offspring indeed of the god") and Ammi-saduqa ("My paternal uncle is righteous") seem reasonably secure, the name of the most illustrious representative of the dynasty, Hammu-rabi, still arouses debate. Most agree that the first element must be Ammu "paternal uncle" (as in Ammi-ditana "My paternal uncle is Ditanu" and Ammi-saduqa), but the second element can be interpreted either as -rabi "great, important" or as -rapi "healer." The consensus now seems to be moving towards Ammu-rapi "the paternal uncle is a healer," although most still adhere to the traditional orthography Hammu-rabi for practical purposes. It is notable that the First Dynasty generally held on to its ancestral Amorite onomastics until the very end.

3.4 Elusive Beginnings

By the beginning of the nineteenth century, more than a hundred years after the fall of Ur, political fragmentation prevailed in Iraq. Nowhere can the extent of this breakdown of central power be better appraised than in northern Babylonia, now illuminated by the appearance of archival documentation at various sites. A number of local dynasts are mentioned in these texts, most of them unknown from any other source. For a long time historians assumed without question that amidst this turmoil Sumu-abum seized power at Babylon in 1894 and founded the First Dynasty. This reconstruction rests chiefly on the evidence from King List B and Date List A, which both recognize him as first king of Babylon with a reign of fifteen (or fourteen) years. King List A, which is broken at the beginning and preserves none of the names of the First Dynasty, still summarizes it with a count of eleven rulers, and therefore must also have started with Sumu-abum. His name has also been partly restored in the *kispum* list of Ammi-saduqa.

All these data are comparatively late. The earliest sources, Date List A and the *kispum* list, both come from the reign of Ammi-saduqa, two centuries after Sumu-abum. Evidence that is contemporary with Sumu-abum for his rule in Babylon is in fact lacking. Textual evidence from Babylon itself begins only with Sin-muballit, Hammu-rabi's father. No building inscription of Sumu-abum has been discovered, though admittedly no king of the First Dynasty has left any before Hammu-rabi. Sumu-abum does appear as sovereign ruler in year names and oath formulas at Sippar and Dilbat in northern Babylonia and also at Kisurra in the south in the early nineteenth century, but none of this evidence associates him with Babylon. In addition, two letters from Sippar-Amnanum (Tell ed-Der) mention Sumu-abum and Sumu-la-el together holding roughly equal rank, which raises obvious problems since they appear to have been contemporaries. King List B, while carefully labeling each ruler of Babylon I as son of his predecessor, curiously fails to make the same claim for Sumu-la-el in relation to Sumu-abum, and later rulers of Babylon I, such as Hammu-rabi, Abi-eshuh and Ammi-ditana, all claim Sumu-la-el, not Sumu-abum, as their forefather.

In consideration of this evidence, historians are now inclined to consider that Sumu-abum did not reign in Babylon but for some reason became eventually integrated in its dynastic history. Perhaps Sumu-la-el ruled at Babylon as vassal or ally of Sumu-abum, who may have controlled a wider territory as tribal over-lord. Both may have belonged to the same Amorite clan. Be that as it may, Sumu-abum obviously left an imprint on the memory of the nascent polity, and later the official historiographers of Babylon I presented him as the founder of the dynasty rather than a contemporary of Sumu-la-el and probably invented some of the year names attributed to him in Date List A, since a number of them duplicate year names of Sumu-la-el almost word for word. This shows that even a practical document such as a date list could be manipulated to rewrite history. However, at least one source appears to maintain a more accurate tradition. The Synchronistic King List ends with a summation of ninety-eight kings who reigned over Babylon "from Sumu-la-el until Kandalanu," thus implicitly rejecting Sumu-abum. Only the discovery of new documents will enable us to assess the role of Sumu-abum in Babylon's political rise.

3.5 Sumu-la-el (1880–1845)

The reign of Sumu-la-el saw Babylon emerge as independent power. Evidence for the political history of his rule rests largely on Date List A, which records a number of military events as well as irrigation projects, pious foundations and, significantly, the erection of fortifications. Before Sumu-la-el's accession an Amorite chieftain named Sumu-ditana had broadened his hegemony from Kazallu (localization uncertain) and Marad to other cities in the north, including Kish and Damrum (near Kish). The latter two eventually fell under the control of another line of dynasts with their seat at Damrum, the so-called Dynasty of Manana, while Sumu-ditana's successor, Halum-pi-umu, remained in control of Kazallu and Marad. The third year name of Sumu-la-el records a victory against this Halum-pi-umu in 1879. This was followed by the capture of Kish in 1869 (year name 13), the expulsion of a new competitor named Yahzir-el from Kazallu in 1864 (year name 18), the tearing down of the walls of Kish in 1863 (year name 19), another victory against Kazallu and the destruction of its walls in 1862 (year name 20), and finally a second successful battle in 1857 against this same Yahzir-el, whose seat of power cannot be precisely located (year name 25). Archival texts corroborate the evidence from Date List A. At Marad three more rulers are attested after Halam-pi-umu (Sumu-atar, Yamsi-el and Sumu-numhim), but in year 21 of Sumu-la-el (1860) scribes started using his year names and transactions now contain oaths by him. At Sippar, where a line of local rulers is attested in the early nineteenth century, Sumu-la-el was recognized as early as his thirteenth year.

Thus, by the end of his reign Sumu-la-el had expanded his kingdom from an initial nucleus around Borsippa, Lagaba, Dilbat, and Kutha into a territorial state that extended from Sippar to Marad and also comprised Kish, Kazallu, and Damrum. Sumu-la-el consolidated his realm by ordering the destruction of the walls of conquered cities to prevent their resurgence (Kish, Kazallu), while launching a program of fortifications for Babylon (building of its wall in 1877, year name 5) and other cities which he originally ruled (walls of Kutha and Anzagar-urgi in 1855, year name 27; wall of Habuz in 1851, year name 31; wall of Dilbat in year name B, chronological placement unknown), or obtained without evidence of conflict (wall of Sippar in 1853, year name 29). Samsu-iluna claims that he restored six fortresses originally created by Sumu-la-el; a place named Dur-Sumu-la-el ("Fort Sumu-la-el") is known from later documents. With Sumu-la-el we also have the earliest indisputable evidence for the cult of Marduk, the patron god of Babylon. Year name 22 commemorates the fashioning of a throne of silver and gold for Marduk in 1860; year name 24 a statue of (or for) Marduk's consort, the goddess Zarpanitum, in 1858. In documents from the north, oaths are now taken in the name of Sumu-la-el and Marduk as well as other deities, whereas Marduk never occurs in oaths taken earlier by Sumu-abum. Sumu-la-el also proclaimed a *mesharum* edict commemorated in his year name C. With these basic outlines of a new Babylonian state now in place in the north, conflict with other rising powers seemed likely to erupt. It is in this context that we must evaluate an important document, the letter of Anam.

3.5.1 The Letter of Anam and the Babylon-Uruk Alliance

This tablet, discovered at Uruk in the palace of Sin-kashid, contains a letter from Anam, king of Uruk, to Sin-muballit, king of Babylon, Hammu-rabi's father. The letter consists of an extensive apologetics by Anam to his ally Sin-muballit, who had sent Babylonian troops to help him fight their common enemy Larsa, but now complained about the poor reception they experienced at Uruk. Anam reminds Sin-muballit of the long standing alliance between the two royal houses since the time of Sin-kashid, a contemporary of Sumu-la-el, and insists that a more formal alliance should now be concluded between Uruk and Babylon in order to avoid any further misunderstanding as to the intentions of each partner. A number of arguments can be invoked against the authenticity of the letter. The text is unusually long (more than 150 lines) and displays too many literary niceties compared with diplomatic letters from that era. Additionally, it was discovered in its alleged point of origin, whereas real letters normally turn up in their place of destination. The letter probably belongs to the genre of fictitious royal correspondence. Yet, we should not disregard it as a source. If the events reported cannot be considered factual, the general circumstances it describes are corroborated by primary sources.

Uruk initially paid allegiance to Isin but fell under Larsa's hegemony with most of southern Babylonia in the early part of the nineteenth century. Then Sin-kashid seized power at Uruk between 1865 and 1860 and founded a royal house that was to last until 1803, when Rim-Sin of Larsa regained control of the city. Sin-kashid claims the titles "king of Uruk" and "king of the Amnanum" in his inscriptions, while the letter of Anam insists that the Babylonians are related to the Amnanum and Yahrurum tribes. This suggests that common ancestry constituted a factor in the alliance between Sumu-la-el and Sin-kashid: "I have known personally, ever since the time of Sin-kashid and since the time I witnessed myself until now, that the army of Amnan(um)-Yahrur(um) has indeed arrived here two or three times for military assistance to this house." The existence of this alliance is proven by a seal impression on clay tablets found at Uruk which reveals that Sumu-la-el gave his daughter Shallurtum in marriage to Sin-kashid. By the middle of the nineteenth century Babylon and Larsa had become the rising powers in Sumer and Akkad, and Sumu-la-el's strategy of allying himself with the tribally related kingdom of Uruk, using it as a buffer against a more powerful contender rising further south, made perfect sense strategically. Indeed, Babylon and Larsa clashed already by the end of Sumu-la-el's reign, as Sin-iddinam of Larsa (Figure 3.2) records a victory against his rival in 1847 in his fourth year name: "the year the army of Babylon was smitten by weapons."

3.6   Half a Century of Stability (1844–1793)

Babylon seems to have enjoyed half a century of relative peace and stability under Sabium, Apil-Sin, and Sin-muballit. However, a tablet from Borsippa datable to the late sixth century paints a rather dismal portrait of the reign of Sabium, recording seven years of anarchy, plague, famine, and threats of usurpation. One should probably disregard this text given its late date and the absence of contemporary evidence corroborating its claims. Date List A still constitutes our

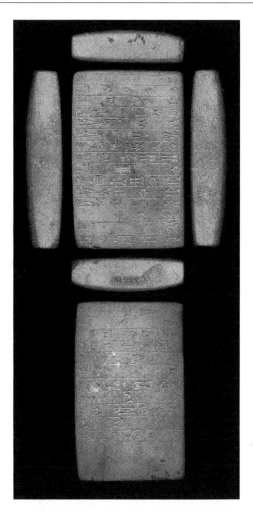

Figure 3.2 Inscription of Sin-iddinam of Larsa. Larsa rose to prominence in the nineteenth century and became a major opponent of Babylon. This inscription of king Sin-iddinam, preserved on a limestone tablet in the Walters Art Museum, Baltimore, commemorates his rebuilding of Ebabbar, the temple of the sun-god in Larsa. It is inscribed in Sumerian. Measurements: H: 5 13/16 ×W: 3 3/4 in. (14.8 × 9.5 cm). *Source*: The Walters Art Museum (Walters 41.222), Public Domain.

main source for the year names of that period, although it is now supplemented by Date Lists S (Sin-muballit years 7–12) and U (Sabium to Sin-muballit). The parts dealing with Sabium contain significant gaps, but these can be filled with dated archival documents. This period witnessed a slow expansion of the kingdom's boundaries. A fairly large number of year names celebrate the repair of sanctuaries and pious endeavors, providing the earliest known mentions of two prominent temples in Babylon: year name 10 of Sabium records work on Esagil, the temple of the god Marduk in 1836; and year names 13 and 14 of Apil-Sin commemorate the rebuilding of Eturkalamma, the temple of the goddess Inanna in 1819. The sun god Shamash of Sippar became the object of regular patronage, while other cities benefited on occasion, notably Dilbat with the temple E-ibbi-Anum dedicated to the god Urash. Only four Babylonian year names of that period record military events: Sabium 7, a victory against Larsa in 1839; Sabium 12, the destruction of the walls of Kazallu in 1834; Sin-muballit 13, another victory against Larsa in 1801; and Sin-muballit 16, the capture of Isin in 1798. None of the year names of Apil-Sin mention any military event.

3.6.1   The Battle for Kazallu

The conflict around Kazallu reveals the intricacies of interregional and inter-tribal politics at that time. Sumu-la-el had subjugated Kazallu and destroyed its walls in 1862, but the Babylonians apparently soon lost influence over the city. In 1840, in the first year of his reign, the king of Larsa Sin-iqisham claims that he restored the divine images of Kazallu (year name 2 of Sin-iqisham): "the year (Sin-iqisham) made (statues) of (or for) the gods Numushda, Namrat and Lugal-apiak and brought them into the city of Kazallu." Yet, three years later in 1837 Sin-iqisham repelled a coalition that included Kazallu, a conflict recorded in his fifth year name: "the year Uruk, Kazallu, the army of the land of Elam and Zambiya the king of Isin were smitten with weapons." A hymn in Sumerian to the god Numushda with a prayer for Sin-iqisham claims that the ruler of Larsa had resettled the population of Kazallu and restored its water supply. This piece may have been composed when he regained control of the city. In 1834 the new king of Larsa Warad-Sin destroyed the wall of Kazallu again (year name 2 of Warad-Sin): "year the wall of Kazallu was destroyed and its army Mutiabal was defeated in Larsa." The following year Sabium laid an identical claim.

The victory of Larsa against Kazallu is also commemorated in a building inscription in the name of Warad-Sin and his father Kudur-Mabuk, who claim that they "smote the army of Kazallu and Mutiabal in Larsa and Emutbal" and "seized Kazallu, tore down its wall, and made it submit." Mutiabal was the name of an Amorite tribe that had settled around Kazallu. A group of letters from the Mari archives sent around 1764–1763 by Yarim-Addu, ambassador of Mari to Babylon, claims that a faction among the Mutiabalites of Kazallu fomented a revolt against Babylon at the instigation of the Elamites. Hammu-rabi suppressed it vigorously. Similar conditions must have prevailed in the preceding century, explaining why neither Babylon nor Larsa could easily control Kazallu, which represented a disputed border zone between two powers and a constant nest of insurgency. Repeated mentions of the destruction of Kazallu's walls must be considered rhetorical claims to some degree, reflecting the wish to neutralize it. In spite of this it seems that Sabium's bid for control in 1833 more or less permanently secured the city for the Babylonians, whose authority was apparently accepted only with reluctance.

3.6.2 The Apex of Larsa

Apil-Sin strengthened the territorial acquisitions of his predecessors, notably with the building of fortifications, starting early in his reign with the wall of Borsippa (year name 1) and a new wall for Babylon (year name 2), and later in his reign with the eastern gate of Babylon (year name 15). His most significant effort, however, is probably the extension of Babylon's territory to the banks of the Tigris, where he built or restored the fortress of Kar-Shamash (year name 12) and especially the city of Upi, later known as Opis (year name C). In a treaty concluded with the king of Eshnunna Silli-Sin, Hammu-rabi later recalled that Apil-Sin established a new march on the Tigris which included Upi and Mankisum. Babylon now threatened to encroach on the territory of its northern rival. Apil-Sin also built a fortress bearing his name northeast of Sippar, Dur-Apil-Sin, which may have been intended to control access to the Tigris although we do not know it precise location. However, some of this new territory was lost later since it had to be reclaimed by Hammu-rabi. The loss possibly occurred in the early years of Naram-Sin of Eshnunna (1818–?), who campaigned along the Tigris and annexed Kakkulatum.

In 1822 Rim-Sin succeeded his brother Warad-Sin on the throne of Larsa and embarked on a vigorous crusade to expand his kingdom. In 1810 Sin-muballit entered a coalition that was defeated by Rim-Sin, who subsequently named his fourteenth year "the year the armies of Uruk, Isin, Babylon, Sutium, Rapiqum, and of Irdanene the king of Uruk were smitten with weapons." Sin-muballit was no less active than Apil-Sin in erecting strongholds along his border, notably the city walls of Murum, Marad, Eresh, and Bas (year names 10, 11, 14, and 17). The creation of a string of Babylonian fortresses must have been viewed as direct provocation by Larsa and Isin. Indeed, the year before, in 1801, Sin-muballit recorded a victorious armed encounter with Larsa (year name 13), and three years later in 1798 the capture of Isin (year name 16), which resulted in temporary occupation only since the local ruler Damiq-ilishu continued to reign, but not for long. The end came for Isin in 1794 with the conquest of the city by Rim-Sin, who named all subsequent thirty-one years of his reign after that momentous event. Rim-Sin had also captured Uruk a few years earlier in 1802 and put an end to the dynasty founded by Sin-kashid. At the time of Sin-muballit's death in 1793, Larsa controlled all of Sumer.

The founder of the new ruling house of Larsa, Kudur-Mabuk, successively installed his two sons Warad-Sin and Rim-Sin as kings and claimed for his part the titles of "father of the Amorite country" and "father of Emutbal," Emutbal becoming an alternative name for the kingdom of Larsa. The tribal affiliation of the Emutbalites remains unclear; some have suggested they were Bensim'alites. Kudur-Mabuk chose Akkadian names for his two sons, while he and his father Simti-Shilhak bore Elamite names, hinting at Trans-Tigridian origins, an area where Ur III sources already locate many of the Amorites. The advent of Kudur-Mabuk and his sons did not provoke a caesura with the previous ruling houses.

Respect continued to be paid to the memory of former kings, and the Larsa King List considered all its members since Naplanum to belong to the same line in spite of frequent changes of ruling family.

At the accession of Hammu-rabi to the Babylonian throne the kingdom of Larsa presented the aspect of two strips of cities along the Tigris and Euphrates, from Eridu and Ur in the south to Nippur and Mashkan-shapir in the north. Excavations at Mashkan-shapir have revealed that it served as northern capital of the kingdom. Kudur-Mabuk probably resided there, and so would later the brother of Rim-Sin when he became the military leader of Larsa in the ultimate conflict against Babylon. Larsa showed some characteristics of a dimorphic kingdom at that point. Larsa and other city states had been integrated within the tribal territory of Emutbal, which probably extended towards the dimorphic zone east of the Tigris. Larsa enjoyed a great period of prosperity at the end of the nineteenth century if we judge from the large size of private houses excavated in the northern part of the city. They present the aspect of nouveau riche villas surrounded by gardens, starkly contrasting with the cramped living quarters that were the norm in Babylonian cities. Control of Ur and the Persian Gulf trade might explain this sudden prosperity, which made Larsa into a bulwark against Babylon's ambitions. The showdown would happen under Hammu-rabi, Sin-muballit's son and successor.

3.7   Hammu-rabi (1792–1750)

Many sources document Hammu-rabi's reign, some important ones published only in the past three decades. Date lists are available in larger numbers than for his predecessors. He is also the first ruler of Babylon who has left royal inscriptions. Archival texts become more numerous during his reign, a fact to be explained mainly by the considerable expansion of his territory in the 1760s. The richest source, however, consists of the large corpus of letters which directly illuminate aspects of his personality as statesman, tactician, and administrator. No fewer than two hundred letters from Hammu-rabi have been discovered, the larger portion of them sent to provincial administrators posted at Larsa after the city's conquest. Several others were discovered among the state correspondence of Mari, but the most significant epistolary corpus from that city are the letters of Yarim-Addu, ambassador of the king of Mari to Babylon. Dating from the years 1764–1763, they contain eyewitness reports on the political life in the palace of Hammu-rabi, often quoting his speeches and interventions on matters of inter-regional relations and domestic affairs. Few other sources from the ancient world afford us such vivid and reliable information on the conduct of government and the role played by individual personalities in political decision-making.

Hammu-rabi transformed Babylon from a kingdom of moderate size into an empire covering the larger part of Iraq. Thus he replicated the accomplishments of the Old Akkadian and Ur III states, ensuring the lasting importance of his city as center of power. It is tempting for historians to explain retrospectively the success of Babylon by highlighting economic, geographic, or environmental conditions that would have made its rise inevitable. Such factors always play a role in history, but none should be considered decisive and Hammu-rabi must also receive some individual credit. A less capable and astute leader might easily have failed, letting other cities make their bid to unify Mesopotamia under a single administration. Indeed, Larsa was not the only competitor on the horizon. Eshnunna posed a much more serious challenge. Located in the Diyala river valley, the city of Eshnunna (modern Tell Asmar) had long harbored its own hegemonic ambitions, which came into full view in the second half of the nineteenth century under the rule of Ipiq-Adad II (1862-1819) and Naram-Sin (1818–?). Eshnunna expanded in two directions: towards upper Mesopotamia, ultimately targeting the Habur triangle; and towards the middle Euphrates, where Yahdun-Lim (1810–1794), the Bensim'alite ruler of Mari, was forced to acknowledge its hegemony. From that period dates the introduction at Mari of the Akkadian dialect and script of Eshnunna, replacing the scribal practices from the time of the *shakkannaku*s, the native rulers of Mari before the Amorite takeover. Another, formidable competitor in northern Mesopotamia was the Amorite leader Samsi-Addu.

3.7.1   In the Shadow of Samsi-Addu (1792–1775)

Samsi-Addu probably originated from the Diyala region, where sources situate the activities of his father Ila-kabkabu and his brother Aminum. His ties with the city of Agade, which he visited probably after the peace with Eshnunna, suggest that he may have been a native of the ancient capital of the Sargonic dynasty. He may even have started his reign in Agade. He ascended the throne around 1833, but the Assyrian King List, which knows him as Shamshi-Adad (I), claims that eventually the ambitions of Naram-Sin of Eshnunna forced him to seek refuge in Babylon. Later he left Babylon and seized the city of Ekallatum, probably located on the Tigris at not too great a distance from Assur. After three years he captured Assur, probably in 1808, deposing the Assyrian ruler Erishum II. Samsi-Addu reigned thirty-three years over Assur, succeeded by his son Ishme-Dagan and his grandson Mut-Ashkur, and this explains why Samsi-Addu and Ishme-Dagan, together with their Amorite tribal ancestors who are in part identical with Hammu-rabi's, found their way in the Assyrian King List. However, Samsi-Addu did not make Assur the seat of his kingship. His ambitions took him to the Habur triangle where he established his new capital at Shehna, which he renamed Shubat-Enlil (modern Tell Leilan), leaving his older son Ishme-Dagan in control of Ekallatum. In the Habur he clashed with Yahdun-Lim, the Bensim'alite ruler of Mari. In 1792, the year of Hammu-rabi's accession, Samsi-Addu finally gained control of Mari and installed there his younger son Yasmah-Addu (1792–1775) as king. Documentary sources from Mari increase during the time of Yasmah-Addu, and this is why we now know many more details about diplomatic and military history. One important text from that period found at Mari is a fragmentary *kispum* ritual which includes the Old Akkadian kings Sargon and Naram-Sin among the recipients of offerings. Historians are now inclined to see this ritual not as a local product, but as an import reflecting the family traditions of Samsi-Addu and his Agadean origins. To be sure, his territorial ambitions surely matched those of the Sargonic kings. By the time of Hammu-rabi's accession Samsi-Addu had assembled a vast kingdom that included all of Upper Mesopotamia and threatened to expand into the middle regions controlled by Eshnunna and Babylon.

In the first year of his reign (1792) Hammu-rabi issued an edict of redress (*mesharum*) canceling debts and obligations (year name 2). He devoted the next few years to the repair and endowment of temples (year names 3 to 6). In 1787 he captured Isin and Uruk, which had fallen to Rim-Sin of Larsa several years earlier (year name 7). We know that this victory did not lead to annexation since documents from Uruk and Isin continued to be dated to Rim-Sin. Hammu-rabi then turned his attention to the Tigris area, claiming a victory against Malgium in 1784 (year name 10). The site of Malgium has not yet been identified, but all evidence points to a location on the Tigris north of Mashkan-shapir, a strategic area on the border of the kingdom of Larsa. The victory was not decisive either and Malgium continued to be mentioned as independent kingdom.

Hammu-rabi achieved a more significant aim in 1783 with the conquest of Rapiqum on the Euphrates northwest of Sippar (year name 11), but here again the situation appears to have been more complex than what transpires from the year name. Rapiqum probably still gravitated in the orbit of Eshnunna at that point. The year before, in 1784, the Eshnunnean ruler Dadusha (?–1779) had captured Mankisum on the Tigris, controlled at that time by Samsi-Addu. A letter from Mari reveals that Dadusha had invited Hammu-rabi to join him in that campaign but met with a refusal. Hostilities persisted. In 1782 Dadusha launched a massive operation along the Suhum, which Samsi-Addu had mostly taken away from Eshnunna a decade earlier. Sources from Mari inform us on the details of that campaign. After initial successes such as the (re)conquest of Rapiqum and the capture of Harbe and Yabliya, the Eshnunneans failed to reach Mari. Ishme-Dagan launched a counter-offensive from Ekallatum and the whole episode ended in a military stand-off and a peace treaty between Samsi-Addu and Dadusha. Samsi-Addu, who had regained the upper hand, conceded to his ally Hammu-rabi joint control of the Suhum between Hit and Rapiqum, which became the seat of a Babylonian resident appointee. A letter from Mari dated a few years later quotes Hammu-rabi recalling that when Samsi-Addu had wrested control of Rapiqum from the Eshnunneans and given it to him, they had agreed both to station troops in the city. Sources from Mari also intimate that after the death of Dadusha in 1779 some tensions may have arisen between Samsi-Addu and Hammu-rabi concerning Rapiqum, but this apparently came to a resolution without serious conflict. In 1777 Hammu-rabi joined Samsi-Addu and the new king of Eshnunna Ibal-pi-El II (1778–1765) in a confrontation against Malgium, capturing several towns and laying siege to the city. A letter from Mari informs us that the ruler of Malgium bought off the assailants with an indemnity of fifteen talents of silver (ca. 1,000 pounds), which all three shared equally after lifting the siege. This event is not mentioned in the seventeenth year name of Hammu-rabi, which commemorates instead the dedication of a statue for the goddess Ishtar of Ilip.

3.7.2   Eshnunna's Bid for Hegemony (1772–1770)

The stand-off between the three powers ended with the natural death of Samsi-Addu in the summer of 1775. Soon his empire began to crumble, causing another shift in the political configuration of the region. The smaller kingdoms conquered by Samsi-Addu recovered their independence. Zimri-Lim, who claimed to be the son, but more likely was the nephew or grandson of Yahdun-Lim, regained for his family the throne of Mari with the help of the king of Aleppo, Yarim-Lim. Sources from Mari become extremely rich during his reign, allowing us to follow events sometimes month by month. Yasmah-Addu disappeared from the scene and his older brother Ishme-Dagan, entrenched at Ekallatum, soon saw himself threatened by Ibal-pi-El of Eshnunna. Ibal-pi-El sent a letter to Zimri-Lim revealing his intent to campaign against Ishme-Dagan but, deploring the fact that Hammu-rabi had decided to send an army of 6,000 soldiers to help his ally, he asked Zimri-Lim to prevent that army from reaching its goal. The outcome of this episode is unknown, but eventually Ishme-Dagan did leave Ekallatum to seek refuge in Babylon, as his father had done in his early career when also threatened by the Eshnunneans. Three years after the death of Samsi-Addu almost nothing remained of his empire, leaving the door open for Eshnunna to resurrect its own territorial ambitions.

Ibal-pi-El set military operations in motion in the fall of 1772 with the capture of Rapiqum, celebrated in his ninth year name. Eshnunnean troops then proceeded along the Suhum, forcing Mari to evacuate Yabliya and Anat. At that point Hammu-rabi resolved to side with Zimri-Lim, fearing that an Eshnunnean victory would pose a permanent threat to his northern border. The Mari archives document the presence of Babylonian troops and envoys at Mari in the winter of 1772–1771. Meanwhile Ibal-pi-El opened a second front in the north. An Eshnunnean army marched along the Tigris to Assur and Ekallatum, already abandoned by Ishme-Dagan, and then proceeded towards the Habur triangle and captured Shubat-Enlil, the former capital of Samsi-Addu. Ibal-pi-El wrote to Zimri-Lim to reveal his ultimate aim: "I will establish my boundaries; I am proceeding to Shubat-Enlil." Reacting swiftly, Zimri-Lim set up his military quarters at Ashlakka in the Habur in the spring of 1771. At the same time Eshnunna suffered an attack coming from Halman in the upper Diyala and Ibal-pi-El's troops retreated to Andariq, located probably south of the Jebel Sindjar. Zimri-Lim besieged them but soon retreated to Mari to deal with renewed agitation among the Benjaminite tribes. Before Zimri-Lim left for the Habur the Babylonian troops had helped him quench some of the unrest. They also followed him to the north. At the conclusion of the war Bunu-Eshtar, the king of Kurda in the region of the Jebel Sindjar, invited them to engage in razzias, but the troops asked

Zimri-Lim for permission to return to Babylon. Zimri-Lim made peace with the Benjaminites and Eshnunna. He signed a treaty which recognized Ibal-pi-El as his superior (his "father") although Mari gained important concessions in the Jebel Sindjar and especially the Suhum, which was completely evacuated by Eshnunna. Hammu-rabi occupied Rapiqum again, while Zimri-Lim's authority over Yabliya, Harbe and Hit was recognized, although the latter had already become an object of dispute between Mari and Babylon before the treaty. One figure would soon play a major role in the political evolution of the region: the *sukkalmah* of Elam, a powerful state in southwestern Iran with one of its political centers located at Susa. The *sukkalmah* intervened as mediator and upheld Zimri-Lim's claims. Hammu-rabi reminded Zimri-Lim's envoys of his good intentions, and the envoys reciprocated the claim on behalf of their master.

3.7.3   A Fragile Equilibrium (1769–1766)

Ibal-pi-El's failure to gain supremacy led to a new balance of power, expressed in an oft-cited letter from a high official of Mari, Itur-Asdu, to Zimri-Lim:

> No king is really powerful on his own. Ten to fifteen kings follow Hammu-rabi, the man of Babylon; Rim-Sin, the man of Larsa; Ibal-pi-El, the man of Eshnunna; and Amut-pi-El, the man of Qatna. However, twenty kings follow Yarim-Lim, the man of Yamhad (Aleppo).[1]

Needless to say, the correspondents implicitly understood Mari to represent the sixth power in that consortium of Amorite rulers. Two of them, Aleppo and Qatna, controlled the Levant, three more, Eshnunna, Babylon, and Larsa, shared power in Sumer and Akkad, while Mari played its traditional role of bridge between Mesopotamia and the West (see Map 3.2). The "ten to fifteen kings" who allegedly followed Hammu-rabi remain indefinable figures, but Itur-Asdu probably used these numbers as rhetorical expedient to express the relative importance of each great ruler and also to confer a preeminent position upon Yarim-Lim of Aleppo, Zimri-Lim's ally.

This new equilibrium could not last long. The Mari archives attest to a sudden intensification of relations between Zimri-Lim and the *sukkalmah* of Elam (also called "king of Anshan") in the eighth and ninth years of Zimri-Lim (1768–1767), as well as with his brother and second-in-rank, Kudu-zulush, king (*sukkal*) of Susa. The *sukkalmah* of Elam, whose foreign sounding name, Siwe-palar-huppak, appears under the bungled form Sheplarpak in the Mari letters, had decided to open hostilities with Eshnunna and now requested military help from Hammu-rabi and Zimri-Lim. We know very little about the history of Elam in that period, but our sources indicate that Eshnunna had clashed with its eastern neighbor in the middle of the previous century during the reign of Ipiq-Adad II. All too content to participate in the demise of their rival, Zimri-Lim and Hammu-rabi sent contingents to side with the *sukkalmah*,

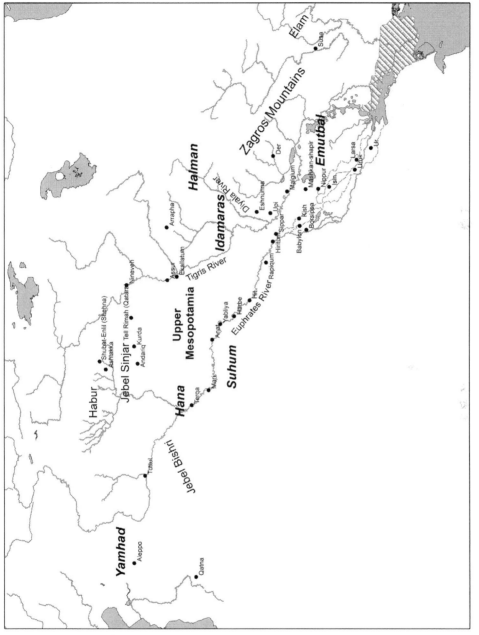

Map 3.2 The Near East in the Age of Hammu-rabi. Map Design: Stephen Batiuk, University of Toronto.

probably not foreseeing that the Elamites would now entertain greater territorial ambitions of their own. The chronology of events remains uncertain, but Eshnunna fell probably in the tenth year of Zimri-Lim (1766).

3.7.4   The Elamite Intervention and its Aftermath (1766–1764)

The events which ensued constitute a major turning point in the history of Babylon. After the capture of Eshnunna Hammu-rabi recuperated Mankisum and Upi, coveted since the time of his grandfather Apil-Sin. This, however, provoked an ultimatum by the *sukkalmah*, who ordered the Babylonians to evacuate the cities he too now considered his. Faced with a refusal, the Elamites took Mankisum by force and laid siege to Upi. Hammu-rabi called for a general conscription and sent envoys to Larsa to seek an alliance. While Rim-Sin's answers remained evasive, the Elamites stirred up rebellion among the Mutiabalite tribe around Kazallu. Hammu-rabi quenched the uprising but had to evacuate Upi. Elamites troops then followed the route taken earlier by Ibal-pi-El along the Tigris, capturing Ekallatum and heading towards the Habur where a representative of the *sukkalmah* named Kunnam was installed at Shubat-Enlil. Mari and Babylon now faced a threat greater than Eshnunna. This induced them to make a formal alliance in spite of their ongoing dispute about the status of Hit and the general sentiment of suspicion which they harbored against each other's political ambitions. Indeed, when Zimri-Lim started his own preventive campaigns against Elamite expansion in the north, he had to reassure Hammu-rabi about his intentions, with his envoys to Babylon insisting that these orders of mobilization were not aimed against him.

As proof of goodwill Mari and Babylon exchanged troops and made a formal alliance against the *sukkalmah*. Documents from Mari inform us on the preliminary negotiations and the details of this treaty, concluded probably in the eighth month of the tenth year of Zimri-Lim. The treaty also involved Yarim-Lim, the king of Aleppo, who died soon after and was succeeded by his son Hammu-rabi, a namesake of the king of Babylon. Zimri-Lim, probably fearing that the conflict would threaten the core of his kingdom, took the unprecedented step to impose a general oath of loyalty on his subjects. Considerable confusion prevailed in the north, where the Elamites tried to eliminate through betrayal and assassination the smaller potentates gravitating in the orbit of Mari, dividing the entire region between pro- and anti-Elamite factions. In the south the military situation had become critical for Hammu-rabi. After taking Upi and leaving it under the control of Eshnunnean troops under his command, the *sukkalmah* sent a message to the northern kings declaring his intention to capture Babylon as well and dispatched an army of 40,000 to besiege Hiritum, halfway between Upi and Hammu-rabi's capital. By now, however, the Elamites faced a broad coalition of Amorite rulers and began to experience setbacks. Zimri-Lim sent troops to support Babylon in the second month of his eleventh year (1765), and the Elamites lifted the siege of Hiritum probably two months later, retreated east of the Tigris and tried unsuccessfully to launch another attack in the north. They finally withdrew to the Diyala, ransacking the entire Eshnunnean territory. From there they returned to Elam, suddenly abandoning their dreams of Mesopotamian hegemony.

After the departure of the Elamites a pro-Babylon party at Eshnunna contemplated offering the crown to Hammu-rabi, which would have in effect united all of Akkad under his rule without further bloodshed. Instead the Eshnunneans bestowed kingship on one of their own, a member of the armed forces of modest origin (a *mushkenum*) named Silli-Sin who immediately initiated a policy of confrontation with Hammu-rabi. Fearful of the normalization of relations between Babylon and Elam, he tried to create dissensions between Hammu-rabi and his allies Zimri-Lim, Ishme-Dagan of Ekallatum, and Hammu-rabi of Kurda (another namesake), but to no avail. Negotiations between Babylon and Eshnunna lingered on the status of Mankisum and Upi, which Hammu-rabi considered his rightful due given the cost of the war against Elam and the claim on the region already made by his grandfather Apil-Sin. The capture of Larsa by the Babylonian troops a year later may have had a persuasive effect on Eshnunna, because soon after they reached an agreement culminating with Silli-Sin's marriage to a daughter of Hammu-rabi.

3.7.5 Showdown with Larsa (1764–1763)

Zimri-Lim had played a key role in the war, and it is dubious whether Babylon could have survived the Elamite onslaught without the help of its ally. However, in his thirtieth year name Hammu-rabi predictably claims sole credit for the expulsion of the enemy and adds the note that, having defeated Elam in one campaign, he had "secured the foundations of Sumer and Akkad." In spite of its formulaic nature, the mention of "Sumer and Akkad" at this precise juncture suggests that Hammu-rabi already planned the conquest of Sumer. Larsa had stood apart during the war against Elam in spite of Babylon's request for help. Several motives may account for Rim-Sin's reluctance to engage: his advanced age, his Elamite ancestry, perhaps his distrust of Hammu-rabi's motives or simply the fact, which historians have pointed out, of an economic decline of the state of Larsa during the second half of his reign, which may have weakened its resources to the point of discouraging military engagements.

Hammu-rabi began with a smearing campaign, complaining to Zimri-Lim that Rim-Sin now violated his territory and ordered razzias in spite of the numerous alleged favors he had granted him since he saved the country from the clutch of the Elamites. War finally broke out. The king of Malgium sided with Hammu-rabi, Der with Rim-Sin. Hammu-rabi laid siege on Mashkan-shapir, defended by Rim-Sin's brother, three generals and thousands of troops. The siege did not last long and the city surrendered on Hammu-rabi's promise of clemency. The core of Rim-Sin's kingdom soon fell under Babylonian control. Texts from Nippur began using Hammu-rabi's dates in the fourth month of his thirtieth year (1763), those from Isin in the following month, while the troops of Emutbal now enthusiastically joined the Babylonian army to besiege Larsa.

Hammu-rabi requested military help from his allies, Mari and Malgium, and established his headquarters at Dildaba. Some details about the progress of operations are known from reports sent to Zimri-Lim by his military envoys, who mention siege towers, ramps and battering rams. Rim-Sin sent messengers to Qatna probably to seek help, but the Babylonians intercepted them. After about six months the grain stocks of the defenders ran out and Larsa fell amidst reports of jubilation on the parts of the troops. The city's capture probably occurred at the end of the year since the earliest text from Larsa dated to Hammu-rabi's reign was written in the twelfth month of his thirtieth year. Hammu-rabi's conquest of Larsa is one of the very few historical events of the First Dynasty remembered in the later cuneiform tradition. Chronicle 40 records it as follows: "Hammu-rabi, king of Babylon, mustered his troops and marched on Rim-Sin, king of Ur. He conquered Ur and Larsa, took away their possessions to Babylon, and brought [Rim-Si]n there in a neck-stock." The chronicle is a very late source (sixth century) and therefore must be handled with caution. However, it seems uncannily close to the two reports sent to Zimri-Lim about the conquest of the city, which confirm that the Babylonian troops captured Rim-Sin alive and took him to Babylon with his belongings. The first report states that "the Babylonian troops entered and the troops [o o] the city wall; in the early morning, the men [o o] entered; and they have brought out Rim-Sin alive"; and the second one that "as the city of Larsa was being seized, they brought Rim-Sin and his [o o together with] his property out to Babylon." Year name 31 of Hammu-rabi records his victory over Rim-Sin:

> The year when king Hammu-rabi, trusting the gods An and Enlil who march in front of his army, and with the supreme power which the great gods have given to him, destroyed the troops of Emutbal and subjugated its king Rim-Sin and brought Sumer and Akkad to dwell under his authority.[2]

For a few years Hammu-rabi maintained a dual regime for the former kingdom, with separate year names, administrative divisions replicating those of the reign of Rim-Sin, and an edict of redress applying specifically to his dominions. In the long term, however, the entire territory of Emutbal became integrated in the Babylonian kingdom. In 1762, the year after the conquest of Larsa, Hammu-rabi claims to have defeated Eshnunna and conquered Mankisum (year name 32). We know little about this campaign, but this time Zimri-Lim did not provide Babylon with military help, sending instead presents to Silli-Sin to show his support. Hammu-rabi's bellicose intentions now appeared clear to him, especially as Babylon had recently intervened directly in the affairs of the Jebel Sindjar which Mari considered to lie within its zone of influence. During the war against Larsa Ishme-Dagan of Ekallatum had initiated hostilities with Atamrum of Andariq, an ally of Zimri-Lim, and obtained the support of Eshnunna after vainly seeking troops from Hammu-rabi. After the fall of Larsa and the ensuing conciliation between Silli-Sin and Hammu-rabi, Ishme-Dagan had to abandon his project and leave Ekallatum, apparently seeking refuge again with the Babylonians in spite of the fact that Hammu-rabi had considered somewhat of a betrayal his recent act of allegiance to Eshnunna. Atamrum had just died heirless and Hammu-rabi sent an army of 20,000 soldiers to settle his succession, dividing his kingdom into two smaller states with the evident intent of neutralizing them. Meanwhile Zimri-Lim had laid siege to Ashlakka in the Habur, a vassal state which had just rebelled under its king Ibal-Addu, and feared that Hammu-rabi would take advantage of the situation to lay siege on Mari.

3.7.6   The Capture and Sack of Mari (1761–1759)

The events that followed prove that Zimri-Lim's fears were entirely justified. Year name 33 of Hammu-rabi records the conquest of Mari:

> Year when king Hammu-rabi dug the canal (called) "Hammu-rabi is abundance to the people" (and when he), the beloved of the gods An and Enlil established the everlasting waters of plentifulness for Nippur, Eridu, Ur, Larsa, Uruk and Isin, restored Sumer and Akkad which had been scattered, overthrew in battle the army of Mari and Malgium and caused Mari and its territory and the various cities of Subartu to dwell under his authority in friendship.[3]

The state archives of Mari, our main source up to that point, do not provide any information on these campaigns. Archaeological evidence points to sack and destruction of the city. Babylonian troops sifted through the archives and removed most of the correspondence sent from Babylon and Aleppo. Tags attached to tablet baskets bear the name of Hammu-rabi's thirty-second year, confirming the year of the city's capture as 1761. We know even less about the capture of Malgium, which had also been an ally of Hammu-rabi in his conflict with Larsa. His thirty-fifth year name (1759) commemorates the destruction of the walls of Mari and Malgium, and an inscription composed later recalls the period when "he (Hammu-rabi) captured Mari and all its villages, destroyed its walls and turned the land into rubble heaps and ruins." We have no clue as to the ultimate fate of Zimri-Lim, who may even have been absent from his capital at the time of its capture. The Babylonians also campaigned in the north (Subartu) and Hammu-rabi may have then reinstalled Ishme-Dagan on the throne of Ekallatum and Assur as vassal since the Assyrian King List claims a reign of forty years for him.

3.7.7   Towards an Empire (1759–1750)

The years 1759 to 1750 are much less well known because the Mari archives no longer document the international situation. The year names of Hammu-rabi record two campaigns in that period: against the armies of Gutium, Sutum,

Turukku, Kakmu, and the land of Subartu in 1757 (year name 37), and against the land of Subartu in 1755 (year name 39). This indicates that the focus of expansion had moved to the Trans-Tigridian region and northern Iraq. In the prologue of his Law Code, promulgated late in his reign, Hammu-rabi claims to have established his rule as far north as Assur and Nineveh. The archives found at Tell al-Rimah (probably ancient Qattara) between the Tigris and the Jebel Sindjar corroborate Hammu-rabi's claim of northern hegemony. About two hundred documents including letters and accounts datable approximately between 1760 and 1754 indicate that the city was administered at that time on behalf of Hammu-rabi by a diviner named Aqba-Hammu whose wife Iltani, the recipient of almost all the letters, was the sister of Asqur-Addu, the previous king of Karana, a city probably not far from Qattara. The extent of Babylonian control beyond Mari and in the Habur triangle cannot be ascertained. In his Code, Hammu-rabi claims to have received control of the Euphrates, including Mari and Tuttul, from the god Dagan. Sometime after his death, however, an independent kingdom arose in the middle Euphrates, with Terqa and perhaps a resurgent Mari as political centers. Those areas made up a buffer zone between Aleppo and Babylon. It seems appropriate at that point to speak of an empire for the territories ruled by Hammu-rabi, who now claimed hegemonic titles such as "king of Sumer and Akkad," adopted after the capture of Larsa, and "king of the four quarters" or "king who made the four quarters obedient," both implying universal dominion. He also assumed the innovative titles of "king of the Amorites" and "king of all the Amorite land," and "eternal seed of kingship," which signals the emergence of a new concept of royal legitimacy derived not solely from divine election, as had been the case since the Early Dynastic period, but also based on lineage and pedigree, a notion probably influenced by the interest of Amorites in tribal and family ancestry (Figure 3.3). Three centuries had elapsed since the epochal reign of Shulgi, and Babylonia was unified again under a single rule. Two important sources shed light on the last decade of Hammu-rabi's reign: the Law Code, and the official correspondence between Hammu-rabi and his officials found at Larsa.

3.7.8   The Code of Hammu-rabi

Hammu-rabi's fame in modern times rests on his Law Code, whose best preserved version was discovered at Susa in southwestern Iran and is in view at the Louvre. Inscribed on a seven-and-a-half foot tall stele of black basalt, it is the largest collection of laws from the Ancient Near East outside the Bible and one of the most impressive legacies of Iraq's past (Figure 3.4). The laws are framed by a prologue and an epilogue which extol the king as lawgiver and provide a moral justification for his intervention in the legal sphere. The ultimate inspiration for the laws, however, resides with the god of justice, the sun god Shamash, who is depicted on top of the stele in a seated position with Hammu-rabi standing before him in a gesture of worship. The laws as such number at least 282 separate articles, but a

Figure 3.3   Inscription of Itur-Ashdum. This limestone slab, probably from Sippar, is preserved in the British Museum (BM 22454). It is inscribed in Sumerian by an official named Itur-Ashdum and dedicated to the goddess Ashratum for the life of Hammu-rabi, who is exceptionally called "king of the Amorites". The figure on the relief is in all probability Hammu-rabi. Measurements: H: 39 ×W 40.64 cm. *Source*: © The Trustees of the British Museum.

gap in the middle of the stele prevents full reconstruction. The style of the laws is mostly casuistic, that is, rather than providing a general abstract formulation, each law presents the essentials of a case. For instance, article 3 reads: "If a man comes forward to give false testimony in a case but does not substantiate his accusation, if that case involves a capital offense, that man shall be killed."

Hammu-rabi's Code represents the culmination of a long tradition. Ur-Nammu of Ur and Lipit-Ishtar of Isin promulgated law codes in Sumerian. A collection of laws in Akkadian discovered at Tell Harmal (ancient Shaduppum) near Baghdad, with a duplicate fragment from Tell Haddad (ancient Me-Turan) in the Diyala, must probably be attributed to Dadusha of Eshnunna, antedating Hammu-rabi's by one generation. Some law collections were not even attached to a particular ruler but circulated as models in scribal schools, evidence that the codes drew their inspiration in part from a scholastic tradition of legal writing. Hammu-rabi's Code truly attained canonical status, replacing in this function Ur-Namma's Code which had been copied in schools until that time. Numerous excerpts have been discovered on clay tablets, a number of them in the library of the Assyrian king Ashurbanipal at Nineveh. Recently a copy of its prologue turned up at Sippar

Figure 3.4   Code of Hammu-rabi. The Code of Hammu-rabi is preserved in the Louvre. It is inscribed on a stele of black basalt topped with a relief showing Hammu-rabi standing before the sun-god Shamash, the god of justice, who is seated on a throne. H: 2.25 m × W 55 cm. *Source*: Photo © RMN-Grand Palais (musée du Louvre) / Franck Raux.

in a temple library dating to the sixth century. Remarkably, the colophon claims that the scribe had copied it from a stele in view at Susa, obviously the same one discovered by French archaeologists in 1901. The stele had in fact been plundered by the Elamite king Shutruk-Nahhunte in the twelfth century after a military raid to northern Babylonia. The Laws of Hammu-rabi influenced the formulation of other laws in the first millennium, including the Neo-Babylonian laws and some portions of the Biblical laws in the Book of Deuteronomy. A literary text composed in the sixth century which depicts a Babylonian ruler, probably Nebuchadnezzar II, as reformer of legal practices, draws its inspiration from the first five articles of Hammu-rabi's Code, presenting the ruler in question as intensely absorbed in the legal issues raised by them.

In spite of its wide influence and circulation, many Assyriologists and historians of law have cast doubt on the status of Hammu-rabi's Code as legislation. Some of their reservations seem fully justified considering that we do not have a single unequivocal reference to the Code in any legal document or court judgment from that period. At the same time, archival documentation makes clear allusions to the binding nature of the edicts of redress (*mesharum*) promulgated by kings of the First Dynasty, and a number of scholars now tend to view these edicts, rather than the codes, as the real product of legislative activity. Where does that leave the Code of Hammu-rabi and indeed all other codes from the Ancient Near East? To view them as mere rhetorical exercises designed to propagate the ruler's fame seems restrictive given their complexity and the intellectual effort that went into their composition. Although the Code of Hammu-rabi does not formulate comprehensive legislation like the Napoleonic Code, neither does it consist of a hodge-podge of cases borrowed from previous sources with no internal organization. In many cases it reformulates, modifies, and reorganizes previous laws. In other areas it also innovates, such as in the introduction of the *lex talionis* ("an eye for an eye"), of which it provides the earliest known examples (articles 195–205). There is also evidence that at least some articles originated from decisions by the king himself, or perhaps by royal courts of justice. One striking example occurs in a letter to Sin-iddinam where Hammu-rabi declares his intention to adjudicate personally a case involving burglars who pierced the wall of a goldsmith's house on two occasions before being caught. The letter does not detail the royal verdict, but it probably provided the material for article 21 of the Code which heads a small section devoted to theft and burglary: "If a man has pierced (the wall of) a house, he shall be executed and hanged in front of that hole." From this angle the Code represents codified jurisprudence rather than codified law. When faced with a new case, judges could no doubt extract principles from the Codes to adjudicate it.

Thus, if the Code of Hammu-rabi did not function as universal binding legislation in a modern sense, its use as legal guidebook may have been encouraged in areas directly under state control such as royal courts and in the administration of royal domains. The Code certainly represents an intrusion of the monarchy in the field of common law with the long term objectives of modifying and unifying legal practices, even if those objectives remained largely theoretical. Such aims are expressed in a letter written by Hammu-rabi to Sin-iddinam, his official in post at Larsa, in which he orders him to adjudicate a case according to the law now applying in the former kingdom of Larsa (Emutbal): "When they arrive look into their affair, take care of their case and grant them justice in accordance with the legal practice (*dinum*) that is now applied in Emutbal and see that proper justice is done to them." The letter does not mention the Code explicitly, which may not yet have been promulgated. Nevertheless, the wording of the royal order implies that instead of the legal practice prevailing formerly in the defunct kingdom of Larsa, Sin-iddinam should adjudicate the case in accordance with the one that is now current. It seems difficult to deny that Hammu-rabi refers in this case to collections of legal decisions (*dinum*) emanating from his authority, such as those assembled in the Code.

3.7.8.1 Old Babylonian society

The Code of Hammu-rabi also affords many insights into the fabric of Old Babylonian society, which it divides into three broad classes: the upper class (*awilum*), the bulk of the free population (*mushkenum*), and the non-free slaves (*wardum*). The boundaries between slaves and the other classes seem clear, and compulsory physical marks such as a special hairdo called *abbuttum* ensured the identification of the former. According to article 226 of the Code, a barber who shaved this hairdo without the consent of the slave's owner could have his hand cut off as punishment. Most slaves were either born in that status or came into it as prisoners of wars. Slaves could buy their freedom or marry into the upper classes, in which case their children were born free (article 175):

> If a slave of the palace or a slave of a *mushkenum* marries a woman of the *awilum* class and she bears children, the owner of the slave will not claim slave status for the children of the woman of the *awilum* class.[4]

The Code also deals with debt slavery which was probably common and could be annulled by *mesharum* edicts. The widespread chattel slavery seen in Greece and Rome or in the plantation economies of the New World in the early modern era does not seem to have taken root in Mesopotamia, except in a punctual manner when large numbers of prisoners of war were put to specific tasks. The majority of the workforce belonged to the intermediate strata of society such as the *mushkenum* class. The *mushkenum* formed the bulk of the agrarian population and probably of the lower echelons of urban society as well, but the finer distinctions between *awilum* and *mushkenum* are still debated. The *awilum* held most official functions and performed the *ilkum* service, which entailed the privilege to hold land in tenure as salary for services rendered to the state. The *mushkenum*, on the other hand, were liable to corvée and taxation. Texts often contrast the *mushkenum* with the palace, which has led some scholars to view affiliation with the palace as the basic feature of the *awilum* class.

The Code sometimes treats classes differently. The *lex talionis* applied only for offences against an *awilum*, while a monetary compensation sufficed for the same offence against members of the lower classes. Thus, articles 196 and 197 read: "If somebody has destroyed the eye of an *awilum*, his eye shall be destroyed," and "If somebody has broken the bone of an *awilum*, his bone shall be broken." Article 198, on the other hand, reduces the penalty if the offence is committed against a *mushkenum*, although the fine contemplated still amounts to a hefty compensation: "If somebody has destroyed the eye of a *mushkenum* or broken the bone of a *mushkenum*, he shall pay one mina of silver." Article 199 further reduces the fine for the slave of an *awilum*: "If he has destroyed the eye of the slave of an *awilum* or broken the bone of the slave of an *awilum*, he shall pay half of his value." The term *awilum* carries an inherent ambiguity since it is also the standard word for "man, person," and sometimes it is difficult to determine whether the Code means *awilum* as "somebody, anybody" or as a reference to the upper class.

The Code mentions several professions and occupations and dwells in detail on certain aspects of society. In view of the frequent state of warfare during Hammu-rabi's reign, it is hardly surprising that a number of articles deal with the army (articles 26–39), composed mainly of two types of soldiers: the *redum* (literally "follower") and the *ba'irum* (literally "fisherman"). The army appears to have been professionalized and subjected to the *ilkum* state service whereby soldiers received a plot of land in tenure as salary. Article 26 imposes the death penalty on deserters or soldiers who hire substitutes to perform their service, in which case the land is reattributed, and article 33 details the same punishment for an officer who accepts substitutes: "If a captain or a lieutenant has tolerated desertion, or if he has accepted a substitute for a royal military mission and commanded him, he shall be killed." A soldier taken prisoner could be replaced by his son (article 28), and if the latter was too young the mother kept one-third of the land until he came of age (article 29). Such laws aimed at preventing the system of military tenure from becoming hereditary and patrimonial. A small archive of twenty-one texts from the town of Supur-Shubula near Kish and dated to the reign of Abi-eshuh offers unusual insights into the life of a *redum* named Ubarum, whose main concern appears to have been the hire of substitutes to cultivate his land legally while he performed his military duties. Such concerns must have been ever present in the minds of soldiers, who could lose their land if they left it fallow. This is clearly stipulated in article 30 of the Code:

> If either a *redum* or a *ba'irum* soldier abandons his field, orchard, or house because of the *ilkum* service and absents himself, then another person takes possession of his field, orchard, or house to succeed to his holdings and performs the service obligation for three years, if he then returns and claims his field, orchard, or house, it will not be given to him; he who has taken possession of it and has performed his service obligation shall be the one to continue to perform the *ilkum* service.[5]

The larger part of the Code (articles 127–94) deals with various aspects of family law (status of women, marriage, inheritance, family patrimony, adoption, sexual offences). Babylonian society allowed male polygamy, although only wealthier members of society could afford it. We have plenty of evidence from Mari for the existence of royal concubines in the palace. Even so, only one wife (*asshatu*) held legitimate status. Marriages were pre-arranged and accompanied by a betrothal gift (*biblum*) and a bride-price (*terhatum*) brought by the groom's family, and a dowry (*sheriktum*) provided for the bride by her father. Divorce and repudiation occurred only under exceptional circumstances. For instance, a man could divorce his barren wife only if he returned her dowry and gave her an amount of silver equivalent to her bride-price (article 138). On the other hand, if the woman contracted the *la'bum* disease (probably a skin disease) after her marriage, her husband was obligated to construct special quarters for her and support her for the rest of her life (article 148). The wife could also repudiate her husband, take her dowry, and return to her father's house if she proved upon investigation to have been virtuous and without blame while her husband belittled her and led a dissolute life (article 142). However, if she became wayward, squandered her household, and disparaged her husband, she could incur the death penalty by being cast into the water (article 143). The Code imposes capital punishment on the adulterous wife and her lover unless the husband intervened in her favor (article 129), while a man earned a sentence of equal severity only if caught having sexual relations with his daughter-in-law (article 155), but a man caught in an incestuous relation with his own daughter incurred only banishment from his city (article 154). Many articles deal with family patrimony and especially inheritance law, reviewing the various situations which could influence the redistribution of inheritance shares, for instance regarding the rights of the children of concubines and slaves (articles 170–6). Other articles deal with adoption, preventing the reclaiming of an adopted child by his biological parents unless the adoptive father fails to teach the child his craft (article 188) or refuses to reckon him on an equal footing with his other children (article 190). A child who constantly seeks his biological mother and father from the time of his adoption could also be reclaimed (article 186).

3.7.9 Hammu-rabi as Administrator

Our knowledge of Hammu-rabi as administrator derives mostly from his correspondence with two officials in post at Larsa after the conquest: Sin-iddinam and Shamash-hazir, the former not to be confused with his namesake who reigned over Larsa in the previous century (Figure 3.2). We owe the survival of this correspondence to violent disruptions at Larsa during the reign of Samsu-iluna which forced the abandonment of institutional buildings with their archives. The correspondence is one-sided in that we have letters from Hammu-rabi to these officials, but not from them to the king. These would have been filed in Babylon. About one hundred letters from Hammu-rabi to Shamash-hazir are known. Shamash-hazir bore the titles of "scribe of the fields" and "registrar" (*shassuku*), two functions that appear to have been more or less identical. Sin-iddinam, also the recipient of about a hundred letters, probably occupied the position of private secretary of Hammu-rabi (*tupshar sakkakkim*) before his appointment at Larsa. One letter informs us that he was in charge of the southern half of the former kingdom of Emutbal, referred to as the "lower province" (*litum shaplitum*), and exercised authority over local governors there.

Hammu-rabi addressed a whole range of issues in his correspondence with Sin-iddinam, who had to deal with the management of the irrigation system (repair and cleaning of canals; regulation of water supply); calendar regulation; the army (recruitment, desertion, assignment of fields to soldiers); tax collection (often farmed out to merchants); levying and management of manpower; shipment of cattle, sheep, and wool from the palace's herds to Babylon; various juridical duties such as the adjudication of cases, and even police work involving the arrest of thieves and the recovery of stolen property. Hammu-rabi sometimes asks him to send people to Babylon to investigate the matter himself. At other times he enjoins Sin-iddinam to apply "(royal) regulations" (*simdatum*), a term which certainly refers to orders issued from the palace, although it is not clear how they relate to law codes and edicts of redress. More important, the correspondence of Sin-iddinam reveals that all the resources of the former kingdom of Emutbal were channeled to the central administration in Babylon; not only taxes, but also the income from the royal estates of the former kings of Larsa, now the private domain of Hammu-rabi.

The correspondence of Shamash-hazir deals mostly with conflicts over assignments of fields, which is consonant with his function as land registrar. Although Shamash-hazir occupied a lower rank than Sin-iddinam in the administration, Hammu-rabi dealt with him directly in matters within his sphere of responsibilities. Once Hammu-rabi even ordered him to come and meet with him in Sippar for an audit of all the records of his administration over the past three years, and to bring along all the surveyors and accountants who worked with him. Such close supervision of officials in intermediate and lower level positions reveals an important side of Hammu-rabi's character as statesman: his tireless micromanagement, which comes forward in many other letters in which he appears to attend personally to complaints filed by ordinary citizens:

> Speak to Sin-iddinam: Thus says Hammu-rabi. Epesh-ilim the palace guard has informed me as follows: "The son of Lu-Asalluhi has claimed from me the field which Shamash-hazir the registrar (*shassuku*) had allotted to me and he has appropriated my barley. Also, he has claimed from me the orchard of Etel-pi-Marduk and he has appropriated my dates." This (is what) he brought to my attention. Herewith I send (you) this Epesh-ilim. Issue a written order that his opponent be summoned to you and take care of the case, and if he has (indeed) been unjustly deprived of his field and orchard, hand him back the field and his barley (and) the orchard and his dates.[6]
>
> Speak to Shamash-hazir: Thus says Hammu-rabi. Ili-ippalsam the shepherd informed me as follows: "For four years Etel-pi-Marduk has been taking from me a field of three *bur*s which had been sealed for me with the seal of my lord, and he has been taking its grain. Moreover I informed Sin-iddinam but it has not been returned to me." Thus he informed me. I have written to Sin-iddinam (that) if it really is as Ili-ippalsam claims, namely, that Etel-pi-Marduk has taken and used for four years the field of three *bur*s which was sealed for him by the palace, there is no matter more harmful than this one. Investigate carefully the circumstances of this matter and return to Ili-ippalsam the field according to the document that was sealed for him by the palace, and moreover, establish by the divine weapon the (quantity of) grain which for four years Etel-pi-Marduk had been taking from that field and give it to Ili-ippalsam the shepherd. Finally send me a report of that case.[7]

If we look at the archival corpus from Larsa covering the last thirteen years of Hammu-rabi and the first twelve years of his son Samsu-iluna, it seems odd that so few letters of the latter have surfaced. This could indicate that Samsu-iluna relied on the upper echelons of his administration to oversee the entire machinery, while Hammu-rabi cared to supervise himself all the details, perhaps to prevent the spread of corruption and the creation of administrative fiefdoms, the plight of all ancient states. This might explain his success as statesman and empire builder.

3.7.9.1 The palace and state economy

Much discussion has been devoted to the role of the palace (or the state) in the economy of the Old Babylonian period. Historians have often assumed that the state controlled and regulated most of the economy, but this impression derives from the one-sided nature of our sources, which stem mostly from large organizations. There must have existed substantial sectors of small, private producers that left no trace in the documentation. The palace entrusted a portion of its estates to agricultural entrepreneurs called *isshiakkum* for the fields producing grain and *shandanakkum* for the date orchards, who in return paid a rent (*biltum*) to the state and hired subcontractors to perform the tasks. The state maintained the infrastructure for irrigation and provided entrepreneurs with traction animals and agricultural implements. Similar practices still prevailed in Babylonia a millennium later and are well attested for temples which owned vast latifundia like the Eanna at Uruk. Evidence for the periodic failure of the system also exists in both periods, with entrepreneurs and tenants accumulating arrears in unpaid rents because of crop failure, forcing rulers of the First Dynasty to remit these debts periodically in their edicts of redress.

Babylonia did not enter the world of monetary economies until the latter part of the first millennium. Since there was no currency, everybody who worked for the state received allocations of food and staples as salary. Some also received a field in tenure for their services, a system which, as we have seen, is well known for soldiers. Our sources refer generally to such fields as *shukussum*, which means literally "(field) for subsistence," but the relation of this institution to the *ilkum* service cannot be assessed easily. All *shukussu* fields may in fact have entailed performance of the *ilkum* service. Recipients of land could cultivate it themselves or hire tenant farmers, a practice documented by the archive of the soldier Ubarum. The state also owned large herds of livestock, and to tend them hired professional herdsmen who had to deliver various products accruing from the herds (wool, skins). Another important participant in the state economy were the merchants (*tamkaru*), most of them private businessmen who offered their services to large institutions such as the temple and palace, although some of them appear as royal functionaries. Merchants performed two important functions for the state: the import of resources that were lacking in the alluvial plain of Babylonia (wood, stones, metals), and the commercialization of surpluses produced on the royal domains (wool, leather, foodstuffs such as fish, dates, grain). An influential school of thought used to deny the existence of a real market in Babylonia, claiming that the state fixed prices and exercised monopolies on basic staples. Such policies existed indeed, but their application was punctual and often aimed at providing equity. The evidence has in fact accumulated for the existence of price fluctuations due to factors not basically different from those regulating market economies. Therefore Old Babylonian merchants operated within a familiar framework of calculated risks and varying profits, very much like their Old Assyrian counterparts whose activities are known in much greater detail.

NOTES

1. After Charpin 2004: 209.
2. After Horsnell 1999, vol. 2: 141–3.
3. After Horsnell 1999, vol. 2: 146–9.
4. After Roth 1995: 115.
5. After Roth 1995: 86–7.
6. After Van Soldt 1994: 39, no. 43.
7. After Kraus 1968: 55, no. 55.

FURTHER READING

Archival sources are listed by the Archibab Project at http://www.archibab.fr/. Royal inscriptions are edited by Frayne 1990. The date lists (year names) of Babylon I are compiled by Horsnell 1999. Law codes are edited and translated by Roth 1995. The letters from the royal archives of Mari are translated by Durand 1997, 1998, and 2000, by Heimpel 2003, and by Sasson 2015. Charpin 2004 is an irreplaceable survey of political history from the fall of Ur III until the end of Babylon I. Stol 2004 offers an in-depth survey of the economy and society of the Old Babylonian period. Van de Mieroop 2004, and especially Charpin 2012 discuss the reign of Hammu-rabi. Specific topics are studied by Van de Mieroop 1987 (transition from Ur III to Isin I), Streck 2000 (the Amorites), Goddeeris 2002 (northern Babylonia before Hammu-rabi), Van de Mieroop 1993 (Rim-Sin I of Larsa), Roth 1994 and Westbrook 1989 (legislative nature of Law Codes). Charpin 2010 offers a series of interesting studies on various aspects of the period.

Charpin, Dominique. 2004. "Histoire politique du Proche-Orient amorrite (2002–1595)." In Attinger, Pascal, et al (eds.), *Mesopotamien - Die altbabylonische Zeit*. Fribourg and Göttingen: Academic Press and Vandenhoeck & Ruprecht: 25–480.
Charpin, Dominique. 2010. *Writing, Law, and Kingship in Old Babylonian Mesopotamia*. Chicago: University of Chicago Press.
Charpin, Dominique. 2012. *Hammurabi of Babylon*. London: I. B. Tauris.
Durand, Jean-Marie. 1997, 1998, 2000. *Les documents épistolaires du palais de Mari*, I, II, and III. Paris: Editions du Cerf.
Frayne, Douglas. 1990. *Old Babylonian Period (2003–1595 BC):* The Royal Inscriptions of Mesopotamia, Early Periods 4. Toronto: University of Toronto Press.
Goddeeris, Anne. 2002. *Economy and Society in Northern Babylonia in the Early Old Babylonian Period (ca. 2000–1800 BC)*. Leuven: Peeters.
Heimpel, Wolfgang. 2003. *Letters to the Kings of Mari: A New Translation, with Historical Introduction, Notes, and Commentary*. Winona Lake, IN: Eisenbrauns.

Horsnell, Malcolm. 1999. *The Year-Names of the First Dynasty of Babylon*, 2 vols. Hamilton, ON: McMaster University Press.

Kraus, Fritz Rudolf. 1968. *Briefe aus dem Archive des Šamaš-hāzir*. Altbabylonische Briefe IV. Leiden: Brill.

Roth, Martha T. 1994. "Mesopotamian Legal Traditions and the Laws of Hammurabi." *Chicago Kent Law Review* 71: 13–39.

Roth, Martha T. 1995. *Law Collections from Mesopotamia and Asia Minor*. Atlanta, GA: Society of Biblical Literature.

Sasson, Jack. 2015. *From the Mari Archives: An Anthology of Old Babylonian Letters*. Winona Lake, IN: Eisenbrauns.

Stol, Marten. 2004. "Wirtschaft und Gesellschaft in altbabylonischer Zeit." In Attinger, Pascal, et al (eds.), *Mesopotamien - Die altbabylonische Zeit*. Fribourg and Göttingen: Academic Press and Vandenhoeck & Ruprecht: 641–975.

Streck, Michael. 2000. *Das amurritische Onomastikon der altbabylonischen Zeit 1*. Münster: Ugarit-Verlag.

Van de Mieroop, Marc. 1987. *Crafts in the Early Isin Period: a Study of the Isin Craft Archive from the Reigns of Išbi-Erra and Šu-ilišu*. Leuven: Peeters.

Van de Mieroop, Marc. 1993. "The Reign of Rim-Sin." *Revue d'assyriologie et d'archéologie orientale* 87: 47–69.

Van de Mieroop, Marc. 2004. *King Hammurabi of Babylon: A Biography*. Oxford: Blackwell.

Van Soldt, Wilfred H. 1994. *Letters in the British Museum, Part 2*. Altbabylonische Briefe XIII. Leiden: Brill.

Westbrook, Raymond. 1989. "Cuneiform Law Codes and the Origins of Legislation," *Zeitschrift für Assyriologie und vorderasiatischen Archäologie* 79: 201–222.

4

Decline of the First Dynasty

At the time of Hammu-rabi's death Babylon ruled the larger part of Mesopotamia either directly or through a system of vassals and clients. This hastily built construction began to crack under Samsu-iluna, whose successors reigned over a kingdom limited to Akkad and the Middle Euphrates. In spite of territorial losses, the late Old Babylonian period represents an important era of creativity that witnessed the blossoming of a new literature in the Akkadian language (Figure 4.1) and the emergence of omen compendia, a genre that will play a significant role in the cultural and political life of Babylonia and Assyria until the first millennium. Date lists provide the essential backbone for the chronology and political history of this period, although with minor gaps and some uncertainties. The main issue concerns the year names of Abi-eshuh, which are known mainly from individual occurrences in archival texts; their chronological sequence is therefore uncertain and scholars have designated many of them by letters (e.g. year name "a"). The other issue concerns the year names of Samsu-ditana; they are preserved only in Date List N, which is incomplete. The order of year names 23 to 27 cannot be established with certainty, and the last four year names (28 to 31) are left blank in Date List N, depriving us of potentially crucial information on the closing events of the First Dynasty.

4.1   The Reign of Samsu-iluna (1749–1712)

The Mari archives tell us that Hammu-rabi had two sons named Sumu-ditana and Mutu-numaha. They spent some time at the court of Mari where they may have served as voluntary hostages to cement the ill-fated alliance between Zimri-Lim and their father. We have no information on Samsu-iluna before his accession. However, he claims primogeniture in one of his inscriptions as

A History of Babylon: 2200 BC–AD 75, First Edition. Paul-Alain Beaulieu.
© 2018 John Wiley & Sons Ltd. Published 2018 by John Wiley & Sons Ltd.

Figure 4.1   Epic of Gilgamesh, Tablet V. During the late Old Babylonian period Akkadian replaced Sumerian as the main language of literature. The Akkadian Epic of Gilgamesh was composed at that time, partly adapting material from previously independent Sumerian tales. This recently discovered cuneiform manuscript, probably from southern Iraq, preserves Tablet V of the Old Babylonian Epic, which tells the story of Gilgamesh and Enkidu's encounter with Humbaba in the Cedar Forest. It is preserved in the Sulaymaniyah Museum (T. 1447) in Iraq. Measurements: H: 11 × W: 9.5 cm. *Source:* Osama Shukir Muhammed Amin: https://commons.wikimedia.org/wiki/File:Tablet_V_of_the_Epic_of_Gligamesh. JPG?uselang=fr (accessed April 10, 2017).

"firstborn son of Hammu-rabi." Samsu-iluna's date of accession can be determined quite closely from archival documents. One text dated V-10 carries a double date by Hammu-rabi (year 43) and Samsu-iluna (year of accession), and another one dated on VI-3 in year 43 of Hammu-rabi contains an oath by Samsu-iluna. These suggest a period of co-regency. A letter from Larsa tells us that Samsu-iluna ascended the throne during his father's illness, whereupon he proclaimed a *mesharum* edict:

> Speak to Etel-pi-Marduk; thus Samsu-iluna: The king, my father, is ill, and I have now seated myself on the throne of my ancestral family to govern the country. And in order to strengthen those who deliver rent (*nashi biltim*), I have remitted the arrears [o o] of the tenant farmers (*isshiakkum*) and the [o o]. I have broken the tablets recording the debts of soldiers (*redum*), fishermen (*ba'irum*) and commoners

(*mushkenum*). I have established equity (*mesharum*) in the land. In the land [o o] nobody shall make demands from a soldier, a fisherman or a commoner. As soon as you read my letter, you and the elders of the land which you administer shall come up here and meet with me.[1]

Little is known about the early part of Samsu-iluna's reign. His year names 1 to 8 mention only the dedication of votive objects and irrigation works. The general impression of stability seems contradicted by the proclamation of a second *mesharum* edict in his eighth year, preserved only in fragmentary copies. A private archive from Sippar contains an important accumulation of unsettled promissory notes dated to years 6 and 7 of Samsu-iluna. These had obviously been canceled by the *mesharum* edict. Similar concentrations of unclaimed promissory notes dating to the same period have been found in other archives, two of them from Lagaba. But the problems were not only economic. Soon rebellions erupted in various parts of the empire.

4.1.1   The Rebellion of Rim-Sin II (1742–1740)

Samsu-iluna claims that he clashed with a certain Rim-Sin, whom he describes as "the agitator of Emutbal who had been elevated to the kingship of Larsa." This Rim-Sin can hardly be identical with the former king of Larsa, already an elderly man when defeated by Hammu-rabi twenty years before, hence we must refer to him as Rim-Sin II, but his adoption of that name indicates that he aimed at restoring the kingdom of Emutbal. The dates and extent of his rebellion can be determined from archival texts. Scribes at Larsa ceased using Babylonian dates after XII-20 in year 7 of Samsu-iluna (early 1742), and resumed at the beginning of year 10 (spring of 1740). During the intervening period, they used year names of Rim-Sin II. Dating formulas of Rim-Sin II are attested also at Kutalla, Ash-dubba, Bad-Tibira, Lagash, Ur, and Nippur. The insurrection probably started at Larsa, feeding on local resentment against Babylonian rule and the memory of the city's political importance until the recent past. However, it seems clear from the formulation of his third (and last) year name that Rim-Sin II eventually moved the seat of his power to the city of Kesh (not to be confused with Kish) in middle or southern Babylonia: "Year in which the goddess Ninmah raised (Rim-Sin) greatly in the temple of Kesh, the foundation of heaven and earth, to kingship over the land." A letter of Rim-Sin found at Larsa corroborates the data from the year name:

Speak to Amurrum-tillati: Thus says Rim-Sin (II). In order to bring light to Emutbal and to gather its dispersed people, the great gods established the foundation of my throne in Kesh, the city of my creatress. Just as the entire country has heard and rejoiced (about it) and has come and met with me, you must also come and meet with me. As soon as you have read my letter come and meet with me. Then I will elevate you to high rank.[2]

The "creatress" mentioned in the letter is Ninmah, known in Akkadian as Belet-ili, a mother goddess who played an important mythological role as creatress of humanity alongside Enki. She was the patron goddess of Kesh. Not much is known about the reign of Rim-Sin II. Texts from Larsa dated to the year of his accession ("Year when Rim-Sin became king") allude to harsh living conditions. Some quotations of high prices fetched by grain suggest a state of near famine. Other texts mention a detention unit (*bit asiri*) presumably set up to hold political prisoners and other captives, where even guards received rations well below the norm, sufficient only to keep body and soul together.

4.1.2   The Rebellion of Rim-Anum (1742–1740)

At about the same time another insurrectionist by the name of Rim-Anum seized power at Uruk and also started using his own year names. His reign of about two years is known mostly from two groups of archival documents. One group was discovered in the palace of Sin-kashid together with the state archives of the defunct kingdom of Uruk. The other group, by far more important numerically, comes from clandestine excavations and is scattered through various museums. It concerns the administration of another detention unit (*bit asiri*), this one holding opponents of Rim-Anum as well as enemy combatants, although the texts also record deliveries of food allotments to messengers and other people engaged in diplomatic and military activities. The last text from Uruk with a Samsu-iluna year name is dated VIII-11 in year 8 of Samsu-iluna, and documents securely dated by the accession year of Rim-Anum ("Year when Rim-Anum became king") are spread from months IX to XII. We can therefore tentatively date his capture of power to the middle of the month VIII in Samsu-iluna's eight year (late in 1742). Samsu-iluna does not mention Rim-Anum by name but claims to have defeated twenty-six rebel leaders during his war against Rim-Sin II. Texts from the detention unit at Uruk reveal the complexity of the political situation. No fewer than twenty different entities occur in the archive: allies, opponents, messengers, and groups of prisoners. They mention three other rebels by name: Daganma-ilum of Mutiabal-Kazallu, and Iluni and Munnawirrum, both designated as ruler (*ensi*) of Eshnunna. It appears that after an initial period of cooperation with Rim-Sin II and other insurgents, Rim-Anum switched sides. Either the rebel coalition turned against him, or he allied himself with Samsu-iluna to secure his future in case of a Babylonian victory. Indeed, references in the *bit asiri* archive to allied rebels such as Daganma-ilum and the people of Mutiabal-Kazallu gradually cease in the second year of Rim-Anum, indicating a reversal of policy reflected in Rim-Anum's third and last year name:

> The year in which king Rim-Anum inflicted a defeat on the troops of the land of Emutbal, the armies of Eshnunna, Isin and Kazallu, all together having presented themselves at Uruk for war. Since time immemorial Uruk had never experienced (such) a dust storm (raised by a foreign army), but after the dust storm settled, he slaughtered (all of them) and by his power ejected (them all) from the homeland.[3]

Rim-Anum did not reap the benefits of this turnaround and was eliminated a few months after the demise of Rim-Sin II, in the tenth year of Samsu-iluna (1740). Textual documentation at Uruk stops completely after his downfall.

4.1.3   The Invasion of the Kassites (1742)

The ninth year name of Samsu-iluna records an armed encounter in 1742 with the Kassites: "Year in which king Samsu-iluna destroyed the foundations of the Kassite troops at Kikalla." Kikalla probably lay in northern Babylonia, in the vicinity of Kish. This is the earliest securely dated mention of the Kassites, a people from the Zagros Mountains that will play a major role in Babylon's history. The second year name of Rim-Sin II, probably contemporary with Samsu-iluna's ninth year name, also mentions the Kassite invasion: "the enemy, the evil Kassites from the foreign lands, who cannot be repelled to the mountains." During the later years of Samsu-iluna we begin to see references to Kassites in Babylonian archives, and afterwards they appear with recurring frequency until the end of the First Dynasty, mostly in documents from Sippar, Dilbat, and Dur-Abi-eshuh. These texts give a fairly consistent picture of the role of Kassites in Old Babylonian society. They seem to have kept for the most part their own tribal organization, living outside large urban centers in settlements designated as "houses," which were extended family units under the authority of a clan leader. Scribes often designate Kassites collectively (and sometimes even individually) with the logogram ERÍN "troops," a term which often has a military connotation. Indeed, some texts highlight the role of Kassites as mercenaries and also their involvement in chariotry, a fact of some significance given the importance of Kassite loanwords in texts dealing with horses and chariots during the time of the Kassite Dynasty. A number of Kassites appear in other occupations as well, especially as seasonal laborers. Some people designated as Kassites bear Akkadian names, reflecting individual efforts at assimilating into the larger society. However, Kassites still living in their own settlements must have kept the use of their native language; a text from the reign of Ammi-saduqa mentions that an interpreter had been sent to a Kassite "house" to gather information on the movement of insurgent tribes.

4.1.4   Samsu-iluna Strikes Back

The Kassite invasion must have delayed Samsu-iluna's response to the southern rebellions. His tenth year name, however, shows that he was on the offensive in 1741: "Year in which king Samsu-iluna, with the great strength of the god Marduk, smote with weapons the troops of Idamaras (variant: Eshnunna), Emutbal, Uruk and Isin." The toponym Idamaras refers here to the Diyala region. Samsu-iluna designates Iluni, king of Eshnunna, as the other major rebel leader besides Rim-Sin II. He also appears in the *bit asiri* archive from Uruk. Rim-Anum of Uruk claims to have fought the same enemies in his last year name, while Samsu-iluna identifies Uruk as one of his opponents. The third and last year name of Rim-Anum must therefore be coeval with Samsu-iluna's tenth, reflecting the following sequence of events: in 1742 the south rebelled against Babylon, with Rim-Sin II and Rim-Anum emerging as leading contenders. Soon other cities followed, creating a zone of insurgency from the Diyala to the Persian Gulf. In 1742 Babylonia was also affected by the Kassite invasion, threatening both Samsu-iluna (year name 9) and Rim-Sin II (year name 2). In that same year the insurrectionists turned against Uruk, but Rim-Anum repelled their onslaught. In 1741–1740 Samsu-iluna emerged victorious after the elimination of Rim-Sin II and Rim-Anum, and his date formulas gradually reappeared at Larsa, Ur, Nippur, and Kutalla. Chronicle 40 preserves a memory of Samsu-iluna's victory in a damaged entry which mentions Rim-Sin (II). Iluni of Eshnunna and most of the other rebels who are not identified by name in Samsu-iluna's account of the war, notably Daganma-ilum of Kazallu-Mutiabal, must have been eliminated around the same time. Complete pacification required more actions. Samsu-iluna's eleventh year name records the destruction of the city walls of Ur and Uruk (1740), his twelfth the defeat of the troops of Sumer and Akkad (1739), his thirteenth the submission of Kisurra and Sabum (1738), and his fourteenth the defeat of the "hateful kings who had brought the people of Akkad to revolt," which might refer to further operations in northern Babylonia (1737).

4.1.5   Sargonic Reveries

Historical events are often viewed by their contemporaries through the lens of past ones. To the minds of Samsu-iluna and his scribes, the great rebellion against Naram-Sin of Agade offered the best framework to explain the events they had just witnessed. The deeds of Sargonic kings had become memorialized in schools with compositions inspired by copies of genuine inscriptions of that period. Sargonic traditions thrived particularly in the Diyala and northern Mesopotamia during the early part of the second millennium. Rulers of Eshnunna and Assur adopted names of Sargonic rulers (Sargon, Naram-Sin) and the *kispum* rituals discovered at Mari invoked the departed spirits of Sargon and Naram-Sin. Royal inscriptions of Eshnunna and Mari emulate Old Akkadian models. Two inscriptions of Yahdun-Lim, the first Amorite ruler of Mari, record his defeat of rebel leaders with literary motifs borrowed from Naram-Sin's inscriptions. Southern Babylonia also cultivated Old Akkadian models. A little known ruler of Uruk in the nineteenth century went by the name of Naram-Sin, and Nippur yielded many Old Babylonian copies of Sargonic inscriptions which became accessible to Babylonian scribes after Hammu-rabi's defeat of Larsa. These may have been the main source for Samsu-iluna's revival of the great rebellion motif in a building inscription commemorating the restoration of the Ebabbar temple at Sippar:

> At that time I (Samsu-iluna) defeated with weapons, eight times within one single year, the entirety of the country of Sumer and Akkad, which had become hostile to

me; I turned the cities of my enemies into heaps of rubble and mounds of ruins; I tore out the foundations of the foes and enemies from the country; I caused the entirety of the country to dwell under my command; whereas since distant days, since the time when the brickwork of Ebabbar was fashioned, Shamash had favored no king among the previous kings, and (therefore) nobody had rebuilt for him the wall of Sippar; Samsu-iluna, the beloved one of Shamash and Aya, the mighty king, the king of Babylon, the king of the four quarters, the king whose command is agreeable to Shamash and Aya, I, at the command of Shamash and Marduk, by levying the army of my land, and during the course of that very same year, I fashioned its brickwork; I raised the wall of Sippar like a great mountain; I restored Ebabbar.[4]

The restoration of Ebbabar and the wall of Sippar are also commemorated in year names 16 and 18 of Samsu-iluna. The building inscription borrows the familiar topoi of Naram-Sin's great rebellion: the universal nature of the rebellion and its suddenness; the defeat of all insurgents within record time, usually one single year; the utter destruction of their cities (heaps of rubble and mounds of ruin); divine favor which made victory possible; reunification of the empire under a single rule. Samsu-iluna provides more specific details in another building inscription for the rebuilding of the wall of Kish, a deed which is also recorded in his twenty-fourth year name. The inscription is also modeled on the genre of the great rebellion:

> Samsu-iluna, the able king, the one who heeds to the great gods, greatly trusted the words which the god Zababa and the goddess Ishtar had spoken to him; he made his weapons ready for slaying his enemies; he set out on a military campaign to annihilate his foes. The year was not half over that he killed Rim-Sin (II), the agitator of Emutbal who had been elevated to the kingship of Larsa, and in the land of Kish he heaped up a burial mound over him. He killed twenty-six rebellious kings, his foes; he annihilated all of them. He captured Iluni, king of Eshnunna, who had been disobedient to him; he carried him off in neck-stocks and destroyed his life; he caused the land of Sumer and Akkad to live in agreement; he caused the four quarters to dwell under his command.[5]

Rim-Sin II had moved his capital to Kesh in southern Babylonia, and the scribes of Samsu-iluna may have played on the assonance of the names Kesh and Kish. Rim-Sin II may in fact have been buried in Kesh. On the occasion of his building works at Kish Samsu-iluna revived the title "king of Kish," probably again to emulate Sargonic rulers. The title appears in an inscription which commemorates the renovation of the ziggurat of the gods Zababa and Ishtar, the city's patron gods.

4.1.6   Loss of Southern Babylonia

Samsu-iluna's suppression of the rebellions did not lead to permanent reoccupation of the south. Although his dating formulas replaced those of Rim-Sin II and Rim-Anum in the reclaimed cities during his tenth year, archival evidence stopped at Ur, Larsa and Bad-Tibira in his twelfth year, suggesting either abandonment or loss of the area to another power, the most likely candidate being Ilumma-ilum, founder of the First Dynasty of the Sealand. Archival evidence from northern Babylonia indicates that an exile of people from the south took place at that time. The best known case is the migration of inhabitants of Uruk to Kish. Urukeans are attested in the documentation from Kish as early as the eleventh year of Samsu-iluna. Texts from Kish dated to the last four kings of the First Dynasty document the maintenance of the cult of Urukean deities such as Ishtar-of-Uruk and Nanaya, indicating that the divine images had moved there accompanied by their priesthood. There is also evidence for migrations from Lagash to Kish, and from Larsa to Babylon. Economic factors have been invoked to explain the migration, in particular a partial collapse of food production due to intensive cultivation and salinization of the soils. The water management policy of Babylonian kings, which may have favored northern cities and reduced the inflow of irrigation water to the south, presents itself as another possible cause. Be that as it may, the southernmost area of Sumer, the area later known as the Sealand, escaped Babylonian control. We owe to these political disruptions the preservation of the state archives of Larsa, including the correspondence of Hammu-rabi with Sin-iddinam and Shamash-hazir. Written documentation at Ur and Larsa resumed only in the later Kassite period. The First Dynasty of the Sealand filled the vacuum under circumstances that are obscure.

4.1.7 Northern Exertions

The fifteenth year name of Samsu-iluna records the restoration of the destroyed wall of Isin (1736), probably as bulwark against further losses in the south. The sixteenth mentions work on the wall of Sippar (1735) and the seventeenth the wall of Emutbal (1734), which must refer to Mashkan-shapir, the former northern capital of Emutbal near Nippur. Samsu-iluna must have proclaimed in that same year a third *mesharum* edict since a reference to its application has been found in a text from Sippar. All these measures aimed at consolidating the Babylonian heartland after the loss of the south. They were soon followed by major military efforts in the northern parts of the empire: the Diyala, Habur, and Middle Euphrates. These projects claimed the attention of Samsu-iluna for the remaining years of his reign.

4.1.7.1 The Diyala region

Samsu-iluna claims to have defeated Eshnunna in his tenth year name. We know nothing about the fate of the region after the suppression of Iluni's rebellion, but Samsu-iluna launched another campaign against Eshnunna in 1731, recorded in his twentieth year name: "Year in which king Samsu-iluna, the foremost king, subdued the country not obedient to him and smote with weapons the army of the land of Eshnunna." In 1727 he erected a fortress in the Diyala named Dur-Samsu-iluna ("Fort Samsu-iluna"), a deed commemorated in his twenty-fourth year name, which also records that the building of Dur-Samsu-iluna was part of a larger military project that included the rebuilding of the wall of Kish:

> Year when king Samsu-iluna, who rules in wisdom, built on the banks of the Euphrates the city wall of Kish, whose splendor covers the enemy countries, and he erected Dur-Samsu-iluna in the land of Warum on the banks of the Turul canal (i.e. Diyala).[6]

Dur-Samsu-iluna has been identified during the University of Chicago excavations in the Diyala in 1938 as mound B at Khafaje thanks to the discovery of an inscription of Samsu-iluna. The inscription mentions the victory against Eshnunna and lays the bold claim that Samsu-iluna "subjugated the land of Idamaras from the border of Gutium to the border of Elam," implying a deep thrust in the piedmont of the Zagros. A small archive from uncontrolled excavations documents military units stationed at Dur-Samsu-iluna, the latest text dating to the twenty-seventh year of Samsu-iluna (1723). Babylonian control of the area continued for at least a few more years since his thirty-second year name records some work on the banks of the Diyala and Taban rivers in 1719.

4.1.7.2   War in the Habur triangle

While still busy in the Diyala, Samsu-iluna took the war far to the north in the Habur triangle. After the collapse of the large kingdom assembled by Samsi-Addu in northern Mesopotamia, Shubat-Enlil (Tell Leilan), his former capital, became a bone of contention between rival powers. A state archive of several hundred tablets discovered there in the Eastern Lower Town Palace documents a local dynasty which postdates the destruction of Mari by Hammu-rabi and includes three rulers: Mutu-abih (mostly in the hypocoristic form Mutiya), Till-abnu and Yakun-ashar. They claim the title of "king of the land of Apum," and during their reigns the city retrieved its original name of Shehna (also Shahna and Shahana). Mutiya was a contemporary of the later years of Hammu-rabi and the early years of Samsu-iluna. Yakun-ashar can be identified as the ruler mentioned in the twenty-third year name of Samsu-iluna, which commemorates the destruction of Shehna in 1728. The state archives of Shehna stop at this point. We certainly owe their preservation to the destructions caused by the armies of Samsu-iluna. We do not know how effectively the Babylonians controlled Shehna after this event, if they did at all. Aleppo probably remained the dominant power in the region, being the one most often mentioned in the archives of Shehna, while Babylon occurs rarely. However, another rival power had emerged in Syria as successor state of Mari, the kingdom of Hana, with renewed pretensions to control the Middle Euphrates and the Habur.

4.1.7.3   The Suhum and the region of Mari

After the fall of Mari, Babylon controlled the Middle Euphrates for about twenty years. During the revolts against Samsu-iluna, however, the region regained its independence under a dynasty known mainly from texts discovered at Terqa (Tell Ashara) upstream from Mari (see Map 4.1). A sequence of rulers with the title "king of the land of Hana" appears in their date formulas. The three earliest rulers are Yapah-Sumu-abum, Isi-Sumu-abum, and Yadih-abum. The latter appears in year name 28 of Samsu-iluna:

> Year in which king Samsu-iluna, by the command of the god Enlil (and) by the wisdom and strength given by the god Marduk, crushed like a mountain with his terrifying *shita*-weapon and his mace the hostile kings Yadih-abum and Muti-hurshan.[7]

Muti-hurshan has not yet been identified in contemporary documents. Finds at Terqa have been complemented by the publication of texts found at Harradum (Khirbet ed-Diniye), ninety kilometers downstream from Mari, and Tabatum (Tell Taban) twenty kilometers south of Hassake on the Habur in northeastern Syria. The conflict between Hana and Babylon can be followed from documents found at Harradum: one text dates to Isi-Sumu-abum, one to Samsu-iluna year 6 (1744), and the bulk of the archive (about 100 texts) from Samsu-iluna year 26 to Ammi-saduqa year 18 (1724–1629). These texts show that Samsu-iluna had lost Harradum during the great revolts against his rule (the text dated to Isi-Sumu-abum must date to this period), and regained it by his twenty-sixth year at the latest (1724). Then he scored a major victory against Yadih-abum in his twenty-seventh year (1723). About twenty-five tablets dated to the reign of Isi-Sumu-abum and one to the reign of Yadih-abum were found at Tabatum; this shows that the kingdom of Terqa had about the same northern reach as the former kingdom of Mari. The site may have been raided by the Babylonians during Samsu-iluna's campaigns against Hana. Indeed, Samsu-iluna commemorates the restoration of the fortifications of Saggaratum in 1718 in his thirty-third year name: "Year in which Samsu-iluna the king at the command of Shamash and Marduk restored completely all the brickwork of the city of Saggaratum." Accepting the current proposed localization of Saggaratum at Abu Ha'ir, about twenty kilometers from the confluent of the Habur and the Euphrates, this year name indicates that Samsu-iluna had extended Babylonian control to the heart of the kingdom of Hana, at least for a certain time. Babylon remained entrenched in the Suhum and even at Terqa until the reign of Samsu-ditana. Although it has long been assumed that the rulers of Hana had made Terqa their capital, there is no definite proof of this. Recent archaeological work has shown that Mari was not completely deserted after the Babylonian conquest and may have continued to function as political center for a while, especially in view of the fact that the god of Mari, Itur-Mer, figures prominently in oath formulas of documents found at Terqa.

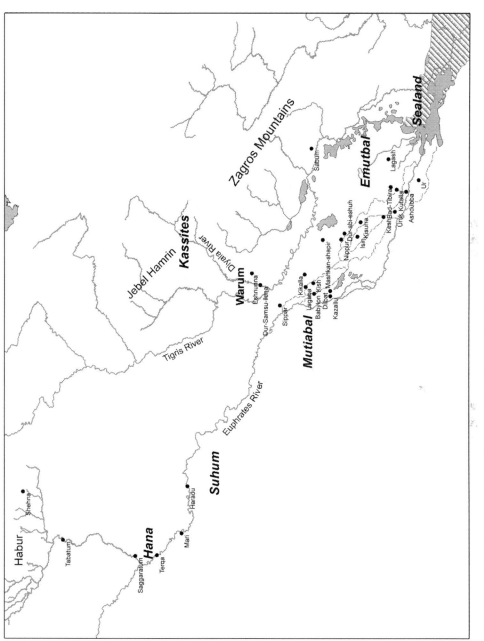

Map 4.1 Iraq in the Seventeenth Century. Map Design: Stephen Batiuk, University of Toronto.

4.1.8   Loss of Central Babylonia and Rise of the Sealand

Further losses in Babylonia overshadowed Samsu-iluna's relative success in the north. Archives stop at Isin in his twenty-ninth year (1721), at Nippur in his twenty-ninth or thirtieth year (1721–1720), at Lagaba in his thirtieth year (1720). There is some evidence for further transfer of cults and their personnel from these cities to northern Babylonia, notably from Isin to Sippar (cults of Gula and Ninkarrak), and from Nippur to Babylon (cult of Enlil), although we cannot exclude that these had long taken root in the north. This abrupt withdrawal from central Babylonia may have been caused by the growing power of the Sealand kingdom. Documents from Nippur which almost certainly date shortly after Samsu-iluna's thirtieth year (1720) bear the dating formulas "Year when Ilumma-ilum became king" and "Year after Ilumma-ilum (became king)." Ilumma-ilum, who appears in kings lists as founder of the First Dynasty of the Sealand, may even be mentioned in a document from Larsa dating to the rebellion of Rim-Sin II. The text mentions a "king of the Sea(land)." His name is nearly lost except for the last sign which can be read /li/, allowing a restoration [Ilumma-i]li, a possible form of the name Ilumma-ilum. Another document from Larsa dated to Rim-Sin II lists soldiers probably detained in the *bit asiri*, some being characterized as "soldiers of the Sealand." These may have been allies of Samsu-iluna during the rebellion, or perhaps they attacked Rim-Sin II independently. Thus, although we can tentatively place the beginning of the First Dynasty of the Sealand around 1720, it may in fact have begun earlier in the areas vacated by the Babylonians after Samsu-iluna's twelfth year, notably in Ur, Uruk and Larsa. Information about the Sealand dynasts that were contemporary with Babylon I is scarce, but an entry in Chronicle 40 mentions a victory of Ilumma-ilum against the armies of Samsu-iluna. Similar encounters with the Sealand Dynasts will occur under Abi-eshuh and Ammi-ditana.

4.1.9   From Sumerian to Akkadian Literature

One consequence of Samsu-iluna's loss of Nippur has been the preservation of the Sumerian literary heritage. Excavations at Nippur uncovered thousands of tablets and fragments in private houses, mostly manuscripts of Sumerian compositions which formed the standard curriculum of apprentice scribes and their teachers. In all probability the majority of the houses had been abandoned with the tablets left in situ during the collapse of Babylonian power in 1720. Three centuries earlier Shulgi claimed to have created scribal academies at Ur and Nippur, and indeed Ur is the only site which has yielded a trove of Sumerian literary texts comparable to Nippur. This corpus includes compositions created in large part during the Ur III and Isin-Larsa periods. Sumerian died out as spoken vernacular long before the time of Samsu-iluna. The manuscripts, probably copied from memory in their majority, reveal inconsistencies which can often be ascribed to the students' approximate knowledge of a dead language.

Yet scribes in training devoted much effort to the study of Sumerian. They learned vocabulary lists and grammatical paradigms with Sumerian verbal forms alongside their Akkadian equivalents. They had also developed a theory of Sumerian grammar with terms denoting the two basic conjugations.

Many compositions have come down to us virtually complete thanks to the profusion of school manuscripts found in the scribes' houses. Thus, we can now read the six short Sumerian epic tales about Gilgamesh and the four epics of Lugalbanda and Enmerkar, all ten compositions forming a legendary cycle about the early history of Uruk; collections of proverbs, fables, hymns to gods and kings, myths, lyrical poetry, in short, a corpus of a few hundred works ranging from a few dozen to several hundred lines and forming the earliest known literary culture in history. If the Babylonians had not suddenly relinquished control of Nippur at that time, the greater portion of this tradition might have been lost since the majority of these texts ceased to be transmitted after the middle of the second millennium, in the same manner as most of the Greek and Latin literary heritage disappeared in late Antiquity. Contemporary with the demise of Sumerian literature in schools we see the rise of a new literature in Akkadian, written in a slightly archaizing language which differs from that of Old Babylonian letters and documents. Two large literary compositions stand out. The myth of Atra-hasis, which contains the most extensive account of the flood story in Mesopotamian literature, and the Old Babylonian version of the Epic of Gilgamesh, partly based on the shorter Sumerian tales but incorporating new motifs and viewpoints (Figure 4.1). The Epic was edited and expanded during the Middle Babylonian period and became the longest literary composition ever created in Babylonia.

4.1.10   Samsu-iluna as Administrator and Legislator

Compared with his father's, the activities of Samsu-iluna as administrator are not well known. Only a dozen letters from him have been preserved. We have more information on his role as legislator. Samsu-iluna proclaimed *mesharum* edicts in his first, eighth, and seventeenth years. A fourth one was apparently issued in his twenty-eighth year; direct evidence for it has not survived, but a number of archives show an unusual accumulation of unclaimed promissory notes in the years preceding his twenty-eighth, a sign that debts had been canceled by royal decree. The most important legislative document from his reign has been handed down in the form of a royal letter addressed to officials in Sippar. In this letter Samsu-iluna addresses two legal cases that had been brought to his attention. The address formula and the second case with the royal decision read as follows:

> Say to Sin-nasir, Nuratum, Sin-iddinam, the merchant board of Sippar and the judges of Sippar-Amnanum, to Awil-Nabium, Sin-iddinam, the *shangu*-priests, the judges, the overseers of the temples, the overseers of the *naditum*s, the [o o] of the judges, and the doorkeepers of the cloister of Sippar-Yahrurum, thus (speaks) Samsu-iluna …:

[Second Case]: I was further informed as follows: The judge Awil-Sin is owed silver by Mar-Shamash, a man of Sippar. Because of non-payment of the silver, he seized Mar-Shamash and spoke to him as follows: "If you keep your possessions (so that) I will not receive anything from you, I will take (as payment) the slave of your daughter, the *naditum* of Shamash, who lives in the cloister." This is what he told him. Thus I was informed.

[Royal Directive]: A *naditum* of Shamash, whose father and brothers gave her food supplies and wrote a tablet for her (to that effect), and who lives in the cloister, is not liable for the debts and the *ilkum* duties of the house of her father and brothers. Her father and brothers will perform their *ilkum* duties and [o o]. As for the creditor who takes hold of a *naditum* of Shamash for the debts or the *ilkum* duties of the house of her father and brothers, such a man is an enemy of Shamash![8]

This letter has survived in four copies. One comes probably from the temple archives of Sippar. The other three were discovered at Sippar-Amnanum in the archive of Ur-Utu, lamentation singer of the goddess Anunitum. Two copies from that archive end with colophons stating that they are duplicates of "a tablet of Samsu-iluna archived in the cloister." The paleography of the three copies from the Ur-Utu archive and their archaeological as well as archival contexts indicate they were made during the reign of Ammi-ditana or Ammi-saduqa. Therefore the letter had been memorialized in a manner not typical for normal correspondence, but without becoming a school text or literary piece either. Why that happened is evident from its unusual formulation. While the king appears as judge in a few letters from that period, Samsu-iluna provides here more than adjudications of a specific legal problem. He draws general guidelines to address analogous cases, although the formulation of the solution remains casuistic. The similarity to law codes is striking. The Code of Hammu-rabi regulates the rights and duties of the *naditum*s, a class of cloistered women that is especially well attested at Sippar, where they numbered about three hundred. These cloistered priestesses often came from wealthy families which provided for them with a lifelong income. A sister of Hammu-rabi named Iltani and one of his daughters were *naditum*s of Shamash at Sippar. The Code does not cover the issues addressed in Samsu-iluna's letter, which must likely be viewed as complementary legislation given its circulation, long-term preservation, and universal formulation. The term *simdatum* refers to such royal regulations, and this letter may in fact be a unique direct witness to the issuance of such provisions.

We do not know much about the last years of Samsu-iluna. His thirty-fourth year name commemorates the building of a new royal palace in 1717; the palace was presumably in Babylon since he qualifies it as his main residence: "Year when king Samsu-iluna built the princely palace, a residence appropriate as the primary location of his kingship." His thirty-sixth year name records a war against the "land of the Amorites" in 1715, perhaps referring to the Middle Euphrates or northeastern Syria, and his thirty-seventh, imperfectly preserved, mentions the Abih (or Ebih) mountain, probably the Jebel Hamrin in the western Zagros, probably in the context of a campaign which would have taken place in 1714.

4.2   The Last Century of Babylon I (1711–1595)

The political history of the last four reigns of the First Dynasty is not well documented. Royal inscriptions become scarce, and year names record only six military encounters, the rest being devoted mostly to public works, pious foundations, and votive offerings. While this could be interpreted as a sign of peace and stability, it seems more likely that military encounters were either avoided or generally not favorable to the Babylonians, and therefore not recorded. Sumer had largely seceded but this did not prevent Abi-eshuh and Ammi-ditana from claiming the title "king of Sumer and Akkad." Hammu-rabi's vast empire, partly maintained by Samsu-iluna with great effort, became an increasingly distant memory. Effective rule appears to have been limited mostly to Akkad, with the addition of the Suhum which Babylon firmly controlled until the reign of Samsu-ditana.

4.2.1   Abi-eshuh (1711–1684)

Samsu-iluna was succeeded by his son Abi-eshuh. His second year name makes allusions to a *mesharum* edict, stating that Abi-eshuh established "goodwill and reconciliation in his land, caused justice (*kittum*) and equity (*mesharum*) to exist and made the land prosper." The existence of this edict is confirmed by a lawsuit preserved in the British Museum dated to the first year of Abi-eshuh. The case concerns Geme-Asaluhi, an uncloistered *naditum* of the god Marduk who had been imprisoned probably for the debts incurred by her father and then released "when king Abu-eshuh established a *mesharum*." She sued her former husband Adad-muballit to retrieve her belongings, and the two spouses became legally divorced by the court. The "chief of the merchants and the judges of Larsa" presided over the court, and they invited the husband to swear an oath in "the temple of Shamash of Larsa," indicating that the lawsuit took place among exiles from Larsa in Babylon. The fourth year name of Abi-eshuh (Year name "d") commemorates a victory against the Kassites, probably in 1709: "The year when king Abi-eshuh, by the supreme command of the gods An and Enlil and the great power of the god Marduk, defeated the Kassite troops." A trial record probably from Babylon and dated to year "q" of Abi-eshuh alludes to this event. The plaintiff, a woman named Nanaya-shamhat, daughter of Uruk-tayyar and Sha-Nanaya, belonged to a family displaced from Uruk and resettled in Kish. Nanaya-shamhat sued to retrieve her freedom which she had lost after coming to Babylon with her family "when the general Mannum-kima-Shamash retreated safely with the troops of Ushanum in face of the Kassite army." In Babylon she was abusively reduced into slavery by a smith named Hazippa. After long deliberations and oaths taken by members of her family, the judges set her free. The circumstances of her tribulations remain partly unclear; most likely she and her family had taken refuge in Babylon with the troops after a Kassite raid on Kish. The earlier encounter of Samsu-iluna with the Kassites had also taken place in the area around Kish, at Kikalla.

Other military clashes occurred during Abi-eshuh's reign. Recently a fuller version of year name "f" of Abi-eshuh has been identified on tablets from Sippar. The year name has been tentatively assigned to his fifth or sixth year and mentions "the army of Elam," which would make this the first officially recorded conflict with the Elamites since the time of Hammu-rabi. A year name tentatively assigned to his seventeenth year mentions a war against Eshnunna, which would have taken place in 1696:

> Year when king Abi-eshuh, by the perfect power of the god Marduk, defeated in a powerful battle the army of the land of Eshnunna on the way from Tashil and took prisoner Ahushina, the king of Eshnunna.[9]

Another year name possibly to be placed two years later records the damming up of the Tigris River: "The year when king Abi-eshuh, by the supreme power of the god Marduk, dammed the Tigris." This year name must be related to an entry in Chronicle 40 which states that Abi-eshuh's purpose in obstructing the flow of the Tigris was to capture Ilumma-ilum of the Sealand: "Abi-eshuh, son of Samsu-iluna, put himself in a position to seize Ilumma-ilu and decided to obstruct the flow of the Tigris. He obstructed the flow of the Tigris but did not [catch] Ilumma-ilu." This operation is further mentioned in an oracular consultation (*tamitu*) preserved in Neo-Assyrian copies in which the diviners inquire whether the soldiers of Abi-eshuh should dam the Tigris on both sides or let the water flow. Visibly this event left a lasting memory in the scribal tradition, perhaps because of the mammoth undertaking involved in diverting the waters of the river. A recently published divinatory text alludes to the same situation; the text comes from Dur-Abi-eshuh, the new military compound created by the king in central Babylonia.

4.2.1.1 Dur-Abi-eshuh

The construction of the fortress of Dur-Abi-eshuh ("Fort Abi-eshuh"), recorded in a year name to be placed probably two years later (year name 21?), was certainly directed against the Sealand kingdom: "Year when king Abi-eshuh built Dur-Abi-eshuh upstream from the marshlands on the bank of the Tigris." A fairly large number of texts written at Dur-Abi-eshuh have surfaced on the antiquities market. The location of the fortress is uncertain given that they originate from uncontrolled excavations, but internal evidence suggests a location near Nippur. The texts situate Dur-Abi-eshuh at the confluence of the Tigris with the canal "Hammu-rabi-is-the-abundance-of-the-people." According to year name 33 of Hammu-rabi this canal provided water for Nippur, Eridu, Ur, Larsa, Uruk, and Isin. This made Dur-Abi-eshuh a strategic location controlling the flow of water to southern cities while protecting northern Babylonia from incursions by the Sealand.

Two, possibly three distinct archives have been identified at Dur-Abi-eshuh. The first archive still awaits publication but its contents have been partly disclosed.

The texts consist of records of the military establishment at the fortress and can be dated mostly to the reign of Abi-eshuh, including a few letters sent by the king. The soldiers involved in chariotry and horses all bear Kassite names, while foot soldiers come from a variety of backgrounds: Isin, Idamaras, Emutbal, Mashkan-shapir, Elam, Arrapha in northeastern Iraq, the Suhum, and even Aleppo. The names of the contingent leaders are mostly Babylonian, however. The second archive has recently been published and concerns mainly the activities of one Enlil-mansum, a *neshakkum* priest of the god Enlil. The archive covers eighty years, from Abi-eshuh 20 until Samsu-ditana 13 (1692–1613), with most of the texts dating to Ammi-saduqa and Samsu-ditana. Enlil-mansum managed a local replica of Ekur, the temple of Enlil at Nippur, created by refugees who came from Nippur after its abandonment by the Babylonians in the thirtieth year of Samsu-iluna (1720). However, while some texts list offerings of animals for this new Ekur at Dur-Abi-eshuh, others mention that animals were taken to Nippur as well. These hints at an ongoing life at Nippur corroborate archaeological data which indicate that the city could still sustain a small population at that time, although the texts remain unclear about its political status.

4.2.2   Ammi-ditana (1683–1647)

The relatively long reign of Ammi-ditana is not well documented. His second year name alludes to the proclamation of a *mesharum* edict: "The year when king Ammi-ditana the pious and obedient shepherd of the gods Shamash and Adad, released (people) from forced service." A fragmentary quotation of a provision of this edict has been tentatively identified in a text from Harradum in the Suhum. Additional historical information can be gleaned from the third archive found at Dur-Abi-eshuh. The texts date to the reign of Ammi-ditana and shed light on life at Nippur. One letter dated to the eleventh year of Ammi-ditana (1673) discloses information about an attack on the city by unidentified enemies. The letter specifies that both assailants and defendants had horses. The enemy eventually evacuated the city after inflicting some damage on the Ekur temple. The wording of the letter implies that Nippur lay outside Babylonian control, yet very close to it. It confirms the data from the archive of Enlil-mansum at Dur-Abi-eshuh that the Ekur temple of Nippur was still functioning.

Year name 17 alludes to the defeat in 1668 of a certain Yarah-abi (or Arahab), who is not known from any other source: "The year when king Ammi-ditana with the great strength (given) by the gods Shamash (and) Marduk [defeated] Yarah-abi, the man of the land." Ammi-ditana engaged in further fortifications of his realm with the construction of three fortresses named Dur-Ammi-ditana, one commemorated in year name 16: "The year when king Ammi-ditana built Dur-Ammi-ditana on the banks of the canal Silakku," the other in year name 35: "The year when king Ammi-ditana built Dur-Ammi-ditana on the banks of the canal Me-Enlil." The construction of a fortress Dur-Ammi-ditana on the canal Sharbit (perhaps Sarbatum) is also commemorated in a building inscription of the king. The localization of these canals remains hypothetical and some of the references might be to one and the same fortress. Another inscription of Ammi-ditana commemorates the erection of a defensive wall at Babylon named "May the god Asaluhi turn into clay in the netherworld the one who makes a breach in the clay (of this wall)," and year name 32 mentions similar work at a locality called Ishkun-Marduk, also on the Silakku canal: "The year when king Ammi-ditana built the city wall of Ishkun-Marduk on the banks of the Silakku canal." Finally year name 37 records the destruction of an important Sealand fortress in 1648: "Year in which (Ammi-ditana) destroyed the city wall of Udinim built by the army of Damiq-ilishu." The city of Udinim might be identical with Udannu, a town mentioned in Neo-Babylonian documents and probably located in the vicinity of Uruk. According to king lists Damiq-ilishu was the third ruler of the First Dynasty of the Sealand.

4.2.3   Ammi-saduqa (1646–1626)

The defeat of Damiq-ilishu at Udinim is the last military event recorded in a year name of the First Dynasty. Year names of Ammi-saduqa still record some public works such as the digging of a canal named "Ammi-saduqa is the abundance of the people" (year name 16), the repair of the upper portion of the ziggurat of the god Shamash at Sippar and work on the temple Eulmash (year name 17 + d), and the building of a fortress named "Dur-Ammi-saduqa" on the Euphrates and the canal "Samsu-iluna is a source of abundance" (year name 11), but the rest of his year names record exclusively votive offerings in temples such as the dedication of royal images and ornaments for the gods (Figure 4.2).

4.2.3.1   The edict of Ammi-saduqa

Like his predecessors Ammi-saduqa proclaimed a *mesharum* edict at the beginning of his reign, but contrary to established practice he promulgated it upon his accession rather than during his first full regnal year and it is therefore commemorated in his first year name: "The year when king Ammi-saduqa, the god Enlil having magnified his princely lordship, rose forth steadfastly like the sun over his country and established justice for all his people." While all other *mesharum* edicts of the First Dynasty have survived in a very fragmentary state or are known merely from mentions in legal documents and reflections of their impact in private archives, the edict of Ammi-saduqa can be reconstructed almost in its entirety from three ancient manuscripts. It contains twenty-two provisions such as these:

> §1 The arrears of the farmers, shepherds, knackers, of the people working in the summer pastures, and of other tributaries of the palace, in order to strengthen them and treat them equitably, are herewith cancelled: the collector must not take any legal action against the household of a tributary.

Figure 4.2   Venus Tablet of Ammi-saduqa. The so-called Venus Tablet compiles observations of the planet Venus made during the reign of Ammi-saduqa. The manuscript comes from the Library of Ashurbanipal, about one thousand years later. Often invoked in the past to establish absolute astronomical dating for the First Dynasty of Babylon, its use for that purpose is limited given the likelihood of textual corruption during its long history of transmission. It is preserved in the British Museum (K. 160). Measurements: H: 17.14 × W: 9.2.
Source: © The Trustees of the British Museum.

§20 If an obligation weighed upon a resident of [the regions] of Numhia, Emutbal, Idamaras, [or of the cities] of Uruk, Kisurra or Malgium, and he had to place his own person, his wife, or his children in servitude for debts in exchange for money, or as a security, he is liberated because of the royal edict of redress (*mesharum*) for the country; his *andurarum* will be carried out.[10]

The edict first cancels the arrears of people working on crown land and obligated to pay a fixed annual rent in nature or silver. It also cancels the arrears of merchants working for the palace and responsible for marketing these products, essentially from agriculture and animal herding. It intervenes in the larger society, canceling non-commercial debts, returning alienated property to their former owners and restoring to their original status individuals who had fallen into debt and servitude, a practice called *andurarum*. A number of letters and juridical documents specifically refer to *mesharum* edicts as the basis for legal action, indicating that they operated as statutes, unlike the law codes. The *mesharum* edicts were enacted frequently, but not at regular intervals. Indeed, a similar measure is recorded in year name 10 of Ammi-saduqa: "Year in which (Ammi-saduqa), the true shepherd, the obedient servant of Shamash and Marduk, released the debts of his country." Their frequency indicates that they served as regulatory mechanism rather than decrees introducing social or legal reform. Indeed, the socio-economic system remained the same after each reenactment, and each new edict tended to repeat measures prescribed in previous ones, even when their context had become anachronistic.

4.2.3.2   Kassites, Bimatites, and Samharites

A group of ten letters, some dated to the fifteenth year of Ammi-saduqa (1632), indicates that the region of Sippar suffered at that time severe attacks inflicted by groups labeled as Samharites, Bimatites, or even simply as "the enemy." The letters in their majority originate from the king or transmit orders given by him to officials at Sippar. Ammi-saduqa warns them about marauding enemies, suggesting various measures to ensure the safety of the town and enjoining people to stay within the city walls and the herdsmen to move their flocks and cattle to a safer place inside the country. One letter refers to the Samharites as main troublemakers:

> To Marduk-mushallim, Marduk-lamassashu and Sin-bel-aplim; thus speaks Ammi-saduqa. The translator who came from the encampment of the Kassites informed me that numerous Samharite troops have already crossed over into the heart of the country in order to attack the herds, flocks and troops coming outside of Sippar-Yahrurum. The matter has been confirmed! Thus I write to you so that you should know about it. [The city gate should not be opened unt]il the sun has risen ... Be on your guard and do not neglect your duty to keep watch over the city. Month of Ululu, eighteenth day, the year when king Ammi-saduqa (brought into the temple Emeteursag, for the god Zababa and the goddess Inanna), his statue (representing him) saying a prayer of peace.[11]

Another letter identifies the Bimatites and the Samharites as a threat to Sippar-Yahrurum, and a third one speaks about two men, one named Puzur-Dagal and the other one Kashtil, who took the leadership of a band of 1,500 Samharites to plunder cattle around the city. The name Kashtil is typically Kassite, suggesting a possible connection between Samharites and Kassites. Also, a text datable to the reign of Samsu-iluna or Abi-eshuh mentions "Kassite Bimatite troops," which can be interpreted either as two different ethnic or tribal groups ("Kassite and Bimatite troops"), or more likely indicates that the Bimatites formed a subdivision within the Kassite troops ("troops of the Bimatite Kassites"). This opens the possibility that the Bimatites and Samharites both belonged to the larger Kassite population that had settled in and around Babylonia. These groups could on occasion turn hostile. At the same time it appears that other Kassites informed the royal messenger and interpreter about the movements of these enemy troops.

4.2.3.3   Trauma at Sippar-Amnanum and Haradum

During the later years of Ammi-saduqa hostile armed groups caused much destruction between Sippar and the Suhum. Excavations at Tell ed-Der, ancient Sippar-Amnanum, uncovered some 2,000 tablets in a house that had been destroyed by fire at the end of the Old Babylonian period. The archaeologists meticulously recorded the find spots of all tablets, providing a unique opportunity to reconstruct the circumstances of the abandonment and destruction of the house. The house and tablets belonged to Ur-Utu, chief lamentation singer (*kalamahhu*) of the goddess Anunitum in Sippar-Amnanum. Ur-Utu inherited this house from his father Inanna-mansum and occupied it from the fifth to the eighteenth year of Ammi-saduqa (1642–1629). The bulk of the tablets dates from the twenty-eighth year of Ammi-ditana until the thirteenth year of Ammi-saduqa (1656–1634); after that the number of tablets declines steadily until the end of the archive in his eighteenth year (1629). There is evidence of disorder among the tablets stored in one archive room, leading some scholars to suggest that Ur-Utu searched in a hurry through the tablets before fleeing, keeping mostly real estate documents; as he abandoned his house precipitously, he apparently dropped forty-nine of them on the way out. The city of Haradum in the Suhum was destroyed by fire at about the same time. The most recent text discovered there is dated to the eighteenth year of Ammi-saduqa (1629), the very same year when the archive of Ur-Utu ends. In spite of these reversals, Ammi-saduqa and Samsu-ditana eventually managed to restore Babylonian authority at Sippar-Amnanum and the Suhum. Documents dated to these two kings have been discovered at Terqa and textual evidence shows that life continued at Sippar-Amnanum until at least the early years of Samsu-ditana, at which time a new chief lamentation singer of the goddess Anunitum named Marduk-muballit is attested.

4.2.4   *Samsu-ditana (1625–1595)*

Samsu-ditana, the last sovereign of the First Dynasty, reigned thirty-one years according to King List B. The order of his year names and their content can be established with certainty until his twenty-second year only, and approximately until his twenty-seventh year. No source records his last four year names. Archival documents from his reign are attested at several sites and their distribution allows us to assess the gradual weakening of Babylonian control. Documentation stops at Supur-shubula near Kish in 1615 (year 11; archive of the soldier Ubarum), Dur-Abi-eshuh in 1613 (year 13), Dilbat and Kish in 1612 (year 14; perhaps as late as year 19 in Kish), Sippar in 1607 (year 19), and finally at Babylon in 1600–1599 (years 26/27). His year names record solely votive offerings, but a longer version of year 5 has recently turned up at Dur-Abi-eshuh which vaguely alludes to a successful military encounter: "The year when king Samsu-ditana, by the great might of the gods Shamash and Marduk, smote(?) evil and wicked-ness(?), and drove out the camp(?) of his enemy." The year name does not further identify the threat faced by Samsu-ditana. This, however, tallies with sources from that period which subsume the opponents of Babylonian kings under the general label of "enemy." Indeed, the "enemy" may have become so polymorphous as to defy more precise categorization. One *tamitu* from Nimrud mentions the siege of an unnamed city and the following grab bag of opponents: the Elamite army, the Kassite army, the army of Idamaras, the army of Hanigalbat, the Samharite army, the Edashushtite army, and a collection of unnamed foreign troops and military corps allied with them, all described as those "who have rebelled against the god Marduk and against Samsu-ditana, son of Ammi-saduqa, king of Babylon and are constantly seeking out stratagems and hostile acts."

While the Edashushtites cannot be identified in contemporary sources, the other groups are well documented, including the Samharites who had become a cause of concern during the later years of Ammi-saduqa. The term Hanigalbat refers probably to the Hurrians, a people at home in the northern confines of Mesopotamia and eastern Turkey and attested since the Old Akkadian period. The state archives of Mari mention a few Hurrian dynasts in northern Mesopotamia. In the seventeenth century the Hurrians started to expand their territory. This process culminated in the sixteenth century with their creation of the kingdom of Mitanni, later known as Hanigalbat, which controlled a large swath of territory from Levantine Syria to northeastern Iraq. The *tamitu* specifies that these armies had rebelled against Samsu-ditana. The kings of the First Dynasty always relied on a system of fortified settlements to protect their territory and resorted to foreign groups like the Kassites to staff these military compounds, Dur-Abi-eshuh providing the best documented example. The situation reported in the *tamitu* may have been a revolt of the mercenaries, combined perhaps with incursions by neighboring powers, notably Elam and Idamaras in the Diyala valley. One neighboring state conspicuously absent from the *tamitu* is the Sealand. However, a recently identified Middle Babylonian epic preserved on a manuscript from Nippur recounts a victorious campaign of Gulkishar, the sixth ruler of the First Dynasty of the Sealand, against Samsu-ditana. Further details will emerge with the publication of the epic. At least it now establishes a synchronism between Gulkishar and Samsu-ditana and promises to shed more light on the circumstances which led to the demise of the First Dynasty of Babylon.

4.2.4.1   The fall of Babylon (1595)

According to a laconic entry in Chronicle 40, it was the Hittites who dealt the final blow to the First Dynasty: "During the time of Samsu-ditana, the Hittites marched on Akkad." Further details are preserved in the Telepinu Proclamation, a Hittite historical text dating to the later part of the sixteenth century. The Proclamation states that the assault on Babylon took place during the reign of the Hittite king Mursili I (ca. 1620–1590):

> And then he (Mursili I) marched to Aleppo, and he destroyed Aleppo and brought captives and possessions of Aleppo to Hattusha. Then, however, he marched to

Babylon, and he destroyed Babylon, and he defeated the Hurrian troops, and he brought captives and possessions of Babylon to Hattusha.[12]

In the late eighteenth and seventeenth centuries the Hittites established their capital at Hattusha (modern Boghazkoi) and gradually extended their rule over Anatolia. The campaign of Mursili concluded this early phase of expansion and aimed at destroying Aleppo and Babylon, the two powers able to block Hittite expansion in Syria and the Middle Euphrates. The sack of Babylon by the Hittites resulted apparently in the removal of the images of the god Marduk and his consort the goddess Zarpanitu from their shrines in the Esagil temple. This can be inferred from the inscription of the Kassite king Agum-kakrime, who claims later to have returned the images to Babylon, refurbished them and granted on the same occasion tax exemptions to various corps of craftsmen. Another late text, the Marduk Prophecy, echoes the inscription of Agum-kakrime by attributing to Marduk an exile of twenty-four years in the land of the Hittites. The conventional date for the fall of Babylon according to the Middle Chronology is 1595, but the last few years of Samsu-ditana remain elusive and his reign may in fact have been shorter than the figure provided by King List B.

4.2.5 The City of Babylon during the First Dynasty

We know much more about cities like Sippar, Nippur, and Larsa during the time of the First Dynasty than about the capital Babylon. German excavations reached a small area in the Old Babylonian levels of Babylon in the Merkes city quarter northeast of the temple precinct of Marduk. These forays uncovered private houses where seven discrete private archives were discovered totaling more than a thousand cuneiform tablets. The largest one includes about 450 tablets belonging to one Marduk-nasir, the head of a scribal school. The purely archival documents date for the most part to the reign of Samsu-iluna. Among the literary texts and school exercises which form the bulk of the tablets one finds excerpts from literary works as well as epics often written in Sumerian, incantations, and copies of older royal inscriptions. The second most important find includes about 240 tablets making up the archives of a merchant (*tamkaru*) named Kuru and his companions. Most of the tablets date from the period 1616–1599, ending four years before the traditional date for the fall of Babylon. Only a small part of these texts has been published. On the layout and architectural aspect of Babylon under the First Dynasty little can be said except for the few references garnered from archival texts and year names. Late Old Babylonian documents from Babylon mention the Gate of Ishtar and the Newtown district northeast of the city. Sumu-la-el, Apil-Sin, and Abi-eshuh claim to have undertaken work on the city wall. Year names mention work on several temples, such as: Esagil temple (Sabium year name 10); temple of Inanna in Babylon (Apil-Sin year name 11); Eturkalamma (Apil-Sin year name 13); temple of Nanna (Hammu-rabi year name 3); Enamhe of Adad in Babylon (Hammu-rabi year name 28); Eturkalamma for An, Inanna and Nanaya (Hammu-rabi year name 34); Ekishnugal for Nanna in Babylon (Abi-eshuh). All these buildings and topographical features are also known later in the first millennium. Our sources also mention a royal palace in Babylon but do not reveal its location.

NOTES

1. After Veenhof 2005: 121, no. 130.
2. After Van Soldt 1994: 47, no. 53.
3. After Michalowski and Beckman 2012: 427.
4. After Frayne 1990: 376–7.
5. After Frayne 1990: 387.
6. After Horsnell 1999, vol. 2: 213–15.
7. After Hornsell 1999, vol. 2: 220–2.
8. After Janssen 1991: 8–9.
9. After Horsnell 1999, vol. 2: 258–9.
10. Adapted from Hallo 2000.
11. Adapted from Richardson 2005: 273.
12. Adapted from Van den Hout 1997: 195.

FURTHER READING

Pientka 1998 is an in-depth historical survey of the period, with discussions of archives and year names (for the latter see also Horsnell 1999), to be complemented with the recent publication of texts from Dur-Abi-eshuh by Van Lerberghe and Voet 2009. Royal inscriptions are edited by Frayne 1990. Royal edicts (*mesharum*) of the period are translated by Hallo 2000. The *tamitu*s are edited by Lambert 2007, and the Proclamation of Telipinu by Van den Hout 1997. On the wars of Samsu-iluna see Charpin 2011 and 2014, Eidem 2011 (archives from Shehna), Michalowski and Beckman 2012 as well as Seri 2013 (rebellion of Rim-Anum). Royal edicts are discussed by Renger 2002, and the other legislative activities of Samsu-iluna by Janssen 1991. The rebellions and wars of the time of Samsu-ditana are discussed by Richardson 2005, and the conflicts of the First Dynasty with the Sealand and other opponents by Zomer 2016. For the kingdom of Hana in the Middle Euhprates see Podany 2002, and for Kassite infiltrations in Babylonia Van Lerberghe 1995.

Charpin, Dominique. 2011. "Le 'Pays de Mari et des bédouins' à l'époque de Samsu-iluna de Babylone." *Revue d'assyriologie et d'archéologie orientale* 105: 41–59.
Charpin, Dominique. 2014. "Chroniques bibliographiques 15. Le royaume d'Uruk et le pays d'Apum, deux voisins de Babylone vaincus par Samsu-iluna." *Revue d'assyriologie et d'archéologie orientale* 108: 121–60.
Eidem, Jesper. 2011. *The Royal Archives from Tell Leilan: Old Babylonian Letters and Treaties from the Lower Town Palace East*. Leiden: NINO.
Frayne, Douglas. 1990. *Old Babylonian Period (2003–1595 BC):* The Royal Inscriptions of Mesopotamia, Early Periods 4. Toronto: University of Toronto Press.

Hallo, William W. 2000. "The Edicts of Samsu-iluna and his Successors." In Hallo, William W. and Lawson Younger, K. (eds.), *The Context of Scripture Vol. 2: Monumental Inscriptions from the Biblical World*. Leiden: Brill: 362–4.

Horsnell, Malcolm. 1999. *The Year-Names of the First Dynasty of Babylon*, 2 vols. Hamilton, ON: McMaster University Press.

Janssen, Caroline. 1991. "Samsu-iluna and the Hungry Naditums." In *Mesopotamian History and Environment: Northern Akkad Project Reports* 5. Ghent: University of Ghent. 3–39.

Lambert, Wilfred George. 2007. *Babylonian Oracle Questions*. Winona Lake, IN: Eisenbrauns [edition of the *tamitu*s].

Michalowski, Piotr, and Beckman, Gary. 2012. "The Promulgation of the Name of the Third Year of Rim-Anum of Uruk." In Boyi, Tom et al., (eds.). *The Ancient Near East, a Life! Festschrift Karel Van Lerberghe*. Orientalia Lovaniensa Analecta 220. Leuven: Peeters. 425–434.

Pientka, Rosel, 1998. *Die spätaltbabylonische Zeit: Abiešuh bis Samsuditana. Quellen, Jahresdaten, Geschichte*, 2 vols. Münster: Rhema.

Podany, Amanda. 2002. *The Land of Ḫana: Kings, Chronology, and Scribal Tradition*. Bethesda, MD: CDL Press.

Renger, Johannes. 2002. "Royal Edicts of the Old Babylonian Period: Structural Background." In Hudson, Michael, and Van de Mieroop, Marc (eds.), *Debt and Economic Renewal in the Ancient Near East*. Bethesda, MD: CDL Press. 139–61.

Richardson, Seth. 2005. "Trouble in the Countryside, *ana tarṣi* Samsuditana: Militarism, Kassites, and the Fall of Babylon I." In van Soldt, Wilfred et al., (eds.), *Ethnicity in Ancient Mesopotamia: Papers Read at the 48th Rencontre Assyriologique Internationale, Leiden, 1–4 July 2002*. Leiden: NINO: 273–89.

Seri, Andrea. 2013. *The House of Prisoners: Slavery and State in Uruk during the Revolt against Samsu-iluna*. Berlin and New York: Walter de Gruyter.

Van den Hout, Theo P. J. 1997. "The Proclamation of Telipinu." In Hallo, William W., and Lawson Younger, K. (eds.), *The Context of Scripture Vol. 1: Canonical Inscriptions from the Biblical World*. Leiden: Brill: 194–8.

Van Lerberghe, Karel. 1995. "Kassites and Old-Babylonian Society: A Reappraisal." In *Immigration and Emigration within the Ancient Near East: Festschrift E. Lipiński*. Leuven: Peeters: 379–93.

Van Lerberghe, Karel, and Voet, Gabriella. 2009. *A Late Old Babylonian Temple Archive from Dur-Abieshuh*. Bethesda, MD: CDL Press.

Van Soldt, Wilfred H. 1994. *Letters in the British Museum, Part 2*. Altbabylonische Briefe XIII. Leiden: Brill.

Veenhof, Klaas R. 2005. *Letters in the Louvre*. Altbabylonische Briefe XIV. Leiden: Brill.

Zomer, Elise. 2016. "Game of Thrones: koningen in strijd in de Laat Oud-Babylonische periode." *Phoenix* 62: 52–63.

5

Kassite Ascendancy

After their raid on Babylon the Hittites withdrew without laying territorial claims to the region. What happened then is unclear. The prologue of a *kudurru* probably dating to the reign of Marduk-shapik-zeri (1077–1065) describes in retrospect the turmoil of that period:

> When the fighting of the Amorites, the insurrection of the Haneans and the army of the Kassites upset the boundaries of Sumer and Akkad during the reign of Samsu-ditana and the ground plans could not be recognized and the borders were not designed.[1]

The prologue does not allude to any specific event, but it suggests that the Kassites profited from the prevailing chaos, while their contribution to the fall of Samsu-ditana may in fact have been minimal. Be that as it may, after a period of uncertainty they captured Babylon and made it the seat of their power.

5.1 The Kassites as Linguistic and Cultural Group

The Kassites referred to themselves as *Galzu*, a term borrowed in Akkadian as *Kasshu*. Their language is known exclusively from personal names and Kassite loanwords in Akkadian texts. Not a single sentence in the Kassite language has survived. However, the Library of Ashurbanipal preserved a bilingual vocabulary giving Akkadian translations of a few Kassite words and a list of Kassite personal names with their Akkadian correspondents. This meager body of evidence has prevented serious linguistic analysis of Kassite, which to this day has not been convincingly related to any known language. Arguments have been advanced for the presence in the Kassite language of loanwords from a group of Indo-Aryans who came into contact with the Kassites as they migrated to the Near East, the

A History of Babylon: 2200 BC–AD 75, First Edition. Paul-Alain Beaulieu.
© 2018 John Wiley & Sons Ltd. Published 2018 by John Wiley & Sons Ltd.

same groups who eventually allied with the Hurrians to create the kingdom of Mitanni in the later part of the sixteenth century. However, these proposed (and sometimes questionable) loanwords are very few and cannot lead to any firm conclusion as to the alleged influence of these groups on the Kassites. The original homeland of the Kassites seems to have been located in the Zagros Mountains and the upper Diyala. Later Greek sources mention a people in that area named the *Kossaioi*, a term probably derived from the Akkadian demonym *Kasshu*. A number of additional clues support the identification of the upper Diyala as homeland of the Kassites. The inscription of the Kassite king Agum-kakrime attributes to him the titles of "king of Padan and Alman" and "king of Gutium," the latter definitely located in the Zagros, while the former might be identical with the toponyms Namar (or Namri) and Halman (or Habban), two localities in the upper Diyala (see Map 5.1). Namar was inhabited by the Kassite tribe of Bit-Karziabku according to a *kudurru* from the reign of Nebuchadnezzar I (1121–1100). This may explain why the Kassites are first attested in texts from northern Babylonia, especially Sippar. Northern Babylonia lay close to the Diyala, which provided the most natural road of infiltration from the Zagros. This pattern continued during the sixteenth century, with Kassite names appearing in substantial numbers in the texts from Tell Muhammad near Baghdad, while they are largely absent from the southern texts dated to the First Dynasty of the Sealand.

Very few sources from the Middle Babylonian period shed light on the culture of the Kassites. It is also not always clear whether innovations and cultural changes which took place at that time should be attributed to Kassite influence or to other factors. Most Kassite loanwords in Akkadian relate to horse breeding and chariotry. A few texts from Nippur, some of them dated to the fourteenth century, record lists of horses with their name, color, and pedigree. Although the lists are in Akkadian the vocabulary is largely Kassite, including the names of the horses and the terms describing their color. The association of Kassites with horses and chariots began during the Old Babylonian period and suggests that they played the leading role in the spread of this technology to Babylonia. The international correspondence from Amarna and Hattusha reveals that by the fourteenth century Babylonia had become highly prized for its horses. In a letter preserved in the Hittite state archives at Hattusha, the Hittite king Hattushili III wrote to the Kassite king Kadashman-Enlil II (1263–1255) that "in the land of my brother horses are more plentiful than straw." In the realm of religion there is no evidence for the imposition of Kassite gods or rituals in Babylonian temples. One notable exception is the pair formed by the god Shuqamuna and the goddess Shumaliya, two deities possibly originating from the Kassite homeland in the Zagros. This origin seems likely in consideration of the portrayal of Shumaliya as a mountain goddess, described in one source as "the lady of the shining mountains, who dwells on the summits (and) treads on snowy paths." Shuqamuna and Shumaliya played the role of dynastic gods. One text depicts their shrine at Babylon as the locus for the investiture of the Kassite king, and the inscription of Agum-kakrime gives him the epithet of "pure seed of Shuqamuna," implying divine descent.

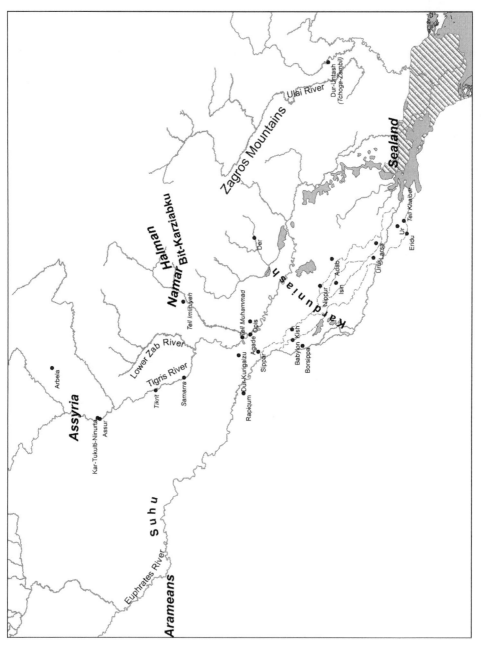

Map 5.1 Kassite Babylonia. Map Design: Stephen Batiuk, University of Toronto.

Some Kassite groups who settled in Babylonia kept their tribal structure intact for a long time. Sources, especially *kudurru*s from the later Kassite period and succeeding dynasties, often refer to Kassite tribal units with the compound *bit PN* "house, household of PN," PN designating the name of the real or supposed ancestor of the clan or tribe. Thus we hear of the Bit-Karziabku "House of Karziabku" and the Bit-Tunamissah "House of Tunamissah." Members of these tribes often designated themselves as "sons" of the tribe's ancestor, for example as Mar Tunamissah "son, descendant of Tunamissah." The system of "houses" probably took shape quite early since Old Babylonian sources mention Kassite "houses" a few times and associate some of them with patronymic ancestors (e.g. Houses of Agum, Houses of Nanakti). Kassites living in cities, on the other hand, appear to have assimilated to the larger population rapidly. This is suggested by the fact that we have numerous examples of individuals with Kassite names giving Akkadian names to their sons, while the opposite is much rarer. Eventually the Kassite ruling house also displayed signs of assimilation by abandoning Kassite personal names in favor of Akkadian ones, as can be seen from Table 5.1, where Kassite names are in Roman, and Akkadian names in Italics. Of the last eight kings of the Dynasty, those who reigned after the Assyrian invasion led by Tukulti-Ninurta I, no fewer than six bear Akkadian names.

5.2   The Early Kassite Period (1595–ca. 1400)

Table 5.1 is based mostly on King List A, which contains a number of gaps for early Kassite rulers. The Synchronistic King List provides additional data, although its state of preservation is also very poor for that period. Archival sources dated to Kassite rulers appear in Babylonia only around 1375. The earliest official Kassite monuments we have are the inscriptions of Kara-indash, which date to the last quarter of the fifteenth century. The scarcity of sources is partly compensated by two collections of archival documents datable to the sixteenth century. One was discovered at Tell Muhammad near Baghdad. The other one, which has come to light more recently as the result of illicit digs in southern Iraq, includes nearly five hundred texts dated to the First Sealand Dynasty.

5.2.1   The Texts from Tell Muhammad

Tell Muhammad (ancient name unknown) is a mound located in the suburbs of Baghdad near the Diyala. Excavations uncovered seven levels at Tell Muhammad. Level I, the most recent, can be ascribed to the early Kassite period; the material culture of levels III and II corresponds to the late Old Babylonian and early Kassite periods. Cuneiform texts uncovered in Levels III and II record mostly loans of silver and grain and contain a number of dating formulas with year names. Year names of Level III commemorate events connected possibly with a local dynasty and mention a king called Hurbazum: for example, "Year in

Table 5.1   The Kassite Dynasty

1. Gandash		
2. Agum I		
3. Kashtiliashu I		
4. (....)		
5. Abirattash		
6. Kashtiliashu II		
7. Urzigurumash		
7a. (Agum II, kakrime)		
8. (Hurbazum ?)		Tell Muhammad Level III (?)
9. (Shipta-Ulzi ?)		Tell Muhammad Level II (?)
10. (...)		
11. Burna-Buriash I		
12. (Ulam-Buriash ?)	ca. 1475	Conquest of Sealand (Ea-gamil)
13. (Kashtiliashu III ?)		
14. (Agum III ?)		Destruction of Dur-Enlil in Sealand
15. Kara-indash	ca. 1415	Earliest genuine Kassite inscriptions
16. Kadashman-Harbe I	ca. 1400	
17. Kurigalzu I		Foundation of Dur-Kurigalzu; earliest *kudurru*s
18. Kadashman-Enlil I	1374?–1360	Amarna correspondence
19. Burna-Buriash II	1359–1333	Amarna correspondence; Nippur archives begin
20. Kara-hardash	1333	
21. Nazi-Bugash	1333	Intervention of Ashur-uballit I of Assyria
22. Kurigalzu II	1332–1308	
23. Nazi-Maruttash	1307–1282	
24. Kadashman-Turgu	1281–1264	
25. Kadashman-Enlil II	1263–1255	
26. *Kudur-Enlil*	1254–1246	
27. Shagarakti-Shuriash	1245–1233	
28. Kashtiliashu IV	1232–1225	Intervention of Tukulti-Ninurta I of Assyria End of Nippur archives
29. *Enlil-nadin-shumi*	1224	Assyrian occupation begins
30. Kadashman-Harbe II	1223	
31. *Adad-shuma-iddina*	1222–1217	
32. *Adad-shuma-usur*	1216–1187	Assyrian occupation ends
33. Meli-Shipak	1186–1172	
34. *Marduk-apla-iddina* I	1171–1159	
35. *Zababa-shuma-iddina*	1158	
36. *Enlil-nadin-ahi*	1157–1155	

which (king) Hurbazum refurbished the gods of Eshnunna," or "Year in which Silli-Adad, son of Shumma-ilu, died." More recent texts from Level II, however, display three different types of dating formulas and mention a king named Shipta-ulzi. The first type commemorates events similar to those from Level III: for example, "Year in which Zalmi was conquered," or "Year in which Ninnahn-eru, son of Burna-Sah, died." The second type consists of double dates, one commemorating an event as in Level III, while the other one follows the pattern "Year X after the resettlement of Babylon:" e.g. "Year 36 after the resettlement of

Babylon; year in which the son of Hurbah was killed in Tupliyash;" "Year 37 after the resettlement of Babylon; year when king Shipta-ulzi … (rest lost);" or "Year 38 after the resettlement of Babylon; year in which the moon became invisible, an eclipse occurred." Finally the third type contains only the formula "Year X after the resettlement of Babylon." Most of the personal names appearing in the texts are Semitic, but a number are Kassite, including those of some personages who appear in the year names (for example, Burna-Sah). The dating formulas "after the resettlement of Babylon" extend from year 36 to year 41 and probably calculate the years elapsing since the installation of the Kassite dynasty in Babylon. Most scholars have interpreted the texts as evidence that after the fall of Babylon I a dynasty of Kassite origin controlled Tell Muhammad and the lower Diyala for some time, but eventually fell under the control of the Kassite line established in Babylon, at which point they started using double dating formulas commemorating their own events jointly with the early dating system of the Kassite dynasty (the era "after the resettlement of Babylon"), until eventually only the latter remained in use (it is attested in the published texts only for year 41), perhaps when Tell Muhammad fell under the full control of Kassite Babylon.

5.2.2 The Early Kassite Rulers (Sixteenth Century)

Reconstructing the sequence and names of early Kassite rulers presents considerable difficulties. King List A and the Synchronistic King List contain several gaps and often disagree. Another source is the inscription of Agum-kakrime, known from a unique manuscript in the Library of Ashurbanipal. The authenticity of this text has generally been doubted, and Agum-kakrime himself does not occur in any other document. However, the inscription includes a genealogy of early Kassite kings which by and large agrees with king lists and should therefore be taken into consideration. The data from all three sources can be tabulated as follows.

The earliest known Kassite ruler, Gandash, occurs only in the two king lists and in a building inscription known from a Neo-Babylonian copy in which his name is spelled Gaddash. The inscription is poorly preserved and difficult to understand and could be a school product of the late periods. Gandash appears in it with the titles "king of the four quarters, king of Sumer and Akkad, king of Babylon," but these must be apocryphal attributions. The second known ruler is Agum I, called "Agum the first" (*Agum mahru*) in King List A, where he is said to be the son of Gandash. The inscription of Agum-kakrime hails him as "Agum the Great" (*Agum rabi*). Some scholars have proposed to identify Agum I with the head of the Kassite tribe known as the "Houses of Agum" mentioned in a letter dating probably to the reign of Samsu-iluna. The letter appears to attribute to this Agum the title of *bukashum* "prince," no doubt a loanword from the Kassite language. The identification seems attractive but cannot be proven. The next Kassite rulers in the lists are even more elusive. Kashtiliashu I and Abirattash appear only in the three sources listed in Table 5.2 and the second Kashtiliashu

Table 5.2 The Early Kassite Rulers

King List A	Synchronistic King List	Inscription of Agum-kakrime
Gandash	Gandash	
Agum I	Agum I	Agum I
Kashtiliashu I	Kashtiliashu I	Kashtiliashu I
[o o o]		
Abirattash	Abirattash	Abirattash
	Kashtiliashu II	
Urzigurumash	Urzigurumash	Urshigurumash
		Agum-kakrime (Agum II)
[o o o]	Hurbazum (?)	
[o o o]	Shipta-ulzi (?)	
[o o o]	[o o o]	
[o o o]	Burna-Buriash I	

is known only from the Synchronistic King List. Urzigurumash (the name can also be read Tazzigurumash) is also unknown outside these three genealogies. Agum-kakrime names him as his father (under the form Urshi- or Tasshiguru-mash) and claims direct descent from Agum the Great through Kashtiliashu I and Abirattash. The inscription credits Agum-kakrime with the return of the statues of Marduk and his consort Zarpanitum from the land of Hana to the Esagil temple in Babylon, from where they had been removed when the city fell in 1595. No outside evidence corroborates this assertion. Also, nothing assures us that the earliest Kassite rulers named in the king lists actually reigned in Babylon, although it was assumed later that they did. It was common practice to include ancestors of a royal family in a king list, the Assyrian King List and the Larsa King List being cases in point.

After Urzigurumash King List A breaks off to resume with Kadashman-Enlil II in the thirteenth century. The Synchronistic King List, however, preserves traces of two names after him. Original editions of the list restored the two names as Harba-shipak (or -shihu) and Tiptakzi, and the third one as Agum (II). Subsequent collations have cast serious doubts on these readings: the first name begins with HAR (with phonetic values *har*, *hur*, and *mur*) and BA followed by two illegible signs; the second name begins with an uncertain sign followed by IB (with phonetic values *ib* or *ip*) and two of three more illegible signs, ending probably with ZI; the third name cannot be read at all. Recently it has been proposed that the two names should in fact be restored as Hurbazum (*hur-ba-zum*) and Shipta-ulzi (*shi-ip-ta-ul-zi*), the two kings attested in the year names from Tell Muhammad. In this case these year names would not belong to a local dynasty, but to the Kassite royal house in Babylon. However, there is much disagreement on the reading of these names and more evidence will be needed to confirm this proposal. The reading of the third name after Urzigurumash as Agum (II) has been abandoned. After Burna-Buriash I the Synchronistic King List breaks off to resume only at the end of the Kassite dynasty.

5.2.3 The First Dynasty of the Sealand (ca. 1725–1475)

During the formative period of the Kassite kingdom in northern Babylonia, the First Dynasty of the Sealand continued to rule Sumer, possibly as far north as Nippur. King Lists A and B subsume this royal line under the label "Dynasty of Urukug." All sources agree on the sequence of rulers except the Synchronistic King List which adds one king with his name written DISH + U-EN, but the reading of the signs remains uncertain. King List A gives abbreviated forms of the names, perhaps because of a broken original (e.g. Itti-ili for Itti-ili-nibi, Gul-ki for Gulkishar, Ea-ga for Ea-gamil). Family ties between the members of the dynasty are unknown with two exceptions: King List A notes that Shusshi was the brother of his predecessor, and King List B that Peshgaldaramesh was the son of Gulkishar, and Ayadaragalamma the son of Peshgaldaramesh. Only King List A provides the length of each reign, with some gaps at the beginning. The evidence from chronographic texts allows the following reconstruction of the dynasty, with Sumerian names in Roman and Akkadian names in italics (see Table 5.3).

The history and identity of the First Dynasty of the Sealand was shrouded in obscurity until the publication in 2009 of an archive of 463 texts dated to the reigns of Peshgaldaramesh and Ayadaragalamma. Unfortunately, the texts came from illicit digs. According to King Lists A and B this dynasty reigned from the city of Urukug, a site which has not yet been identified. The texts do not yield sufficient internal evidence to determine their place of origin; they could stem from a provincial administrative center rather than the capital. However they contain a number of clues, especially divine names, which definitely point to southern Babylonia as the original locus of the archive. Many of the texts bear dating formulas, some with year names and others with year numbers. The few texts dated to Peshgaldaramesh adhere to the latter pattern and come from his twenty-seventh and twenty-ninth years (e.g. "The twenty-seventh year after Peshgaldaramesh became king"). Fifteen date formulas of his

Table 5.3 The First Dynasty of the Sealand

1. *Ilumma-ilu*	x years
2. *Itti-ili-nibi*	x years
3. *Damiq-ilishu*	26? years
4. Ishkibal	15 years
5. Shusshi (brother of Ishkibal)	24 years
6. Gulkishar	55 years
6a. DISH + U-EN (one source only)	
7. Peshgaldaramesh (son of preceding)	50 years
8. Ayadaragalamma (son of preceding)	28 years
9. Ekurduanna	26 years
10. Melamkurkurra	7 years
11. *Ea-gamil*	9 years

successor Ayadaragalamma occur on the tablets, some recording only year numbers and others commemorating historical events or pious deeds (e.g. "Year when, Aydaragalamma being king, his land rebelled against him," or "Year when king Ayadaragalamma installed wooden statues overlaid with red gold for the gods Enlil and Enki"). It is possible that the dating formulas which record only year numbers were used concurrently with year names. Thus the archive covers a rather limited period in time, fifteen years at most. King List A assigns a reign of fifty years to Peshgaldaramesh, but this would imply an unexplainable gap of twenty-one years in the archive between his twenty-ninth year and the accession year of Ayadaragalamma. Therefore it seems probable that King List A assigned to his reign a round number of fifty years, possibly in imitation of his father Gulkishar, and that he reigned in fact only twenty-nine years.

The Sealand Dynasty texts contain no information on the historical events of that period outside the restricted data from year names. They consist mostly of administrative records, including deliveries of animals for sacrifices to the gods and ledgers dealing with agricultural taxation. The texts mention a palace, but we cannot determine whether they refer to the main royal residence or a provincial palace. All the texts are written in Akkadian and they continue the Old Babylonian script and dialect but with some signs adhering to Middle Babylonian conventions. Most of the personal names belong to the Akkadian onomastics, with a small number of Elamite and Kassite names. Some high ranking officials appear with Sumerian names (e.g. Anam-dingirra, Urash-hegal, Lu-enshegbara), perhaps in emulation of the ruling dynasty whose rulers often adopted pedantic Sumerian names unknown in the earlier Sumerian onomastics (e.g. Gulkishar "conqueror of the world," from Sumerian *gul* "to destroy, smash" and *ki-shar* "totality"). However, celebration of the Sumerian heritage seems to have been largely symbolic. A collection of scholarly texts has come to light from the same site and period, three of which contain colophons with dates of Peshgaldaramesh and Ayadaragalamma. Most of them are divinatory; a small number are lexical and literary, including an episode from the cycle of Gilgamesh. With the exception of a few bilingual, mostly lexical texts and one liturgical text in Sumerian, all other texts are written in Akkadian and reflect late Old Babylonian scholarly traditions. The placement of the Sealand Dynasty texts within the chronology of that period is uncertain given the paucity of secure chronological data. However, the recent discovery of a synchronism between Gulkishar and Samsu-ditana allows us to posit a date for them about two generations after the fall of Babylon I (Table 5.4). Thus it seems likely that the Sealand texts are roughly contemporaneous with those from Tell Muhammad. Another, smaller archive of Sealand texts was discovered recently at Tell Khaiber near Ur during regular excavations. A few texts are dated to Ayadaragalamma, indicating that the whole group is probably contemporary with the archive published in 2009. Tell Khaiber was undisturbed before the regular digs. Therefore the archive from the illicit dig must come from another site.

Table 5.4 Synchronisms between Sealand I, Babylon I, and Kassites

Sealand I	Babylon I	Kassites
Ilumma-ilu	Samsu-iluna (1749–1712)	First Kassite invasion (1742)
	Abi-eshuh (1711–1684)	Second Kassite invasion (ca. 1709)
Itti-ili-nibi		
Damiq-ilishu	Ammi-ditana (1683–1647)	
Ishkibal		
Shusshi		
Gulkishar	Samsu-ditana (1625–1595)	
DISH+U-EN		Kassites capture Babylon (ca. 1570?)
Peshgaldaramesh		
Ayadaragalamma		
Ekurduanna		
Melamkurkurra		
Ea-gamil		Kassites conquer Sealand (ca. 1475)

5.2.4   The Reunification of Babylonia

During the first half of the fifteenth century the Sealand Dynasty came to an end and the Kassites unified Babylonia under their rule. Our main source at this point is Chronicle 40, which reports on these events in two laconic entries. The first entry mentions the demise of Ea-gamil, the last ruler of the Sealand Dynasty: "Ea-gamil, king of the Sealand, fled to Elam; later, Ulam-Buriash, brother of Kashtiliashu (III), the Kassite, mustered his army, conquered the Sealand (and) governed the country." Most scholars identify this Ulam-Buriash as Ula-Burariash, son of Burna-Burariash, who appears with the title "king of the Sealand" in an inscription on a stone knob found at Babylon. His father Burna-Burariash should therefore be identified as the Kassite king Burna-Buriash I, known only from the Synchronistic King List. Kashtiliashu (III), the brother of Ulam-Buriash, appears again in the other entry of Chronicle 40 dealing with the Sealand: "Agum (III), son of Kashtiliashu (III), mustered his army and marched on the Sealand; he conquered Dur-Enlil (and) desecrated E-galga-sheshna, Enlil's temple there." Although the Chronicle does not clearly states this, Ulam-Buriash, Agum (III) and Kashtiliashu (III) may all have reigned in succession as Kassite kings in Babylon and could be inserted in the chronographic tradition in the gap between Burna-Buriash I and Kara-indash. According to Chronicle 40 the reunification of Babylonia came gradually. First Ea-gamil fled to Elam perhaps because of internal strife (a year name of Ayadaragalamma already hints at rebellion), after which Ulam-Buriash, having presumably succeeded Burna-Buriash I on the throne of Babylon, marched south and seized the kingship of the Sealand. Although the Sealand Dynasty then came to an end, it seems that the region retained a spirit of independence for a while since Agum (III) campaigned there and destroyed Dur-Enlil, which some scholars have proposed to identify with the fortress Dur-Abi-eshuh near Nippur.

More evidence on the transition between Sealand I and the Kassites has come to light at the site of Qal'at al-Bahrain in the Persian Gulf, where a French archaeological expedition discovered about one hundred Middle Babylonian administrative texts, some with date formulas. They share many features with the texts from the Sealand Dynasty. One text is dated to the fourth year of a king named Ea-gamil, who is evidently identical with the last ruler of Sealand I; others are dated to Agum and Kadashman-Sah, two Kassite names. This Agum should probably be identified as Agum (III) who allegedly put an end to the Sealand Dynasty, but no evidence for the rule of Kadashman-Sah has come to light outside these texts. He may have been a transitional Kassite ruler with local power only. Be that as it may, the demise of the Sealand Dynasty should be viewed as a momentous event in the history of Babylon. Babylonian unity became then irreversible, and although Babylonia was to experience periods of political weakness, regional fragmentation, and foreign occupation, never again would the country become split between rival dynasties.

5.3   Kassite Babylonia: The Documentary Evidence

After the demise of the Sealand Dynasty the Kassites ruled Babylonia almost uninterruptedly for another three hundred years, establishing its longest lived and most stable regime. However, only the last two centuries of the Kassite dynasty (1360–1155) are documented by reasonable amounts of textual evidence. One unfortunate innovation of the Middle Babylonian period for modern scholarship is the abandonment of year names in the fourteenth century in favor of regnal years (e.g. "Tenth year of king Shagarakti-Shuriash" or "Fifth year of Nazi-Maruttash"). Although the new system makes it easier to put documents in chronological sequence, which may well have been the main reason for its introduction, it deprives us of an invaluable source for political history. Three chronicles compensate partly but poorly for the loss of year names: the Synchronistic History, an Assyrian source which surveys the relations between Assyria and Babylonia from the fifteenth century onward, especially regarding the fixing of their common boundary; Chronicle 45, which reflects similar interests and represents a Babylonian version of, or a response to the Synchronistic History; and Chronicle 46, which covers the last Kassite kings and the Second Dynasty of Isin. Some letters to and from Kassite kings have been retrieved in the international correspondence of the Egyptian capital at Tell el-Amarna and in the Hittite state archives at Hattusha. Kassite royal inscriptions are few and generally succinct and they rarely allude to contemporary events.

Middle Babylonian archives cannot compare to those of the Old Babylonian period in terms of number, variety, richness, and geographic spread. Few sites have yielded texts in any significant quantity. The largest one is Nippur where more than 12,000 texts dating to Kassite rulers have been recovered, making up the bulk (90 percent) of the Middle Babylonian archival record. The texts range from 1360 (first year of Burna-Buriash II) to 1225 (last year of Kashtiliashu IV), with some tablets dating from the accession and first year of Kadashman-Harbe II (1224–1223). The largest group, possibly around 10,000 tablets, apparently stems from a building of the Kassite period which may have housed the administration of the *shandabakku*, the governor of Nippur. Several distinct sub-archives or files can be identified within this vast group. The texts record mostly the income and redistribution of agricultural produce, but we also have legal documents and letters. Only about one fifth of the texts from Kassite Nippur have been published. The main cut-off date for the archive is the end of the reign of Kashtiliashu IV, and this must be due to the disruptions caused by the Assyrian invasion under Tukulti-Ninurta I. Also, more than 450 Middle Babylonian texts from uncontrolled excavations have recently published. Their time range is roughly the same as that of the Nippur archives. They probably originate from a site named Dur-Enlile, which appears to have been dependent on Nippur for certain aspects of its economy and administration and was probably located near that city. Other Middle Babylonian archives date to the thirteenth or early twelfth century. The Kassite royal residence at Dur-Kurigalzu has yielded about 220 texts which are still unpublished in their majority and date between 1254 and 1225, with another group dating between 1171 and 1159. An important archive of seventy-five tablets from Ur, all of them published, record activities of the brewers of the god Sin; it consists mostly of legal texts and some court records dating between 1267 and 1166. We also have a small agricultural archive of forty-five tablets, all published, from Tell Imlihiye in the Diyala and dating from the thirteenth century (1263–1255 and 1227). Excavations at Babylon have recovered archives in private houses in the Merkes dating between the fourteenth and twelfth centuries, but these texts, numbering 567, still remain almost entirely unpublished. This somewhat meager harvest may be supplemented by a new type of source which appears during the Kassite period, the *kudurrus*.

5.3.1 A New Source: The Kudurrus

The Akkadian term *kudurru* means "heir" as well as "boundary" and also refers to a type of stele, usually made of stone (rarely of clay), roughly ovoid in shape and with a height of up to three feet. Some later examples occur on stone tablets imitating originals in clay. The word *kudurru* is not the only designation for these objects; other terms occur such as *naru* or *asumittu* "stele" and even *abnu* "stone," but these are generic terms and *kudurru* seems to have been more specific to that particular genre. Typically a *kudurru* is inscribed on a substantial portion of its surface and many have an iconographic section. The inscription records a legal transaction, usually a royal grant of land, less often a tax exemption, and ends with curses against potential violators. In the course of time other types of transactions were recorded on *kudurrus*, such as royal adjudications and private sales of real estate. There is wide variation in the structure and appearance of the *kudurrus*, hardly a surprising fact since they range from the fourteenth to the seventh century. Their greatest concentration, however, occurs during the late Kassite and Isin II periods; fewer examples date to the first millennium. Thirty-two *kudurru*s from the Kassite period are known. In the past, historians referred to *kudurru*s as "boundary stones" on the assumption that they were planted in the soil to mark the limits of properties. While the appearance of these monuments may have been inspired by the use of boundary markers in the shape of pegs and stones, it is clear that this was not their primary function. There is concrete evidence that the transactions recorded on *kudurru*s also existed on clay tablets, making the stone monument legally superfluous. Most *kudurru*s were in fact probably deposited in temples where they served as iconic guarantees for the transactions. The *kudurru*s constitute an important source for studying the development of religious iconography since gods appear on them mostly in the form of symbols or emblematic animals, and some *kudurru*s even bear captions identifying the symbols with divine names. The curse sections sometimes specify that the gods depicted on the stele stand as protectors of the transaction; this is the case in a *kudurru* from the time of the Kassite king Meli-shipak (1186–1172): "May all the gods whose names are invoked, whose altars are depicted and whose designs are drawn on this stele, uproot his (i.e. the violator's) name, seed and offspring." Some *kudurru*s also have depictions of the king and the beneficiary of the grant.

Why do *kudurru*s suddenly appear under the Kassites? Real estate transactions were sometimes recorded on stone monuments in the third millennium and scholars often apply the term *kudurru* to these artifacts as well (Figure 2.2), but they bear only a distant relation to the later *kudurru*s, which truly constitute an innovation of the Kassite period. Some have cogently argued that the demise of the state apparatus at the end of Babylon I and the ensuing period of anarchy favored the creation of the *kudurru*s because of their durability, and this might also explain the practice of depositing them in temples, institutions which had long proven more perennial than monarchies. However, *kudurru*s do not systematically record all types of land transactions but heavily concentrate on royal grants and also on transactions where the king appears as adjudicator or guarantor. Therefore the practice of engraving deeds on stone monuments may also have been motivated by the prestige of the benefactor and the desire to memorialize and even sacralize his deeds. The exceptional, almost magical nature of *kudurru*s is further suggested by the fact that some were given names which are recorded on the objects themselves, for instance: "The name of this stone stele is: Do not transgress the borders, do not disturb the boundary, hate evil and love truth!" (*kudurru* from the time of Enlil-nadin-apli, 1099–1096). Their geographic range varies over time. During the Kassite and Isin II periods most *kudurru*s come from northern and eastern Babylonia, while first millennium examples stem in their majority from the southern and western parts of the country. This may reflect a power shift from areas where most Kassites had settled to those later inhabited by Chaldeans. The Kassite monarchy apparently favored the development of the regions along the Tigris and allotted tracts of land there which had no previous recorded owner. The size of the estates granted varies and donations of as many as 1,000 hectares are attested, but most properties range from eighty to 250 hectares. The recipients were Kassites or Babylonians, including members of the royal family, officials, courtiers, generals, priests, and temple administrators. Some historians have interpreted these donations as a sign of an emerging feudal system. The *kudurru*s do not really provide evidence that a feudal structure pervaded all elements of Babylonian society under the Kassites such as the one that prevailed in France and England in the Middle Ages. Feudalism is an elastic concept, however, and certain types of feudal relations are undeniably present in the *kudurru*s since the monarchy expected, in return for these grants, continued loyalty and services. However, similar reciprocal relations can flourish in any complex agrarian society where land constitutes the main source of wealth. The appearance of the first *kudurru*s in the fourteenth century indicates that the Kassite state had stabilized and its monarchs, now fully in control of the country and its institutions, wielded sufficient power to grant large properties to individuals and guarantee these donations in perpetuity.

5.4   Karduniash: A New Babylonia

The earliest Kassite king for whom we have evidence contemporary with his rule is Kara-indash, who reigned in the last quarter of the fifteenth century. A number of inscribed bricks found at Uruk record his restoration of a shrine in the Eanna temple for the goddess Inanna:

> To Inanna, the lady of the Eanna temple, his lady, Kara-indash, the mighty king, king of Babylon, king of Sumer and Akkad, king of the Kassites, king of Karduniash, built a chapel in the Eanna temple.[2]

Excavations of the shrine have uncovered a frieze of tall, thin figures lodged in niches recalling similar figures on Kassite cylinder seals (Figure 5.1). Like the majority of early Kassite royal inscriptions, Kara-indash's bricks are in Sumerian, a language favored by the Kassite dynasty as a linkage to the most ancient traditions of Babylonia, and perhaps also as legitimization of their recent conquest of the Sealand. The titulature of Kara-indash reveals the dual nature of his rulership since he claims to be leader of the Kassites alongside traditional titles such as "king of Babylon" and "king of Sumer and Akkad." In this respect the Kassites behaved no differently than the Amorite rulers of the First Dynasty. Kara-indash also introduced the title "king of Karduniash," a term which seems to have originally referred to the territories ruled by the Kassite monarch in northern Babylonia, but eventually became a synonym for all Babylonia.

In Assyrian sources Karduniash is used until the seventh century as a territorial concept equivalent to "Assyria" (*mat Ashur*). The Synchronistic History records one of the earliest examples of this usage, reporting that Kara-indash concluded a treaty and border agreement with the Assyrian king Ashur-bel-nisheshu: "King

Figure 5.1   Uruk frieze of Kara-indash. The restoration work of king Kara-indash (end of fifteenth century) at Uruk is the earliest architectural activity known for the Kassite dynasty. This frieze of baked bricks from the temple of the goddess Inanna (Ishtar) depicts gods with flowing vases in the "elongated" style typical of that period. The frieze is reconstructed in the Vorderasiatisches Museum, Berlin. *Source*: Erich Lessing / Art Resource, NY.

Kara-indash of Kard[uniash] and king Ashur-bel-nisheshu of Assyria concluded a mutual accord and took a reciprocal oath, specifically on the matter of this boundary." The Amarna correspondence offers evidence that Kassite Babylonia had reached international stature under Kara-indash; in a letter to Amenophis IV (Akhenaten) the Kassite king Burna-Buriash II (1359–1333) later reminded the pharaoh that Egypt and Babylonia had enjoyed very good relation since his reign. Chronicle 45 claims that the successor of Kara-indash, Kadashman-Harbe I, waged war against the semi-nomadic Sutians. The Chronicle is partly garbled, however, since it makes him the son of the later Kassite king Kara-hardash, probably confused in the manuscript tradition with Kara-indash, who may in fact have been the father of Kadashman-Harbe I. Yet, a *kudurru* probably from the reign of Marduk-shapik-zeri also records Kadahsman-Harbe's efforts to expel the Sutians from Babylonia. An isolated document from Nippur predating the beginning of Kassite archival documentation there by two or three generations contains a year name of Kadashman-Harbe I which commemorates the digging of a canal in the city of Diniktum in the Diyala. This document indicates that the transition to year numbers had not yet fully taken place.

5.4.1   Kurigalzu I

The name Kurigalzu, which means "shepherd of the Kassites" according to the Kassite-Akkadian list of personal names, was borne by two kings: Kurigalzu I son of Kadashman-Harbe I, who probably succeeded his father in the early part of the fourteenth century, and Kurigalzu II son of Burna-Buriash II, who reigned from 1332 to 1308. The majority of extant royal inscriptions from the Kassite period belong to the two Kurigalzus, but few contain genealogical indications that allow us to ascribe them for certain to Kurigalzu I or II. A number of votive inscriptions on small objects such as beads and cylinders belong to Kurigalzu son of Burna-Buriash and therefore can be ascribed with certainty to Kurigalzu II. Building inscriptions in the name of Kurigalzu (I or II) stem from Babylon, Kish, Sippar, Nippur, Isin, Adab, Uruk, Ur, possibly Eridu, Der in the Trans-Tigridian region, and even the ancient Sargonic capital of Agade, not to mention Dur-Kurigalzu, the new Kassite royal residence created in the fourteenth century, but none of them contains genealogical information. Although in the past many of these inscriptions were assigned to Kurigalzu II, a consensus has formed that Kurigalzu I should in fact be viewed as the main engineer of the renewal of Babylonian cities and temples after the decline which followed the end of Babylon I. According to a letter found at Tell el-Amarna and dating to the reign of Burna-Buriash II, Kurigalzu I had received gold from a predecessor of the pharaoh Amenophis IV (Akhenaten) and refused to join the Canaanites in an alliance against Egypt. One problematic source is the "Donation of Kurigalzu" preserved on two clay prisms from the first millennium. The text records a large endowment of land to the goddess Ishtar of Uruk by Kurigalzu, son of Kadash-man-Harbe. The identity of the donor as the first Kurigalzu seems thus assured; the authenticity of the text, on the other hand, still remains in doubt. As is the case with late copies of texts recording grants of privileges to temples and their personnel, there is always the possibility that the document is a forgery designed to increase royal endowments of temples. One achievement of Kurigalzu I cannot be doubted, however, and this is the creation of a new Kassite royal residence at Dur-Kurigalzu.

5.4.2   Dur-Kurigalzu: A Kassite Royal Residence

Dur-Kurigalzu lies thirty kilometers west of Baghdad and 100 kilometers north of Babylon. Joint excavations during World War II by the Iraqi Directorate of Antiquities and the British School of Archaeology in Iraq revealed a large walled site that may have reached a size of 225 hectares. We do not know how densely Dur-Kurigalzu was occupied. Two key areas have been identified: Aqarquf, the largest mound, which housed the religious district, and Tell al-Abyad, a smaller mound with royal palaces and administrative buildings. The two districts lie about one kilometer apart. The name of the city means literally "Fort-Kurigalzu" and recalls a number of similar foundations created at the time of the First

Figure 5.2 Ziggurat of Dur-Kurigalzu. The Kassite king Kurigalzu I created a new royal residence at Dur-Kurigalzu, now Aqarquf west of Baghdad. The new capital included royal palaces and religious buildings dedicated mostly to the gods of Nippur. Only the core of the ziggurat has survived from ancient times, but the first story was restored by the Iraqi Directorate of Antiquities. *Source*: US Army photo by Spc. David Robbins: https://commons. wikimedia.org/wiki/File:The_ziggurat_at_Aqar_Quf.jpg (accessed April 10, 2017).

Dynasty (e.g. Dur-Samsu-iluna). However, Dur-Kurigalzu achieved more ambitious proportions and became the second capital of the Kassite kingdom, complete with court in residence, central administration, and religious buildings, the most imposing one being the ziggurat. Its core has partly survived to this day and the first floor terrace has been restored by the Iraqi Government (Figure 5.2). Works of art discovered during the excavations in the area of the palaces attest to the flourishing of a courtly life, notably paintings depicting officials in attendance. The founding of Dur-Kurigalzu can be attributed for certain to Kurigalzu I since the city is mentioned in an extispicy report datable to the reign of Burna-Buriash II, the father of the second Kurigalzu.

The creation of new royal cities away from historical political centers characterizes the Late Bronze Age. In Egypt the heretic pharaoh Amenophis IV Akhenaten (1353–1336) moved the capital from Thebes to his new city Akhetaten "Horizon of the Aten" (Tell el-Amarna), where he built palaces and a great temple to his god Aten. Untash-Napirisha, king of Elam, also created a new city named Dur-Untash in the late fourteenth or thirteenth century at the site of Tchoga-Zambil thirty kilometers west of the Elamite capital Susa. Dur-Untash included several religious buildings including a well preserved ziggurat dedicated to the god Inshushinak "the lord of Susa." The Assyrian king Tukulti-Ninurta I (1243–1207) also created his own residence on the Tigris, Kar-Tukulti-Ninurta ("Port-Tukulti-Ninurta"), a few kilometers north of the capital Assur. Besides a palace it also included a temple of the god Ashur. The creation of Dur-Kurigalzu in the early part of the fourteenth century appears therefore as a precursor.

The most salient aspect of Dur-Kurigalzu lies in the religious sphere. All the temples built by Kurigalzu in his new capital were dedicated to Enlil and his consort Ninlil, the chief gods of Nippur, and to their son Ninurta. The transfer of the cults of Nippur to other centers hardly ranked as a novelty. We saw that after the city fell in the orbit of the Sealand Dynasty at the end of the reign of Samsu-iluna the cult of Enlil had migrated to Babylon, and slightly later the cults of Nippur and their priesthood moved to Dur-Abi-eshuh. However, the Kassite kings paid unusual devotion to Enlil and other gods of Nippur. No fewer than five members of the dynasty bore names honoring Enlil (Kadashman-Enlil I and II, Kudur-Enlil, Enlil-nadin-shumi, and Enlil-nadin-ahi). If we take into account the evidence from the Kassite Akkadian vocabulary, which equates the Kassite gods Harbe and Maruttash with Enlil and Ninurta, we can add more names to the list (Kadashman-Harbe I and II, Nazi-Maruttash). Devotion to Enlil and his family may have served to affirm Kassite control over Nippur and southern Babylonia after they eliminated the Sealand kings. Enlil still ranked as the most important Babylonian god and Nippur enjoyed the status of religious capital, and one may posit that the Kassites, being relative newcomers, sought to legitimize their rule by appealing to these traditions. Similar reasons may also explain the preference of early Kassite kings for Sumerian in their building inscriptions. Others have highlighted the fact that the Kassites may have felt a special kinship with Enlil because he was considered a mountain god, suggestive of a connection with the Zagros. The temple of Enlil at Nippur was called Ekur, which means "House (that is a) Mountain," and we find among his epithets such names as "Great Mountain" and "Lord of the Foreign Lands." Thus, it seems obvious that the creation of the new capital served among other purposes to proclaim a specific theological program favored by the Kassite monarchs, a form of state building that is also plainly evident at Akhetaten, Dur-Untash, and Kar-Tukulti-Ninurta.

Excavations at Dur-Kurigalzu have uncovered about 220 texts in the royal palaces, of which more than fifty have been published. The larger group dates mostly to Kashtiliashu IV (1232–1225) with a few texts from the reign of Kudur-Enlil (1254–1246). The cut-off date for this group corresponds to the end of the Nippur archives and must likewise be attributed to the turmoil caused by the Assyrians when Tukulti-Ninurta I invaded Babylonia. The other group of texts is much smaller and dates to the reign of Marduk-apla-iddina I (1171–1159), only a few years before the destruction of the palace by fire during the Elamite invasion. Stray texts have been found at other locations on the site, as well as one *kudurru* from the reign of Nazi-Maruttash and fragments of a statue with an inscription of one of the two Kurigalzus. One letter details the whereabouts of two Assyrian envoys, one of whom was apparently detained in Hatti for a period of three years. Another fragment of a letter addressed to Kadashman-Enlil (I or II), king of Karduniash, by a correspondent who claims to be "his brother," that is to say, the ruler of a kingdom of equal importance such as Egypt or Hatti, suggests that Dur-Kurigalzu housed an archive of international diplomatic correspondence similar to the ones discovered at Amarna and Hattusha. The administrative texts that have been published consist mostly of receipts of gold, silver, and precious stones by jewelers and goldsmiths working on the decoration of the palaces during the reign of Kashtiliashu IV. Inscriptions on door-sockets found at Dur-Kurigalzu give the official name of one palace as Egal-kisharra "palace of the entire world," but the administrative texts mention the receipt of gold to plate doors for the "palace of the mountain sheep" as well as carnelian and lapis lazuli to make objects in the shape of stags and birds for the "palace of the stag," suggesting that the Kassite kings created residences evoking their homeland in the Zagros and its fauna. One text mentions that an Elamite fugitive was brought "before the king in Babylon," indicating that Babylon had not relinquished its status as royal residence. The relative importance of Babylon and Dur-Kurigalzu as capitals cannot easily be assessed. The title "king of Babylon" remained a relatively frequent title of Kassite monarchs and one document (the Kurigalzu Text) states that the Kassite king was crowned in Babylon. On the other hand, the administrative archives of Nippur, the third most important city in the Kassite kingdom, contain much more evidence of direct and habitual connections with Dur-Kurigalzu than with Babylon. This suggests that Dur-Kurigalzu, at least during the lifetime of the Nippur archives, functioned as main royal residence and administrative capital of the Kassites.

5.5   The Age of Amarna

More than a century ago cuneiform tablets, mostly letters, came to light at the site of Tell el-Amarna in Egypt. The letters, almost four hundred in total, belong to the state and diplomatic correspondence deposited in the archives of the short-lived capital created by the pharaoh Akhenaten during the heyday of Egypt's New Kingdom in the fourteenth century. The bulk of the correspondence comes from the Egyptian vassals of the Syro-Palestinian corridor. A smaller portion, no more than fifty items in total, forms the remnants of the international correspondence of the pharaohs, mostly letters from the kings of Babylon, Hatti, Mitanni, Assyria, and Alashia (Cyprus). Usually referred to as "the Amarna letters," this corpus represents a primary source of great importance for the study of international relations. Written mostly in Akkadian, which had attained the status of international language during the late Bronze Age, and couched in a highly formalized language, the Amarna letters provide a trove of details on the exchange of gifts and greetings between courts, dynastic marriages, and especially the existence of an internationally recognized hierarchy of states led by a restricted club of "great kings" ruling the major powers of the time. The letters

spread over a period of about thirty years, from the later part of the reign of
Amenophis III until the first year of Tutankhamen, when the Egyptian court
returned to Thebes and the archive was abandoned. The expression "Age of
Amarna" in reference to the world of the letters is a bit of a misnomer because
the international system they describe certainly existed before and after their
limited time range. Indeed, the Babylonian correspondence alludes to the fact
that exchange of letters with the Egyptian court had occurred already under
Kara-indash and Kurigalzu I. The specific features of the international system
that is reflected in the Amarna correspondence are broadly characteristic of the
Late Bronze Age. Similar letters dating to the thirteenth century have been discovered at Hattusha and, as we have seen, one fragmentary example probably
from the same period came to light at Dur-Kurigalzu.

Two Kassite kings appear as correspondents in the Amarna letters: Kadashman-
Enlil I (1374?–1360) and Burna-Buriash II (1359–1333), the two successors of
Kurigalzu I. They are always addressed as "king of Karduniash." The corpus
includes three letters from Kadashman-Enlil I to Amenophis III and two from
Amenophis III to Kadashman-Enlil I, and among the six letters sent by Burna-
Buriash II, one is addressed to Amenophis III, four to Akhenaten, and one to
Tutankhamen. The address formulas of the letters are not always well preserved
and some of the attributions remain open to discussion. The subjects revolve
mostly around the exchange and treatment of messengers and dynastic marriages. Exchanges of gifts are routinely mentioned, with the Babylonian sending
horses, chariots, and lapis lazuli, and the Egyptians mostly gold and luxury
furniture. Gifts of Egyptian gold seem to have been much appreciated although
occasional complaints are voiced about its lack of purity. The most recent letter
in the corpus, from Burna-Buriash II to Tutankhamen, contains revealing
information on the relations between Assyria and Babylon and the international
status sought by the two kingdoms:

> Say to Nibhurrereya (= Tutankhamen), the king of Egy[pt, my brother]: Thus
> speaks Burna-Buriash (II), the king of Kard[un]iash, your brother. For me all goes
> well. For you, your household, your wives, your sons, your country, your magnates,
> your horses, your chariots, may all go very well … In the time of Kurigalzu (I), my
> ancestor, all the Canaanites wrote here to him, saying: "C[om]e to the border of
> the country so we can revolt and be allied [wi]th you." My ancestor sent them this
> (reply), saying: "Forget about being allied with me. If you become enemies of the
> king of Egypt, and are allied with anyone else, will I not then come and plunder
> you? How can there be an alliance with me?" For the sake of your ancestor my
> ancestor did not listen to them. Now, as for my Assyrian vassals, I was not the one
> who sent them to you. Why on their own authority have they come to your country?
> If you love me, they will conduct no business whatsoever. Send them off empty-
> handed. I send you as your greeting gift three minas of genuine lapis lazuli and five
> teams of horses for five wooden chariots.[3]

The Amarna corpus preserves two letters from the Assyrian king Ashur-uballit I
(1363–1328); they convey in unequivocal terms his desire to be recognized as a

"great king," on a par with Egypt and Babylon. In response Burna-Buriash enjoins the pharaoh to dismiss the Assyrians, pointing out as a paragon of upright behavior his ancestor Kurigalzu I, who had spurned an invitation by the Canaanites to join them in an alliance against Egypt, thus denouncing the Assyrian bid as nothing less than open rebellion. Events would soon prove the concerns of Burna-Buriash well founded.

5.6   The Rise of Assyria

After the fall of Babylon I and the Hittite retreat to central Anatolia, a new power emerged in the north: Mitanni. The Hurrians formed the dominant group in Mitanni, although some linguistic clues indicate that they had mingled with Indo-Aryans who probably came through the Iranian plateau. At its height around 1500 under king Barattarna, Mitanni encompassed most of northern Mesopotamia and Syria as well as a large portion of southeastern Anatolia in a network of directly administered and vassal territories. The core of Mitanni revolved around its capital Wasshukanni, a site which has not yet been securely identified but almost certainly lay in the Habur triangle. For a long period the kings of Assur ruled only as vassals of the kings of Mitanni, and in the middle of the fifteenth century the Mitannian king Saushtattar II launched a punitive campaign against Assur, sacking and looting the city. As Mitannian power began to wane at the end of the fifteenth century, however, Assur reasserted its independence, and by the time of Ashur-uballit I a renewed and confident Assyrian state had emerged. No longer a city state drawing its wealth mostly from commercial ventures, Assur had already become under his reign a territorial kingdom named *mat Ashur* "the land of (the god) Ashur," a term we translate as "Assyria." The new status gained by the Assyrian state manifested itself in the first Assyrian intervention in Babylonian affairs. Our sources, the Synchronistic History and Chronicle 45, contradict each other on a few points and even contain some internal inconsistencies.

Synchronistic History:

> In the time of Ashur-uballit (I), king of Assyria, Kassite troops rebelled against Kara-hardash, king of Karduniash, son of Muballitat-Sherua, the daughter of Ashur-uballit (I), and killed him. They appointed Nazi-Bugash, a Kassite, son of nobody, as king over them. Ashur-uballit (I) marched to Karduniash to avenge Kara-indash (error for Kara-hardash), his grandson. He killed Nazi-Bugash, king of Karduniash, appointed Kurigalzu the Younger (= Kurigalzu II), son of Burna-Buriash (II), as king and put him on the throne of his father.

Chronicle 45:

> [Kadashman-Har]be (I), son of Kara-indash, son of Muballitat-Sherua, [the daughter of] king Ashur-uballit (I) of Assyria, ordered the overthrow of the Sutians from east to west and annihilated their large forces. He strengthened the fortresses

in Mount Sharshar (= Jebel Bishri). He dug wells and settled people on fertile lands in order to reinforce the guard. Later the Kassites revolted against him and killed him. They appointed Shuzigash, a Kassite, the son of nobody, as king over them. [King] Ashur-uballit of Assyria marched to Karanduni[ash] in order to avenge Kadashman-Harbe, his daughter's son. [He killed] Shuzigash the Kassite, [and made Kurigalzu (II), son(?) of Kadash]man-Harbe, ascend the thr[one of his father].

Most historians adhere to the account of the Synchronistic History. Burna-Buriash II had a son named Kara-hardash from his marriage to Muballitat-Sherua, the daughter of the Assyrian king Ashur-uballit I. This Kara-hardash ascended the throne at his father's death but a rebellion broke out among the Kassites, who killed Kara-hardash and put on the throne a certain Nazi-Bugash. This prompted the intervention of Ashur-uballit who killed Nazi-Bugash and installed on the throne Kurigalzu II, who claims in his votive inscriptions to be the son of Burna-Buriash II and must therefore have been the brother of Kara-hardash. Chronicle 45 conflates this episode with the war against the Sutians which took place under Kadashman-Harbe I, son of Kara-indash, about three generations before. As discussed earlier, a recently published *kudurru* provides independent confirmation that a war against the Sutians did take place during his reign. It appears therefore that a confusion occurred in the manuscript tradition between Kara-IN-dash and Kara-HAR-dash (the signs IN and HAR look somewhat alike in certain scribal hands), and this is supported by the Synchronistic History, which begins by stating that the Kassite troops had rebelled against Kara-hardash, but in the next entry affirms that Ashur-uballit marched to Babylonia to avenge Kara-indash. The compilers of Chronicle 45 picked up the same error and went one step further, confusing Kara-hardash (reigned 1333) with Kadashman-harbe I, the son of Kara-indash (ca. 1415), who thus became anachronistically the grandson of Ashur-uballit I. Chronicle 45 contains other errors attributable to textual corruption, such as the name Shuzigash for the rebel ruler. Kara-hardash and Nazi-Bugash are not attested outside Chronicle 45 and the Synchronistic History. King List A is broken at this point and we do not know if the Kassite king list recognized them.

5.7 The Middle Kassite Period (1332–1225)

The period of about one hundred years between Kurigalzu II (1332–1308) and Kashtiliashu IV (1232–1225) is the best documented one of the Kassite era in terms of archival texts. Its political history, on the other hand, is very poorly known. The Synchronistic History relates a clash with Assyria between Kurigalzu II and the new Assyrian king Enlil-nirari I (1327–1318), which ended allegedly with a Babylonian defeat and the drawing of a new boundary. Chronicle 45 moves the same episode to the reign of Adad-nirari I (1305–1274), possibly confusing him with Enlil-nirari I, and, contrary to the Synchronistic History, claims a victory for the Babylonians. It also relates a conflict between Kurigalzu II and a certain Hurbatila, king of Elam, who is not mentioned in any other source. A recently discovered dedicatory inscription of Kurigalzu II records a rebellion which affected the temple E-sag-dingirene in Nippur:

> A certain nobody mobilized a wicked foe in the land, who had no name and held no goods precious, and he took troops from Der to be his allies, and he dared go in the courtyard of E-sag-dingirene and draw a blade, and he spilled like water the blood of Nippur's citizens.[4]

The Synchronistic History mentions a war between Nazi-Maruttash (1307–1282) and Adad-nirari I which is also reported in fragments of an Assyrian epic. The Synchronistic History records, unsurprisingly, an Assyrian victory, stating that "Adad-nirari (I) brought about the defeat of Nazi-Maruttash and conquered him. He took away from him his camp and his standards."

Further light comes from two letters found in the Hittite capital Hattusha. One is fragmentary and was sent from Kadashman-Turgu (1281–1264) to the Hittite king Hattushili III. The other one, from Hattushili III to Kadashman-Enlil II (1263–1255), is well preserved. It addresses a number of issues, including complaints by Hattushili about the undue influence at the Babylonian court of an official named Itti-Marduk-balatu, who may have acted as regent during the minority of Kadashman-Enlil II and seems to have viewed unfavorably the alliance with the Hittites, initiated by Kadashman-Turgu. We hear about Kadashman-Turgu's pledge of support for the Hittites in case of an Egyptian attack and the fact that he even broke relations with the pharaoh (probably Ramses II) because of the latter's refusal to hand over to the Hittites an enemy who had taken refuge in Egypt. Hattushili also writes concerning messengers between the two countries being interrupted by the Assyrians and by the Ahlamu (Arameans). The letter deals also with the treatment of merchants, the reception of a Babylonian doctor and an incantation priest at the Hittite court and concludes with the usual queries about the possibility of receiving horses and lapis lazuli from Babylonia as gifts. The letter shows that the status of Babylon as international power had remained unchanged since the Amarna period.

Sumerian remained the dominant language of building and votive inscriptions until the reign of Burna-Buriash II. With Kurigalzu II, however, Akkadian began to appear in a number of inscriptions and became the preferred language under his successor Nazi-Maruttash, although Sumerian remained in occasional use until the end of the dynasty and beyond (Figure 5.3). As we have seen earlier the Kassite kings adopted the traditional titles of Babylonian kings (e.g. king of Babylon, king of Sumer and Akkad) and innovated with such titles as "king of Karduniash" and "king of the Kassites." Starting with Kadashman-Enlil I and especially Burna-Buriash II the title "king of the totality" (*shar kisshati*) became a regular epithet of Babylonian kings until the tenth century. The title made its appearance at the same time in Assyria, although it is already attested under Shamshi-Adad I (Samsi-Addu) in the eighteenth century.

Figure 5.3   Dedicatory inscription of Adad-shuma-usur. This brick bears an inscription of the Kassite king Adad-shuma-usur (1216–1187). It was discovered during the 1957–58 Joint Expedition to Nippur by the American Schools of Oriental Research and the Oriental Institute of the University of Chicago. Typical of many Kassite royal inscriptions this one is written in Sumerian. It records the restoration of Ekur, the temple of the god Enlil in Nippur. Measurements: Brick: 13.2 × 10.8 × 7.2 cm (5 1/4 × 4 1/4 × 2 7/8 in.); Inscription: 10.6 × 8.6 cm (4 1/8 × 3 3/8 in.). *Source*: The Metropolitan Museum of Art, NYC (MMA 59.41.82), Public Domain.

5.7.1   Ruralization of Babylonia

The picture of Kassite Babylonia which emerges from archaeological surveys and the limited textual evidence we have is very different from the one that prevailed during the third and early second millennia. Babylonia had been a land of relatively high urban density until the time of Hammu-rabi and Samsu-iluna, with a complex settlement hierarchy ranging from large cities to provincial centers, towns of varied size, forts, and villages. The economic and environmental crisis of the mid-second millennium reshaped the country, which became polarized between a few important urban centers and the countryside made up of large cultivated areas and small rural communities. We can glean information on the taxation structure of the countryside from *kudurru*s, which sometimes detail the burdens imposed on landowners and villages, or in a number of cases the tax exemptions granted by the king. Taxes were levied on the increase of herds, on grain, straw, and fodder. Corvée duty involved building and maintaining roads, bridges, city walls, and the irrigation system as well as quartering and supplying the military. We also hear of obligations to provide transportation vehicles, animals, and workers. Some large land grants included entire villages, but it is not clear to what degree the grantee, whether private or institutional, received any form of authority over these communities other than the right to receive the proceeds of taxation and corvée. In spite of the resettlement of provincial centers such as Ur and Uruk, Kassite Babylonia had only three major cities: Babylon, Dur-Kurigalzu, and Nippur, and their importance derived in large part from their political status.

5.7.2   Nippur as Southern Capital

Most of the archival sources dated to the Kassite kings stem from Nippur and any description of the social or economic structure of Kassite Babylonia necessarily depends on these texts. Nippur had been largely abandoned during the reign of Samsu-iluna and survived only as a sparsely inhabited settlement until its revival in the early fourteenth century during the reign of Kurigalzu I. During the fourteenth and thirteenth centuries it played the role of southern capital and recovered its status of religious metropolis of Babylonia. The importance of Nippur is further underscored by the fact the Kassite kings made regular pilgrimages to the site around the time of the New Year festival. The Nippur archives stem mostly from an institutional context and cover about five generations (1360–1225), but only about one fifth of the texts have been published and their nature as terse bookkeeping records, yielding only tidbits of useable information, makes their study strenuous and unrewarding. An official named the *shanda-bakku* headed the administration of Nippur; he seems to have occupied almost a vice-regal function, second only to the king in the state hierarchy. We know a number of *shandabakku*s by name; it appears that the office became hereditary since we have evidence for a father to son succession with the second, third and fourth incumbents in the list (Table 5.5).

The last two governors are attested only in *kudurru*s, as the Nippur archives end during the reign of Kashtiliashu IV. The *shandabakku*'s administration

Table 5.5 The Governors (*shandabakku*) of Nippur

Governor	King
Amilatu	Kurigalzu I (?)
Ninurta-nadin-ahhe	Kurigalzu I (?) to Burna-Buriash II
Enlil-kidinni, son of Ninurta-nadin-ahhe	Burna-Buriash II
Enlil-alsa, son of Enlil-kidinni	Nazi-Maruttash
Uzi-Shu[gab]	after Nazi-Maruttash
Amil-Marduk	Shagarakti-Shuriash and Kashtiliashu IV
Enlil-zakir-shumi	Adad-shuma-iddina
Enlil-shuma-imbi	Adad-shuma-usur

controlled the revenues of Nippur and its countryside. The income came mostly from villages in the form of agricultural products. The payments recorded in the ledgers involve large quantities, enabling the administration to provide rations and salaries for thousands of employees and dependents, including troops, crafts-men, workers of various sorts, and temple personnel. The *shandabakku* super-vised the administration of temples and we know that at least three of them also bore the title of *neshakku* of the god Enlil, a priestly office closely connected with the cult of Enlil and Ninlil at Nippur. Among the work force employed by the *shandabakku* we find unfree laborers numbering in the thousands. The administration kept detailed rosters of this servile population and went to great lengths to prevent escapes, which are frequently documented in the archive, and to replenish constantly the workforce by acquiring new slaves through purchase or assignment of war captives. The *shandabakku* Enlil-kidinni appears himself as buyer in a number of sales of slaves from the reign of Burna-Buriash II. This evi-dence paints a rather dismal social portrait of Kassite Babylonia, but one must be wary not to extend the conditions prevailing in that very specific institutional context to the entire country. One document from Nippur mentions that the Kassite king Shakarakti-Shuriash had released from slavery all women origi-nating from Nippur who had fallen into servitude, thus allowing one woman serving in another household to return to her married status. This shows that the role of the monarchy as social regulator, well attested under the First Dynasty, continued in some fashion under the Kassites.

5.8   The Intervention of Tukulti-Ninurta I and its Aftermath

Assyria had become a major territorial power in the thirteenth century, espe-cially after the annexation of Hanigalbat, the successor state of Mitanni by Shalmaneser I (1273–1244). His son Tukulti-Ninurta I (1243–1207) continued his expansionist policy, campaigning in northern Syria and southeastern Anatolia where he clashed with the Hittite king Tudhaliya IV. After a few years the conflict came to a resolution, giving Tukulti-Ninurta I free reins to attack the Kassite king Kashtiliashu IV (1232–1225). The cause of the war is obscure, but its outcome and consequences are reflected in a number of contemporary and later sources, a rare occurrence for any political event of the Kassite period. Historians long posited that Kashtiliashu had taken advantage of Tukulti-Ninurta's involvement in Anatolia to attack Assyria on its southern flank. However, a fragmentary letter found at Hattusha now casts doubt on this interpretation. The letter comes from the latter part of the reign of Tukulti-Ninurta. Although the names of the correspondents are lost, there is no doubt that the Assyrian king must be identified as the sender, and the recipient as the last Hittite king Suppiluliuma II, a son of Tudhaliya IV. Tukulti-Ninurta appears to justify his invasion of Babylonia. Reviewing the history of the Kassite dynasty before his intervention, he mentions Kurigalzu (II), Kudur-Enlil, somebody pretending to be the son of Kudur-Enlil, and finally Shagarakti-Shuriash and his sons, who appear to be the main protagonists of the narrative. Tukulti-Ninurta then blames Tudhaliya and probably his sons for not having intervened when someone seized the throne in Babylon. He also refers to an enigmatic figure designated as the "slave of the land of Suhi," who appears to play a central role in the episode. Another fragment of the letter mentions that the sons of Shagarakti-Shuriash were killed or murdered and that somebody seized the throne. The narrative is poorly preserved and difficult to interpret. Some claim that Kashtiliashu must be identified as the "slave of the land of Suhi," usurper of the Babylonian throne and murderer of the sons of Shagarakti-Shuriash, others that the designation refers in fact to Adad-shuma-usur who emerged as independent Babylonian ruler during the Assyrian intervention.

According to the Assyrian Epic of Tukulti-Ninurta I, the conflict began because Kashtiliashu had broken an oath by the sun-god Shamash, although the content of this oath is not revealed in the extant portions of the epic. The god Enlil became furious, left his shrines at Nippur and Dur-Kurigalzu and commissioned Tukulti-Ninurta to avenge the gods' honor. Babylonian merchants, perhaps spies, were arrested in Assyria, but Tukulti-Ninurta released them as gesture of good will. He wrote to Kashtiliashu, charging him with violation of a treaty, but possibly ended the letter on a conciliatory note. Kashtiliashu replied insolently, withheld Assyrian messengers and threatened Tukulti-Ninurta. After an exchange of correspondence between the two kings Tukulti-Ninurta proceeded to invade. Assyrian victory followed, accompanied with plunder. An inscription of Tukulti-Ninurta describes how Kashtiliashu was taken captive to Assyria:

> At that time I approached Kashtiliashu, king of Karduniash, to do battle. I brought about the defeat of his army. In the midst of that battle I captured Kashtiliashu, king of the Kassites, (and) I brought him bound as captive into the presence of the god Ashur, my lord. Thus I became lord of Sumer and Akkad in its entirety (and) stood over them (i.e. its inhabitants) with joy and excellence.[5]

Tukulti-Ninurta is acknowledged as king of Babylon in a single administrative document from Nippur dated to his accession year. After the conquest of Babylon, Tukulti-Ninurta adopted a lengthy string of titles, including "mighty king, king of Assyria and king of Karduniash, king of Sumer and Akkad, king of Sippar and Babylon, king of Dilmun and Meluhha, king of the Upper and Lower Seas." This is the first instance of an Assyrian king claiming Babylonian kingship, setting a precedent in the relations between the two countries. At this point Chronicle 45 becomes our main source. Tukulti-Ninurta apparently destroyed Babylon's wall and slaughtered many Babylonians, plundered the property of the Esagil temple and removed the statue of the god Marduk to Assyria, where it allegedly stayed for sixty-six(?) years before returning to its abode in the reign of the Assyrian king Ninurta-tukulti-Ashur. Chronicle 45 also claims that Tukulti-Ninurta appointed his own governors in Karduniash and ruled it for seven years, after which Babylonian officers rebelled and put Adad-shuma-usur on his ancestral throne while Tukulti-Ninurta was assassinated in a conspiracy led by his son Ashur-nasir-apli; thereafter he was succeeded by his other son Ashur-nadin-apli (1206–1203), then by the latter's son or nephew Ashur-nirari III (1202–1297), and finally by a third son named Enlil-kudurri-usur (1196–1192). Seven years is only a little less than the period which King List A assigns to the three successors of Kashtiliashu IV, namely Enlil-nadin-shumi (1224), Kadashman-Harbe II (1223) and Adad-shuma-iddina (1222–1217). Historians have therefore generally assumed that they ruled as puppets of Tukulti-Ninurta until the advent of Adad-shuma-usur, who would have expelled the Assyrians from Babylonia right at the end of that period and is credited with a reign of thirty years (1216–1187) in King List A.

The publication of Chronicle 46 has cast doubt on this interpretation. It seems to assume that Tukulti-Ninurta and Adad-shuma-usur ruled Babylonia concurrently, the former controlling Sippar, Babylon and Karduniash (i.e. northern Babylonia and the Diyala), and the latter probably entrenched in the south since he is described as rebuilding the wall of Nippur. Brick inscriptions of Adad-shuma-usur record his building activities there on the Ekur temple (Figure 5.3) and one of them claims that he was the son of Kashtiliashu. Chronicle 46 then describes the defeat inflicted by Adad-shuma-usur on the Assyrian king Enlil-kudurri-usur, a conflict also briefly mentioned in the Synchronistic History, and details his victorious march on Babylon where an unnamed usurper had briefly seized the throne: "Adad-shuma-usur raised a revolt, and, enjoying eternal divine protection, he entered Babylon and he became ruler of the land and established himself on his royal throne." All this resulted in Adad-shuma-usur finally gaining control of Babylon, apparently for the first time since his accession. This implies a much longer period of Assyrian control over the city than the seven years mentioned in Chronicle 45 and raises the possibility that Adad-shuma-usur reigned over a reunited Babylonia only for the last few years of his rule. It is possible in this case that King List A presents as successive, rulers who in fact reigned concurrently.

The situation in Babylonia in the wake of Tukulti-Ninurta's attack seems to have been chaotic at times. Chronicle 45 mentions that the king of Elam, Kiten-Hutran (written Kiten-Hutridish), led two separate attacks against the vassal rulers appointed by the Assyrians. One attack targeted Enlil-nadin-shumi, whose short rule is barely attested in contemporary sources:

> At the time of king Enlil-nadin-shumi, Kiten-Hutran, the king of Elam, attacked. He went into action against Nippur and scattered its people. He destroyed Der and E-dimgal-kalamma, carried off its people, drove them away and eliminated the suzerainty of king Enlil-nadin-shumi.

The second attack took place under Adad-shuma-iddina but the entry in Chronicle 45 is poorly preserved; it mentions actions against the cities of Isin and Marad. Elamite intervention may in fact have weakened the Assyrian hold on the country and facilitated the rise of Adad-shuma-usur in the south.

Adad-shuma-usur left his mark on posterity. An Epic of Adad-shuma-usur is known from several fragments. It mentions a rebellion against Adad-shuma-usur which is unattested in contemporary sources. Important aspects of Babylonian religion and kingship appear in the Epic for the first time, notably the formal prayer and confession of sins which the king presents before the god Marduk in the Esagil temple, as well as the pilgrimage he undertakes to the three cities of Babylon, Borsippa, and Kutha and which will become a regular feature of Assyrian and Babylonian royal devotion in the first millennium. These, however, might be apocryphal attributions since the fragments of the Epic date to Persian and Seleucid times. Another source of uncertain value is a letter from Adad-shuma-usur to the Assyrian king Ashur-nirari III and to his vizier Ili-hadda, preserved in a Neo-Assyrian fragment. Adad-shuma-usur is depicted in a position of superiority and hurls abuse at his correspondents. Some commentators have assumed on this basis that Adad-shuma-usur held a hegemonic position over Assyria during the troubled years which followed the assassination of Tukulti-Ninurta. However, the document belongs in all probability to the genre of fictitious royal correspondence and need not be taken at face value.

5.9   End of the Kassite Regime (1186–1155)

Adad-shuma-usur was followed by his son Meli-Shipak (1186–1172). Dated to his reign are archival documents found at Ur and Babylon and two *kudurrus* which record donations of land, one to his son and eventual successor, the crown prince Marduk-apla-iddina, near the ancient city of Agade, and the other one to his daughter Hunnubat-Nanaya (Figure 5.4). Like many other Kassite kings his building activities are recorded at Nippur, but also at Isin. A single document from the Syrian town of Emar on the Euphrates is dated by his reign, although it seems dubious that his rule extended that far in the northwest. Meli-Shipak was succeeded by his son Marduk-apla-iddina I (1171–1159) whose reign seems to have generally been peaceful and is known mostly from seven *kudurrus* recording large grants of land in northern and northeastern Babylonia. The downfall of the Kassite kingdom came swiftly in the wake of separate attacks by the Assyrians and Elamites. The Synchronistic History records that the Assyrian king Ashur-dan I (1178–1133) invaded Babylonia and defeated Zababa-shuma-iddina (1158), the ephemeral successor of Marduk-apla-iddina I. The final years of the dynasty are described in a fragmentary historical-literary text preserved in a later copy which records that the Elamite king Shutruk-Nahhunte, now claiming the Babylonian throne because of his marriage to a daughter of Meli-Shipak, raided northern Babylonia, plundered gold, silver and other goods from the cities of Dur-Kurigalzu, Agade, Sippar, and Opis, and put an end to the rule of Zababa-shuma-iddina. It is on this occasion that the Code of Hammu-rabi, the Stele of Naram-Sin and numerous *kudurrus* were taken to the Elamite capital Susa. Babylonian resistance continued for three years under the last king of the Kassite dynasty, Enlil-nadin-ahi (1157–1155). According to the same text Shutruk-Nahhunte appointed as regent his son Kuter-Nahhunte, who eventually captured Enlil-nadin-ahi and carried him off to Elam together with the statue of the god Marduk. Around 1155 Kuter-Nahhunte formally succeeded his father to the Elamite throne. Thus ended the Kassite regime, which had ruled a unified Babylonia for more than three centuries.

Figure 5.4 *Kudurru* of Meli-Shipak. This *kudurru* records a donation of land by the Kassite King Meli-Shipak (1186–1172) to his daughter Hunnubat-Nanaya. The relief depicts Meli-Shipak introducing his daughter to a goddess seated on a throne, probably Nanaya. The astral symbols on top refer to the goddess Isthar (the planet Venus), the god Sin (the lunar crescent), and the god Shamash (the sun). The monument is preserved in the Louvre Museum (Sb 23) and was found at Susa. *Source*: Photo © RMN-Grand Palais (musée du Louvre) / René-Gabriel Ojéda.

5.10 Akkadian Literature under the Kassites

The period of Kassite rule witnessed a remarkable flowering of Babylonian literature which continued under the Second Dynasty of Isin. Indeed, some of the most significant works of literature in the Akkadian language were composed during that era. First and foremost one must mention the Standard Babylonian version of the Epic of Gilgamesh, known in ancient times as *Ishkar Gilgamesh* "the Series of Gilgamesh" and also by its incipit *Sha nagba imuru* "He who Saw the Deep". It considerably expanded on the Old Babylonian version and became the most widely accepted edition of the Epic, represented by numerous manuscripts in the Library of Ashurbanipal at Nineveh. With eleven tablets and over three thousand verses Gilgamesh is also the longest literary composition from ancient Mesopotamia. Later tradition ascribed authorship of the Epic to a certain

Sin-leqe-unninni, an exorcist or lamentation singer who might well have been a historical figure living during the Kassite period. Nothing is known about him from Middle Babylonian sources but an influential priestly family attested at Uruk from the Neo-Babylonian until the Hellenistic period claimed descent from him. Another masterpiece from the Kassite era is *Ludlul bel nemeqi* "Let me praise the Lord of Wisdom." Often known as The Babylonian Job or The Poem of the Righteous Sufferer, *Ludlul* illustrates one aspect of the universal theme of theodicy, the suffering of the just in the face of the seeming arbitrariness of divine retribution. It ranks as one of the most elaborate and sophisticated works of Akkadian literature. *Ludlul* praises Marduk as the lord of wisdom, thus bearing witness to the increasing importance of the god under the Kassite kings. The composition has not been fully preserved but its original length may have reached 480 verses divided into four tablets. The name of the protagonist of the poem, Shubshi-meshre-Shakkan, is of a very rare type, and two prominent individuals with that very same name occur in documents from the time of the Kassite king Nazi-Maruttash. Therefore it is tempting to seek the historical setting of the text during his reign. Both Gilgamesh and *Ludlul* were written in a literary idiom known as Standard Babylonian, largely derived from the Hymnic Epic dialect of Old Babylonian literature with a number of Middle Babylonian innovations. Standard Babylonian was not a spoken language but became during the late second millennium the accepted official medium for literature and royal inscriptions in Babylonia and Assyria and retained that status until the end of the cuneiform tradition.

NOTES

1. Adapted from Paulus 2013b: 296–7.
2. After Brinkman 1976: 378.
3. After Moran 1992: 18.
4. After George 2011: 118.
5. After Grayson 1987: 276.

FURTHER READING

Sources for the Kassite period are surveyed by Brinkman 1976 and Paulus 2013a. The *kudurru*s are edited and discussed by Paulus 2013b. There is still no comprehensive edition of the royal inscriptions of that period, although there is a study by Bartelmus 2010. The Sealand dynasty texts are edited by Dalley 2009; for an analysis of the archive and the history of the dynasty see Boivin forthcoming. The archives from Nippur are examined by Sassmannshausen 2001; and social and economic conditions there by Tenney 2011. For a translation of the Amarna letters see Moran 1992. The origin, language and culture of the Kassites are discussed by Balkan 1954, Sassmannshausen 2000, Sommerfeld 1985, and 1995, and Zadok 2005. A general survey of Babylonia during the Kassite period is Bartelmus and Sternitzke 2017. The installation of Kassite power is studied by Boese 2008 and Van Koppen 2010. The pivotal reign of Kurigalzu I is studied by Clayden 1996.

Balkan, Kemal. 1954. *Kassitenstudien I. Die Sprache der Kassiten*. New Haven: American Oriental Society.

Bartelmus, Alexa. 2010. "Restoring the Past: A Historical Analysis of the Royal Temple Building Inscriptions from the Kassite Period." *KASKAL* 7: 143–71.

Bartelmus, Alexa, and Sternitzke, Katja (eds.). 2017. *Karduniaš. Babylonia under the Kassites. Babylonien zur Kassitenzeit*. Berlin: de Gruyter.

Boese, Johannes. 2008. "Harbašipak, Tiptakzi, und die Chronologie der älteren Kassitenzeit." *Zeitschrift für Assyriologie und vorderasiatischen Archäologie* 98: 201–10.

Boivin, Odette. Forthcoming. *The First Dynasty of the Sealand in Mesopotamia*. Berlin: de Gruyter.

Brinkman, John Anthony. 1976. *Materials and Studies for Kassite History, Vol 1: A Catalogue of Sources Pertaining to Specific Monarchs of the Kassite Dynasty*. Chicago: The Oriental Institute of the University of Chicago.

Clayden, Tim. 1996. "Kurigalzu I and the Restoration of Babylonia." *Iraq* 58: 109–21.

Dalley, Stephanie. 2009. *Babylonian Tablets from the First Sealand Dynasty in the Schøyen Collection*. Bethesda, MD: CDL Press.

George, Andrew R. et al. 2011. *Cuneiform Royal Inscriptions and Related Texts in the Schøyen Collection*. Bethesda, Maryland: CDL Press.

Grayson, Albert Kirk. 1987. *Assyrian Rulers of the Third and Second Millennia*. RIMA 1. Toronto: University of Toronto Press.

Moran, William L. 1992. *The Amarna Letters*. Baltimore and London: The Johns Hopkins University Press.

Paulus, Susanne. 2013a. "The Limits of Middle Babylonian Archives," In Faraguna, M. (ed.), *Archives and Archival Documents*. Trieste: Edizioni Università di Trieste. 87–103.

Paulus, Susanne. 2013b. *Die babylonischen Kudurru-Inschriften von der kassitischen bis zur frühneubabylonischen Zeit*. Munster: Ugarit-Verlag.

Sassmannshausen, Leonhard. 2000. "The Adaptation of the Kassites to the Babylonian Civilization." In Van Lerberghe, Karel and Voet, Gabriela (eds.), *Languages and Cultures in Contact: At the Crossroads of Civilizations in the Syro-Mesopotamian Realm. Proceedings of the 42th RAI*. Louvain: Peeters. 409–24.

Sassmannshausen, Leonhard. 2001. *Beiträge zur Verwaltung und Gesellschaft Babyloniens in der Kassitenzeit*. Mainz: Verlag Philip von Zabern.

Sommerfeld, Walter. 1985. "Der Kurigalzu-Text MAH 15922." *Archiv für Orientforschung* 32: 1–22.

Sommerfeld, Walter. 1995. "The Kassites of Ancient Mesopotamia: Origins, Politics, and Culture." In Sasson, Jack, et al. (eds.), *Civilizations of the Ancient Near East II*. New York: Scribner's. 917–30.

Tenney, Jonathan. 2011. *Life at the Bottom of Babylonian Society: Servile Laborers at Nippur in the 14th and 13th Centuries B.C.* Leiden: Brill.

Van Koppen, Frans. 2010. "The Old to Middle Babylonian Transition: History and Chronology of the Mesopotamian Dark Age." *Egypt and the Levant* 20: 453–63.

Zadok, Ran. 2005. "Kassites." In *Encyclopedia Iranica*: online edition, 2015, available at http://www.iranicaonline.org/articles/kassites.

6
Second Dynasty of Isin

After the fall of the last Kassite king the Elamites occupied parts of the country for some time and the transfer of power to the Second Dynasty of Isin occurred in obscure circumstances. The new royal line derives its name from King List A which sums it up as *palê Ishin* "Dynasty of Isin." It is called "Second" by modern historians to differentiate it from the First Dynasty of Isin which ruled Babylonia after the Third Dynasty of Ur. Contrary to Isin I, however, rulers of the Second Dynasty of Isin never claim the kingship of Isin in their inscriptions, and no evidence has yet surfaced that the city held the role of capital. However, the fact that the governor of Isin often appears in a leading position in lists of witnesses on *kudurru*s from that period, suggests that the new dynasty had some connection to Isin and may have started its bid for power there before transferring its seat to Babylon. Isin II rulers definitely recognized Isin as the preeminent regional center, perhaps a southern capital in the same manner as Nippur had functioned during the Kassite period. The replacement of Nippur by Isin also seems reflected in the archaeological record. Surveys show an increase in population at Isin at the end of the second millennium and a simultaneous decrease at Nippur, which became again largely deserted until its revival in the eighth century. The list of Isin II rulers can be reconstructed as follows (Table 6.1), mainly from King Lists A and C.

Scholars have usually placed the beginning of the dynasty in 1157 and assumed an overlap of two years with the last Kassite ruler. However, recent studies of contemporaneous Assyrian sources have argued for lowering Isin II chronology by four years. The main argument hinges on Chronicle 15, which mentions that the death of Marduk-nadin-ahhe and the accession of Marduk-shapik-zeri took place at least one year before a campaign of Tiglath-pileser I against Katmuhu. Since the absolute dates for Tiglath-pileser I can be established almost certainly as 1114–1076, the death of Marduk-nadin-ahhe must therefore have occurred in 1078. These conclusions, however, must still be considered provisional.

A History of Babylon: 2200 BC–AD 75, First Edition. Paul-Alain Beaulieu.
© 2018 John Wiley & Sons Ltd. Published 2018 by John Wiley & Sons Ltd.

Table 6.1 The Second Dynasty of Isin

Name of Ruler	Revised Chronology	Old Chronology
Marduk-kabit-ahheshu	1153–1136	1157–1140
Itti-Marduk-balatu	1135–1128	1139–1132
Ninurta-nadin-shumi	1127–1122	1131–1126
Nebuchadnezzar I	1121–1100	1125–1104
Enlil-nadin-apli	1099–1096	1103–1100
Marduk-nadin-ahhe	1095–1078	1099–1082
Marduk-shapik-zeri	1077–1065	1081–1069
Adad-apla-iddina	1064–1043	1068–1047
Marduk-ahhe-eriba	1042	1046
Marduk-zer(?)-x	1041–1030	1045–1034
Nabu-shumu-libur	1029–1022	1033–1026

The Second Dynasty of Isin makes up the fourth dynasty ruling at Babylon according to King List A. It is also the first truly native Babylonian dynasty, at least insofar as we rely on the names of the rulers which are, for the first time in the city's history, all Akkadian. Whether all members of the dynasty formed one family cannot be ascertained except for the sequence from the third to the seventh king in the list where we have evidence for a succession from father to son. Sources for the Second Dynasty of Isin are sparse. Disconnected fragments of political history can be gleaned from king lists, chronicles, mentions of events affecting Babylonia in the inscriptions of Assyrian kings, as well as historical-literary texts available in later copies. Isin II royal inscriptions contain little historical information. A number of them consist of building and votive inscriptions often written in Sumerian, while others record mere ownership on bronze daggers found in Iran (e.g.: "Belonging to Marduk-nadin-ahhe, king of the totality, son of Ninurta-nadin-shumi, king of Babylon"). These inscribed daggers are attested from the time of Adad-shuma-usur (1216–1187) until Eulmash-shakin-shumi (1004–988) of the Bazi Dynasty. No agreement has been reached on their original function, some advocating that they were manufactured as gifts to mercenaries or allies of the Babylonians, others that they originated as votive offerings in Babylonian temples or even local sanctuaries in the Zagros. The complete lack of archives from that period forms the main gap in our sources. Only handfuls of legal and administrative texts are dated to Isin II kings. However, twenty-seven *kudurru*s can be securely assigned to that period (Figure 6.1). This body of material is supplemented with references in later texts to the role of Isin II kings as sponsors of literature and scholarship.

The sources bear witness to a degree of cultural and institutional continuity between the Kassite and Isin II periods. Kassite individuals continued to occupy important posts at the court and in the provincial administration. The data from *kudurru*s show the same division into provinces which existed under the Kassites and many of the same officials appear in them; one exception is the *shandabakku* of Nippur who almost completely disappears from the documentation, his role

Figure 6.1 Caillou Michaux. The Caillou Michaux ("The Michaux Stone") is one of the earliest Mesopotamian antiquities to have reached Europe. It was acquired in 1786 by the French botanist André Michaux south of Baghdad, probably near the site of Ctesiphon, and subsequently bought by the French state. It now belongs to the Bibliothèque Nationale in Paris. This beautifully preserved *kudurru* records a private donation of land. Internal evidence suggests a dating to the reign of Marduk-nadin-ahhe (1095–1078). The top of the stone is carved with the symbols of the gods preserving the transaction. Measurements: H: 46 cm. *Source*: Reproduced with permission of Bibliothèque nationale de France.

being filled by the governor (*shaknu*) of Isin. One title which now becomes common is *bel biti* (literally "head of the house," probably "clan, tribal leader") to refer to the governor of a tribal area (as opposed to the *shaknu* for urban areas). These existed mostly east of the Tigris where Kassite tribal organization still prevailed. The size of the land granted or sold on *kudurru*s is generally smaller than during the Kassite period, but the data are admittedly restricted. Archaeological surveys indicate a general decrease in population and cultivated areas until the beginning of the first millennium except for the city of Isin and its vicinity. Excavations have not revealed any major building program linked to the Isin II kings anywhere. Aramean and Sutian invasions probably contributed to the general decline, and climatic changes have been advanced as another cause of the economic problems which faced Babylonia at that time, causing a dry climate in the Near East which considerably diminished the agricultural output. The fact that no cuneiform archive from that period and the ensuing centuries has been discovered in Babylonia is in all likelihood not accidental, but reveals the weakness or even breakdown of large institutions.

6.1   Marduk and Nabu

Important theological changes took place under the Second Dynasty of Isin. We saw that during the time of the Kassites the god Enlil had retained royal favor and kept its status as leader of the pantheon. Only one Kassite king bore a name honoring Marduk: Marduk-apla-iddina I, which means "Marduk has provided me with an heir." Isin II monarchs depart radically from this pattern with six Marduk names and only one Enlil name. The rise of Marduk began during the Old Babylonian period and continued throughout the Middle Babylonian period. By the end of the Kassite regime Marduk had become the main god worshiped by the literary elite and the court, paving the way for the sudden rise of Marduk in the royal onomasticon under Isin II. The other significant innovation is the introduction of the god Nabu in the royal onomastics. The god appears in two royal names: Nabu-shumu-libur "O Nabu, may the progeny stay healthy," and Nebuchadnezzar I, the dynasty's most illustrious representative. Nebuchadnezzar is the Biblical form of the name Nabu-kudurri-usur "O Nabu, protect my heir," borne also centuries later by Nebuchadnezzar II (605–562), the main architect of Babylon's imperial power. Nabu appeared first during the time of Hammu-rabi, and sources from that period already depict him as god of writing. Although Nabu eventually became the patron god of the city of Borsippa and its temple Ezida, Old Babylonian sources mention Tutu, a form of Marduk, as god of that city, while Nabu's main shrine was apparently located in the Esagil temple in Babylon at that time. During the late Kassite period Nabu became the son of Marduk and heir of Esagil and is mentioned with Marduk in the curse sections of *kudurru*s. The migration of Nabu to Borsippa probably occurred after the fall of the Kassites. The earliest testimonies are a Sumerian inscription of Marduk-shapik-zeri which commemorates the restoration of the Ezida temple in Borsippa and depicts Nabu (under his learned name Mudugasa) as "lion of Esagil and Ezida, lord of Borsippa, who dwells in Ezida," and a bilingual inscription of Adad-apla-iddina which records the dedication of a belt to the cult statue of Nabu at Borsippa, praising him as follows:

> Offspring of the god Dumu-duku (i.e. Marduk), perfect heir, honored son, offspring of the goddess Eru'a (= Zarpanitu, Marduk's wife), the one who has gathered to himself all rites and ordinances, who makes secure the throne, the scepter, and the crown, who establishes the reign, who decrees kingship, the lord of Borsippa, who dwells in the Ezida temple, his helper, his august protector, who makes him triumph, his lord.[1]

Some of the most important traits of Nabu are listed here: his status as son of Marduk, his control of all rites and ordinances which justified his increasingly exalted status in the first millennium, and his role as upholder of the monarchy who confers the insignias of kingship. In the Neo-Babylonian period the coronation of the king took place in the temple of Nabu in Babylon, the E-niggidri-kalamma-summa "House which bestows the Scepter of the Land." According to Chronicle 51 the temple already existed at the turn of the first millennium, and one may therefore assume that it became the locus for the coronation of the Babylonian king under Isin II.

6.2   Renewed Conflict with Assyria

Little is known about the first three Isin II rulers. The reign of Marduk-kabit-ahheshu is variously recorded as seventeen or eighteen years in king lists. He was followed by his son Itti-Marduk-balatu, who bears in a dedicatory inscription the epithet of "king of kings," unusual for that period, and the more traditional title of "viceroy of Babylon" (*shakkanak Babili*). Their relation to the third ruler, Ninurta-nadin-shumi, cannot be established. A fragmentary literary letter from an unknown Babylonian ruler to the Assyrian king Mutakkil-Nusku, who reigned for about one year in 1132, sheds some light on that period. However, it is difficult to identify the sender for certain: either Itti-Marduk-balatu or Ninurta-nadin-shumi. The letter belongs to the genre of fictitious royal correspondence and is known from two manuscripts: one from the Library of Ashurbanipal and the other one probably from Babylon and of a later date. The letter alludes to the captivity of the god Marduk which followed the invasion of Tukulti-Ninurta I and possibly deals with his return to Babylon. As we saw earlier Chronicle 45 claims that Marduk reintegrated his shrine during the reign of a certain Tukulti-Ashur, whom most historians identify as Ninurta-tukulti-Ashur; he reigned for about one year in 1133. According to the Assyrian King List, Ninurta-tukulti-Ashur lost his throne in a coup led by his brother Mutakkil-Nusku, who then exiled him to Babylonia. The fictitious letter to Mutakkil-Nusku mentions Ninurta-tukulti-Ashur in unclear context and also complains about the Assyrian failure to show up at a previously agreed meeting at the border town of Zaqqa.

The two brothers eventually disappeared from the scene and Ashur-resha-ishi I (1132–1115), son of Mutakkil-Nusku, became king of Assyria. According to Chronicle 14 Ashur-resha-ishi marched on the city of Arba'il (Arbela) to prevent a Babylonian invasion led by Ninurta-nadin-shumi. The city of Arbela probably belonged to Assyria in that period and one may wonder why the Assyrian king would march against it unless it had become a hotbed of political unrest. Archival evidence from Assyria seems in fact to indicate that the city rebelled against Ashur-resha-ishi around the tenth year of his reign (1123–1222) under the leadership of its governor, Bere, who acted as eponym for that year. This could explain the Babylonian intervention, which aimed perhaps at supporting the rebellion to gain territorial advantages. A much damaged entry in Chronicle 46 appears to refer to that campaign and claim that Nebuchadnezzar took advantage of the situation to lead a coup against his father Ninurta-nadin-shumi, who was killed by the conspirators upon his return to Babylon. This interpretation rests on extensive restorations in the chronicle and must be considered provisional. If we adopt it, the alleged rebellion and accession of Nebuchadnezzar would have taken place in 1122. This reconstruction of events fits only the revised chronology which places Nebuchadnezzar's accession in that year, and his first full regnal year in 1121.

6.3   Nebuchadnezzar I (1121–1100)

The conflict with Assyria continued since the Synchronistic History claims that Nebuchadnezzar I campaigned twice against the Assyrians, trying to capture the border fortresses of Zanqu and Idu, probably located on the lower Zab River:

> Nebuchadnezzar took his siege engines and went to conquer Zanqu, a fortress in Assyria. Ashur-resha-ishi, king of Assyria, mustered his chariots to go against him. To prevent the siege engines being taken from him, Nebuchadnezzar burnt them. He turned and went home. This same Nebuchadnezzar with chariots and infantry went to conquer Idu, a fortress of Assyria. Ashur-resha-ishi sent chariots and infantry to help the fortress. He fought with Nebuchadnezzar, brought about his total defeat, slaughtered his troops and carried off his camp.

Given the pro-Assyrian bias of the Synchronistic History one may doubt the routine narrative of easy Assyrian triumph. Eventually they made peace and Nebuchadnezzar went on a state visit to Assyria; the trip is indirectly documented by an administrative document from Assur which mentions deliveries made "on the day when Nebuchadnezzar, king of Karduniash, arrived." The main achievement of Nebuchadnezzar's reign, however, was the campaign against Elam and the triumphal return to Babylon of the statue of Marduk, which had been plundered from the Esagil temple by Kuter-Nahhunte one generation earlier. These events are commemorated in both contemporary and later sources, including two *kudurru*s from the reign of Nebuchadnezzar, and historical-literary compositions which, although available only in later copies, probably originate in the official scriptoria of the Isin II dynasty.

6.3.1   *The Elamite Campaign and the Return of Marduk*

The most detailed account of the campaign is preserved in the *kudurru* of Shitti-Marduk, the *bel biti* of Bit-Karziabku, a Kassite tribal area in the province of Namar in the upper Diyala. This *kudurru* records the grant of tax exemptions to the towns of Bit-Karziabku and the reinstatement of its previous independent status from the provincial administration of Namar as a reward for the heroic deeds of Shitti-Marduk during the Elamite campaign. The *kudurru* contains an unusual prologue in epic style which extols the virtues of Nebuchadnezzar, provides details on the conduct of the war and puts much emphasis on Shitti-Marduk's achievements. The campaign started in the month of Duzu (June–July) at Der across the Tigris. Marching under scorching heat, the Babylonian army reached the river Ulai where it clashed with the king of Elam, Hulteludish-Inshushinak. The encounter resulted in a resounding Babylonian victory, and the prologue credits Shitti-Marduk with a decisive role in the battle:

> Shitti-Marduk, the head of the house (*bel biti*) of Bit-Karziabku, whose chariot was on the right flank of the king, his lord, did not lag far behind, but kept his chariot ready. He did not fear the battle, but went down against the enemy. Moreover, he penetrated deep into the enemy of his lord. By the command of the goddess Ishtar and the god Adad, the gods (who are) the lords of battle, he put Hulteludish, the king of Elam, to flight (and) he (Hulteludish) disappeared. Thus, king Nebuchadnezzar stood in triumph; he seized the land of Elam (and) plundered its property.[2]

Another, tablet-shaped *kudurru* contains a prologue claiming that Nebuchadnezzar undertook the campaign on behalf of the beneficiaries of the grant, two priests who had fled Elam to seek refuge in Babylonia. The prologue briefly describes the campaign and adds one crucial element: the victory against Elam allowed Nebuchadnezzar to bring back the statue of Marduk, named Bel "the lord" in the inscription. More than the campaign itself, the return of Marduk became the main achievement celebrated in the literary tradition about Nebuchadnezzar. A historical-literary text from the Library of Ashurbanipal, copied according to its colophon from a Babylon original, describes a fretful Nebuchadnezzar who entreats Marduk to return to his land:

> In Babylon dwells Nebuchadnezzar, [the king]. He rages like a lion (and) thun[ders] like the god Adad. Like a lion, he frigh[tens] his distinguished nobles. [His] supplications go to the god Marduk, lord of Babylon: "Have pity on me, one who is dejected and prost[rate]! Have pity on my land, which weeps and mourns! Have pity on my people, who wail and weep! O lord of Babylon, how long will you dwell in the land of the enemy? May beautiful Babylon be remembered by you! Turn your face back to Esagil, which you love!".[3]

The rest of the text has lacunas, yet it is clear that Marduk hearkens to Nebuchadnezzar's prayer and orders him to wage war in order to bring him back to Babylon, a mission which the king dutifully accomplished: "[I grasped] the hand of the great lord, [the god Marduk, and] caused him to take the road towards his own country." Another text preserved in a later copy found at Babylon is couched as a letter sent by Nebuchadnezzar from Elam after his victorious campaign; the Epic of Nebuchadnezzar, an elaborate bilingual composition (Sumerian and Akkadian) preserved in later manuscripts from Nineveh and Babylon, furnishes lavish details on Marduk's triumphal return to Babylon. These two texts offer a deeper reflection on the significance of the event, elaborating a theology of divine anger and absence. Marduk had become estranged from his land and people because of their sinful demeanor and allowed the Elamites to remove him from his shrine. But now at last, ceding to the entreaties of Nebuchadnezzar, he had relented and granted him victory over the enemy, letting the pious king take him back to his city.

Babylonian historical-literary sources claim that the statue of Marduk had been stolen twice before: when the Hittites captured Babylon in 1595, and when Tukulti-Ninurta I attacked the city in 1225–1224. The statue captured during the latter assault allegedly returned to Babylon during the reign of Itti-Marduk-balatu or Ninurta-nadin-shumi and cannot therefore be the same as the one captured by the Elamite king Kuter-Nahhunte at the end of the Kassite regime. Probably new statues had been consecrated in temporary replacement of those that had been spoliated. The Marduk Prophecy, a literary text probably composed during the reign of Nebuchadnezzar, puts the three captures of Marduk on the same level, arguing each time that the god had left his land of his own volition. The core of the matter resides not so much in the importance of the object itself that was captured, but more in the motives lying behind the historical memorialization of the event. And in Nebuchadnezzar's mind, the motif of the statue's return undoubtedly inspired a larger project, the exaltation of Marduk to the highest position in the pantheon.

6.3.2 Enuma Elish and the Supremacy of Marduk

Several stories about the creation and organization of the universe existed in Mesopotamia. Yet Enuma elish, commonly known in English as the Babylonian Epic of Creation (it was known in ancient Babylonia after the first two words of its initial verse, *Enuma elish la nabu shamamu* "When on high heavens had not been named"), ranks as the most important for several reasons. Mainly, it is the longest (more than 1,100 verses) and most ambitious in its thematic complexity, and also, it assumed near canonical status in the first millennium, to the extent that it became integral part of the New Year festival in Babylon, when the king was ritually confirmed in his office. Enuma elish explains how Marduk was promoted to the status of king of the gods as a reward for vanquishing the primeval forces of chaos and creating an organized and stable cosmos. It also offers an etiology of the foundation of Babylon as center of the world and cosmic node, where the gods travel on their journey between heaven, earth, the netherworld, and the Abzu (the watery abyss). Thus Enuma elish embodies basic beliefs of many ancient civilizations, which viewed the state as coextensive with the cosmos and the ruler as the earthly counterpart of the demiurge. The king was responsible for upholding the political order in the same way as the demiurge maintained cosmic stability.

The Second Dynasty of Isin put much greater emphasis on the god Marduk than the Kassite kings, who generally adhered to a traditional divine hierarchy that gave Enlil the leading role. The inscriptions of Nebuchadnezzar I reflect a major shift in the status of Marduk. For the first time in an official context they praise Marduk as "king of the gods," an epithet which had begun to appear during the Kassite period only in personal names (e.g. Marduk-shar-ili "Marduk is king of the gods"). The epithet figures prominently in the Shitti-Marduk *kudurru* and the bilingual Epic of Nebuchadnezzar. The Epic insists that the gods had abandoned Babylonia at the command of Marduk, who is portrayed as their absolute master, the god who determines fates and wields cosmic power. Enuma elish is the earliest literary composition which ascribes these same qualities to Marduk. For these reasons, the reign of Nebuchadnezzar I seems the most likely date for its composition, and in spite of occasional criticism this view has gained broad acceptance. The oldest extant manuscripts of Enuma elish date from the ninth century. Linguistically the composition displays an ornate form of Standard Babylonian, the literary dialect which became dominant after 1400. Contrary to the Epic of Gilgamesh, Enuma elish has no forerunners in Sumerian or Old Babylonian. Even if one questions the precise dating to the reign of Nebuchadnezzar I, because of its stylistic unity and the absence of any clear parallels or even allusions to its contents in previous works, one must still recognize Enuma elish as the creation of a single mind active between the late Kassite period and the beginning of the first millennium.

Further arguments to date Enuma elish to Isin II can be advanced in consideration of one of the main themes of the Epic, the assumption of Enlil's persona by Marduk, who became the "Enlil (i.e. leader) of the gods." The earliest contemporary reflection of this syncretism occurs in an inscription of Adad-apla-iddina (1064–1043) which commemorates the repair of the wall of Nippur and names it Nemetti-Marduk "bulwark of Marduk." According to later sources the wall of Babylon was Nemetti-Enlil "bulwark of Enlil." Therefore it seems that before the reign of Adad-apla-iddina the fortification wall of each city was named after the other city's patron deity with the purpose of syncretizing the two gods. Similar evidence surfaces in an inscription of Simbar-Shipak (1021–1004). The inscription commemorates the making of a throne for Enlil in the shrine Ekur-igigal at Nippur, but specifies that Marduk is the god who sits on that throne to decree fates. In Enuma elish, decreeing fates instead of Enlil is the main prerogative bestowed on Marduk as a reward for his victory against Tiamat, the personified force of chaos and rebellion. By the time of these two rulers the shift to a Marduk centered theology had already occurred, adding more weight to the hypothesis that the reign of Nebuchadnezzar I marked the watershed in these developments. The Marduk Prophecy, very probably a product of Isin II scriptoria, contains similar speculations since it renames the temple of Marduk, E-sag-il "House which raises its head," as Ekur-sag-il "Ekur which raises its head," E-kur "House which is a mountain" being the temple of Enlil in Nippur.

Enuma elish represents a milestone in the intellectual history of Babylonia. For the first time in the Ancient Near East a religious tradition attributed the creation and organization of the entire universe, including the creation of humankind, to one single god. Having no real antecedents, Enuma elish burst into history like the Gospels or the Quran, assuming the status of revealed text. It became incontrovertible, forcing other traditions to answer its challenge. A response came in the seventh century when the Assyrian king Sennacherib sponsored the redaction of a new version of Enuma elish which gave the leading role in creation to Ashur, the national god of Assyria, instead of Marduk. The Biblical account of creation in Genesis 1 very probably constitutes another response to the Babylonian challenge, attributing the role of demiurge to the god of Israel in a narrative which bears a close resemblance to the account of the creation of the world by Marduk in Enuma elish.

6.3.3   Nebuchadnezzar I and Royal Legitimacy

By presenting Babylon as cosmic center and bond between all regions, a role previously filled by Nippur (a common learned name for Nippur in Sumerian is Dur-an-ki "bond of heaven and the netherworld"), Enuma elish provided the city with a conceptual tool to claim exclusive control of Babylonia and extend its hegemony to the larger Near East, a goal that will be achieved lastly in the sixth century. The inscriptions of Nebuchadnezzar I and the historical-literary tradition about him reflect a parallel change in their view of kingship, which is emphatically re-centered on Babylon and acquires a definite sacral character. In addition to the traditional Isin II titles ("king of the totality," "king of Babylon," "king of Sumer and Akkad"), Nebuchadnezzar claims the epithets of "scion of Babylon" (*zer Babili*) and "creature of Shuanna" (*binut Shuanna*), Shuanna being a learned name for Babylon. Distant and prestigious lineage becomes an essential constituent of royal authority. The Epic of Nebuchadnezzar describes him as "distant descendant of kingship" (*lipu ruqu sha sharruti*), "seed preserved since before the flood" (*zeru nasru sha lam abubi*), and traces his ancestry back to the mythical antediluvian king En-me-duranki, whose name means literally "high-priest of the rites of the bond of heaven and the netherworld." It also highlights the religious responsibilities of the Babylonian king, presenting Nebuchadnezzar as the one "who administers correctly all cult centers and confirms the regular offerings." In his inscriptions Nebuchadnezzar revives epithets of the First Dynasty, particularly those of Hammu-rabi such as "king of justice" (*shar mesharim*), "true shepherd" (*re'u kinu*), and "sun-god of his land" (*Shamash matishu*).

In spite of the rhetoric projecting the image of a strong, centralized kingship, Nebuchadnezzar had to share his authority with local officials, especially Kassite tribal leaders. Shitti-Marduk, the head of the Kassite clan of Bit-Karziabku, obtained the reinstatement of his district's autonomy with increased tax exemptions, and the prologue of his *kudurru*, while acknowledging the preeminence of Nebuchadnezzar, celebrates his own exploits in an epic style normally the prerogative of the king. The Hinke *kudurru* records a grant to the mayor of Nippur; while cursorily acknowledging Nebuchadnezzar, it portrays a Kassite official named Baba-shuma-iddina of the Hunna clan (Bit-Hunna) as the actual granting authority. The same Baba-shuma-iddina is later attested as governor of Babylon in the Shitti-Marduk *kudurru*.

6.4 Sealand Memories under Enlil-nadin-apli (1099–1096)

Very little is known about Enlil-nadin-apli. A *kudurru* dated to the last year of his reign records the return of a disputed strip of land along the Tigris to the temple of the goddesses Namma and Nanshe in the Sealand province. Nabu-shuma-iddina, the high-priest of the temple, complained that Ekarra-iqisha, the governor of the province of Sin-magir, initiated a survey of land tenure and tampered with the boundary markers in order to appropriate the land in question. The *kudurru* specifies that the land had initially been granted by Gulkishar, the sixth ruler of the First Sealand Dynasty, and it even indicates the time elapsed between Gulkishar and Nebuchadnezzar I:

> (Land which) [Gulki]shar, king of the Sealand, had delimited [as] territory [for] the goddess Nanshe, his lady, and [since the time] of Gulkishar, king of the Sealand, (until) Nebuchadnezzar (I), king of Babylon, 696 years (had passed).[4]

The matter was brought to the attention of the king who ordered Ekarra-iqisha and the governor of the Sealand province, one Eanna-shuma-iddina, to investigate the matter. The inquiry confirmed the return of the land to the temple of Namma and Nanshe. The count of 696 years from Gulkishar to Nebuchadnezzar I is erroneous; we know that Gulkishar was a contemporary of Samsu-ditana (1625–1595). Kist List A ascribes 120 years to the successors of Gulkishar in the First Sealand Dynasty, then 576 years and nine months to the Kassite Dynasty. The total arrives at 696 years exactly and therefore the scribes of the *kudurru* may have used that as a round figure, omitting the thirty-two years covering the beginnings of Isin II until Nebuchadnezzar I, and assuming that the Sealand and Kassite dynasties had reigned consecutively with no overlap. At the same time the scribes acknowledged that the two dynasties held different centers of power since they reckoned Gulkishar specifically as "king of the Sealand" and Nebuchadnezzar I as "king of Babylon." These data suggest that the sources for King List A were already circulating at that time. A damaged entry in Chronicle 46 seems to imply that a rebellion broke against Enlil-nadin-apli not too long after the settlement of that land dispute and brought to power his uncle Marduk-nadin-ahhe, the brother of Nebuchadnezzar I.

6.5 Marduk-nadin-ahhe (1095–1078)

The reign of Marduk-nadin-ahhe (Figure 6.2) was dominated by the ongoing conflict with Assyria, which enjoyed a renewal of its power under Tiglath-pileser I (1114–1076). Initially Babylon seems to have gained the upper hand. The Bavian

Figure 6.2   *Kudurru* of Marduk-nadin-ahhe. Representations of Babylonian kings are rare and most of them are found on *kudurrus*. This one depicts the Isin II ruler Marduk-nadin-ahhe wearing the feathered cylindrical tiara common to kings and deities. The *kudurru* is preserved in the Walters Art Museum, Baltimore, and records a sale of land. Measurements: 11 × 8 1/4 × 4 1/4 in. (28 × 21 × 10.8 cm). *Source*: The Walters Art Museum (21.10), Public Domain.

inscription of the Neo-Assyrian king Sennacherib (704–681), composed in the year 688 or slightly later, contains the following account:

> In the time of Tiglath-pileser (I), king of Assyria, Marduk-nadin-ahhe, king of Akkad, had taken Adad and Shala, the gods of Ekallate, and carried them off to Babylon. Four hundred and eighteen years later, I (Sennacherib) brought them out of Babylon and returned them to their places in Ekallate.[5]

The number of years given by Sennacherib, 418, is slightly inaccurate. Calculating years backwards from 688–681, the time period during which the statues had presumably been retrieved, bring us back between 1106 and 1099. The event probably took place during the first half the reign of Marduk-nadin-ahhe since a *kudurru* dated to his tenth year mentions "the victory over Assyria." Soon, however, Tiglath-pileser struck back, engaging against Babylonian forces in two separate battles reported in the Synchronistic History:

> (Concerning) Tiglath-pileser I, king of Assyria, and Marduk-nadin-ahhe, king of Karduniash: twice Tiglath-pileser drew up a battle array of chariots, as many as were by the Lower Zab, opposite Ahizuhina, and in the second year he defeated Marduk-nadin-ahhe at Gurmarritu, which is upstream from Akkad. Dur-Kurigalzu, Sippar-of-Shamash, Sippar-of-Anunitu, Babylon and Opis, the great urban centers, he captured together with their forts. At that time, he plundered Ugarsallu as far as Lubda. He ruled every part of Suhu as far as Rapiqu.

The History spreads the events over two years, with an initial engagement near the border at the Lower Zab, and a second one during which the Assyrians sacked Babylon and other cities in the north. Inscriptions of Tiglath-pileser record the campaigns with different details, claiming that the first campaign also involved the capture of several towns in the Suhu, and that the second one culminated in the capture of Babylon and the torching of Marduk-nadin-ahhe's palaces. This detail constitutes the most conclusive evidence that the Second Dynasty of Isin had abandoned Dur-Kurigalzu as principal royal residence:

> By the command of the god Ninurta, who loves me, I marched to Karduniash. I conquered the cities of Dur-Kurigalzu, Sippar-of-Shamash, Sippar-of-Anunitu, Babylon (and) Opis, which is on the far side of the Tigris, the great towns of Karduniash together with their fortresses. I brought about the defeat of their multitudes (and) took prisoners without number from them. I captured the palaces of Babylon which belonged to Marduk-nadin-ahhe, king of Karduniash, (and) burnt them. In the eponymy of Ashur-shumu-erish (and) in the eponymy of Ninuaya, twice, I drew up a battle line of chariots against Marduk-nadin-ahhe, king of Karduniash, (and) defeated him.[6]

The chronological placement of Ashur-shumu-erish and Ninuaya among the eponyms of the reign of Tiglath-pileser cannot be determined. However, since they do not appear in a text listing the last eleven eponyms of his reign we must place the events before 1087 and therefore immediately in the wake of Marduk-nadin-ahhe's initial successes. A recently discovered inscription of Tiglath-pileser adds more details about the war, including a counter-attack by Marduk-nadin-ahhe:

> I demolished the palaces of the city of Babylon that belonged to Marduk-nadin-ahhe, king of Karduniash, (and) carried off a great deal of property from his palaces. Marduk-nadin-ahhe, king of Karduniash, relied on the strength of his troops and his chariots, and he marched after me. He fought with me at the city of Shitula, which is upstream from the city of Agade on the Tigris River, and I dispersed his numerous chariots. I brought about the defeat of his warriors (and) his fighters in that battle. He retreated and went back to his land.[7]

The battle at Shitula must be the same one recorded at Gurmarritu in the Synchronistic History. Evidence from other sources suggests a location near the Tigris for these two localities, between modern Tikrit and Samarra. Soon, however, Assyria became entangled in a protracted conflict with the Arameans, a new wave of invaders pressing at the western border of the kingdom. As a result, Tiglath-pileser became unable to continue the war with Babylon.

6.5.1 Aramean Invasions

The earliest mentions of the Arameans occur in texts from Kassite Babylonia where they appear as seasonal workers. Cuneiform sources refer to them as Ahlamu or Aramu, and sometimes by a combination of both terms, Aramu gradually becoming the more widely accepted designation. The Arameans belonged linguistically to the West Semitic branch. Their original homeland, like that of the Amorites, probably lay in the Jebel Bishri, where the Annals of Tiglath-pileser I locate several of their home cities. During his reign their presence suddenly became overwhelming, threatening the stability of both Assyria and Babylonia. Tiglath-pileser claims to have waged numerous battles against the Ahlamu Aramu in a vast territory stretching along the Euphrates. Although there is no direct evidence for any clash between Marduk-nadin-ahhe and the Arameans, Chronicle 15 seems to connect his demise with the turmoil they caused:

> [In the eponymy of o o o, the peop]le ate one another's flesh [o o o o o o] the Aramean houses [increased], plundered [o o o o o], conquered and took [many fortified cities of] Assyria. [People fled to]ward the mountains of Habruri to (save their) lives. They (= the Arameans) took their [gold], their silver, (and) their possessions. [Then Marduk-nadin-ahhe, the king of] Karduniash, disappeared. Marduk-[shapik]-zeri acceded to hi[s father's throne]. Eighteen turns of office (= years of reign) of Marduk-[nadin-ah]he.

6.6 Marduk-shapik-zeri (1077–1065)

Chronicle 15 claims that Marduk-nadin-ahhe "disappeared." In fact the succession to the throne may not have run smoothly. A *kudurru* dated to the first year of his son and successor Marduk-shapik-zeri records a grant of land to the prefect of the palace gate, one Shiriqti-Shuqamuna, son of Nazi-Marduk. The document specifies that the land had been confiscated from the previous holder of that office, a certain Uzib-Shiparru, son of Abirattash. In addition, the high office holders listed in the *kudurru* are mostly new individuals if we compare them with the holders of the same offices in the *kudurru*s from the reign of Marduk-nadin-ahhe. It would be premature to draw far-reaching conclusions from these facts, but minimally we can say that the accession of the new king was accompanied by the abrupt dispossession of at least one high official and the dismissal of several others. How that relates to the "disappearance" of Marduk-nadin-ahhe remains unclear. The reign of Marduk-shapik-zeri left a positive image in later chronicles. The Synchronistic History claims that "in the time of Ashur-bel-kala, king of Assyria, Marduk-shapik-zeri was the king of Karduniash. They made an entente cordiale together." The new climate of peace between Assyria and Babylon may have been prompted by their common fear of the Arameans. The same claim occurs in Chronicle 47, a Babylonian document, which adds further positive assessments of his rule:

> Marduk-shapik-zeri, the son of Marduk-nadin-ahhe, rebuilt the wall of Babylon. He conquered the kings of the lands. During his reign, the people of the land enjoyed prosperity. He made an entente cordiale with Ashur-bel-kala, king of Assyria. At that time, the king went from Assyria to Sippar.

6.7   Adad-apla-iddina (1064–1043)

Assyrian and Babylonian sources tell different stories about the origins of the next ruler of Babylon, Adad-apla-iddina. The Synchronistic History lays the following claim:

> At the time of Ashur-bel-kala, king of Assyria, Marduk-shapik-zeri, king of Karduniash, passed away. Ashur-bel-kala appointed Adad-apla-iddina, son of Esagil-shaduni, son of nobody, as sovereign over the Babylonians. Ashur-bel-kala, king of Assyria, married the daughter of Adad-apla-iddina, king of Karduniash, and took her with a vast dowry to Assyria. The peoples of Assyria and Karduniash were joined together.

The two Babylonian sources, Chronicles 46 and 47, insist on the contrary that Adad-apla-iddina was the son of, or descended from one Itti-Marduk-balatu, who might be the second Isin II ruler. In this case Adad-apla-iddina would have belonged to a collateral line of the ruling family. The two chronicles further claim that during his reign the Arameans and an unnamed usurper rebelled against him and desecrated the sanctuaries of Babylonia, specifically naming Agade, Der, Nippur, Sippar, and Dur-Kurigalzu. They also mention attacks by the Sutians, whose depredations at Sippar had long term consequences since they are also mentioned two centuries after the fact in the Sun-God Tablet of Nabu-apla-iddina. Adad-apla-iddina seems to have been quite active himself in repairing the damage wrought by the invaders; his inscriptions attest to his activities at Babylon, Borsippa, Nippur, Ur, Isin, Larsa, and Kish. The Assyrian claims of friendly relations recorded in the Synchronistic History are partly contradicted in an inscription of the Assyrian king Ashur-bel-kala, the Broken Obelisk. The inscription speaks about numerous campaigns against the Arameans but also boasts of conquests from Babylon and Akkad all the way to the Mediterranean Sea and mentions a raid against Babylonia during which the governor of the province of

Dur-Kurigalzu, one Kadashman-Buriash, son of Itti-Marduk-balatu, was captured. Some historians have noted that this Itti-Marduk-balatu might be the father of Adad-apla-iddina rather than the Isin II king of the same name, in which case the governor Kadashman-Buriash (a Kassite name) would have been his brother.

Later sources remembered Adad-apla-iddina as patron of scholarship and literature. Saggil-kinam-ubbib, the author of the Babylonian Theodicy, lived at the time of Adad-apla-iddina according to a catalogue of texts and authors from the Library of Ashurbanipal. A text from Uruk dating to the Seleucid era names him "chief scholar" (*ummanu*) of Nebuchadnezzar I and Adad-apla-iddina. Another important scholar of that period is Esagil-kin-apli, who compiled *Sakikku*, the most important medical treatise from Mesopotamia, known from many manuscripts found in Assyrian and Babylonian libraries of the first millennium. A colophon of *Sakikku* claims that Esagil-kin-apli created the treatise during the reign of Adad-apla-iddina in order to put diagnoses at the disposal of the king; it also attributes to Esagil-kin-apli the title of "chief scholar" of Sumer and Akkad. All this evidence seems to confirm the importance of Isin II in the intellectual history of Babylonia, with a number of foundational texts created at that time.

6.8   The End of Isin II (1042–1022)

The last three rulers of the dynasty: Marduk-ahhe-eriba (1042), Marduk-zer(?)-x (1041–1030) and Nabu-shumu-libur (1029–1022), are to us little more than names in king lists. From the reign of Nabu-shumu-libur comes a sale of land to the *shandabakku* of Nippur, one Nusku-zera-iddina, son of Nazi-Enlil (a Kassite name), the only mention of that office for the entire Isin II period. The person who sells the land, Mudammiqu, son of Ulam-gadida (a Kassite name too), had been redeemed by the *shandabakku* from captivity, hinting at the troubled conditions of that period. The selling price of the land may have been in fact reimbursement (totally or in part) for the redemption price paid by the *shandabakku*. Northern Babylonia may have been affected again by Aramean and perhaps Sutian invasions, while the dynasty vanished in obscure circumstances, with the center of power moving south again, to the Sealand.

NOTES

1. After Frame 1995: 55.
2. After Frame 1995: 34.
3. After Frame 1995: 18.
4. Adapted from Paulus 2013: 521.
5. After Grayson and Novotny 2014: 316.
6. After Grayson 1991: 43–4.
7. After George et al. 2011: 131.

FURTHER READING

Sources are edited by Paulus 2013 (*kudurru*s) and Frame 1995 (royal inscriptions and historical literature). Brinkman 1968 offers the only detailed historical survey of the period. Specific topics are covered by Nielsen 2012 (war of Nebuchadnezzar I against Elam), Brinkman 1968 (structure of provincial administration), Finkel 1988 (intellectual history), Neumann and Parpola 1987 (economic crisis of the late second millennium). For all question related to Enuma elish see the recent edition and discussion by Lambert 2013: 1–277, and 439–65.

Brinkman, John Anthony. 1963. "Provincial Administration in Babylonia under the Second Dynasty of Isin." *Journal of the Social and Economic History of the Orient* 6: 233–42.

Brinkman, John Anthony. 1968. *A Political History of Post-Kassite Babylonia (1158–722 B.C.).* Rome: Biblical Institute Press.

Finkel, Irving. 1988. "Adad-apla-iddina, Esagil-kīn-apli, and the Series SA.GIG." In Leichty, Erle, et al. (eds), *A Scientific Humanist, Studies in Memory of Abraham Sachs.* Philadelphia: University Museum. 143–59.

Frame, Grant. 1995. *Rulers of Babylonia: From the Second Dynasty of Isin to the End of Assyrian Domination (1157–612 BC):* The Royal Inscriptions of Mesopotamia, Babylonian Periods 2. Toronto: University of Toronto Press.

George, Andrew R. et al. 2011. *Cuneiform Royal Inscriptions and Related Texts in the Schøyen Collection.* Bethesda, MD: CDL Press.

Grayson, Albert Kirk. 1991. *Assyrian Rulers of the Early First Millennium BC I (1114–859 BC).* RIMA 2. Toronto: University of Toronto Press.

Grayson, Albert Kirk, and Novotny, Jamie. 2014. *The Royal Inscriptions of Sennacherib, King of Assyria (704–681 BC), Part 2.* RINAP 3/ 2. Winona Lake, IN: Eisenbrauns.

Lambert, Wilfred George. 2013. *Babylonian Creation Myths.* Winona Lake, IN: Eisenbrauns.

Neumann, J., and Parpola, Simo. 1987. "Climatic Change and the Eleventh–Tenth Century Eclipse of Assyria and Babylonia." *Journal of Near Eastern Studies* 46: 161–82.

Nielsen, John. 2012. "Nebuchadnezzar I's Eastern Front." In Galil, Gershon et al. (eds.), *The Ancient Near East in the 12th–10th Centuries BCE: Culture and History.* Münster, Ugarit-Verlag: 401–11.

Paulus, Susanne. 2013. *Die babylonischen Kudurru-Inschriften von der kassitischen bis zur frühneubabylonischen Zeit.* Münster: Ugarit-Verlag.

7

Arameans and Chaldeans

The period from the demise of the Second Dynasty of Isin until the Assyrian takeover of Babylonia in the second half of the eighth century bathes in relative obscurity. King List A divides it into four dynasties: three short ones between 1021 and 975, and the so-called Dynasty of E from 974 to 732. During that period Babylonia truly "hit bottom." The economic decline that had begun during Isin II continued until the middle of the eighth century. Archaeological surveys have determined that urban life reached its nadir during the first quarter of the first millennium, when no major building phase can be identified anywhere. Documentary sources also become very scarce. The internal chronology of the period presents numerous gaps since our sole source for the length of individual reigns, King List A, breaks off almost entirely between Nabu-mukin-apli (974–939) and Nabu-nadin-zeri (733–732). Royal inscriptions are found mostly on daggers from Iran or votive objects such as cylinder seals. Archival documentation reappears only after the middle of the eighth century, a tell-tale sign of the incapacity of the monarchy to uphold state institutions at the local level. Most of our data come from fifteen *kudurrus*, but this represents a small number considering that they spread over nearly three centuries. Bits of information found in chronicles and various Assyrian documents, mainly royal inscriptions and annals, complement this meager harvest. The settlement of two new ethnic groups, the Arameans and the Chaldeans, constitutes the most important event in the history of Babylonia during that period. Kassite influence seems to have waned by the middle of the ninth century, at about the same time when the Chaldeans first appear in our sources. These changes ushered into a new cultural period for Babylonia, the Neo-Babylonian period.

A History of Babylon: 2200 BC–AD 75, First Edition. Paul-Alain Beaulieu.
© 2018 John Wiley & Sons Ltd. Published 2018 by John Wiley & Sons Ltd.

7.1 The Arameans

As we have seen earlier, the most common designation for Arameans in first millennium sources is Aramu. Information on Aramean penetration in Babylonia after the end of Isin II remains sketchy. The few references in Babylonian chronicles depict them as hostile and intrusive. The inscriptions of Shamash-resha-usur and Ninurta-kudurri-usur, who ruled the Suhu as virtually independent sovereigns during the first half of the eighth century, describe at length their wars against the Aramean tribes of the Tu'manu and the Hatallu, who seem to have posed a major threat along the Middle Euphrates. The inscriptions of the Assyrian king Tiglath-pileser III (745–727) list thirty-six Aramean tribes he subjugated during his campaigns to Babylonia. In his summary inscription from Kalhu he claims to have conquered "all of the Arameans on the banks of the Tigris, Euphrates and Surappu rivers, as far as the Uqnu river, which is by the shore of the Lower Sea," implying that Arameans were to be found everywhere in Babylonia. Other sources indicate that the area along the Tigris constituted in fact the zone of heavier Aramean penetration. Two of the most influential Aramean tribes settled there: the Puqudu along the Uqnu River and in the marshy areas between Babylonia and Elam, and the Gambulu between Ur, the Uqnu River and the Elamite border. Both tribes still wielded considerable influence in the sixth century and a prominent Puqudu leader, Neriglissar, became king of Babylon in 560.

The lifestyle of Arameans in Babylonia bore some resemblance to that of the Amorites. The areas along the Tigris lay in the dimorphic zone, well adapted to the life of semi-nomadic pastoralists, and there is little doubt that some Arameans kept that lifestyle long after their arrival in Babylonia. An inscription of the Assyrian king Sargon II describes the road from Assyria to the city of Babylon as infested with lions and jackals, adding that "Arameans and Sutians, tent-dwellers, fugitives, criminals and thieves, had established their lodgings in that desert and made the route through it desolate." Yet many Arameans eventually developed a sedentary economy combining agricultural and pastoralist activities. During his war against Marduk-apla-iddina II in 710 Sargon II claims to have raided Aramean settlements in the Gambulu district:

> The remainder of the rebellious Arameans who lived in their district (Gambulu) and had listened to Marduk-apla-iddina and Shutur-Nahhunte and had sought refuge at the Uqnu River, a distant territory, I destroyed their settlements like a flood and cut down the date palms, their support, and the groves, the pride of their district, and fed my troops with (the grain of) their granaries.[1]

Several other sources describe Arameans as owners of fields and date groves and in some cases specify that these had been stolen from urban dwellers. Individual Arameans can be designated by the demonyms Aramu and Aramayu (also Armayu). However, the more common practice was to refer to them by tribal affiliation (e.g. Puqudu or Puqudayu "Puqudean," Gambulu or Gambulayu "Gambulean"). Sources refer to Aramean tribal leaders as *nasiku*, loosely translated as "sheikh."

The most significant impact of the Arameans in Babylonia (and in Assyria as well) happened at the linguistic level. At the turn of the first millennium the Aramean states of northern Syria promoted Aramaic as language of administration and lapidary inscriptions. Aramaic was written with an alphabet derived from the Phoenician. In the ninth and eighth centuries Assyria annexed these states one after the other, often deporting large swaths of their population. By the end of the eight century Assyria had in effect become a bilingual state, where Assyrian cuneiform and alphabetic Aramaic, the latter written mostly on scrolls, coexisted in the administration (Figure 8.1). The presence of an important Aramean population in Assyria and Babylonia further increased the influence of Aramaic, which gradually gained ground as common vernacular. The Neo-Assyrian and Neo-Babylonian dialects of Akkadian begin to show signs of Aramaic influence in the eighth century, and starting in the seventh century, during Assyria's late imperial phase, Aramaic had begun to replace Akkadian as everyday language all over Iraq. The Babylonian imperial administration in the sixth century also used Aramaic extensively, but this documentation has all perished because of the fragility of the writing surfaces it used. Eventually Akkadian died out as living language like its predecessor Sumerian, although it continued to be written well into the Hellenistic and Parthian periods. Most scholars now agree that Aramaic had become the common everyday language in Babylonia at the latest by the end of the Achaemenid period in the fourth century.

7.2   The Chaldeans

The word Chaldean derives from Akkadian *Kaldu*, which refers both to the Chaldeans as a people and to Chaldea (see Map 7.1), the territory they inhabited (*mat Kaldu*). The demonym *Kaldayu* is also used for Chaldeans. The earliest cuneiform documents related to the Chaldeans date to the ninth century and portray them as already settled in Babylonia. Their region of origin and the circumstances which brought them to Babylonia remain unknown. The Chaldeans were divided into five major groups named after the head of a tribe. These follow the pattern *bit* PN "house of PN," which as we have seen is well attested also for the Kassites. The three largest groups, Bit-Amukani, Bit-Dakkuri, and Bit-Yakin played a pivotal role in the history of Babylonia, providing six of its rulers in the eighth and early seventh centuries. The other two groups, Bit-Sha'alli and Bit-Shilani, seem to have disbanded at the end of the eighth century, although Bit-Shilani occurs in an inscription of Nebuchadnezzar II in the early sixth century, perhaps as a historical reference. Chaldea extended along the Euphrates from Sippar and Babylon all the way south to the Persian Gulf, an area which included most of the major cities of Babylonia. Bit-Amukani lay between Uruk and Babylon and appears to have been the largest Chaldean group. According to the inscriptions of the Assyrian king Sennacherib (704–681) it included thirty-nine cities and 350 villages. Bit-Dakkuri lay south of Babylon, more specifically between Borsippa and Marad. Assyrian sources of the ninth century refer to Bit-Dakkuri as Bit-Adini, after the name of its then ruler, but

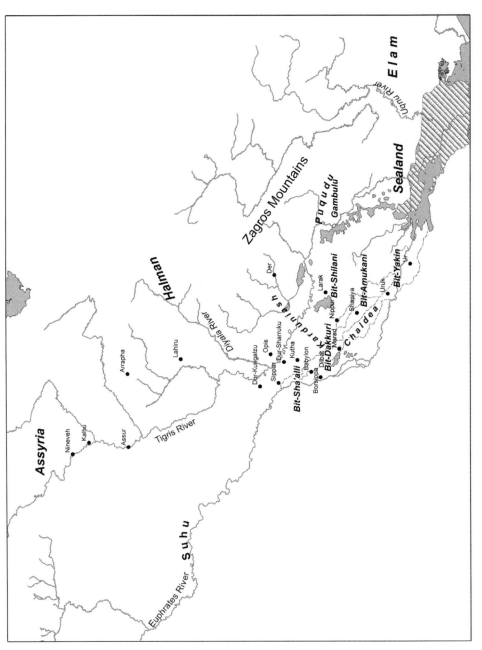

Map 7.1 Babylonia in the Early First Millennium. Map Design: Stephen Batiuk, University of Toronto.

this designation was later abandoned. Bit-Adini was also the name of an Aramean kingdom in northern Syria. Sennacherib ascribes thirty-three cities and 250 villages to Bit Dakkuri and eight cities and 100 villages to Bit-Sha'alli. The latter lay near Babylon and seems to have been dissolved and partly absorbed by Bit-Dakkuri around that time. Bit-Shilani was located near Larak and Nippur but little information has survived on its composition. Finally Bit-Yakin lay in the southernmost part of Babylonia and became closely identified with the Sealand. Sennacherib ascribes eight cities and 100 villages to Bit-Yakin. We do not know how representative these numbers are. They amount to suspiciously round figures. However, they still convey an image of Chaldea as densely populated area. The bronze gates erected by the Assyrian king Shalmaneser III at Balawat depict his armies capturing Chaldean walled settlements flanked with defensive towers. Chaldeans were also known to reside in the old urban centers of Babylonia.

The Chaldeans must have been related to Arameans, but we can resort only to linguistic criteria to investigate the question. The material at hand is restricted to the names of the five Chaldeans tribes, the names of individuals identified as Chaldean, and the names of cities that belonged to Chaldean territories and which followed the patterns *Bit* PN "House of PN" and *Dur* PN "Fort of PN." Most Chaldeans bore Babylonian names, which reflects their rapid acculturation. However, in the fifteen known instances where a Chaldean bore a name that is not Babylonian, the name can be classified broadly as West Semitic and in some cases as probably or definitely Aramean. The same applies to the names of the five Chaldean tribes: Dakkuru is very probably an Aramean word; Shilanu, Sha'allu, and Yakin are West Semitic and could well be Aramean; the etymology of Amukanu is unclear. We find a similar proportion of West Semitic and specifically Aramean names among the seventeen towns which belonged to Chaldean territories and were named after individuals. Thus, it appears that the Chaldeans belonged to the larger family of West Semitic peoples, and probably constituted a branch of the Arameans. However, our sources always carefully distinguish between Chaldeans and Arameans and maintain them as separate groups. For instance, an oracular consultation from the time of the Assyrian king Ashurbanipal asks whether Assyria's enemy of the moment will "fight and do battle with the men and army of Ashurbanipal, king of Assyria, or with the Assyrians, or the Akkadians (i.e. Babylonians), or the Chaldeans, or the Arameans." Contrary to Arameans, individual Chaldeans are designated in cuneiform sources as descendants (literally "sons") of the eponymous founder of their tribe. Thus a Dakkurean, a member of the Bit-Dakkuri, was designated as *mar Dakkuri* "descendant of Dakkuru," rather than Dakkurayu. A member of Bit-Yakin was a *mar Yakin* "descendant of Yakin." Chaldeans thus designated were often tribal leaders. Also, while the term *nasiku* referred to Aramean chieftains, Chaldean ones were called collectively *rash'anu* (or *ras'anu* in Assyrian sources). In sum, even if we assume that the Chaldeans were Aramaic speakers, it appears that historical factors favored the rise of a distinctive identity and social structure among them which set them apart from Arameans. At the same time, it seems certain that they contributed to the linguistic Aramaization of Babylonia, even though they embraced its traditional culture. Indeed, during the Persian and Hellenistic periods, Chaldea and Chaldean became synonym with Babylonia and Babylonian among the Greeks, and the term Chaldean acquired an even more specific meaning, referring to a specialist of the traditional lore of Babylonian sages, especially astrology and astronomy.

7.3　Three Short Dynasties

King List A and the Dynastic Chronicle agree on the basic chronological scheme and also on the names of the three dynasties which arose successively after the fall of Isin II. In modern terminology they are referred to as the Second Dynasty of the Sealand (Table 7.1), the Dynasty of Bazi (Table 7.2), and the Elamite Dynasty (Table 7.3). All three cover a period of less than fifty years.

King List A summarizes the three kings of the Second Dynasty of the Sealand as follows: "twenty-one (years and) five months, three kings, *palû* of the Sealand." The Dynastic Chronicle gives a slightly different figure: "three kings, *palû* of the Sealand; they reigned twenty-three years." Chronicle 47 claims that the founder of the dynasty was the son of a certain Eriba-Sin; this is confirmed by an inscription of Simbar-Shipak on a bronze arrow head. According to the Dynastic Chronicle, however, Eriba-Sin was not his father, but a distant ancestor: "Simbar-Shipak, a soldier resident of the Sealand, descendant of Eriba-Sîn, a soldier who died in combat during the reign of Damiq-ilishu, reigned seventeen years; he was buried in Sargon's palace." This Damiq-ilishu must probably be identified as the third ruler of the First Dynasty of the Sealand and the entry must reflect an attempt to connect the new royal house of the Sealand with the first one. According to an inscription of Nabu-apla-iddina, Simbar-Shipak tried to restore the cult of the god Shamash at Sippar which had been disrupted during the Aramean invasions. Chronicle 47 claims that he also made the throne of the god

Table 7.1　Second Dynasty of the Sealand

Simbar-Shipak	1021–1004
Ea-mukin-zeri	1004
Kasshu-nadin-ahhe	1003–1001

Table 7.2　Dynasty of Bazi

Eulmash-shakin-shumi	1000–984
Ninurta-kudurri-usur I	983–981
Shirikti-Shuqamuna	981

Table 7.3　Elamite Dynasty

Mar-biti-apla-usur	980–975

Enlil in the Ekur-igigal, and this is confirmed by an inscription of Simbar-Shipak known from a later copy. The inscription contains interesting historical details on the disruptions caused by the Arameans and Sutians:

> (Concerning) the throne of the god Enlil in Ekur-igigal, which Nebuchadnezzar (I), a previous king, had made, during the reign of Adad-apla-iddina, king of Babylon, the Aramean and Sutian foe, the enemy of Ekur and Nippur, the desecrator of Duranki (= Nippur), the one who upset their rites in Sippar, the ancient city and abode of the great judge of the gods (= Shamash), plundered the land of Sumer and Akkad and overthrew all the temples.[2]

The inscription also claims that the Assyrians returned to Nippur the goods plundered by the Arameans, and it ends with a description of the god Marduk taking his seat on the restored throne of Ekur-igigal in his quality as "Enlil of the Gods," the replacement of Enlil with Marduk being the outcome of the theological reforms initiated by Nebuchadnezzar I, who is named in the inscription as the original maker of the throne. Simbar-Shipak may have died a violent death since his successor Ea-mukin-zeri was a usurper according to the Dynastic Chronicle: "Ea-mukin-zeri, a usurper, a son of Hashmar, reigned three months; he was buried in the marshland of Bit-Hashmar." The Chronicle claims that the last ruler of the Dynasty, Kasshu-nadin-ahhe, was son of a certain Sippaya (or Sappaya), perhaps a shortened form of the name Simbar-Shipak. All three rulers of Sealand II appear to have had some Kassite background. The name Simbar-Shipak is purely Kassite. The usurper Ea-mukin-zeri bears an Akkadian name but he stemmed from Bit-Hashmar. Hashmar means "falcon" in Kassite according to the Kassite-Akkadian vocabulary from the Library of Ashurbanipal. The last ruler has an Akkadian name honoring a god named "the Kassite deity," *kasshu* being the demonym for Kassite: Kasshu-nadin-ahhe means "the Kassite god provides brothers." A governor of the Sealand who probably lived in the same period and left a dedicatory inscription on a cylinder seal known from a later copy, bears the name Kasshu-bel-zeri "the Kassite god is the lord of the progeny."

The Dynastic Chronicle sums up the dynasty which followed Sealand II as: "[Three king]s, the *palû* of Bit-Bazi; they [rei]gned twenty years and three months." King List A agrees with the count: "twenty (years and) three months, three kings, *palû* of Baz[u!]." The Dynastic Chronicle specifically qualifies each of its kings as "descendant of Bazi" (*mar Bazi*). Chronicle 20 claims that Shirikti-Shuqamuna reigned for three months over Babylon and that he was the brother of Nabu-kudurri-usur, a mistake for Ninurta-kudurri-usur. Bit-Bazi is attested during the Kassite and Isin II period as a clan which probably derived its name from the town Baz on the Tigris River. Some high officials under Isin II belonged to that clan. One of them is a certain Eulmash-shakin-shumi, descendant of Bazi, a homonym of the first king of the Dynasty of Bazi; he appears in two *kudurrus* from the reign of Marduk-nadin-ahhe. A Kassite connection for the Dynasty of Bazi might be inferred from the name of its last king, Shirikti-Shuqamuna "gift of the god Shuqamuna," which, although linguistically Akkadian, honors the patron god of the former Kassite dynasty.

King List A credits the ruler who succeeded the Dynasty of Bazi, a certain Mar-biti-apla-usur, with a reign of six years. The Dynastic Chronicle provides the same figure and ascribes Elamite ancestry to him, although his name is fully Akkadian: "[Mar-biti-apla-usu]r, a distant descendant of Elam, reigned six years; he was buried in Sargon's palace. [One king], the *palû* of [Ela]m; he reigned six years." Nothing else is known about his reign.

7.4   The Dynasty of E

The next dynasty according to King List A is the so-called Dynasty of E, the term E referring probably to Babylon. King List A contains a major gap at this point, preserving only the length of the reign of the first king (Nabu-mukin-apli) and the partly broken names of the last five kings (from Eriba-Marduk to Nabu-shuma-ukin II). It then sums up the royal line as *palû* of E. The designation "Dynasty of E" occurs only in King List A. The Dynastic Chronicle assigns rulers of that period to shorter dynasties, but unfortunately its preserved portion covers only the eighth century. The Dynasty of E hardly formed a cohesive royal line. Very little information has survived on the family relations between successive rulers. One major trend which deserves notice is the predominance of Nabu (seven instances) and Marduk (five instances) in royal names, a sharp contrast with the preceding three dynasties. The following Table 7.4 of rulers is reconstructed from various sources. The lengths of reigns cannot be ascertained for most of them.

Table 7.4   Dynasty of E

Name of Ruler	Dates	Origin	Royal Filiations
Nabu-mukin-apli	974–939	Babylonian	
Ninurta-kudurri-usur II	939	Babylonian	son of Nabu-mukin-apli
Mar-biti-ahhe-iddina	938–x	Babylonian	son of Nabu-mukin-apli
Shamash-mudammiq		Babylonian	
Nabu-shuma-ukin I		Babylonian	
Nabu-apla-iddina		Babylonian	son of Nabu-shuma-ukin I
Marduk-zakir-shumi I		Babylonian	son of Nabu-apla-iddina
Marduk-balassu-iqbi	x–813	Babylonian	son of Marduk-zakir-shumi I
Baba-aha-iddina	812–x	Babylonian	
Interregnum			
Ninurta-apla?-x		Babylonian	
Marduk-bel-zeri		Babylonian	
Marduk-apla-usur		Chaldean	
Eriba-Marduk		Chaldean (Yakin)	
Nabu-shuma-ishkun	760?–748	Chaldean (Dakkuru)	
Nabonassar	747–734	Babylonian	
Nabu-nadin-zeri	733–732	Babylonian	son of Nabonassar
Nabu-shuma-ukin II	732	Babylonian	

A Babylonian origin is presumed for each ruler unless sources specify another background. This is the case only for Marduk-apla-usur, Eriba-Marduk and Nabu-shuma-ishkun, all of Chaldean origin, Eriba-Marduk belonging to Bit-Yakin and his successor to Bit-Dakkuri.

7.4.1   Nabu-mukin-apli (974–939)

King List A ascribes thirty-six years to Nabu-mukin-apli, the first ruler of the Dynasty of E. The main sources for his reign are three *kudurrus* and Chronicle 51. The chronicle begins at least as early as Nabu-shumu-libur, the last Isin II ruler, and its preserved part covers the three ensuing dynasties, ending with Nabu-mukin-apli. It reports mainly ominous sightings in Babylon and disruptions of the New Year Festival. Thus we learn that the festival did not take place in the seventh and eighth years of Nabu-mukin-apli because the Arameans showed enmity, and that it was cancelled for nine more consecutive years later in his reign. A recently published *kudurru* from his sixteenth year (959) records the sale of two fields in or near Dur-Sharrukin, later known as Dur-Sharrukku near Opis. The payment is in kind but silver equivalents are provided. The list of officials witnessing the transaction recalls those of Isin II *kudurrus*; the governor of Isin heads the list, and two high officials are of Kassite descent (from Bit-Karzi-abku and Bit-Tunamissah). Another *kudurru* from his twenty-fifth year (950) deals with a dispute between two prominent families, one belonging to the Kassite clan of Abirattash. The background of the dispute involved arrears of taxes owed since the second year of Ninurta-kudurri-usur I (982). The settlement provided for payment of the arrears, again in kind, with high silver equivalents for grain, suggesting deteriorated economic conditions. The *kudurru* has a full length representation of the king with a caption reading "image of Nabu-mukin-apli, king of the totality, king of Babylon." Three sons of the king witnessed the transaction, two of whom, Ninurta-kudurri-usur (II) and Mar-biti-ahhe-iddina, succeeded their father on the throne. Nothing is known about their short reigns.

7.4.2   Assyrian Resurgence

The reign of the next Babylonian ruler, Shamash-mudammiq, is known almost exclusively from Assyrian sources. He was a contemporary of Adad-nerari II (911–891), who reasserted Assyrian power after the Aramean invasions. The Neo-Assyrian Canon of Eponyms starts with the reign of Adad-nerari, providing historians with an absolute chronology for Assyria which ties in with Babylonian chronology after 747. In his Annals Adad-nerari boasts of resounding victories over Babylonia:

(Adad-nerari II), conqueror of the entire land of Karduniash; who brought about the defeat of Shamash-mudammiq, king of Karduniash, from mount Yalman to the river Turan (= Diyala); (the region) from the city of Lahiru to Ugar-sallu was added

to the boundary of Assyria; I conquered the entire land of the city of Der; I brought
back the cities Arrapha and Lubdu, fortresses of Karduniash, into the boundaries
of Assyria.[3]

The Assyrian war against Babylonia, which resulted in the occupation of the
Trans-Tigridian region, is summarized at the beginning of his Annals and precedes the more detailed year by year account of his later campaigns beginning
with the eponymy of Dur-mati-Ashur in the year 901. The Synchronistic History
also reports on the events and adds that Shamash-mudammiq died and was
succeeded by Nabu-shuma-ukin I (erroneously called Nabu-shuma-ishkun). The
History claims that the conflict with Babylonia continued under Nabu-shuma-
ukin but eventually concluded with a peace agreement and diplomatic marriages
which cancelled off most of the territorial gains reported in the Annals of Adad-
nerari:

> They mutually gav[e] their daughters for wives. They concluded a mutual agreement
> and a total peace. The peoples of Assyria and Akkad were brought together. They
> establi[shed] a permanent boundary line from Til-Bit-Bari, which is up-river on the
> Zab, as far as Til-sha-Abtani and <Til>-sha-Zabdani.

The descendants of Nabu-shuma-ukin I occupied the throne for most of the
ninth century and the country experienced a revival under their rule.

7.4.3   Nabu-apla-iddina

Nabu-shuma-ukin I was succeeded by his son Nabu-apla-iddina, who reigned at
least thirty-two years according to a *kudurru* preserved in the Louvre. Since he was
a contemporary of the Assyrian kings Ashurnasirpal II (883–859) and Shalmaneser III (858–824) and his death occurred at the latest in 851, when Shalmaneser
III led a campaign to Babylonia to help his son Marduk-zakir-shumi quell a rebellion, Nabu-apla-iddina must have acceded to the throne in the 880s. His relations
with Assyria seem to have been generally peaceful, although the Annals of Ashurnasirpal II report on a campaign to the Suhu where he claims to have captured the
Babylonian governor together with the troops of Nabu-apla-iddina and their
commanding officer, a diviner named Bel-apla-iddina. The campaign took place
during the eponymy of Dagan-belu-nasir in the year 878, therefore early during
the reign of Nabu-apla-iddina, and the account of it in Ashurnasirpal's Annals is
notable for providing the earliest known reference to the Chaldeans: "fear of my
dominion reached as far as Karduniash, awe of my weapons overwhelmed Chaldea (*mat Kaldu*)." There is no evidence of ulterior conflict and the Synchronistic
History claims that Shalmaneser III and Nabu-apla-iddina "concluded a mutual
agreement and a total peace." A *kudurru* shaped in the form of a stone tablet and
dated to the twentieth year of Nabu-apla-iddina records a confirmation of land
ownership in Babylon to a priest with the same name. The relief carved on the

Figure 7.1 *Kudurru* of Nabu-apla-iddina. This tablet-shaped *kudurru* made from diorite is preserved in the British Museum (BM 90922). Coincidentally, the beneficiary of the donation, a priest named Nabu-apla-iddina, bears the same name as his royal benefactor. The two figures are identified with captions and the symbols of the gods who protect the transaction appear on top. The *kudurru* is dated in Babylon, I-20 in the twentieth year of the king. Measurements: 17.5 × 10.6 × 3.5 cm. *Source*: www.BibleLandPictures.com / Alamy Stock Photo.

obverse shows the priest greeting the king, who is depicted for the first time wearing the tasseled bonnet of early Neo-Babylonian kings (Figure 7.1). The *kudurru* also contains the last attestation of the governor of Isin heading the list of witnesses in a legal document.

7.4.3.1 The Sun-God Tablet

A *kudurru* known as the Sun-God Tablet of Nabu-apla-iddina ranks as the most remarkable Babylonian artifact of this period. Recorded on a stone tablet and dated at Babylon in the thirty-first year of the king (ca. 855), the transaction contains a historical prologue which recalls the vagaries of the cult of Shamash at Sippar since the days of Adad-apla-iddina in the eleventh century, when the Sutians (i.e. Arameans) desecrated the Ebabbar temple and caused the disappearance of the statue of the god. After an unfruitful inquiry into the features of the original image of Shamash, Simbar-Shipak installed a sun disk in the temple and established regular offerings for it, but these were interrupted during the reign of Kasshu-nadin-ahhe because of economic hardship. The high priest petitioned his successor Eulmash-shakin-shumi, who reinstated the offerings and granted him a prebend. Then during the reign of Nabu-apla-iddina the new high priest, Nabu-nadin-shumi, presented to the king a clay model of the original image of Shamash accidentally discovered on the bank of the Euphrates. Nabu-apla-iddina ordered the making of a new image and the full restoration of the cult of Shamash in Ebabbar with detailed prescriptions for offerings and ceremonies. The relief on the tablet depicts Nabu-apla-iddina being led by a protective deity into the presence of the god Shamash, who is seated under a dais with the large sun disk symbol standing on an altar in front of him (see book cover). The style of the relief harks back to the art of earlier periods, particularly the presentation scenes of Ur III and Old Babylonian cylinder seals. The antiquarian taste of the relief reflects nostalgia for an idealized past in the face of persistent disorder and settlement of foreign populations. A later copy of an administrative text shows that Nabu-apla-iddina also reorganized certain aspects of the cult at Uruk, specifically the distribution of sacrificial meat to prebendaries, including the king.

7.4.4 Marduk-zakir-shumi I

According to the Synchronistic History, Nabu-apla-iddina died during the reign of the Assyrian king Shalmaneser III and was succeeded by his son Marduk-zakir-shumi who soon faced a rebellion led by his brother Marduk-bel-usate. Shalmaneser went to his aid and defeated the insurgency, after which the two kings made a peace agreement. Apparently Marduk-bel-usate had captured a large swath of territory east of the Tigris. The Annals of Shalmaneser contain more details on the crushing of the rebellion, which necessitated two separate campaigns in his eighth and ninth years (851–850), the second one being decisive:

> In my ninth regnal year, in my second campaign (to Babylonia), I captured the city of Gannanate. To save his life Marduk-bel-usate went up to the city of Halman. I pursued him and put to the sword Marduk-bel-usate together with the treacherous soldiers who were with him. (Then) I marched to Babylon and made sacrifices in Babylon, Borsippa and Kutha. I went down to Chaldea and captured their cities. I marched to the sea called the Bitter River and received tribute in Babylon from Adinu, descendant of Dakkuru, and Mushallim-Marduk, descendant of Amukanu: silver, gold, ebony, and elephant tusks.[4]

Excavations at Kalhu, which had become the main Assyrian royal residence under Ashurnasirpal II, uncovered a throne base with a relief depicting Marduk-zakir-shumi and Shalmaneser III shaking hands, a unique instance of the Assyrians portraying a foreign ruler as an equal. Two of the epigraphs on the throne base report on the rest of the Babylonian campaigns with details similar to the Annals. However, they refer to the Chaldean leaders as "kings of Chaldea," and add tin, bronze, elephant hides and *meskannu*-wood to their tribute list, composed mainly of items not found in Babylonia and therefore probably obtained from the trade which passed through the Chaldean territories. The virtually independent status of Chaldean rulers in the south is reflected in a bronze bowl with an inscription of an official of the Chaldean ruler Adinu: "(Property) of Abdi-il, *shaknu* official of Adinu, descendant of Dakkuru."

In spite of its apparent beneficial effect and the display of equality between the two monarchs, Shalmaneser's intervention in Babylonian affairs encouraged the fragmentation of the country and its subordination to Assyria. Chaldea, albeit nominally part of Babylonia and subject to its monarch, had become in his view a separate territory ruled by local kings who brought tribute to the Assyrians in Babylon. Shalmaneser even travelled about the country performing sacrifices in its major shrines. The door had effectively opened for a takeover of the Babylonian monarchy by the Assyrians. Nevertheless, relations apparently stayed cordial for the entire duration of the reign of Marduk-zakir-shumi. Legal documents from his reign include two *kudurru*s dated to his second and eleventh years. The earliest one records a royal grant of land and prebendary office to Ibni-Isthar, a temple official at Uruk who was a lamentation singer of the goddess Ishtar, high priest of the goddess Usur-amassu and head scribe of the Eanna temple. The grant suggests that Marduk-zakir-shumi continued the reorganization of local cults initiated by his father. Heading the list of witnesses is the crown prince Marduk-balassu-iqbi who eventually succeeded his father, followed by Nabu-ahhe-iddin, a palace official, and interestingly a certain Iddin-Marduk, descendant of Amukanu, testifying to the growing influence of the Chaldeans. Other sources include a large cylinder seal of lapis lazuli dedicated to the god Marduk and a fragmentary tax exemption for the city of Borsippa. It mentions that tax-exempt status had been granted to Babylon in his accession year but that a similar privilege for Borsippa had to wait until his sixteenth year, apparently because of the trouble caused by the rebellion of Marduk-bel-usate.

7.4.5   Descent into Anarchy (819–770?)

The final years of Shalmaneser III were overshadowed by a rebellion in Assyria led by his son Ashur-da'in-aplu. It broke out in the year 827 and continued under various forms until the year 820, well into the reign of his other son and successor Shamshi-Adad V (823–811). The cause and course of the rebellion are not well known. It seems to have had some repercussions in Babylonia, reflected in a poorly preserved treaty between Shamshi-Adad and Marduk-zakir-shumi found at Nineveh; it dates probably from the early years of the rebellion since it does not give Shamshi-Adad the title of king. The details of the treaty are lost, but its most likely background would have been a request for support against the rebels, presumably in reciprocity for Shalmaneser's help in securing the Babylonian throne for Marduk-zakir-shumi a generation earlier. However, the alliance did not pay off. Once in control Shamshi-Adad turned against Babylon, where Marduk-balassu-iqbi had succeeded his father Marduk-zakir-shumi. The invasion of Babylonia is mentioned in the Neo-Assyrian Canon of Eponyms, the Synchronistic History and the Annals of Shamshi-Adad V, but these sources do not agree on the details. The Canon mentions three campaigns: in 814 to the city of Der across the Tigris (eponymy of Bel-lu-balat), in 812 to Chaldea (eponymy of Ninurta-ashared) and in 811 to Babylon (eponymy of Shamash-kamua). According to his Annals, Shamshi-Adad campaigned to Babylonia during three consecutive years. In his fourth campaign (814) he engaged in northeastern Babylonia with Marduk-balassu-iqbi who had mustered an impressive array of allies; the Annals mention the Kassites, the Arameans, the Elamites, and Namri. The Babylonians were defeated at Dur-Papsukkal. In his fifth campaign (813) Shamshi-Adad marched again to northeastern Babylonia and after some failed attempts captured Marduk-balassu-iqbi at Der and deported him to Nineveh together with the city's divine statues. Finally in his sixth campaign (812) he captured the new Babylonian king Baba-aha-iddina and deported him to Assyria. The Synchronistic History conflates this campaign with the one to Der and adds that Shamshi-Adad traveled to Kutha, Babylon, and Borsippa to perform sacrifices and then marched to Chaldea where he received the tribute of its kings.

During the last year of his reign (812–811) Shamshi-Adad took up the title of "king of Sumer and Akkad," which is recorded on several inscribed bricks from Nineveh and Assur and also on his sarcophagus found at Assur. The Neo-Assyrian Canon of Eponyms mentions another campaign to Babylonia but nothing more is known about it. Shamshi-Adad was succeeded by his son Adad-nerari III (810–783). After the capture of Baba-aha-iddina, who reigned probably not more than a year, the Babylonian throne seems to have become vacant. At this point Chronicle 47 has an entry stating that "there was no king in the country." An isolated administrative document which might belong to that period bears the date formula "Month Kislimu, twenty-first day, fourth year when there was no king in the land." During this interregnum of indeterminate length Chaldean princes asserted their independence. A cylinder seal depicting a bearded male figure coiffed with a round cap and carrying a staff is inscribed in the name of "Marduk-shakin-shumi, son of Marduk-zera-uballit, descendant of Yakin." The figure displays aspects of royal iconography and the owner of the seal might be the father of Eriba-Marduk, the leader of Bit-Yakin who became king of Babylon in the eighth century. The Bit-Dakkuri also harbored royal ambitions reflected in a jadeite stone weight inscribed as

Figure 7.2   Inscribed Weight of Nabu-shuma-lishir. This ovoid weight made from feldspar was purchased in Cyprus between 1865 and 1872. The inscription reads: "One-third mina, correct (weight), Palace of Nabu-shumu-lishir, the Dakkurian". The object bears witness to the nearly independent status of Chaldean territories in Babylonia. Measurements: W: 4.28 in. (10.87 cm). *Source*: The Metropolitan Museum of Art (MMA 74.51.4426). Public Domain.

follows: "One third mina, correct (weight); palace of Nabu-shumu-lishir, descendant of Dakkuru" (Figure 7.2). Guaranteeing weights and claiming a palace as residence amounted to usurping royal status. The Assyrians also took advantage of the power vacuum to impose their suzerainty over the country. This is what Adad-nerari III claims in an inscription on a stone slab from Kalhu:

> All the kings of Chaldea became my vassals and I imposed upon them in perpetuity tax and tribute. At Babylon, Borsippa and Kutha they brought to me the remnant offerings of the gods Bel, Nabu and Nergal. [I made] pure sacrifices.[5]

Receiving remnants of sacrificial meals constituted a royal privilege and signaled the takeover of the Babylonian crown by the Assyrians, at least nominally. Indeed, Assyria entered a period of relative weakness which prevented it from fully exploiting the situation, although the Synchronistic History, compiled around that time, ends its narrative with a note that Adad-nerari allowed the deported inhabitants (of Babylonia) to return home, granting them income, privileges, and food rations.

In the end the Babylonian monarchy proved its resilience and reemerged as rallying institution for the country, but under increasing Chaldean control. King List 14 names three rulers who can be inserted between the interregnum and the accession of Eriba-Marduk: one Ninurta-apla(?)-x, nothing more than a broken name in the list; one Marduk-bel-[zeri], whose full name is known from an administrative text dated to his accession year which constitutes the only other source for his reign; and one Marduk-apla-usur. The Dynastic Chronicle resumes at this point and lists Marduk-apla-usur as the single member of a Dynasty of Chaldea (*palê Kaldi*). A third mention of Marduk-apla-usur occurs in the pamphlet against Nabu-shuma-ishkun where he is given the epithet of "Chaldean" (LÚ *Kaldi*). Therefore it seems that Marduk-apla-usur must be reckoned as the first Chaldean king of Babylon.

7.4.6   Eriba-Marduk

After Marduk-apla-usur the Dynastic Chronicle includes Eriba-Marduk as the sole representative of a Sealand Dynasty (*palê Tamti*), the third one in the history of Babylon. The Sealand was the home of the Chaldean tribe of Bit-Yakin. The Chaldean king of Babylon Marduk-apla-iddina II, who stemmed from Bit-Yakin, names Eriba-Marduk as his forefather, on which basis we may assume that Eriba-Marduk was also a "descendant of Yakin." A legal document was drafted at Babylon in the ninth year of his reign, which ended around 1760, the assumed accession year of his successor Nabu-shuma-ishkun. Marduk-apla-iddina II refers to Eriba-Marduk as "king of justice" and as one "who reestablished the foundations of the land." Such claims are supported by Chronicle 47:

> Eriba-Marduk, son of Marduk-shakin-shumi, in (his) second year, took the hand of the god Bel (Marduk) and of the son of the god Bel (Nabu). He joined battle and defeated the Arameans who, (amidst) the disorder(?) and anarchy, had appropriated the fields of the inhabitants of Babylon and Borsippa. Having retaken from them their fields and gardens, he gave them to the inhabitants of Babylon and Borsippa. The same year, in the Esagil and the Ezida temples [o], he installed the [thro] ne of the god Bel.

A recently published inscription of Eriba-Marduk corroborates these claims, although it is preserved in a fragmentary state. Eriba-Marduk bears the titles of "king of Babylon" and "king of righteousness" and the narrative centers on the refurbishing of the attire of a god, probably Marduk. According to the Assyrian king Esarhaddon, Eriba-Marduk also restored E-hili-anna, the sanctuary of the goddess Nanaya at Uruk. Nabonidus also mentions that during the reign of Eriba-Marduk the citizens of Uruk had removed the old cultic image of the goddess Ishtar from the Eanna temple and replaced it with an inappropriate one, but the scribes of Nabonidus possibly misinterpreted their sources and the episode most likely happened during the reign of his successor Nabu-shuma-ishkun. One *kudurru* is dated to the reign of Eriba-Marduk.

7.4.7   Nabu-shuma-ishkun (760?–748)

The Dynastic Chronicle records a change of dynasty after Eriba-Marduk, listing one single ruler stemming from Chaldea (*mat Kaldi*). The name of the ruler is lost but King List A and King List 14 know him as Nabu-shuma-ishkun. His reign ended in 748 and must have begun at the latest in 760 since an economic document is dated to his thirteenth year. Two important texts shed light on his reign. They also inform us that he stemmed from the Chaldean clan of Bit-Dakkuri. One is a later copy of a building inscription from Borsippa which records repairs in the storehouse of the Ezida temple and attributes the responsibility for the work to the governor of Borsippa, one Nabu-shuma-imbi, who also appears as witness in a *kudurru* from Borsippa dated to the king's eighth year. The inscription reports on disturbances at Borsippa:

> Disorders, disturbances, revolt and turmoil occurred in Borsippa, the city of truth and justice. During the reign of king Nabu-shuma-ishkun, descendant of Dakkuru, the Babylonians, the Borsippeans and (the citizens of) the town Duteti on the bank of the Euphrates, all the Chaldeans, the Arameans (and) the people of Dilbat whetted their weapons (against) one another and slew one another during many days. They also fought with the Borsippeans over their fields.[6]

The text describes how Nabu-shuma-imbi and a priest named Nabu-shuma-iddin withstood the assault of the trouble-makers. The state of strife it describes recalls Chronicle 47 on the reign of Eriba-Marduk and probably reflects a frequent scenario during that period, groups of urban residents fighting over resources with Chaldeans and Arameans as well as among each other. The absence of effective royal authority seems remarkable considering the proximity of Borsippa to the capital and reflects the chaotic conditions then prevailing. Borsippa seems to have been the theater of prolonged disturbances. Chronicle 19 claims that in the fifth and sixth years of Nabu-shuma-ishkun the statue of the god Nabu could not even leave Borsippa to participate in the New Year Festival in Babylon.

Far more dramatic events transpire from a text discovered at Uruk and dating to the late fourth century. It details various crimes and sacrileges attributed to Nabu-shuma-ishkun in the form of a chronicle of his reign (Chronicle 52), constituting a veritable *damnatio memoriae* that is almost unique in Babylonian historiography. The charges include various cultic outrages he committed at Borsippa such as covering the god Nabu with the garment of Marduk and proposing the latter's marriage to Tashmetu, Nabu's wife, and force-feeding leeks, the sacred food of Nabu, to the priests of the Ezida temple. In his sixth year Nabu-shuma-ishkun apparently plundered the treasury of the Esagil in Babylon to give it to the gods of the Sealand, of the Chaldeans, and of the Arameans. In his seventh year he even turned against his own constituency, the Bit-Dakkuri. The catalogue of misdeeds is substantial and one wonders how much of this is reliable. The text is a copy from an earlier manuscript and there is little doubt that it goes back to the reign of Nabu-shuma-ishkun or shortly thereafter, as some charges seem too specific, even referring to individuals by name, to be the product of later invention. It credits Nabu-shuma-ishkun with actual power, but this seems contradicted by the Borsippa inscription which depicts him wielding only nominal authority. One misdeed ascribed to Nabu-shuma-ishkun left a lasting memory at Uruk and may explain why the pamphlet against him was discovered there. As we have just seen an inscription of Nabonidus claims that the goddess Ishtar was removed from a shrine at Uruk during the reign of Eriba-Marduk, giving specific details about her appearance. In a damaged passage the pamphlet reports on some misdeed against the goddess Ishtar and describes her sitting on a throne with seven lions. Since these details correspond closely to those of the Nabonidus inscription it seems probable that some confusion occurred in the transmission of the historical tradition and that the event probably occurred during Nabu-shuma-ishkun's reign.

7.4.8 Nabonassar (747–734)

The accession of Nabonassar constitutes a milestone in ancient chronography since the Ptolemaic Canon begins with him. The conventional form Nabonassar derives from the Greek spelling Nabonassaros found in the Canon and other classical sources. In Babylonian his name was Nabu-nasir "the god Nabu is the protector." No evidence links Nabonassar to his predecessor or to any of the Chaldean tribes of Babylonia and therefore the general assumption is that the throne reverted to a native Babylonian family after the death of Nabu-shuma-ishkun, even though we do not know the circumstances which brought Nabonassar to power. The Dynastic Chronicle breaks off at this point and does not preserve his name, but it does assume a change of dynasty after Nabu-shuma-ishkun. Our main source for the reign of Nabonassar and his two successors is Chronicle 16. The most significant event it records is the accession of the Assyrian king Tiglath-pileser III (745–727) in Nabonassar's third year (745) followed by his invasion of northern Babylonia, where he raided the towns of Rabbilu and Hamrana and captured the gods of Shapazza. The Annals of Tiglath-pileser inscribed on the walls of his palace at Kalhu tell a somewhat different story, claiming that he subjugated several Aramean tribes, deported many of their members, annexed large swathes of Babylonia from Sippar and Dur-Kurigalzu to the river Uqnu in the southeast and appointed a governor over them. The campaign followed some logic since it took place in the area where Aramean tribes were most active, from the Suhu to the border of Elam, and they, rather than Babylonia itself, may have been its main target. Indeed, Tiglath-pileser still allowed Nabonassar to rule southwestern Babylonia along the Euphrates, but these areas seem to have only loosely recognized his authority. Chaldean territories retained their semi-independent status and Chronicle 16 claims that Borsippa rebelled against Nabonassar, although it does not furnish any additional detail on the event, nor does it attempt to date it. A building inscription from Uruk dated to his fifth year (743) records the repair of the *akitu* temple of the goddess Usur-amassu, insisting on the fact that it had long been neglected. Although the inscription acknowledges the rule of Nabonassar, his involvement in the project is inexistent and two leading citizens of Uruk receive all the credit for it. Yet, for all his relative weakness, Chronicle 16 tells us that Nabonassar was still able to pass the scepter on to his son Nabu-nadin-zeri, who lost it two years later in a coup, however:

> The fourteenth year (of his reign), Nabonassar became ill and went to his destiny (i.e. died) in his palace. Nabonassar reigned fourteen years over Babylon. His son Nadin (= Nabu-nadin-zeri) ascended the throne of Babylon. The second year (of his reign), Nadin was killed during an insurrection. Nadin reigned two years over

Babylon. Shuma-ukin (= Nabu-shuma-ukin II), a governor and leader of the insurrection, ascended the throne. Shuma-ukin reigned one month (and) two days(?) over Babylon. Mukin-zeri (= Nabu-mukin-zeri), descendant of Amukanu, removed him and took the throne.

King List A gives the full name of Nabonassar's son as Nabu-nadin-zeri and that of his successor as Nabu-shuma-ukin. The short form Nadin entered the Ptolemaic Canon as Nadios. King List A also assigns a very short reign to Nabu-shuma-ukin II ("one month and thirteen days") but claims him to be the son of his predecessor, in which case the compiler possibly meant "son of Nabonassar." The reign of Nabu-shuma-ukin II was too brief to be recorded in the Ptolemaic Canon. A Chaldean prince named Mukin-zeri (short form of Nabu-mukin-zeri), the leader of Bit-Amukani, grabbed the scepter. During the reign of Nabonassar archival sources reappear after a hiatus of several centuries, and we can follow the career of this Mukin-zeri before his accession to the throne in two groups of letters, one from Nippur, and the other one from Kalhu.

7.4.8.1 The Nippur letters

In the fall of 1973 the University of Chicago excavations at Nippur uncovered a group of 113 letters in secondary context. None of them is dated but their language and contents allow us to place them in the middle of the eighth century. Several letters mention a prominent individual named Mukin-zeri and one of them associates him with the city of Shapiya. According to King List A and the inscriptions of Tiglath-pileser III, Shapiya was the city of origin of the Chaldean king Mukin-zeri, therefore it seems clear that most references to Mukin-zeri in the Nippur letters should be to that same individual. However, they never give him the title of king and must date before his accession in 732, suggesting that the bulk of the correspondence belongs to the reign of Nabonassar and his two ephemeral successors. An important individual named Nabu-nasir also appears as correspondent in a few letters and some have proposed to identify him with Nabonassar the king, but the context and tone of the letters make that dubious. The opinion originally prevailed that the letters stemmed from the archives of the governor of Nippur (the *shandabakku*), but this view has since been largely abandoned. The majority of them deals with commerce, the kidnapping and redemption of captives, and originates from mid-level administrators and private parties with institutional connections. Chaldean and Aramean tribes are mentioned several times in the context of trade and military activities, confirming the portrait of Babylonia as an unstable polity where tribal leaders wielded considerable power.

7.4.8.2 The Kalhu letters

British excavations at Nimrud (ancient Kalhu) uncovered letters from the state correspondence of Tiglath-pileser III and Sargon II. A portion of the letters deals with the affairs of Babylonia, especially the fight against Mukin-zeri after his accession to the throne. However, two letters might contain references to Nabonassar and his son Nabu-nadin-zeri. One alludes to events involving a conflict between Babylon and Borsippa:

> Earlier Nabu-nasir wrote to the king (of Assyria as follows): "Mukin-zeri has moved horses from the gate of Borsippa against Babylon, so nobody can leave Babylon and we cannot cultivate (our fields)." After that the king (of Assyria) wrote (as follows): "Make peace between Babylon and Borsippa." I and the chieftains of Chaldea went and brought out the horses from Borsippa.[7]

The names of the two correspondents are unknown and there is no assurance that the Nabu-nasir they mention is identical with Nabonassar the king, but the letter alludes to circumstances which recall the revolt of Borsippa against him reported in Chronicle 16. The other letter, which also does not preserve the names of the correspondents, ends with a poorly preserved note concerning the celebration of the New Year Festival: "News of Babylon: the god Marduk left (his temple) in procession on the twenty-fifth day of the month of Addaru. The son of Nabu-nasir has given the [...]." Considering the level of royal involvement in the festival there is a strong possibility that this Nabu-nasir is indeed the same as the king, in which case his son would probably be Nabu-nadin-zeri before or during his short rule.

7.4.8.3   The era of Nabonassar

In spite of its lack of luster, the reign of Nabonassar was remembered in the classical tradition as a turning point in the development of Babylonian science and scholarship. Berossus provides the earliest testimony for this view: "Nabonasaros collected together and destroyed the records of the kings before him in order that the list of the Chaldean kings might begin with him." This curious statement may have originated as an explanation for the general dearth of written sources before Nabonassar. Astronomical observations certainly began to be recorded systematically during his reign. Ptolemy had access to complete records of eclipses at Babylon back to his accession year and some cuneiform tables of eclipses including the Saros Canon also begin at that time. The case is less clear for astronomical diaries since the earliest example we have dates to the middle of the seventh century, but we have very few diaries before the fourth century. The information recorded in chronicles also becomes more plentiful at that time, probably reflecting a more methodical collection of data and observations. The fact that the Ptolemaic Canon begins with Nabonassar constitutes the most eloquent evidence of these changes. Some have argued that scribes and chronographers recognized an "era of Nabonassar," but its use seems to have been limited to ancient astronomers, the main evidence coming from Ptolemy's Almagest.

NOTES

1. Adapted from Fuchs 1994: 329–30.
2. After Frame 1995: 72–3.
3. After Grayson 1991: 148.
4. After Grayson 1996: 37.
5. After Grayson 1996: 213.
6. After Frame 1995: 124.
7. After Luukko 2012: 135–6.

FURTHER READING

Sources are edited by Frame 1995 (royal inscriptions) and Paulus 2013 (*kudurru*s). The Nippur letters are edited by Cole 1996, and the Kalhu letters by Luukko 2012. Specific sources are discussed by Woods 2004 (Nabu-apla-iddina) and Cole 1994 (Nabu-shuma-ishkun). Brinkman 1968 covers the political history and the settlement of Arameans and Chaldeans. On these two groups see also Fales 2011, Frame 2013, Lipínski 2000, Rowton 1987, and Zadok 2013. On the concept of the "era of Nabonassar" see Hallo 1988.

Brinkman, John Anthony. 1968. *A Political History of Post-Kassite Babylonia (1158–722 B.C.)*. Rome: Biblical Institute Press.

Cole, Steven W. 1994. "The Crimes and Sacrileges of Nabû-šuma-iškun." *Zeitschrift für Assyriologie und vorderasiatischen Archäologie* 84: 220–52.

Cole, Steven W. 1996. *The Early Neo-Babylonian Governor's Archive from Nippur*. Chicago: The Oriental Institute of the University of Chicago.

Fales, Frederick Mario. 2011. "Moving around Babylon: On the Aramean and Chaldean Presence in Southern Mesopotamia." In Cancik-Kirschbaum, Eva, et al. (eds.), *Babylon. Wissenskultur in Orient und Okzident*. Berlin: De Gruyter. 91–111.

Frame, Grant. 1995. *Rulers of Babylonia: From the Second Dynasty of Isin to the End of Assyrian Domination (1157–612 BC)*: The Royal Inscriptions of Mesopotamia, Babylonian Periods 2. Toronto: University of Toronto Press.

Frame, Grant. 2013. "The Political History and Historical Geography of the Aramean, Chaldean, and Arab Tribes in Babylonia in the Neo-Assyrian Period." In Berlejung, Angelika, and Streck Michael (eds.). *Aramaeans, Chaldaeans, and Arabs in Babylonia and Palestine in the First Millennium B.C.* Wiesbaden: Harrassowitz. 87–121.

Fuchs, Andreas. 1994. *Die Inschriften Sargons II. Aus Khorsabad*. Gottingen: Cuvillier Verlag.

Grayson, Albert Kirk. 1991. *Assyrian Rulers of the Early First Millennium BC I (1114–859 BC)*. RIMA 2. Toronto: University of Toronto Press.

Grayson, Albert Kirk. 1996. *Assyrian Rulers of the Early First Millennium BC II (858–745 BC)*. RIMA 3. Toronto: University of Toronto Press.

Hallo, William W. 1988. "The Nabonassar Era and other Epochs in Mesopotamian Chronology and History." In Leichty, Erle et al. (eds), *A Scientific Humanist: Studies in Memory of Abraham Sachs*. Philadelphia: The University Museum. 175–90.

Lipínski, Edward. 2000. *The Aramaeans: Their Ancient History, Culture, Religion*. Leuven: Peeters.

Luukko, Mikko. 2012. *Correspondence of Tiglath-pileser III and Sargon II from Calah/Nimrud:* State Archives of Assyria 19. Helsinki: Helsinki University Press.

Paulus, Susanne. 2013. *Die babylonischen Kudurru-Inschriften von der kassitischen bis zur frühneubabylonischen Zeit.* Munster: Ugarit-Verlag.

Rowton, Michael B. 1987. "The Role of Ethnic Invasion and the Chiefdom Regime in Dimorphic Interaction: The Post Kassite Period (ca. 1150–750 B.C.)." In Rochberg-Halton, Francesca (ed.), *Language, Literature, and History: Studies Erica Reiner.* New Haven: American Oriental Society. 367–78.

Tadmor, Hayim, and Yamada, Shigeo. 2011. *The Royal Inscriptions of Tiglath-Pileser III (744–727 BC) and Shalmaneser V (726–722 BC), Kings of Assyria.* Winona Lake, IN: Eisenbrauns.

Woods, Christopher E. 2004. "The Sun-God Tablet of Nabû-apla-iddina Revisited." *Journal of Cuneiform Studies* 56: 23–104.

Zadok, Ran. 2013. "The Onomastics of the Chaldean, Aramean, and Arabian Tribes in Babylonia during the First Millennium." In Berlejung, Angelika, and Streck, Michael (eds.). *Aramaeans, Chaldaeans, and Arabs in Babylonia and Palestine in the First Millennium B.C.* Wiesbaden; Harrassowitz. 261–336.

8

The Assyrian Century

The rise of the Chaldean leader Mukin-zeri ushered in a century-long period of Assyrian supremacy. The Neo-Assyrian state of the late eighth and seventh centuries represented a new phenomenon, arguably the first centralized bureaucratic empire in world history. Neo-Assyrian rulers also laid claims to universal dominion, paving the way for subsequent multinational empires in the Near East. Although Assyria succeeded in establishing political and military control over Babylonia, the Assyrian empire rapidly collapsed at the end of the seventh century to give way to a renewed Babylonian state which stepped into the role of hegemonic power. Compared with the previous centuries, the period of Assyrian dominance is relatively well documented mainly because of the discovery at Nineveh of thousands of letters from the state correspondence of the kings of Assyria (Figure 8.1). Other sources include Babylonian archival documents, the Annals of Assyrian kings and their building inscriptions from Babylonia, and finally chronicles and king lists. King List A subsumes all kings recognized in Babylon between 731 and 626 under one unnamed group which has been labeled "Ninth Dynasty of Babylon" in modern historiography. Table 8.1 lists all these rulers with the length of their tenure, their ethnic origin, and their filiations.

King List A recognizes the lack of cohesion of the so-called Ninth Dynasty since it adds supplemental dynastic notations for all rulers until the sack of Babylon by Sennacherib in 689 (Table 8.2). These notations are introduced by the terms *palû* "dynasty" or *sabu* "troops, army," or else by filiation "son of." Their meaning is not always clear. Two of them, the *palû* of the Sealand and the *palû* of E, occur as designations of previous Babylonian dynasties in King List A. Some rulers have no such affiliation but it is quite evident that in these cases they must form a group with their successor. This is the case for Tiglath-pileser III, who

A History of Babylon: 2200 BC–AD 75, First Edition. Paul-Alain Beaulieu.
© 2018 John Wiley & Sons Ltd. Published 2018 by John Wiley & Sons Ltd.

Figure 8.1   Cuneiform and Alphabetic Scribes. This scene on gypsum relief from the South-West palace of Nineveh (Room XXVIII, Panel 9) dates to the seventh century. It probably depicts an episode in the wars of Ashurbanipal (or, less likely, Sennacherib) against Babylonia. Prisoners are led through date palm orchards to the Assyrian camp where a soldier has brought enemy heads. Two scribes record the scene. One holds a writing board or tablet, writing in cuneiform Assyrian, and the other one a scroll, for Aramaic. The relief is preserved in the British Museum (BM 124955). Measurements: H: 1.524 × W: 1.632 m. *Source*: © The Trustees of the British Museum.

forms a *palû* of Baltil (i.e. Assur) with his son and successor Shalmaneser V; for Sargon II and his son Sennacherib, subsumed under a *palû* of Habigal, a designation also applied to Sennacherib's son Ashur-nadin-shumi; and finally for Nergal-ushezib and Mushezib-Marduk, who both belonged to a *palû* of E although they came from different backgrounds.

Another important document is the Ptolemaic Canon, which includes a list of Babylonian kings from 747 to 539, from the first year of Nabonassar until the fall of Babylon to the Persians. The Canon contains data which are slightly at variance with King List A and must therefore be taken into consideration. Table 8.3 lists the names of rulers as they appear in their corrupt Greek forms, followed by their original names and the length of their reigns according to the Canon.

Table 8.1   Ninth Dynasty of Babylon (731–626)

Nabu-mukin-zeri	731–729	Chaldean (Amukanu)	
Tiglath-pileser III (Pulu)	728–727	Assyrian	
Shalmaneser V (Ululayu)	726–722	Assyrian	son of Tiglath-pileser III
Marduk-apla-iddina II	721–710	Chaldean (Yakin)	son of Eriba-Marduk
Sargon II	709–705	Assyrian	son(?) of Tiglath-pileser III
Sennacherib	704–703	Assyrian	son of Sargon II
Marduk-zakir-shumi II	703	Babylonian	son of Arad-(Ea/Enlil)
Marduk-apla-iddina II	703	Chaldean	son of Eriba-Marduk
Bel-ibni	702–700	Babylonian	descendant of Rab-bani
Ashur-nadin-shumi	699–694	Assyrian	son of Sennacherib
Nergal-ushezib (Shuzubu)	693	Babylonian	descendant of Gahal
Mushezib-Marduk (Shuzubu)	692–689	Chaldean (Dakkuru)	
Sennacherib	688–681	Assyrian	son of Sargon II
Esarhaddon	680–669	Assyrian	son of Sennacherib
Ashurbanipal	668	Assyrian	son of Esarhaddon
Shamash-shumu-ukin	667–648	Assyrian	son of Esarhaddon
Kandalanu	647–627	Babylonian (?)	
Interregnum	626		
Sin-shumu-lishir		Assyrian	
Sin-sharru-ishkun		Assyrian	son of Ashurbanipal

Table 8.2   Dynastic affiliations for the "Ninth Dynasty of Babylon"

Nabu-mukin-zeri	731–729	Dynasty of Shapiya
Tiglath-pileser III (Pulu)	728–727	—
Shalmaneser V (Ululayu)	726–722	Dynasty of Baltil
Marduk-apla-iddina II	721–710	Dynasty of the Sealand
Sargon II	709–705	—
Sennacherib	704–703	Dynasty of Habigal
Marduk-zakir-shumi II	703	Son of Arad-(Ea/Enlil)
Marduk-apla-iddina II	703	Soldier of Habi
Bel-ibni	702–700	Dynasty of E
Ashur-nadin-shumi	699–694	Dynasty of Habigal
Nergal-ushezib	693	—
Mushezib-Marduk	692–689	Dynasty of E
Sennacherib	688–681	
Esarhaddon	680–669	
Ashurbanipal	668	
Shamash-shumu-ukin	667–648	
Kandalanu	647–627	
Interregnum	626	
Sin-shumu-lishir		
Sin-sharru-ishkun		

Table 8.3 The Ptolemaic canon (747–539)

Greek name	Original name	Length of Reign
Nabonassaros	Nabu-nasir	14 years (747–734)
Nadios	Nabu-nadin-zeri	2 years (733–732)
Chinzeros and Poros	Nabu-mukin-zeri and Pulu	5 years (731–727)
Ilulayos	Ululayu	5 years (726–722)
Mardokempados	Marduk-apla-iddina (II)	12 years (721–710)
Arkeanos	Sharru-ukin	5 years (709–705)
First interregnum	—	2 years (704–703)
Belibos	Bel-ibni	3 years (702–700)
Aparanados	Ashur-nadin-shumi	6 years (699–694)
Regebelos	Nergal-ushezib	1 year (693)
Mesesemordakos	Mushezib-Marduk	4 years (692–689)
Second interregnum	—	8 years (688–681)
Asaridinos	Ashur-ahu-iddin	13 years (680–668)
Saosdouchinos	Shamash-shumu-ukin	20 years (667–648)
Kiniladanos	Kandalanu	22 years (647–626)
Nabopolassaros	Nabu-aplu-usur	21 years (625–605)
Nabokolassaros	Nabu-kudurru-usur	43 years (604–562)
Illoaroudamos	Amel-Marduk	2 years (561–560)
Nerigasolassaros	Nergal-sharru-usur	4 years (559–556)
Nabonadios	Nabu-na'id	17 years (555–539)

8.1 The Rebellion of Mukin-zeri

King List A credits Mukin-zeri with a reign of three years (731–729). The Ptolemaic Canon knows him as Chinzeros and attributes to him a joint reign of five years with Tiglath-pileser III, named Poros; this figure was obtained by adding the two years of Tiglath-pileser as king of Babylon to the three years of Mukin-zeri. King List A further characterizes Mukin-zeri's reign as the Dynasty of Shapiya, the capital of Bit-Amukani in central Babylonia. Previous and subsequent Chaldean rulers of Babylonia, as far as we know, all stemmed from Bit-Dakkuri and Bit-Yakin. When Mukin-zeri rebelled against the ephemeral Babylonian king Nabu-shuma-ukin II and seized the throne, Tiglath-pileser III was campaigning in Syria against Damascus. Already deeply engaged in Babylonian affairs, Tiglath-pileser devoted the next three years to eradicating Mukin-zeri and his supporters. Epistolary sources from Kalhu and the Annals of Tiglath-pileser allow us to trace the unfolding of the campaign in some detail, although there is much uncertainty regarding the chronology of the letters. It seems that initially the Assyrians sealed off the eastern border of Babylonia to thwart Elamite support for the rebellion. Then Tiglath-pileser subdued several Aramean tribes as well as the Chaldean clans of Bit-Shilani and Bit-Sha'alli, claiming to have deported them in the tens of thousands. By 730 the struggle for the control of Babylon had started. A letter sent to Tiglath-pileser by his agents in Babylonia probably dates to this phase; it describes the Assyrian envoys standing outside the walls, asking the Babylonians to open the city gate and promising them that the king of Assyria would grant them amnesty and even establish their privileged status with tax and corvée exemptions, but the Babylonians rejected the offer. It is clear from the letter that Mukin-zeri was not in Babylon at that point but probably directing the war from Shapiya, where the Assyrian army eventually besieged him in 729. Tiglath-pileser III relates this final episode in his Annals: "I confined Mukin-zeri, the Amukanite, to Shapiya, his royal city. I inflicted a heavy defeat upon him before his city gates." This segment of the Annals is contained in summary inscriptions from Kalhu, probably composed in 729. The death of Mukin-zeri is mentioned in a letter to Tiglath-pileser:

> To the king, my lord, your servant Ashur-shallimanni: Good health to the king, my lord! We got together on the twenty-sixth, stood in the presence of the commander-in-chief and gave orders to one another. We arrived within the (city) gate and inflicted a defeat: Mukin-zeri has been killed and Shumu-ukin, his son, had also been killed. The city is conquered. The king, my lord, can be glad.[1]

One Babylonian document is dated to the twenty-sixth day of the third month in the fourth year of Nabu-mukin-zeri, almost certainly the same as Mukin-zeri. It is therefore possible that Mukin-zeri continued to resist until 728 and that his reign overlapped with that of Tiglath-pileser as king of Babylon. The confusion then prevailing might explain why the Ptolemaic Canon computed his reign jointly with the Assyrian king's. The Annals claim that after the subjugation of Bit-Amukani, Tiglath-pileser received tribute from Bit-Dakkuri and also from Marduk-apla-iddina, the leader of Bit-Yakin, who became a few years later a staunch opponent of the Assyrians.

8.2   The *palû* of Baltil (728–722)

As the defeat of Mukin-zeri appeared certain, Tiglath-pileser III assumed the title of "king of Babylon," becoming the first Assyrian to be recognized as such in the chronographic tradition. Chronicle 16 records the event as follows: "The third year of Mukin-zeri, Tiglath-pileser went down to Babylonia (Akkad), ravaged Bit-Amukani and captured Mukin-zeri. Mukin-zeri reigned three years over Babylon. Tiglath-pileser ascended the throne of Babylon." King List A assigns Tiglath-pileser a reign of two years (728–727) and includes him and his son Shalmaneser V in a Dynasty of Baltil, a name for the city of Assur. Four Babylonian documents are dated to his reign, three from his first year and one (with duplicate) from his second year. King List A gives him the name Pulu, which also appears in the Ptolemaic Canon as Poros and in the Bible as Pul (2 Kings 15:19). Pulu may have been Tiglath-pileser's actual name before he seized the throne, or a nickname. Tiglath-pileser participated in the rituals of the Babylonian monarchy, and even accompanied the statue of Marduk during the New Year Festival according to his Annals. The assumption of Babylonian kingship marked a new phase in Assyro-Babylonian relations. Tiglath-pileser transformed Assyria into a centralized empire and for the next century no polity in the Near East remained unaffected by its aggressive expansionism. Because of their cultural and religious deference to Babylonia, the Assyrians could not just reduce it to the status of mere province like many of their other conquests. The creation of a double kingship, a personal union not unlike that of England and Scotland in modern times seemed the best solution within an imperial framework, since it preserved both Assyrian interests and Babylonian particularism. After the death of Tiglathpileser in 727 his son Shalmaneser V succeeded him as king of Babylon. King List A knows him as Ululayu (literally "of the month Ululu," probably the month of his birth), which became Ilulayos in the Ptolemaic Canon. Little is known of the situation in Babylonia during his five-year reign (726–722). Assyrian efforts were directed mostly at the Levant and the major achievement of his reign was the capture of Samaria, the capital of the northern kingdom of Israel, which occurred in 722, shortly after the death of Shalmaneser.

8.3   Marduk-apla-iddina II and Chaldean Resistance (721–709)

Marduk-apla-iddina II, sometimes known by his Biblical name Merodach-Baladan, was the son or grandson of the Chaldean king Eriba-Marduk. Eriba-Marduk belonged to Bit-Yakin and Marduk-apla-iddina became the second ruler of that clan to occupy the Babylonian throne. As we have seen his earliest appearance in historical sources dates to the reign of Tiglath-pileser III, who calls him "king of the Sealand," a designation corroborated by King List A which defines his reign as "dynasty of the Sealand," while the Dynastic Chronicle attaches the same label to his forebear Eriba-Marduk. Marduk-apla-iddina took advantage of the dynastic troubles which followed the death of Shalmaneser V to reclaim the crown of Babylon from the Assyrians, asserting that he had been selected by the god Marduk to rule his city. According to Chronicle 16 he ascended the throne in Babylon in the month Nisannu (March–April) of 721, less than three months after Sargon II prevailed in the battle for succession in Assyria:

> The fifth year (of the reign of Shalmaneser V), in the month of Tebetu, Shalmaneser went to his destiny. Shalmaneser reigned five years over Akkad and Assyria. In the month of Tebetu, the twelfth day, Sargon (II) ascended the throne of Assyria. In the month of Nisannu Marduk-apla-iddina (II) ascended the throne of Babylon.

Chronicle 16 also reports that in the second year of Marduk-apla-iddina (720) Sargon clashed with the Elamites at Der across the Tigris in eastern Babylonia. The encounter resulted in a defeat for the Assyrians, even though they retained control of Der. The chronicle adds that Marduk-apla-iddina came to the aid of the king of Elam but did not arrive in time for the battle and withdrew. The

Assyrians left Babylon and Elam alone for the ensuing decade and focused their military efforts on the Levant and on the northern state of Urartu, on which Sargon inflicted a crushing defeat in 714.

Babylonian economic and administrative documents increase moderately under Marduk-apla-iddina. Among the three *kudurru*s dated to his reign one stands out for its literary and iconographic qualities. The prologue begins with a hymn to Marduk which describes his choice of Marduk-apla-iddina as ruler and the latter's efforts to bring just government to Babylonia. It insists on the care he fostered on the temples, his continuance of tax-exempt status for Babylon and Borsippa, and the fact that he returned to native Babylonians fields they had previously lost, by now all familiar themes. The *kudurru* records in its main part the grant of a domain to one Bel-ahhe-eriba, the governor of Babylon, and is witnessed by an impressive array of dignitaries including the king's son and the high-priest of Esagil. The transaction is dated on the twenty-third day of the month Duzu in the seventh year of his reign (summer of 715). The finely carved relief on top of the monument shows Marduk-apla-iddina and the beneficiary of the grant facing one another (Figure 8.2). His most important building inscription records work at Uruk on the Eanna temple. The text takes a jibe at the Assyrians, stating that they had ruled Babylonia for seven years (i.e. two years of Tiglath-pileser III and five years of Shalmaneser V) only because of Marduk's anger at his land.

Sargon too viewed Marduk-apla-iddina as a usurper, and once he asserted Assyrian military superiority in the Near East he turned against Babylonia, referring to his nemesis as "a descendant of Yakin, a Chaldean, (and) the likeness of a demon." He portrays his rule as illegitimate and contrasts it with his own election by the god Marduk, who appointed him to expel Marduk-apla-iddina from Babylon and rule in his stead:

> Twelve years he (Marduk-apla-iddina II) ruled and governed Babylon, the city of the Enlil (of the gods), against the will of the gods. Marduk, the great lord, saw the evil deeds of the Chaldean whom he despised, and the taking away of his royal scepter and throne was established on his lips. He (Marduk) chose me, Sargon, the reverent king, among all kings, and he justly appointed me. He selected me in the land of Sumer and Akkad. In order to undermine the Chaldean, the evil enemy, he strengthened my weapons. On the orders of Marduk, my great lord, I prepared the weaponry, pitched my camp, and ordered [my soldiers] to march against the evil Chaldean.[2]

Thus Sargon declared war on Marduk-apla-iddina. Two Biblical passages mention the embassy sent to the Judean king Hezekiah by Marduk-apla-iddina, whose name appears as "Merodach-Baladan, son of Baladan, king of Babylon" (Isaiah 39:1; Berodach-Baladan in 2 Kings 20:12). The embassy probably took place shortly before the start of the war and testifies to the Chaldean king's effort to muster a wide coalition against Assyria. The Neo-Assyrian Canon of Eponyms for the year 710 records that after a swift campaign to northern Babylonia, Sargon

Figure 8.2 *Kudurru* of Marduk-apla-iddina II. This monument ranks as one of the finest examples of royal portraiture from the Ancient Near East. Contrary to the *kudurru* of Nabu-apla-iddina (Figure 7.1), the king is shown here in significantly larger size than the beneficiary of the grant. He is identified by a caption above him which reads "Image of Marduk-apla-iddina, king of Babylon." Divine symbols appear in the upper register. It is preserved in the Vorderasiatisches Museum in Berlin (VA 2663). Measurements: H: 45 × W: 32 cm. *Source*: bpk Bildagentur / Vorderasiatisches Museum, Staatliche Museen, Berlin, Germany / Photo: Olaf M. Tessmer / Art Resource, NY.

established his quarters in Kish. He must have received the allegiance of Nippur soon after since a document from that city is dated to the twenty-ninth day of the month Ululu in his accession year as king of Babylon (710). The Annals of Sargon now become our main source for the progress of the war. By the end of that year Sargon had subjugated the Aramean tribes of eastern Babylonia, effectively cutting the route for Elamite support to the Chaldeans. He then stormed the Chaldean territory of Bit-Dakkuri south of Babylon and forced Marduk-apla-iddina to leave the capital by night, after which Babylon and Borsippa surrendered to him.

The Neo-Assyrian Canon of Eponyms labels the following year (709) the one when "Sargon took the hand of the god Bel," signifying that the Assyrian king had now been recognized legitimate ruler in Babylon and was thus entitled to lead the god Marduk in the New Year's procession. In his Annals Sargon insists that the citizens and priesthood of Babylon and Borsippa welcomed him with open arms. Meanwhile Marduk-apla-iddina sought refuge in the Chaldean territory of Bit-Yakin, forcing Sargon to march to the Sealand to dislodge him from his hometown of Dur-Yakin. The siege lasted from 709 until 707. The Assyrians eventually crossed the defensive moat, captured the city which was looted and torched while Marduk-apla-iddina fled to Elam. In the wake of his victory Sargon confirmed and extended the traditional privileges of Babylon and Borsippa, and also of cities located in the Sealand such as Ur, Uruk, and Eridu. Sargon was now officially recognized as legitimate ruler of Babylonia, a function he exercised until his death in 705 (see Map 8.1). In order to prevent any tribal resurgence he claims to have deported as many as 108,000 Chaldeans and Arameans to various parts of his empire and to have transplanted people from Kummuhu (i.e. Commagene) to the Sealand.

8.4 The *palû* of Habigal (709–694)

King List A attaches the label "Dynasty (*palû*) of Habigal" to Sargon, Sennacherib and Ashur-nadin-shumi. The term Habigal might be a veiled reference to Hanigalbat, a rump state of the kingdom of Mitanni annexed by Assyria in the thirteenth century. Sargon may well have been a usurper, perhaps a member of a collateral branch of the royal family, and this may explain the change of terminology in King List A, which seems ironic since Sargon claims in his inscriptions to be "seed of Baltil" (i.e. scion of Assur). Sargon is the first Assyrian king of Babylon of whom we have building inscriptions from Babylonia. They record the restoration of the defensive walls of Babylon and repair work on the Eanna temple at Uruk. In these texts Sargon claims traditional titles such as "king of Babylon" and "viceroy of Babylon" as well as "king of Sumer and Akkad."

Sargon lost his life on the battlefield in 705. The chronographic tradition varies on his son and successor Sennacherib. The Ptolemaic Canon does not mention him and instead labels the periods of his two Babylonian reigns (704–703 and 688–681) as "without kings," while King List A recognizes him as regnant for the same two periods. The years 704 and 703 appear to have been recognized as his first two full years of reign in Babylon but soon the political situation began to deteriorate. In 703 a usurper named Marduk-zakir-shumi (II) arose in Babylonia and held power for one month according to King List A. The list labels him as "descendant of Arad," an incomplete name which can be restored as Arad-Ea or Arad-Enlil. The former hypothesis seems attractive in light of the mention of a provincial governor named Marduk-zakir-shumi, descendant of Arad-Ea, twelve years earlier in a *kudurru* of Marduk-apla-iddina II; he could be the same as the usurper. Arad-Ea was the name of a prominent Babylonian clan.

In that same year Marduk-apla-iddina II returned from Elam and attempted a return to power. This time King List A labels him "soldier of Habi", possibly an abbreviation for Habiru, a term denoting groups of marauders and soldiers operating outside state control, and credits him with a reign of nine months.

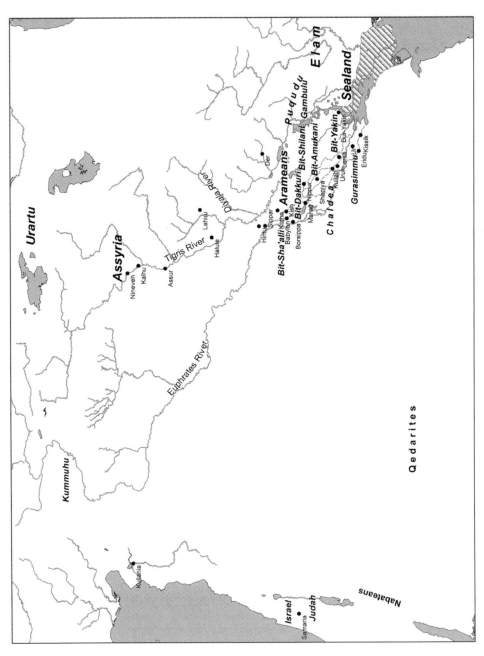

Map 8.1 Babylonia in the Assyrian Empire. Map Design: Stephen Batiuk, University of Toronto.

The final ousting of Marduk-apla-iddina formed the goal of the first campaign reported in the Annals of Sennacherib:

> On my first campaign, I brought about the defeat of Marduk-apla-iddina, king of Karduniash, together with the troops of Elam, his allies, in the plain of Kish. In the midst of that battle he abandoned his camp, fled alone, and saved his life. I seized the chariots, horses, wagons (and) mules that he had abandoned in the thick of battle. I joyfully entered his palace, which is in Babylon, then I opened his treasury and brought out gold, silver, gold (and) silver utensils, precious stones, all kinds of possessions (and) property without number, a substantial tribute, (together with) his palace women, courtiers, attendants, male singers, female singers, all of the craftsmen, as many as there were, (and) his palace attendants, and I counted (them) as booty.[3]

Sennacherib plundered numerous fortified cities of Chaldea and their satellite towns; then he emptied Uruk, Nippur, Kish, Kutha, and Sippar of their Chaldean and Aramean combatants and also of their collaborationist citizens. He claims to have subdued numerous Aramean tribes of eastern Babylonia on his return. The number of deportees from that campaign reached 208,000 people and countless animals. One may doubt the accuracy of these figures, but they still give us an idea of the magnitude of Sennacherib's ambition to reconfigure Babylonia into a docile dependency of the Assyrian empire. This campaign did not signal the end of Marduk-apla-iddina, who remained entrenched in the Sealand with Elamite support for a few more years, until Sennacherib during his fourth campaign in 700 dislodged him from Bit-Yakin and destroyed his remaining strongholds. Marduk-apla-iddina died a few years later, probably as a refugee in Elam. However, three of his sons and grandsons, Nabu-shuma-ishkun, Nabu-zer-kitti-lishir, and Nabu-bel-shumati led various guerillas against the Assyrians between the years 691 and 646.

After the success of his first campaign Sennacherib departed from previous policy and resolved to appoint a Babylonian ruler to the throne. His choice fell on one Bel-ibni, whom he describes as "a descendant of a Rab-bani and a scion of Shuanna (i.e. Babylon) who had grown up like a young puppy in my palace." This statement leaves little doubt as to the subordinate role the Assyrians envisaged for Bel-ibni. Individuals with the ancestral name Rab-bani belonged to important Babylonian urban families. Thus Sennacherib may have wanted to create a political counterweight to Chaldean and Aramean influence. Accordingly, Bel-ibni receives the label *palû* of E "Dynasty of Babylon" in King List A. We know little about his reign (702–700), but he may not have been as compliant with Assyrian demands as expected because Chronicle 16 states that Sennacherib removed him after three years:

> The third year (of the reign) of Bel-ibni, Sennacherib went down into Akkad and sacked Akkad. He took Bel-ibni and his nobles into exile in Assyria. Bel-ibni reigned three years over Babylon. Sennacherib made his son Ashur-nadin-shumi ascend the throne of Babylon.

Bel-ibni's removal and replacement by Ashur-nadin-shumi, Sennacherib's eldest son, occurred in the wake of the Assyrian campaign to uproot Marduk-apla-iddina from the Sealand in 700. An entry in the Synchronistic King List states that a rebellion in Babylonia induced Sennacherib to put Ashur-nadin-shumi on the throne, providing further evidence of Bel-ibni's possible duplicity. Ashur-nadin-shumi receives, like his father, the label *palû* of Habigal in King List A. His six-year rule over Babylon (699–694) is poorly documented. No royal inscription from his reign has been discovered and only one fragment of a *kudurru* and a few economic documents have survived. His tenure seems to have been generally peaceful as no major disturbance in Babylonia is recorded in chronicles or Assyrian Annals.

8.5 The Two Shuzubus (694–689)

The situation, however, changed for the worse in 694. The events which followed are known from the Annals of Sennacherib (his sixth campaign) on the Assyrian side and Chronicle 16 on the Babylonian side. In that year Sennacherib decided to pursue the Chaldean exiles of Bit-Yakin who had sought asylum in Elam. Sennacherib and his army crossed the Persian Gulf into Elamite territory and after wholesale destruction of a number of cities brought back booty and numerous Elamite and Chaldean captives to Assyria. Chronicle 16 tells us that the king of Elam launched a counter-offensive in northern Babylonia:

> King Hallushu-(Inshushinak) of Elam went to Akkad; at the end of (the month of) Tashritu he entered Sippar (and) massacred the inhabitants. The god Shamash did not leave the Ebabbar. Ashur-nadin-shumi was captured and deported to Elam. Ashur-nadin-shumi reigned six years over Babylon. The king of Elam made Nergal-ushezib ascend the throne of Babylon. He brought about the re[trea]t of Assyria.

Although the Chronicle seems to imply that the Elamites captured Ashur-nadin-shumi during the battle for Sippar, a letter from the state archives of Nineveh datable around 670 claims that Sennacherib's son was in fact betrayed by a group of Babylonians who were still active one generation later; the main conjurer was denounced to Esarhaddon in the following terms: "He has assembled the people who had captured Ashur-nadin-shumi and delivered him to Elam, and he concluded a treaty with them, adjuring them by (the planet) Jupiter and (the star) Sirius." No source tells us about the fate of Ashur-nadin-shumi after his deportation. His successor Nergal-ushezib was a Babylonian from the Gahal family. The Annals of Sennacherib state that on the return from his sixth campaign the Assyrian king clashed in a pitched battle with "Shuzubu (= Nergal-ushezib) the Babylonian" and his Elamite allies. The Annals conflate the years 694 and 693 into one campaign since Nergal-ushezib, who reigned less than one full year, was still active in Babylonia in 693. According to Chronicle 16 he captured and plundered Nippur on IV-16 in the year 693, but was finally defeated by an Assyrian army near the city three months later (VII-7, 693) and carried off to Assyria. During the same campaign the Assyrians plundered Uruk and Larsa. In an inscription on a stone tablet from Nineveh Sennacherib claims that his soldiers "captured Shuzubu, the king of Babylon, alive, threw him in a neck-stock (and) fetters and brought him before me. At the Citadel Gate of Nineveh, I bound him with a bear." The Assyrians took advantage of political troubles in Elam to raid that country before returning home, but failed to assert full control of northern Babylonia where a new contender for the crown emerged, one Mushezib-Marduk, a Chaldean from Bit-Dakkuri.

Sennacherib refers to two different kings of Babylon with the nickname Shuzubu: Nergal-ushezib (693) is "Shuzubu the Babylonian," and Mushezib-Marduk (692–689) is "Shuzubu the Chaldean." The practice of giving nicknames was widespread in Babylonia among the urban elites. Indeed, Nergal-ushezib is called "Shuzubu descendant of Gahal" in a letter sent by the citizenry of Babylon to Esarhaddon two decades later, and Sennacherib refers to him by the same designation once in the stone tablet from Nineveh. Nergal-ushezib means "the god Nergal has saved," and the form *shuzubu* is an adjective of the same verb meaning "the saved one." The name of his successor Mushezib-Marduk means "the god Marduk is a savior," and accordingly Sennacherib refers to him as "Shuzubu the Chaldean" to differentiate him from his predecessor. King List A also associates the two Shuzubus with one another, including both in a *palû* of E, a "Dynasty of Babylon," even though Mushezib-Marduk was a Chaldean.

This second Shuzubu became a fierce opponent of Assyria. Originally he had served as subordinate of the Assyrian governor of Lahiru. During his mop-up operation against Bit-Yakin in 700, Sennacherib encountered him as agitator in the Sealand: "In the course of my (fourth) campaign, I defeated Shuzubu the Chaldean who lives in the marshes at the city Bittutu." However, he failed to capture him. Mushezib-Marduk resurfaced in 693, seized the Babylonian throne and gathered a broad coalition to defy the Assyrians. From 693 until to the capture of Babylon in 689, "Shuzubu the Chaldean" held Sennacherib in check. However, the sequence of events involved numerous actors and their chronology cannot be pinned down very precisely. Chronicle 16 is strangely muted at this point. It notes that the king of Elam led Babylonian and Elamite forces in a battle against the Assyrians at Halule "in an unknown year" (probably in 691), and then mentions the capture of Babylon (689). The Annals of Sennacherib provide many more details in the account of the eighth campaign, which begins with a retrospective survey of Babylonian misdeeds going back to 693, "after Shuzubu (the Chaldean) had rebelled and the citizens of Babylon, the evil demons, had locked the city gates (and) plotted to wage war." Various episodes follow, including an initial siege of Babylon, the flight of Mushezib-Marduk to Elam and his return to Babylon whose inhabitants, to Sennacherib's dismay, "inappropriately placed him (back) on the throne." In order to bribe the king of Elam into striking an alliance with them, the Babylonians sent him all the silver and gold found in the treasury of Esagil. The Elamites then led a vast coalition of Iranian states and

Arameans and Chaldean tribes, including Sam'una, one of the sons of the now deceased Marduk-apla-iddina II, and they proceeded to Babylon:

> In their multitude, they took the road to Akkad and, as they were advancing towards Babylon, they met up with Shuzubu the Chaldean, king of Babylon, and banded their forces together. Like a spring invasion of a swarm of locusts, they were advancing towards me as a group to do battle. The dust of their feet covered the wide heavens like a heavy cloud in the deep of winter. While drawing up in battle-line before me at the city Halule, which is on the bank of the Tigris River, (and) keeping me from the water source, they sharpened their weapons.[4]

The Annals conclude with an account of the battle in literary style, claiming a resounding victory for Sennacherib. Chronicle 16, on the other hand, mentions a retreat of the Assyrians. A stand-off seems therefore probable. However, the Assyrians picked up new strength rapidly and were laying siege on Babylon by the summer of 690. One Babylonian document dated V-28 in the year 690 (year 3 of Mushezib-Marduk) describes the dire straits endured by the population:

> In the reign of Mushezib-Marduk, king of Babylon, there were siege, famine, hunger, starvation and hard times in the land. Everything had changed and become non-existent. One shekel of silver was worth two liters of barley. The city gates were locked and there was no exit in (all) four directions. The corpses of people filled the squares of Babylon because there was no one to bury (them).[5]

The siege nonetheless went on for another fifteen months. Chronicle 16 laconically mentions the capture of the city on the first day of the month Kislimu in the fourth year of Mushezib-Marduk (fall of 689) and his deportation to Assyria. The cliff inscriptions of Sennacherib near Bavian in northern Iraq give further details: "I besieged the city. Its people, young and old, I did not spare. I filled the city squares with their corpses. I carried off alive to my land Shuzubu, king of Babylon, with his family." Sources are silent on the ultimate fate of "Shuzubu the Chaldean."

8.6   Sennacherib's Desecration of Babylon (689–681)

By his own account in the Bavian inscription, Sennacherib wrought a terrible vengeance on the city. Intent on eradicating it, he demolished the walls, the temples and the ziggurat from their foundations to their crenellations, diverted the canal Arahtu and flooded the city so that its ground plan could not be recognized in the future. Like the Deluge he claims to have dissolved it in water and turned it into a meadow. Sennacherib's rhetoric may be somewhat inflated. Life certainly continued in the fallen capital. Nevertheless, archaeological evidence has provided confirmation of destructions at that time even though these levels cannot be dated very precisely and do not confirm the Assyrian claim of complete obliteration. Sennacherib's desecration of Babylon was still remembered generations later. A literary letter known in copies from the Hellenistic period and allegedly sent by Nabopolassar to the Assyrian king Sin-sharru-ishkun denounces Sennacherib as "the plunderer of Akkad" and accuses him of having executed the elders of Babylon and carried off booty to Assyria. The letter belongs to the genre of fictitious correspondence, yet it shows that Sennacherib's sacrilegious deeds provided later a justification for bringing down the Assyrian empire and avenging Babylon. Without naming him, Naboni-dus also alludes to Sennacherib as one "who plotted evil against the land," destroyed the sanctuaries of Babylon and took the statue of Marduk captive to Assyria. Sennacherib never assumed the title "king of Babylon" for the balance of his reign, nor did he adopt any of the traditional titles implying rule over Babylonia, such as "viceroy of Babylon" and "king of Sumer and Akkad." This agrees with the claim of kingless years laid by the Ptolemaic Canon. The few documents from Babylonia which belong to that period adhere to other chronological schemes. For example, two texts from Borsippa are dated in the twelfth and thirteenth years "after Ashur-nadin-shumi," that is to say, 682 and 681, still acknowledging the last ruler considered legitimate by Assyrians and Babylonians alike. Chronicle 16 refers to the year 681 as "the eighth year that there was no king in Babylon."

Having effectively abolished Babylonian kingship, Sennacherib proceeded to give his political designs firm theological foundations. The creation of Enuma elish by the scholars of the Isin II dynasty had provided Babylon with a powerful, incontrovertible, and almost revealed sacred text which endowed the city with cosmological primacy and its god Marduk with the role of demiurge. Sennacherib launched a religious reform aimed at displacing Babylon's central role in favor of the old Assyrian capital Assur and also of Nineveh, the new royal residence and political capital of the empire. He promoted the identification of the Assyrian national god Ashur with the primeval deity Anshar, thus making Ashur the ancestor of all the gods. Parallel to this development he sponsored an edited version of Enuma elish in which Marduk is replaced by the god Ashur. Since Anshar appears as the ancestor of Marduk at the beginning of Enuma elish, Anshar became the ancestor of Ashur, that is to say, of himself. In accordance with this Sennacherib ordered a new statue of the god to be made and dedicated new cultic personnel to it, naming the new deity "the self-originate." He erected new sacred buildings in the city of Assur which replicated those of Marduk in Babylon, notably a *bit akiti* decorated with a scene where Ashur/Anshar replaced Marduk as champion of order battling the forces of chaos represented by the primeval monster Tiamat. Earth taken from Babylon was deposited in those buildings to symbolize the replacement of Babylon with Assur. With Babylon crushed, Sennacherib hoped in this manner to answer the challenge posed by Enuma elish. But fate did not allow him to pursue his theological-political dreams further. A palace conspiracy designed by his son Arad-Mullissu led to his assassination in 681, and after a few weeks of clashes between factions at court Arad-Mullissu fled and another son of Sennacherib, Esarhaddon (Ashur-ahu-iddin), ascended the throne.

8.7   Esarhaddon Restores Babylon (681–669)

In his *res gestae* Esarhaddon claims that, although a younger son, he had been selected by his father to succeed him. Not long after his accession he proceeded to reverse his father's policy and restore Babylon. In his account of the resettlement, however, Esarhaddon rewrites history in order to exonerate Sennacherib, ascribing the destruction of the city not to human but solely to divine agency. He notes that "in the reign of a previous king" (i.e. Mushezib-Marduk) the people of Babylonia had become treacherous and neglected their gods. They plundered the treasury of Esagil and sold it off to the Elamites. The god Marduk became furious and punished Babylon, allowing the Arahtu canal to overflow its banks and wipe out the city. But Marduk eventually relented:

> The merciful god Marduk wrote that the calculated time of its (i.e. Babylon's) abandonment (should last) seventy years, (but) his heart was quickly soothed, and he reversed the numbers and (thus) ordered its (re)occupation to be (after) eleven years.[6]

In cuneiform writing the sign for the numeral "one" is a vertical wedge. The vertical wedge can also count for "sixty" because of the sexagesimal nature of the Babylonian numerical system. The number "seventy" is written "sixty + ten," but if we reverse the numerals the vertical sign, now coming after a larger digit, must be read "one" instead of "sixty." Thus we have "ten + one," arriving at the figure of eleven years wished by Esarhaddon. Indeed, with this permutation the resettlement of Babylon roughly coincided with the beginning of his reign. A key agent of the project was Ubaru, put in command of Babylon by Esarhaddon after his accession. One document from that period was drafted at Babylon "in the eponymy of Ubaru, the governor of Babylon," a rare example of Assyrian dating methods applied to Babylonia. The state archives of Nineveh preserve a letter sent by the same Ubaru, praising Esarhaddon for the resettlement:

> To the king, my lord: your servant, Ubaru, the governor of Babylon. May the gods Nabu and Marduk bless the king. Now I pray every day to the god Marduk and the goddess Zarpanitu for the life of the king, my lord. I have entered Babylon. The people of Babylon welcome me, and they bless the king every day, saying: "(He is) the one who returned Babylon's captives and booty." Also the chiefs of Chaldea from Sippar to the mouth of the sea (i.e. the Persian Gulf) bless the king, saying: "(He is) the one who resettled Babylon." All the lands are happy before the king, my lord.[7]

Emulating his grandfather Sargon, Esarhaddon sponsored building projects in Babylonia and commemorated them with building inscriptions in his own name. In Babylon his activities included the Esagil temple, the ziggurat Etemenanki, the processional way of Babylon leading to Esagil, and the temple of Nabu-sha-hare, E-niggidri-kalamma-summa. Esarhaddon also mentions that he rebuilt the walls of Babylon, remitted debts for the inhabitants, confirmed their tax exemptions, and redeemed those who had become slaves. He returned their looted possessions and encouraged them to resettle the city, build houses, plant orchards, and dig canals. Esarhaddon's activities extended also to Borsippa (temple of the goddess Gula), Nippur (Ekur, the temple of Enlil; and E-bara-durgarra, the temple of Ishtar as Queen-of-Nippur), and especially to Uruk, where many inscriptions relate the restoration of the Eanna temple of the goddess Ishtar, of her chapel Enirgalanna and of the chapel of the goddess Nanaya, Ehilianna. Esarhaddon initiated the return of the deities of Uruk abducted to Assyria when Sennacherib raided the city in the fall of 693, including the goddesses Ishtar, Nanaya and Usur-amassu. A letter to him datable to the fall of 671 reports on refurbishing the images of the gods of Uruk: "[The decoration of the goddess N]anaya is incomplete. Furthermore, (while) the face and the hand[s of the goddess Usur]-amassa have been overlaid with gold, the figure [and the feet] have not." The Assyrians enjoyed considerable support at Uruk, which may explain why Esarhaddon and his successors lavished so much attention on the city. Archival sources from Uruk dated to the sixth century reveal that the god Ashur was worshiped there under the form Anshar. This suggests that the cult of Ashur/Anshar had been transplanted to Uruk at that time.

In addition to his Assyrian royal titles, Esarhaddon often adopts traditional Babylonian titles such as "king of Babylon," "viceroy of Babylon" and "king of Sumer and Akkad." However, in economic texts from Babylonia he bears the title "king of Babylon" only once, preferring "king of Assyria," "king of the totality," "king of the lands" or simply "king." Nevertheless, the evidence clearly indicates his readiness to revive the institution of Babylonian kingship, and this is unanimously acknowledged in the chronographic tradition. The chronology of the building works of Esarhaddon in Babylonia is uncertain and it is only at the end of his reign that Babylon's revival came to full fruition with the return of Marduk's statue. The event is reported in Chronicles 18 and 20 in almost identical words:

> For eight years (during the reign of) Sennacherib, for twelve years (during the reign of Esarhaddon), twenty years (altogether), the god Bel (i.e. Marduk) stayed in Baltil (i.e. Assur) and the *akitu*-festival did not take place. The god Nabu did not come from Borsippa for the procession of the god Bel. In the month of Kislimu, Ashurbanipal, his (i.e. Esarhaddon's) son, ascended the throne in Assyria.

8.7.1 A New Generation of Opponents

In spite of his goodwill, Esarhaddon's rule did not unfold peacefully in Babylonia. Chronicle 16 mentions an attack mounted in his first year (680) by Nabu-zer-kitti-lishir (also known as Zer-kitti-lishir), one of the sons of Marduk-apla-iddina II, against the city of Ur in the Sealand. Zer-kitti-lishir failed to capture the city and when the Assyrian army came he fled to Elam, where he was put to death. The *res gestae* of Esarhaddon report that after his murder his brother Na'id-Marduk fled from Elam to seek refuge in Assyria, where Esarhaddon pardoned him and appointed him governor of the entire Sealand. Esarhaddon claims that afterwards he brought yearly tribute to Nineveh. A group of four letters from the Nineveh state archives inform us that later the Elamites invaded the Sealand in support of another son of Marduk-apla-iddina II, one Nabu-ushallim. The outcome of this episode is not known; later a certain Nabu-etir appears as "governor of the northern Sealand" in a letter from Nineveh. Relations with Elam seem to have gradually improved in the second half of his reign. According to Chronicle 16 an Elamite army invaded Babylonia and entered Sippar in 675, slaughtering many residents. The king of Elam died shortly after and his successor tried to pacify the Assyrians by sending back to Agade the divine images which had been captured earlier. A letter from the Nineveh archives refers to a peace treaty between Elam and Assyria: "Having listened to one another, the king of Elam and the king of As[syria] have made peace with one another at Marduk's command and become treaty partners." The treaty must date to the later years of Esarhaddon since the letter in question was sent by "the crown prince of Babylon," an expression which can only refer to Shamash-shumu-ukin. Assyrian military efforts after 673 were directed mostly at the conquest of Egypt, and the peace treaty with Elam must probably be seen in this context.

Bit-Yakin and the Sealand were not the sole locus of Chaldean unrest. The Annals of Esarhaddon report that in 678 a certain Shamash-ibni, the Chaldean leader of Bit-Dakkuri, took control of land belonging to the inhabitants of Babylon and Borsippa. Esarhaddon reacted swiftly:

> I plundered the land of Bit-Dakkuri, which is in Chaldea, an enemy of Babylon. I captured Shamash-ibni, its king, a rogue (and) outlaw, who did not respect the oath of the lord of lords (and) who took away fields of the citizens of Babylon and Borsippa by force and turned them over to himself. Because I know the fear of the gods Bel and Nabu, I returned those fields and entrusted them to the citizens of Babylon and Borsippa. I placed Nabu-shallim, son of Balassu, on his throne and he (now) pulls my yoke.[8]

Chronicles 16 and 18 give further details, stating that Shamash-ibni was not only captured in 678 but also taken to Assyria and executed. The victory against Shamash-ibni is also mentioned in a building inscription of Esarhaddon for the temple of Gula at Borsippa. Shamash-ibni and his successor Nabu-ushallim occur in several state letters from Nineveh. Although appointed by Esarhaddon, Nabu-ushallim soon became over-ambitious. We hear about his attempts to take control of the city of Marad south of Borsippa, and one letter mentions his reluctance to hand over former servants of Shamash-ibni to Assyrian representatives:

> As for the renegade scholars, eunuchs, and soldiers of Shamash-ibni, who are (now) with Nabu-ushallim, about whom the king, my lord, wrote to me. When I spoke to him, he refused to give them up to me, saying: "I will not give them up to you without a sealed document from the king and without a bodyguard".[9]

The state correspondence from Nineveh mentions other agitators, notably a certain Sillaya active mostly in northern and central Babylonia, but their activities cannot really be followed because of the patchy state of the evidence. Recurrent instability did not plague only Babylonia. Chronicle 16 and 18 record that in the penultimate year of his reign (670), Esarhaddon "put his numerous officers to the sword in Assyria." Two years earlier Esarhaddon had made arrangements for the imposition of Succession Treaties throughout the empire, leaving the crown of Babylon to his son Shamash-shumu-ukin and the crown of Assyria to his other son Ashurbanipal, who was in fact the younger sibling. Esarhaddon's exorcist and close advisor, Adad-shumu-usur, wrote as follows to his master in bewilderment:

> What has not been done in heaven, the king, my lord, has done upon earth and shown us: you have girded a son of yours with headband and entrusted to him the kingship of Assyria; your eldest son you have set to the kingship in Babylon. You have placed the first on your right, the second on your left side![10]

Whether disapproval can be detected in the reaction of the royal advisor is uncertain. Be that as it may, Esarhaddon's decision was to prove disastrous for the maintenance of imperial unity.

8.8 Regnant Siblings (669–652)

The Succession Treaties of Esarhaddon have roused considerable interest since their discovery in multiple copies at Kalhu in the 1950s, an interest rekindled with the find of another duplicate at Tell Tayinat (ancient Kullania) near Antakya, Turkey in 2009. They consist essentially of oaths of loyalty (adê) sworn by officials and vassals, describing their obligations to Ashurbanipal and Shamash-shumu-ukin after the death of their father. According to the Annals of Ashurbanipal the treaties were sworn on II-12 (March–April) in the year 672. Actual surviving copies are dated to the sixteenth and eighteenth days of that month, suggesting that the oath ceremonies went on for several days since they involved a large number of people and complex ritual procedures. Esarhaddon died three years later in the fall of 669 on his way to conquer Egypt and Ashurbanipal immediately ascended the throne of Assyria. Chronicles 16 and 18 record that the following spring Shamash-shumu-ukin formally ascended the throne in Babylon, returning the statue of Marduk which had been held captive for twenty years in Assyria. The significant delay in the latter's assumption of power is reflected in the Ptolemaic Canon, which recognizes Esarhaddon posthumously as king of Babylon for one more year, while transactions recorded at Uruk four months after Esarhaddon's death are dated according to the accession year of Ashurbanipal as "king of the lands."

We do not know if Esarhaddon made specific plans to delineate the responsibilities of the two brothers. Not long after his death the queen mother Zakutu imposed on Shamash-shumu-ukin a formal oath of loyalty to Ashurbanipal which defined the relationship between the two brothers for the balance of their joint reigns. Shamash-shumu-ukin became little more than a vassal of his

Figure 8.3   Ashurbanipal Restores the Ezida Temple. This inscribed stele of Ashurbanipal in the British Museum (BM 90865) commemorates the restoration of Ezida, the main temple of the god Nabu in Borsippa. In the stele Ashurbanipal claims Assyrian and Babylonian royal titles while stating that he appointed his brother Shamash-shumu-ukin to the kingship of Babylon. A very similar stele in the name of Shamash-shumu-ukin was discovered in the same room of the Ezida temple, but with the relief defaced, probably after the rebellion was suppressed. Ashurbanipal is depicted here carrying the work basket on his head, a motif going back to the ED period (Figure 2.3). Measurements: H: 39 × W: 15.5 cm. *Source*: Erich Lessing / Art Resource, NY.

brother, who even takes credit for having installed him on the throne of Babylon, passing over in silence Esarhaddon's instructions to that effect (Figure 8.3). Ashurbanipal kept exclusive control of international relations and the military. In the state correspondence from Nineveh we see individuals in Babylonia writing directly to Ashurbanipal on domestic and foreign affairs, especially Elam, and even spies reporting to him on Shamash-shumu-ukin. Babylonian cities sent deputations directly to the Assyrian king. The governor of Ur, Sin-balassu-iqbi, son of the previous governor Nikkal-iddin, sponsored building works at Ur and wrote inscriptions in his own name which acknowledge Ashurbanipal but not Shamash-shumu-ukin. Ashurbanipal's authority extended to religious matters as well. His inscriptions from Babylonia report on his repair of sanctuaries in his own name at Babylon, Borsippa, Sippar, Nippur, and

Uruk, and the state correspondence shows him closely supervising the restoration of cults in those cities, even minutiae of the refurbishing of divine images. Ashurbanipal claims exclusive credit for having completed the rebuilding of the temple of Marduk in Babylon, which his father had initiated. He also confirmed the tax exemptions of the citizens of Babylon. Although the statue of Marduk had been returned to Babylon at his accession, Shamash-shumu-ukin had to wait according to Chronicle 19 until the fifteenth and sixteenth years of his reign (654–653) for the cultic bed and sacred chariot of the god to leave Assyria, suggesting that Ashurbanipal long tarried with their release. No sphere of activity was immune to direct supervision by Ashurbanipal. And yet, Shamash-shumu-ukin was not left without responsibilities, if nominal. Like his brother he sponsored repair works and left a few building inscriptions at Borsippa and Sippar. With one exception, economic and administrative documents are always dated to his reign, never to Ashurbanipal's, at least until civil war broke out in 652. He is also sole bearer of the title "king of Babylon," Ashurbanipal claiming only Assyrian titles and epithets in his inscriptions from Babylonia. Three kudurrus, the last known such documents, acknowledge Shamash-shumu-ukin as ruler.

Babylonia enjoyed a period of relative calm from 669 to 652. The sole major disruption recorded in our sources is an Elamite invasion probably in 664. The episode is known mainly from the Annals of Ashurbanipal. Prompted by Bel-iqisha, the leader of the Aramean tribe of Gambulu, and with the complicity of the governor of Nippur Nabu-shumu-eresh and an official named Marduk-shumu-ibni, the Elamite king Urtak launched an attack on Babylonia. Ashurbanipal took a while to react, in part because of openings for negotiations made by Urtak. In the end, however, the Assyrian army moved in and repelled the invaders. A document from Nippur is dated V-29 in the fifth year of Ashurbanipal (summer of 664). This is the sole Babylonian document dated by Ashurbanipal after the accession of Shamash-shumu-ukin in 668 and before the outbreak of the civil war in 652. Therefore it must date just after the recapture of the city from the supporters of Elam. According to Ashurbanipal's Annals the local collaborators of the Elamites all died within a single year from external causes: Bel-iqisha from "the bite of a rat," Nabu-shumu-eresh, the treacherous governor of Nippur, from dropsy, and Marduk-shumu-ibni from an unspecified "heavy penalty" imposed by the god Marduk. Urtak died shortly after the failed invasion and a coup d'état in Elam brought to power a fiercely anti-Assyrian ruler named Teumman. Chronicle 19 reports that on VII-12 in the fourth year of Shamash-shumu-ukin (fall of 664), the son of the king of Elam had fled to Assyria. He must be identified as Humban-nikash II, son of Urtak, whom Ashurbanipal sheltered at Nineveh together with his brother Tammaritu. Ashurbanipal waited until 653 to attack Elam, dispatch Teumman, whose head was displayed at the gate of Nineveh, and install the two refugee princes as vassal rulers. By that time, however, Assyria's control of Egypt, still a recent conquest, had effectively ended and the first signs of imperial decline begun to appear.

8.9   Civil War (652–648)

In 652 Shamash-shumu-ukin led Babylonia into a rebellion against his brother which lasted until the year 648. Its most likely cause, besides the long standing and widespread opposition to Assyrian rule among Babylonians and Chaldeans, may have been Shamash-shumu-ukin's discontent at his subordinate status. The earliest hint at the coming rebellion occurs in a letter from Ashurbanipal to the citizens of Babylon dated II-23 in the year 652 (early spring; eponymy of Ashur-duru-usur). Ashurbanipal tries to persuade them not to listen to his brother's lies and join the rebellion. He also promises to pardon those who have already sided with him. Ashurbanipal then considered a preemptive strike since two months later, on IV-17 his diviners performed an oracular consultation which determined that Shamash-shumu-ukin would not be captured if Assyrian troops moved into Babylon. According to Chronicle 20, open hostilities began only six months later, on X-19, and soon the Babylonian troops suffered a major defeat at Hiritu near Sippar on XII-27 (early in 651):

> In the month of Tebetu, the nineteenth day, Assyria and Akkad went to war. Slipping away from the enemy, the king (Shamash-shumu-ukin) returned to Babylon. In the month of Addaru, the twenty-seventh day, the army of Assyria and the army of Akkad joined battle at Hiritu. The army of Akkad stopped fighting, and a crushing defeat was inflicted on it. A state of war was prolonged; there was a succession of battles.

The battle of Hiritu is also recorded in the earliest surviving Astronomical Diaries, dating to the year 652–651: "the army of Akkad and the army of Assyria joined battle together at Hiritu in the province of Sippar. The army of Akkad retreated and suffered great losses." Sources for the history of the conflict are relatively abundant, but few yield precise chronological information. The Annals of Ashurbanipal rarely provide dates for events, and successive editions tend to rearrange and conflate episodes according to literary and geographic schemes with little regard for historical accurateness. Chronicle 20 contains no information after the battle of Hiritu, only repeating, for every year of the conflict, that the New Year Festival did not take place. Thirteen reports of oracular consultations, all extispicy and with dates often preserved, inform us on specific concerns on the conduct of the war at the court of Nineveh, and several more deal with related subjects. State correspondence provides numerous details but the contents of the letters are often elusive and offer no chronological perspective. Babylonian economic documents tell us who was recognized as ruler in specific cities during the conflict.

According to "Edition A" of Ashurbanipal's Annals, Shamash-shumu-ukin rallied to his cause the inhabitants of Akkad, Chaldea, the Sealand, the Arameans, the king of Elam, and the rulers of Gutium (i.e. the Zagros), Amurru (the West, including Arabs) and Meluhha (Ethiopia). Among these groups, however, not everyone backed the rebellion. Shamash-shumu-ukin could rely on the major

northern cities, especially Babylon, Borsippa, and Sippar, which locked their
gates to the Assyrians at the beginning of the war. Nippur sided with him as well
since local documents acknowledge him as ruler during the early phase of the
conflict. The Chaldeans of northern and central Babylonia also generally supported him. In the south the Assyrians relied mainly on cities such as Ur, Uruk,
Kullab, Kissik, and Eridu, all in the Sealand. The countryside of the Sealand,
however, being largely identical with the Chaldean territory of Bit-Yakin, joined
the insurrectionists under the leadership of Nabu-bel-shumati, a grandson of
Marduk-apla-iddina II, who became the staunchest supporter of Shamash-
shumu-ukin. An oracular consultation dated I-4 in the year 651 shows him about
to get involved in the conflict with Elamite military support. Among the Arameans
the Puqudu tribe also joined the rebels. At Uruk one document acknowledges
the rule of Ashurbanipal as early as II-15 in the year 651, less than two months
after the Babylonian defeat at Hiritu, and other documents dated in the years
650 and 649 show continued loyalty to Assyria. The city, led by its governor
Nabu-ushabshi, became in fact the nerve center for Assyrian operations in the
south. At Ur the situation seems to have been more complex. Sin-sharru-usur,
son of Nikkal-iddin, a scion of the local line of hereditary governors, was probably in place at the beginning of the war, but a letter from Nineveh casts doubts
on his loyalty. Soon the Assyrians replaced him with his brother Sin-tabni-usur.
Two oracular consultations with broken dates deal with the latter's appointment,
also voicing concerns about his trustworthiness: "Will Sin-tabni-usur, son of
Nikkal-iddin, be reliable? If [he is ap]pointed [ov]er Ur, will he make common
cause [with] Shamash-shumu-ukin?" In fact, Sin-tabni-usur held out against the
rebels for at least two years. At some point the cities of Kullab and Eridu and the
tribe of the Gurasimmu, normally under the jurisdiction of the governor of Ur,
defected to the enemy. In the end Assyrian troops came from Uruk and other
areas to relieve pressure on the city, and Sin-tabni-usur may still have been in
charge of Ur by the time the war ended.

Elamite support for the rebels caused additional problems for the Assyrians.
Humban-nikash II and Tammaritu, who had been installed by Ashurbanipal as
rulers of Elam, joined the Sealanders led by Nabu-bel-shumati and their allies
the Puqudu as soon as the war started. The political situation in Elam seems to
have been very unstable, and confused at times. Eventually a new ruler seized
power, Humban-haltash III, who also pursued anti-Assyrian policies. In the Seal-
and, Nabu-bel-shumati, well in the tradition of his ancestors, proved a particularly adept and elusive opponent for the Assyrians, who constantly spew venom
at him in the state correspondence. In the spring of 650 Ashurbanipal at last
sent a military commander to the Sealand, a Babylonian named Bel-ibni who
gradually but with great difficulty regained the upper hand for the Assyrians.
Meanwhile in the north the war took a more favorable turn for Ashurbanipal at
the end of 651. Documents from Nippur show that the city had switched allegiance to him by XI-18 in his eighteenth year (beginning of 650). According to
Chronicle 19 the Assyrians laid siege on Babylon on IV-11 in the eighteenth year
of Shamash-shumu-ukin (early summer 650). Four months later on VIII-13 a

document from Babylon acknowledges the state of siege: "At that time, famine and hardship were established in the land and a mother would not open (her) door to (her own) daughter." Arab troops from the Qedarite tribe that had come to the assistance of Shamash-shumu-ukin left the besieged capital but the Assyrians inflicted heavy casualties on them. The siege went on for two more years. A document written X-9 in his nineteenth year (late in 649) reflects the deteriorating conditions: "At that time, the enemy was besieging the city; famine and hardship [were established] in the land; [and] people were dying from lack of food." Another one dated II-29 in his twentieth year (spring of 648) alludes to a black market for basic foodstuffs: "At that time, the enemy was encamped against the city; famine was established in the land; and the market rate was three liters of barley for one shekel of silver, purchased in secret." Ashurbanipal's Annals give even more gruesome descriptions of the famine, with people chewing on leather straps and turning to cannibalism, eating the flesh of their sons and daughters. The last documents dated to the reign of Shamash-shumu-ukin come from Borsippa on V-28, year 20, and Babylon two days later (early summer 648).

No source gives us the date of the fall of Babylon, but circumstantial evidence indicates that the capital was taken in the late summer or autumn of 648. Other cities surrendered at about the same time. Sources are unclear as to the ultimate fate of Shamash-shumu-ukin. Ashurbanipal claims that the gods threw him in a fire, but the implications of this statement are disputed; while suicide or assassination cannot be ruled out, it is also possible that he perished accidentally in a conflagration during the sack of the capital. We find a garbled memory of his death in the writings of the Greek historian Ctesias, who transferred the motif to the last Assyrian king Sardanapalus (= Ashurbanipal), dying on a funeral pyre in self-immolation with his eunuchs and concubines during the siege of his capital Nineveh. Ashurbanipal claims that he took away his brother's regalia and palace furnishings. A bas-relief from the North Palace at Nineveh illustrates the event, with Ashurbanipal standing in his chariot while his brother's crown, scepter, chariot and women are paraded before him. Administrative documents dated in January and March 647 record a major wave of acquisitions made in Babylonia for the Library of Ashurbanipal. These were probably confiscated from families who had viewed the rebellion favorably.

8.10   Ashurbanipal and Kandalanu (647–630/27)

The capture of Babylon and the death of Shamash-shumu-ukin did not mark the end of the war. Elam still supported guerilla actions by Nabu-bel-shumati in southeastern Babylonia while Arab tribes who had sided with the rebels remained at large. Between 647 and 645 the Assyrians launched two destructive campaigns against Elam. Susa was ransacked and the tombs of the Elamite kings desecrated. Humban-haltash III eventually agreed to hand over his ally Nabu-bel-shumati to the Assyrians. The latter preferred to commit suicide and Humban-haltash sent his body preserved in salt to Nineveh as proof of goodwill. Around 645 the

Assyrians campaigned against Arabs who had supported Shamash-shumu-ukin. Abiyate and Ayamu surrendered and the Qedarites handed over their sheikh, Uaite, to the Assyrians. The Nabateans (Nabatayu) also eventually submitted. The Annals of Ashurbanipal remain our sole narrative source for this period, but they come to an end with their most recent edition around 643. After that we know almost nothing about international events or the political history of Babylonia until 627. Ashurbanipal's policy towards Babylon seems to have been generally conciliatory once the threat of secession had been removed. In his Annals he claims to have appointed governors over Babylonia: "I imposed upon them the yoke of the god Ashur which they had cast off; I appointed over them governors and officials whom I had selected." Some of Ashurbanipal's appointees had already been in his service during the civil war, such as Kudurru, the governor of Uruk, and Bel-ibni, the opponent of Nabu-bel-shumati in the Sealand.

In 647 Ashurbanipal installed a new king of Babylon named Kandalanu, who is known only from chronographic texts and date formulas in economic and administrative documents. During his tenure which lasted until 627, all royal inscriptions from Babylonia were exclusively in the name of Ashurbanipal and, after the latter's death, of his son and successor Ashur-etel-ilani. Transfer of power to Kandalanu, albeit largely symbolic, was made only gradually. Ashurbanipal dates continue at Uruk until IV-12 in his twenty-second year (summer of 647), at Borsippa until IX-28 also in his twenty-second year (end of 647), and at Dilbat until I-29 in his twenty-third year (spring of 646). After that Kandalanu dates are exclusively attested in Babylonia except at Nippur, which remained under direct Assyrian administration for the rest of the reign of Ashurbanipal and that of Ashur-etel-ilani. This suggests that the Assyrians had selected Nippur as base for future military operations in Babylonia. The date of Ashurbanipal's death is disputed. Babylonian chronographic texts and the Ptolemaic Canon provide no data since they do not recognize him as ruler of Babylonia except for one year at the time of his accession. The most likely date is around 630 since the four-year long reign of Ashur-etel-ilani must have ended before 625. An inscription from Babylonia records that Ashur-etel-ilani returned the corpse of the Chaldean leader Shamash-ibni to the burial grounds of Bit-Dakkuri. This may have been intended to garner support from this important Chaldean tribe, a sign that Assyrian authority was already slipping in the years preceding the seizure of power by Nabopolassar in Babylon.

NOTES

1. After Luukko 2012: 84.
2. Adapted from Fuchs 1994: 327.
3. After Grayson and Novotny 2012: 172.
4. After Grayson and Novotny 2012: 182.
5. After Brinkman 1984: 64.
6. After Leichty 2011: 196.

7. After Reynolds 2004: 18.
8. After Leichty 2011: 18.
9. After Reynolds 2004: 43.
10. After Parpola 1993: 152.

FURTHER READING

The history of this period is covered in detail by Brinkman 1984 and 1991, and also Frame 1992 (with in-depth discussion of sources). On the interpretation of King List A for this period see Fales 2014. Assyrian sources form an important corpus; royal inscriptions are edited by Fuchs 1994 (Sargon II), Grayson and Novotny 2012 and 2014 (Sennacherib), Leichty 2011 (Esarhaddon), Borger 1995 (Annals of Ashurbanipal), and Frame 1995 (Babylonian inscriptions of Assyrian kings); the relevant state correspondence is edited by Dietrich 2003, Luukko 2012, Parpola 1993, and Reynolds 2004; Parpola and Watanabe 1988 edit the treaties, succession treaties, and oaths of vassality.

Borger, Rykle. 1996. *Beiträge zum Inschriftenwerk Assurbanipals: Die Prismenklassen A, B, C=K, D, E, F, G, H, J, und T sowie andere Inschriften.* Wiesbaden: Harrassowitz.
Brinkman, John Anthony. 1984. *Prelude to Empire: Babylonian Society and Politics, 747–626 B.C.* Philadelphia: University Museum.
Brinkman, John Anthony. 1991, "Babylonia in the Shadow of Assyria (747–626 B.C.)." In Boardman, John, et al. (eds.), *The Cambridge Ancient History*, 2nd ed., volume III/2. Cambridge, UK: Cambridge University Press. 1–70.
Dietrich, Manfred. 2003. *The Babylonian Correspondence of Sargon and Sennacherib.* Helsinki: Helsinki University Press.
Fales, Frederick Mario. 2014. "The Two Dynasties of Assyria." In Gaspa, Salvatore et al. (eds.), *From Source to History: Studies G. B. Lanfranchi.* Münster: Ugarit-Verlag. 201–37
Frame, Grant. 1992. *Babylonia 689–627 B.C.: A Political History.* Leiden: NINO.
Frame, Grant. 1995. *Rulers of Babylonia: From the Second Dynasty of Isin to the End of Assyrian Domination (1157–612 BC):* The Royal Inscriptions of Mesopotamia, Babylonian Periods 2. Toronto: University of Toronto Press.
Fuchs, Andreas. 1994. *Die Inschriften Sargons II. Aus Khorsabad.* Gottingen: Cuvillier Verlag.
Grayson, Albert Kirk, and Novotny, Jamie. 2012 and 2014. *The Royal Inscriptions of Sennacherib, King of Assyria (704–681 BC), Part 1 and 2.* Winona Lake, IN: Eisenbrauns.
Leichty, Erle, 2011. *The Royal Inscriptions of Esarhaddon, King of Assyria (680–669 BC).* Winona Lake, IN: Eisenbrauns.
Luukko, Mikko. 2012. *Correspondence of Tiglath-pileser III and Sargon II from Calah/Nimrud:* State Archives of Assyria 19. Helsinki: Helsinki University Press.
Parpola. Simo. 1993. *Letters from Assyrian and Babylonian Scholars.* Helsinki University Press.
Parpola, Simo, and Watanabe, Kazuko. 1988. *Neo-Assyrian Treaties and Loyalty Oaths.* Helsinki: Helsinki University Press.
Reynolds, Frances. 2004. *The Babylonian Correspondence of Esarhaddon and Letters to Assurbanipal and Sin-šarru-iškun from Northern and Central Babylonia.* Helsinki: Helsinki University Press.

9

Imperial Heyday

The period which began with the accession of Nabopolassar in 626 and ended with the entrance of Cyrus into Babylon in 539 covers less than a century, but it witnessed dramatic changes in the geopolitical and cultural landscape of the Near East. The disappearance of Assyria at the end of the seventh century left a huge political vacuum which Babylon swiftly set out to fill. Under Nebuchadnezzar II the city ruled an empire almost as vast as the Assyrian and became the commercial and political hub of the Near East. Nebuchadnezzar embellished his capital with spectacular monuments that left a lasting imprint on later generations, but his death in 562 ushered in a political crisis that ended in 556 with the usurpation of Nabonidus, who proved unable to contain the growing power of the Persians. The latter, under the leadership of Cyrus the Great, conquered the Babylonian empire in the fall of 539, bringing the history of ancient Mesopotamia as an independent civilization to a sudden end.

Significant cultural shifts occurred during this period. After the fall of Nineveh, Assyria became a backwater and cuneiform disappeared from the north, leaving Babylonia as sole torchbearer of Mesopotamian traditions. The Neo-Babylonian vernacular dialect of Akkadian, referred to as Late Babylonian in its ultimate phase, eventually gave way to Aramaic and some have argued that it had already died out as spoken language by the middle of the sixth century. The rise of a strong monarchy and the creation of a centralized state significantly impacted the political and administrative structure of Babylonia. The Neo-Babylonian kings forced cities and temples, which had been granted fiscal and corvée exemptions by the Assyrians, to relinquish much of their autonomy. The economy of Babylonia prospered in the sixth century, enabling them to launch vast building programs and restore temples in many cities. They also reasserted the homogeneity and antiquity of Babylonian civilization in the face of increasing ethnic and linguistic diversity. The official theology of that era centered on the gods Marduk

A History of Babylon: 2200 BC–AD 75, First Edition. Paul-Alain Beaulieu.

Table 9.1   The Neo-Babylonian Dynasty

Nabopolassar (Nabu-aplu-usur)	626–605
Nebuchadnezzar II (Nabu-kudurru-usur)	604–562
Amel-Marduk	561–560
Neriglissar (Nergal-sharru-usur)	559–556
Labashi-Marduk	556
Nabonidus (Nabu-na'id)	555–539

and Nabu in their role as upholders of the cosmic order and on the position of Babylon as center of the universe. In a sense, the exercise of imperial power gave Babylon, if only for a short while, the concrete expression of the claims long laid by its theologians.

The combined evidence of chronographic sources allows us to reconstruct the tenth and last dynasty of Babylon as shown in Table 9.1. The names of these kings are known mostly by their Greek or Hebrew (Biblical) forms, and these conventions are generally followed here, with native forms between parentheses.

9.1 Sources

With the fall of Assyria two of our richest sources for political history come to an end: the annals of the Assyrian kings, and the state archives of Nineveh with their detailed correspondence between the king and his officials, advisors, and scholars. No equivalent exists for the Babylonian empire or the period of Persian and Greek rule. For political history Babylonian chronicles remain our single most important source. However, they are only about half preserved for that period, leaving a huge gap for most of the reign of Nebuchadnezzar II (years 12–43). This is a deplorable loss since no other source provides us with data on the political history of Babylon during the reign of its most famous ruler. Table 9.2 shows that extant manuscripts contain only about half of the yearly entries for the period 626–529.

The Neo-Babylonian dynasty has left a large number of official inscriptions, but they yield very little historical information. The main genre is still the building inscription, which usually consists of a long list of royal titles and epithets, followed by an account of the building and a prayer to the patron deity

Table 9.2   Chronicles of the Babylonian Empire

Nabopolassar	Years 0–3, 10–21 preserved	Years 4–9 missing
Nebuchadnezzar II	Years 0–11 preserved	Years 12–43 missing
Amel-Marduk	none preserved	Years 0–2 missing
Neriglissar	Year 3 preserved	Years 0–2, 4 missing
Labashi-Marduk	none preserved	Year 0 missing
Nabonidus	Years 1–3, 6–11, 17 preserved	Years 0, 4–5, 12–16 missing

of the temple. A few inscriptions of Nebuchadnezzar record the building of palaces and fortifications in Babylon, but these too are almost entirely devoid of historical data. Classical and Jewish sources sometimes yield supplemental information. However, apart from the Biblical account of the conquest of Judah by Nebuchadnezzar and the brief history of the Neo-Babylonian dynasty by Berossus, this evidence seems sketchy and not always reliable. Finally we must add cuneiform literary texts. The rise of a new native dynasty favored the composition of hymns, epics, and literary propaganda extolling the virtues and achievements of kings. Under the Persians, court writers even created counter-propaganda demonizing Nabonidus, but largely as a foil to celebrate the achievements of Cyrus. This body of literature entered the stream of tradition and is known mostly from late Achaemenid and Hellenistic copies. In spite of its tendentious nature it constitutes an invaluable source for the political and cultural history of the Babylonian empire.

9.1.1   Neo-Babylonian Archives

The single most important cuneiform source for that period consists of archives. A rough count of the published and unpublished archival texts and fragments from Babylonia dated between the eighth and second centuries reaches more than 60,000 items, of which only the smaller part have been published (ca. 17,000). The bulk of the material dates to the time of the Babylonian empire and the early Achaemenid period down to second year of the reign of Xerxes, that is to say between 626 and 484. The texts stem from Babylon, Borsippa, Dilbat, Dur-sharrukku, Isin, Kissik, Kish and Hursagkalamma, Kutha, Larsa, Nippur, Sippar, Ur, Uruk, as well as a few small localities. Isolated cuneiform documents have also surfaced outside Babylonia. In spite of its size and distri-bution this material presents limitations. The only state archive we have consists of about 300 texts discovered in the storerooms of the South Palace in Babylon. The texts, few of which have been published, record deliveries of commodities and date mostly between the tenth and twenty-eighth years of Nebuchadnezzar II (595–577). Other institutional archives stem from temples. The archive of Ebabbar, the temple of the sun-god Shamash in Sippar, has been evaluated at some 35,000 texts and fragments dating in their majority between 626 and 484. The archive of Eanna, the temple of the goddess Ishtar in the city of Uruk, includes at least 8,000 texts and an unknown number of fragments. Its time range is shorter, most of the texts falling between 626 and 520. These two archives alone compose the bulk of the Neo-Babylonian documentation and provide historians with considerable data on the social and economic history of the period, as well as some significant information on the political and administrative history of the empire.

Private archives make up the other side of our documentation. The archive of the Egibi business family in Babylon includes 1,700 transactions that have been identified so far and could surpass a count of 2,000 texts, the largest Neo-Babylonian private archive known to date. Several archives of median size (100 to 400 texts) are known, for example those of the Nappahu family from Babylon (ca. 300 texts), of the Re'i-alpi family from Borsippa (ca. 400 texts), of the Ea-ilutu-bani and Ili-bani family, also from Borsippa (ca. 325 texts), of Itti-Shamash-balatu and his son from Larsa (ca. 200 texts), and the Shangu-Shamash archive from Sippar (ca. 160 texts). A large number of smaller archives include less than a hundred texts, many of them comprising only a handful of transactions. The time range of the larger private archives can be considerable, covering five or six generations in some cases. The archives of the Egibi, the Ea-ilutu-bani/Ili-bani, and the Re'i-alpi all begin in the seventh century and end in the first two years of the reign of Xerxes (486–484), encompassing an era that witnessed various political upheavals. Private archives document mostly the life of a restricted segment of the Babylonian urban elites, the majority of them prebend holders in temples. They formed an important social group alongside Aramean and Chaldean tribes and wielded great social and cultural prestige. They also controlled the administration of temples and cities. While ultimately dependent on the monarchy for nominations to priestly and municipal offices, their role in shaping the politics of Babylonia must have been substantial. Indeed, the fourth ruler of the dynasty, Neriglissar, an Aramean from the Puqudu tribe in eastern Babylonia, married off his daughter Gigitu to the high-priest of the Ezida temple of Borsippa in a probable attempt to shore up his legitimacy among them.

9.1.2   Spread of Aramaic

The spread of the Aramaic language eventually led to the demise of Late Babylonian as spoken vernacular. Already in the sixth century we find frequent references to the *sepiru*, a loanword from the Aramaic language meaning "scribe, secretary." The term *sepiru* can be translated as "alphabet scribe" or "parchment scribe" and refers to a class of professionals who wrote documentation in Aramaic using parchment or papyrus. Neo-Assyrian palatial art often depicts two scribes standing side by side, one holding a tablet and stylus and writing in Assyrian cuneiform, the other a scroll and pen and recording the same information in Aramaic. During the time of the Babylonian empire most of the *sepiru*s worked for the royal administration, which was probably bilingual like the late Assyrian bureaucracy. However, the perishable nature of the writing media used by the *sepiru*s, especially in the harsh climate of Iraq, explains why the Aramaic documentation has not survived. Temples, on the other hand, appear to have been far more conservative, and the rare mentions of *sepiru*s attached to them in the sixth century indicate that they continued to use cuneiform Babylonian as main administrative language. Therefore the documentation on clay tablets, in spite of its relative abundance, gives us a partial view of Babylonian society and culture at that time.

9.2 Power Struggle for Babylonia (630–620)

Ashurbanipal died probably in 630, leaving the empire in the hands of his heir Ashur-etel-ilani, who reigned only four years. In or around 628 another son of Ashurbanipal, Sin-sharru-ishkun rebelled against his brother and laid claim to the Assyrian throne. By 627–626 the political situation showed further instability with the rise of another pretender called Sin-shumu-lishir, who did not stem from the royal family. To add to the confusion the Babylonian puppet ruler Kandalanu died in 627, leaving the throne unoccupied. Some legal documents from the year 626–625 are dated by "the year after Kandalanu" and Chronicle 21 states that "for one year there was no king in the country." Soon, however, a new claimant to the Babylonian throne by the name of Nabopolassar (Nabu-aplu-usur "O Nabu, preserve the heir") appeared on the scene. According to the Uruk King List, Sin-shumu-lishir and Sin-sharru-ishkun reigned one year concurrently between Kandalanu and Nabopolassar. Chronicle 20 states that "after Kandalanu, the year of Nabopolassar's accession, troubles took place in Assyria and Akkad; a state of war was prolonged; there was a succession of battles." Chronicle 21 and Babylonian documents reckon the balance of the year 626–625 as the "accession year of Nabopolassar, king of Babylon," the official date of his accession being the twenty-sixth day of the month Arahsamnu (eighth month), corresponding to November 23, 626 in the Julian calendar.

The disappearance of Ashur-etel-ilani and Kandalanu, and the swift elimination of Sin-shumu-lishir, left Nabopolassar and Sin-sharru-ishkun sole competitors in Babylonia. Two documents from Uruk dated to the accession year of Nabopolassar predate his recognition in Babylon by several months, and Chronicle 21 states that one month prior to his official accession to the throne, Nabopolassar retreated to Uruk in the face of the Assyrian offensive and defeated his opponents there. The later tradition that Nabopolassar originated from the Sealand province and rose in that region against the Assyrians, a view echoed in Berossus, coheres with the evidence that one of his initial bases of operation was Uruk, although the city appears to have been divided between a pro-Assyrian and a pro-Nabopolassar camp for a while. There is a possibility that Nabopolassar's family originated from Uruk and occupied some administrative functions there, but the evidence is not conclusive. The political and military situation after his initial bid for power seems to have been quite confused for a number of years. Texts from Uruk indicate that Nabopolassar was recognized there during his accession year and his first two years (626–623). During the next three years (623–620) date formulas generally acknowledge the rule of Sin-sharru-ishkun, with only one text dated to the fourth regnal year of Nabopolassar. In addition, several documents refer to an alternative dating system according to "the year of the closing of the (city) gate" or "the year of hostilities in the land," hinting at a highly volatile situation. By the year 620 at last, Nabopolassar had achieved full control of Uruk and possibly of all Babylonia. Assyrian and Babylonian forces also competed for several years over the control of Nippur, Assyria's main operational base in Babylonia, but the date of the final Assyrian withdrawal from the city cannot be ascertained.

9.3   A Chaldeo-Aramean Empire

It seems dubious that Nabopolassar foresaw the destruction of Assyria. His bid
for Babylonian independence stood in direct line with several previous attempts
at shaking off the Assyrian yoke, starting with the Chaldean king Marduk-apla-
iddina II a century earlier and ending with the rebellion of Shamash-shumu-ukin
and the guerilla warfare led by the Chaldean chieftain Nabu-bel-shumati in the
middle of the seventh century. The prominence of the Chaldeans in the fight
against the Assyrians, and the fact that the Bible sometimes labels Nebuchadnezzar II as "king of the Chaldeans" have induced many scholars to assume that
Nabopolassar was also a Chaldean. As a result the terms "Chaldean Dynasty"
and "Chaldean Empire" have often been applied to this period in spite of the fact
that no conclusive evidence has yet surfaced on the origins of the new royal
house. In his inscriptions, Nabopolassar styles himself "son of nobody," a standard designation for upstarts with no blood ties to a royal or princely house. Such
blank admission of humble background may seem surprising, but it coheres well
with the larger claim which Nabopolassar puts forward, that of having been
selected by the god Marduk to avenge Babylonia from Assyrian depredations and
restore its shrines. Such appeal to divine election to assert one's legitimacy
derived from a long tradition going back to the Early Dynastic period:

> When I was young, although I was the son of nobody, I constantly sought the sanc-
> tuaries of my lords the gods Nabu and Marduk. My mind was preoccupied with
> the establishment of their prescriptions and the complete performance of their rit-
> uals. My attention was directed at justice and equity. The god Shazu (= Marduk),
> the lord who fathoms the hearts of the gods of heaven and the netherworld, who
> constantly observes the conducts of mankind, perceived my inner thoughts and ele-
> vated me, me the servant who was anonymous among the people, to a high status
> in the country in which I was born. He called me to the lordship over the country
> and the people. He caused a benevolent protective spirit to walk at my side. He let
> (me) succeed in everything I undertook. He caused the god Nergal, the strongest
> among the gods, to march at my side; he slew my foes, felled my enemies. The
> Assyrian(s), who had ruled Akkad because of divine anger and had, with his heavy
> yoke, oppressed the inhabitants of the country, I, the weak one, the powerless one,
> who constantly seeks the lord of lords, with the mighty strength of the gods Nabu
> and Marduk my lords I removed them from Akkad and caused (the Babylonians)
> to throw off their yoke.[1]

However, even if the Chaldean origin of Nabopolassar cannot be established,
there is evidence that Chaldean and Aramean tribes continued to play an
important role during Babylon's imperial era. The *Hofkalender* of Nebuchadnezzar II, listing the territorial "dignitaries of Babylonia" (*rabuti sha mat Akkadi*),
includes the leaders of Dakkuru and Amukanu in the roster alongside prominent
Aramean tribes such as Puqudu and Gambulu. The Bit-Dakkuri and Bit-
Amukani also occur many times in the documentation from the Eanna temple at
Uruk. The epic on the coronation of Nabopolassar depicts the "dignitaries of

Babylonia" (*rabuti sha mat Akkadi*) playing the leading role during the ceremony. It also mentions the "princes of the land" (*rubu sha mati*), possibly an alternative designation for the same group. Neriglissar, imitated by Nabonidus later, refers to his father Bel-shumu-ishkun, the tribal leader of Puqudu, as a "wise prince" (*rubu emqu*). The book of Jeremiah (35:11) claims that during the Babylonian invasion of 587–586 Nebuchadnezzar came to Jerusalem with an army of Chaldeans and Arameans, suggesting that these tribes wielded significant military power. This fact may account for the ease with which Neriglissar, now chief of the Aramean Puqudu tribe, usurped the throne from Amel-Marduk only two years after the death of Nebuchadnezzar. Thus, in spite of the fact that the cultural, religious, and political institutions of the new state were very traditionally Babylonian (with some Assyrian components), the influence of long-established Chaldeans and Arameans in its fabric may justify the appellation of Chaldean, even of Chaldeo-Aramean, for the Babylonian Empire.

9.4 The Fall of Assyria (616–609)

The experience of the past century probably instilled fear of an Assyrian return, but destroying the weakened, yet still powerful northern state seemed beyond the abilities of Nabopolassar. Soon, however, convenient allies appeared on the horizon: the Medes, an Iranian people living east of Assyria. According to Berossus, Nabopolassar concluded a matrimonial alliance with the Median king Cyaxares, who married off his granddaughter to the crown prince Nebuchadnezzar. While we do not know to what degree this information is reliable, the succession of events clearly indicates that the two powers eventually struck a deal to eliminate Assyria from the map.

We can follow the trajectory of Assyrian demise with the help of Chronicle 22 covering the years 616 to 609. In 616 the Babylonian armies campaigned in the middle Euphrates region and routed the Assyrians near the town of Balihu. A few months later the stage of military operations moved east of the Tigris where the Babylonians scored another victory in the region of Arrapha. This opened the Assyrian heartland to them and in 615 they were already laying siege on the city of Assur. The Assyrians counterattacked and pushed the Babylonians back south to the city of Tikrit on the Tigris. At this point the Medes entered the stage, moving westward from Iran into the region of Arrapha and then to the town of Tarbisu, which they captured, and finally to Assur, which was apparently taken and sacked in 614. Nabopolassar joined them there and made a formal alliance with Cyaxares. In 613 Nabopolassar suppressed an uprising in the land of Suhu. The German excavators found some monuments originating from that area during the excavations of the North Palace of Babylon. These finds included a stele of Shamash-reshu-usur, one of the semi-independent governors of the Suhu in the eighth century, and a statue of Puzur-Ishtar, an early ruler of Mari. They probably came to Babylon as war trophies in the wake of Nabopolassar's victorious campaign. Finally in the summer of 612 Medes and Babylonians joined forces against Nineveh which fell after a siege of three months. Sin-sharru-ishkun perished as the victors sacked and burned the once invincible capital. The new Assyrian king Ashur-uballit II tried to organize resistance at Harran in northern Syria with the help of the Egyptians, now wary of Babylon's growing power. But Harran fell in turn to the coalition of Medes and Babylonians in 610. The failure of Ashur-uballit and his Egyptian allies to recapture the city in their ultimate campaign of 609 brought the long history of Assyria to a close.

The fall of the Assyrian Empire, unimaginable even a generation before, resonated deeply in the consciousness of Near Eastern peoples. The Biblical prophet Nahum, a contemporary of the events, gloats vengefully over the fall of the imperial city: "Nineveh is devastated; who will bemoan her?" (Nahum 3:7). He also greets the demise of the king of Assyria with glee, stressing his inhumanity (3:18–19):

> Your shepherds are asleep, O king of Assyria; your nobles slumber. Your people are scattered on the mountains, with no one to gather them. There is no assuaging your hurt, your wound is mortal. All who hear the news about you clap their hands over you, for who has ever escaped your cruelty?

Similar judgments are echoed by the prophet Zephaniah. The portrayal of Nineveh as arrogant and corrupt imperial hub finds its ultimate literary expression in the book of Jonah, albeit certainly a later work. Punishment was meted out on Assyria for her brutality and iniquity. In the end only those who put their faith in the god of Israel emerged vindicated. But are such judgments unique to the Bible? Babylonian sources also point to Assyrian brutality and moral failings. The inscriptions of Nabopolassar, reflecting on the demise of the mighty empire, propose a theology of history which emphasizes the pious and contemplative life, exhorting future rulers to shun feats of arms and trust instead in the designs of Marduk:

> Any king, at any time, whether a son or a grandson who will succeed me, (and) whose name Marduk will call to exert rulership of the country, do not be concerned with feats of might and power. Seek the sanctuaries of Nabu and Marduk and let them slay your enemies. The lord Marduk examines utterances and scrutinizes the heart. He who is loyal to Bel (= Marduk), his foundations will endure. He who is loyal to the son of Bel (= Nabu) will last for eternity.[2]

Such rhetoric provided the new Babylonian state with a foundation myth reflected in the official inscriptions of the dynasty and also in the later historical tradition. Two literary letters from Babylon dating to the Hellenistic era preserve alleged correspondence between Nabopolassar and the Assyrian king Sin-sharru-ishkun, who is portrayed as a submissive prince almost ready to acknowledge himself as vassal of the new Babylonian king. The better preserved part of the exchange contains an elaborate exposition of the reasons prompting Nabopolassar to take up arms against Assyria. He recalls the harsh treatment which Sennacherib inflicted on Babylon and the crimes he committed against the god Marduk, even carrying off the property of the Esagil temple to Assyria. Nabopolassar proclaims himself the avenger of Babylon, promising to punish the Assyrians and their arrogant capital Nineveh for their past sacrilege.

9.5   Nabopolassar and the Restoration of Babylonia

Nabopolassar initiated the ambitious building program which symbolizes Babylon's imperial era, although his efforts concentrated mostly on Babylon and Sippar and appear modest in comparison with those of his successors. In Babylon he sponsored work on the walls Imgur-Enlil and Nemetti-Enlil, the royal palace, the ziggurat Etemenanki, the Ehursagtila temple of the god Ninurta, and various repairs and improvements on the canal and river system. His building inscriptions show a stylistic break with the preceding era. He adopted the practice of editing inscriptions in two scripts, one in the contemporary Neo-Babylonian script, and the other one in an archaizing script imitating the monumental script of the Old Babylonian period. The scribes resurrected titles, formulas, and spellings found in inscriptions of the First Dynasty of Babylon to link the new royal house to a glorious past. Old Akkadian inscriptions also provided occasional inspiration for the inscriptions of Nabopolassar, sometimes via Old Babylonian intermediaries but in some cases probably also as direct borrowings from inscriptions of Sargon and his successors. The best known example of Old Akkadian revival is the Cruciform Monument of Manishtushu, a textual forgery concocted by the priests of Sippar in the time of Nabopolassar. The inscription displays reasonably accurate imitations of Old Akkadian paleography, spelling, and grammar, proving that the scribes had ancient texts at their disposal which they studied and understood quite well. Historians refer to this cultural practice as antiquarianism. Attachment to tradition had always been very strong in Mesopotamia, and the remembrance of the past a strong component of the culture. In the Neo-Babylonian period the antiquarian discourse gained renewed strength, with more insistence on the retrieval and revival of long forgotten cultural and religious practices. Reverence for the past also played an instrumental role in the legitimization of the new dynasty.

9.6   Nebuchadnezzar in the Levant

After the fall of Harran in 610, Babylon and Egypt both tried to exploit the situation. According to Chronicle 23 Nabopolassar campaigned in Urartu and in the vicinity of Carchemish between 608 and 606, encountering limited resistance and with apparent lack of Median interference. In 605 a decisive military engagement occurred at Carchemish, where the crown prince Nebuchadnezzar inflicted a crushing defeat on the Egyptians in a battle that set Babylon on the path to controlling the Levant. Nebuchadnezzar succeeded his father soon after.

The sequence of events after Carchemish is detailed in Chronicle 24, which covers the first eleven years of Nebuchadnezzar. The entries for the years 605, 604, 603, and 601 all record that Nebuchadnezzar and his army marched victoriously through the Levant, receiving tribute and other marks of obedience. The relatively easy royal progress encountered little opposition in areas which had been turned into Assyrian provinces earlier. The Babylonian armies faced more resistance in the southern Levant. The Chronicle reports that in 604 Nebuchadnezzar marched against the city of Ashkelon on the Philistine coast, captured its king, plundered the city, and reduced it to a heap of rubble. Excavations at Ashkelon have largely confirmed that the city was completely destroyed at that time. Egypt tried to prop the small states of the region against the Babylonian advance. A papyrus found at Saqqarah in Egypt contains a letter addressed to the pharaoh in which a ruler named Adon asks for help against the advance of the king of Babylon, who has reportedly reached the city of Aphek. The place ruled by Adon is not preserved but some have suggested the inland Philistine city of Ekron, which also suffered severe destruction around that time.

The kingdom of Judah, with its capital Jerusalem safely ensconced in the highlands of Palestine, stood at the epicenter of the competition between the two powers. In 601, counting on Egyptian support, the king of Judah Jehoiakim openly challenged Babylon. Nebuchadnezzar's response came in 598 with a military assault on Jerusalem which is reported not only in the Bible but also in Chronicle 24:

> The seventh year (of Nebuchadnezzar), in the month of Kislimu, the king of Akkad mustered his troops, marched to the Levant, and set up his quarters facing the city of Judah (Jerusalem). In the month of Addaru (early in 597), the second day, he took the city and captured the king. He installed there a king of his choice. He colle[cted] its massive tribute and went back to Babylon.

Jehoiakim died during the siege and was replaced by his son Jehoiakin, who was taken prisoner to Babylon together with a first wave of deportees. Jehoiakin appears as recipient of foodstuffs in a text from Nebuchadnezzar's palace at Babylon dated in the year 592–591 (Nebuchadnezzar year 13). He is still listed as "king of the land of Judah" together with his retinue while his uncle Zedekiah, installed in his stead by Nebuchadnezzar as vassal ruler, was waiting for the opportune moment to throw off the Babylonian yoke. Egyptian involvement in Palestine intensified again during the reign of Psammetichus II (595–589), and his successor Apries (Hophra) openly encouraged rebellion against Nebuchadnezzar. The outcome is known only from the Bible since Chronicle 24 breaks off in 594. Nebuchadnezzar marched again on Jerusalem. The siege lasted from the ninth to the eleventh year of Zedekiah (II Kings 25:1–2) and the city was captured probably in the summer of 586. The suppression of this second rebellion resulted in the sack and destruction of Jerusalem, the abolition of the Judean monarchy, and a second exile to Babylonia. Some Judean administration remained at Mizpah (probably Tell en-Nasbeh) with Gedaliah nominally in charge, but under close Babylonian monitoring.

The degree to which Judah became an "empty land" has been the subject of much debate among Biblical scholars and archaeologists, but it also has importance for Babylon's history since it reflects on the policies of Nebuchadnezzar in the Levant. Surveys indicate that Jerusalem and the surrounding areas were indeed destroyed and depopulated, as well as the Shephelah and the military forts protecting the western border of Judah. Some have claimed that the intensity of destruction in Judah, Ashkelon, Ekron, and other sites proves that Nebuchadnezzar implemented a deliberate scorched earth policy to prevent the Egyptians from gaining a foothold in Palestine. Jeremiah (52:30) mentions a third deportation of Judeans in 582, in the twenty-third year of Nebuchadnezzar. Gedaliah was assassinated around that time, and Jeremiah (40:14) alludes to the participation of the king of Ammon, Baalis, in the plot. In addition, Josephus claims that, also in the twenty-third year of his reign, Nebuchadnezzar led an expedition against Ammon and Moab as part of a larger effort to invade Egypt, so all these events may be connected. Epigraphic evidence recently uncovered in Egypt supports the existence of a war with Babylon in that year. Archaeological evidence confirms that Moab was destroyed and largely abandoned around the middle of the sixth century (eastern Kerak plateau), but this could also have happened during the campaigns of Nabonidus in Transjordan and Arabia.

Further north, the port city of Tyre met with a different fate. It had already accepted vassal status by 598–597 since it is mentioned in the *Hofkalender* of Nebuchadnezzar as a contributor to the construction of the South Palace in Babylon. After the second capture of Jerusalem, and largely in response to Egyptian manipulations in the Levant, Nebuchadnezzar laid siege to the city, but the evidence for the length and date of the conflict comes mainly from Josephus and is subject to debate. It seems that eventually both parties came to an agreement and Tyre continued to be ruled by local kings under renewed and probably heavier Babylonian vassalage. A number of cuneiform texts written at Tyre in the last decade of the reign of Nebuchadnezzar indicate that the city had become a center for Babylonian military operations in the region. Thus, by the middle of his reign, and largely through his conquests in the Levant, Nebuchadnezzar had transformed Babylon from a rump state of the Assyrian Empire into the new Near Eastern hegemon.

9.7 The Climax of Babylon

The excavations led at Babylon by the German archaeologist Robert Koldewey from 1899 until the outbreak of World War I in 1914 revealed the architectural wonders of Nebuchadnezzar's capital. In fact, the image of Babylon propagated in modern books on history and archaeology reflects mostly the appearance of the city after the extensive rebuilding which took place during his reign. His building inscriptions record the restoration of numerous temples, including E-niggidri-kalamma-summa; Emah, the temple of the mother goddess Ninmah located at the city's main entrance; and of course Esagil, the temple of Marduk. Nebuchadnezzar also completed Etemenanki, the ziggurat of Marduk. For this

Figure 9.1   Lion of Babylon. Nebuchadnezzar II rebuilt in grandiose style the processional entrance way to Babylon passing through the Gate of Isthar. Glazed brick panels lined up the highway with figures of lions, symbols of the goddess Ishtar. A large number of them were recovered and restored during the German excavations before World War I. *Source*: The Metropolitan Museum of Arts (MMA 31.13.1), Public Domain.

latter project, begun by the Assyrian kings Esarhaddon and Ashurbanipal and continued by Nabopolassar, Nebuchadnezzar claims to have imposed the corvée throughout the empire. Indeed, much of the architectural extravagance of his reign was sustained by the spoils of imperial conquest.

Civil and military structures were not neglected. The most impressive projects were launched around the Gate of Isthar, the monumental entrance north of the city. They included the restoration of the South Palace located inside the city walls; the building of a new palace, the North Palace, on the other side of the walls facing the Gate of Isthar; and the Processional Way leading through the Gate of Isthar towards the temple complex of the god Marduk in the center. The Gate of Isthar was rebuilt in grandiose style and covered with blue and yellow glazed bricks alternately depicting the bull of the god Adad and the mythical dragon of the god Marduk. Similar glazed bricks adorned the walls around the processional way with depictions of lions, a symbol of the goddess Isthar (Figure 9.1). The walls in the throne room of the South Palace were also covered with panels of glazed bricks representing tall stylized palm trees with lions striding at their base. These monuments have been reconstructed from thousands of fragments and can be seen in the Vorderasiatisches Museum in Berlin (Figure 9.2). Babylon must have been an impressive sight for visitors, rising like a jewel above the plains. No surprise that Greek writers echoed its splendor in their lists of wonders of the world, which included the city's defensive walls and the famed Hanging Gardens which Nebuchadnezzar allegedly built around his palace, but for which no contemporary evidence has yet surfaced, archaeological or textual.

Nebuchadnezzar also lavished particular attention on Borsippa, the city of the god Nabu. Several of his inscriptions commemorate the rebuilding of Ezida, the

Figure 9.2   Gate of Ishtar. The Gate of Ishtar has been partly reconstructed in the Vorderasiatische Museum, part of the Pergamon Museum, Berlin. A large inscription of Nebuchadnezzar II on glazed bricks appears on the side of the gate. Such displays must have made a considerable impression on visitors to the city, spreading its fame throughout the ancient world. *Source*: Gryffindor: https://commons.wikimedia.org/wiki/File:Pergamon_ Museum_Berlin_2007085.jpg?uselang=fr (accessed April 25, 2017).

temple of Nabu, of E-urme-imin-anki, the ziggurat of Ezida, and of Etila, the temple of Gula, as well as a number of shrines and smaller temples. His rock relief inscription at Wadi Brissa in Lebanon also mentions work on the city walls of Borsippa. The archives of the Borsippa families Ea-ilutu-bani and Ili-bani include texts detailing their participation in the building ventures of Nabopolassar and especially Nebuchadnezzar (years 12–21). The texts record mostly contracts to deliver bricks, although it is not clear whether they participated as independent contractors or in fulfillment of corvée obligation.

The inscriptions of Nebuchadnezzar provide unfortunately sparse details on the logistics of these building projects, but archival texts sometimes supplement official accounts and illustrate a different side of the story. The best such source for the reign of Nebuchadnezzar consists of a group of about forty documents dated between years 18 and 27 of his reign. The texts stem from the archive of the Eanna temple at Uruk and document the city's participation in the building of the North Palace as part of the corvée. The authorities of Uruk were responsible for building a segment of the palace and shipped bricks and building materials to Babylon that were stored in a warehouse at the Gate of Enlil across the Euphrates River from the building site. They also sent to Babylon a labor force composed of temple dependents supplemented with hired workers paid in silver. The texts record expenditures in detail, including the salaries paid to architects, and mention some interesting details such as using torches to illuminate trenches for workers on the night shift. The texts confirm the claims which Nebuchadnezzar and other kings sometimes put forward in their inscriptions, that they imposed the corvée throughout their dominions to carry out large building projects.

9.7.1   Economic Expansion

Nebuchadnezzar reigned over a prosperous realm. Archaeological surveys have shown that more than half of the population lived in settlements of more than ten hectares, usually considered the threshold between village and city. Babylonia had finally recovered from its demographic slump of the early Iron Age. The royal administration encouraged agricultural growth with hydrological works and land reclamation. The development of these projects can be followed in the region of Sippar, where we have a combination of official sources in the form of building inscriptions and an abundance of archival documents from the temple Ebabbar. Nabopolassar started work on the Nar-Shamash which brought water from the Euphrates close to the city. This allowed gardens for the prebendaries of the Ebabbar temple (the *rab-bane*) to be allocated in the accession year of Nebuchadnezzar. Early in his reign work started on the Royal Canal (also known as Nebuchadnezzar's Canal), an important waterway linking the Euphrates to the Tigris. It completely changed the patterns of agriculture in that region but was not completed until late in the reign of Nabonidus. The new canal ran south of the Median Wall, a defensive structure built at the same time to prevent incursions into northern Babylonia. Important temple estates producing mainly grain lay along the canal. It was part of a land reclamation project in an area that had probably suffered greatly from the wars between Assyria and Babylonia in the seventh century. These projects were carried out as corvée duty, with not only Sippar contributing but also more distant constituencies such as Borsippa and Uruk. The reclaimed land was cultivated mostly by rent farmers. Although such rapid expansion of the agricultural base cannot be observed in southern Babylonia, the archives of the Eanna temple at Uruk, one of the largest landowners in that region, also reflect an interest of the monarchy in agricultural development since the royal administration intervened directly in the management of the temple's agricultural domains. They encouraged on a large scale the system of rent farming whereby entrepreneurs, often royal favorites, leased tracts of land from the temple and sub-leased them in parcels to tenants, promising temple authorities a fixed return on the harvest. Agricultural expansion also favored the establishment of a new system of military land tenure which made its first appearance under Nebuchadnezzar and expanded considerably under the Achaemenids.

Another development of the period which has come under full view in recent research is the monetization of the Neo-Babylonian economy. The kings of Lydia in Asia Minor introduced the first known coinage in the seventh century. From there it spread to the Greek cities of the Aegean coast and to the Greek mainland. The Neo-Babylonian kings did not mint coinage. However, use of silver money spread considerably in the sixth century, with the silver shekel becoming the basic accounting device to assign market value in the trade, exchange and allocation of goods and commodities. Large institutions such as temples, which traditionally functioned as autarchic economic units with internal redistributive systems, became more integrated in the surrounding economy. As a result the Ebabbar at Sippar and the Eanna at Uruk increasingly depended on the sale of cash crops (dates at Sippar, wool at Uruk) to raise the silver needed to pay hired labor and also to acquire the goods they did not produce. Starting with the reign of Nebuchadnezzar, references to the purity of silver become regular, the most common being to silver with one-eight alloy. Increased monetization also facilitated the integration of Babylonia in the vast trade networks which linked the Near East to the Mediterranean world. The Babylonian empire became a major economic power with the subjugation of Levantine harbors and increased control over the lucrative trade of Transjordan and north Arabia. Not surprisingly, the holder of the important office of Chief of the Royal Merchants (*rab tamkari sha sharri*) according to the *Hofkalender* of Nebuchadnezzar bore the typical Phoenician name of Hanunu. Babylonia in the sixth century enjoyed a comparatively high standard of living. Wages paid to hired laborers reached almost double what they were in the late third and early second millennia. Neo-Babylonian houses were on average much larger than Old Babylonian ones, another indication of greater means of living. Dowry and inheritance documents also show that Neo-Babylonian families owned many more household goods and material possessions than their Old Babylonian counterparts. At the same time there is a much larger range of house sizes in the first millennium, surely a mark of increased social inequality.

9.7.2 Administration of Babylonia

The palaces of Babylon have not yielded archives of any significance and therefore numerous aspects of state administration remain unknown. Our main source on the high officialdom is the *Hofkalender* of Nebuchadnezzar. This document belongs to a building inscription on a clay prism dated to the seventh year of Nebuchadnezzar (598–597). The inscription commemorates the restoration and enlargement of the South Palace in Babylon and provides a list of high officials who contributed to the task: first the high officials of the palace, then the dignitaries of Babylonia (*rabuti sha mat Akkadi*), also mentioned as a group in the Nabopolassar Epic, and finally the provincial and city governors of Babylonia and vassal rulers of the Levant. Several officials mentioned in the list also appear in contemporary archival documents with the same functions, and two are even mentioned in the Bible as being present at the second siege of Jerusalem (Nebuzeraddan and Nergalsharezer). Not surprisingly many of these functions have an Assyrian origin.

The personal names of the officials listed in the *Hofkalender* deserve more than passing notice. The palace officials, those closer to the king, bear in their majority names honoring the god Nabu. Other groups show different patterns, with few Nabu names. In the sixth century Nabu had become in many respects the most important god of Babylon and enjoyed a close tie to the monarchy, presiding over the coronation of the king in the temple E-niggidri-kalamma-summa. The names of three contemporary rulers are formed with the god Nabu (Nabopolassar, Nebuchadnezzar, and Nabonidus), and bearing a Nabu name was very probably an additional means of expressing devotion to the king. The proliferation of eunuchs (*sha reshi*) among royal officials also reflects the elaboration of a pyramidal structure of power binding all its members personally to the monarch, eunuchs having no personal family ties and therefore no competing allegiance. This structure was further reinforced by the widespread imposition of oaths of loyalty (*adê*) to the king, even in the lower echelons of local administrations.

Other influential groups existed alongside the royal bureaucracy. Chaldeans and Arameans dominated much of the countryside with their own tribal organization. There is no evidence for any significant conflict between them and the state and they seem to have been well integrated in the larger society. The traditional urban elites formed compact groups claiming descent from pedigreed ancestors (the *mar bani*); they controlled the temples, and the administration of cities as well to some degree. They certainly wielded some influence, although the monarchy increased its control over the temples considerably during the reigns of Nebuchadnezzar and Nabonidus, especially with the creation of new offices staffed by royal appointees, often eunuchs. Ultimately all priests owed their appointments to the king. This imposed serious restrictions on the independence of temples, but the royal bureaucracy appears to have favored a shared model of administration which safeguarded both the privileged status of urban elites and the interests of the state.

Another area where royal intervention can be detected is law. Here too the Babylonian Empire continued Assyrian practices with the same titles for the two highest judicial officials, *sukkallu* and *sartennu*. Centralization of procedures is evident in the creation of royal courts and the appointment of royal judges. Law and judicial procedure seem to have become standardized since we find no evidence for the survival of local practices, and legal institutions display a higher level of systematization and abstraction, all signs of a rational effort at state building. A small collection of Neo-Babylonian laws has survived; the manuscript is from Sippar and dates roughly to the early seventh century, well before the rise of the Babylonian Empire. Only fifteen articles are preserved. As in the

Code of Hammu-rabi the *awilum* (*amelu* in Neo-Babylonian) still occupies the upper social strata; slaves are called *amelutu*, a term which appears in the Kassite period. Other social groups are not mentioned. In texts from everyday legal practice, however, it is the term *mar bani* which designates the privileged class, or "free class." Several documents record the manumission of members of the lower social strata into the *mar bani* class. The other social group that is frequently mentioned, especially in temple archives, are the *shirku*. Although often translated erroneously as "temple slave," the term probably refers to a class of people who owed service to institutions and the larger community, such as performing corvée labor, but without falling under the legal status implied by slavery; their numerical importance in the general population is difficult to assess. Some could rise quite high in the social hierarchy; at Uruk a few *shirku*s became rent farmers for the temple. Other people fell under the status of *arad-sharrutu* "condition of royal servant," presumably individuals tied to royal service. Membership in any of these classes prevented the sale of a person as slave. Slaves were designated by various terms (*ardu, amelutu, lamutanu*). Large scale chattel slavery was apparently unknown.

9.7.3   Methods of Imperial Control

Babylon replaced Assyria as imperial power in the space of one generation and for the first time in its history controlled territories west of the Euphrates (see Map 9.1). In some areas Babylon simply reclaimed the Assyrian imperial structure. This process is well documented by the finds at Dur-Katlimmu, the modern site of Tell Sheikh-Hamad on the lower Habur River in Syria. There we find evidence for the reuse of an Assyrian administrative building by the Babylonians, the so-called Red House, and cuneiform tablets still written in the Assyrian dialect but dated to the fourth year of Nebuchadnezzar, the year 601. In the Levant the situation is less clear. No evidence has yet surfaced for a well-organized provincial system of governance on the Assyrian model. We simply do not know how the Babylonians ruled the western part of their empire. We have evidence for systematic destruction of a number of sites in Palestine and Transjordan, but also of vassal status being imposed on a number of cities and smaller states of the region. Some have suggested that Babylon loosely controlled Syria and Palestine and raided the region periodically only to collect tribute, but this is contradicted by evidence suggesting permanent occupation. In Lebanon Nebuchadnezzar erected monuments in four separate localities which at times proclaim how the imposition of Babylonian rule benefited the inhabitants of the region. The evidence from Tayma in northern Arabia and the efforts displayed by Nabonidus to secure the region of Harran from the Medes and restore the city and the Ehulhul temple to their former glory certainly reflect a plan to integrate the conquered regions more firmly into the imperial system. Recently textual evidence has surfaced that the temple Ebabbar at Sippar managed agricultural estates in the Habur region, implying some form of colonization.

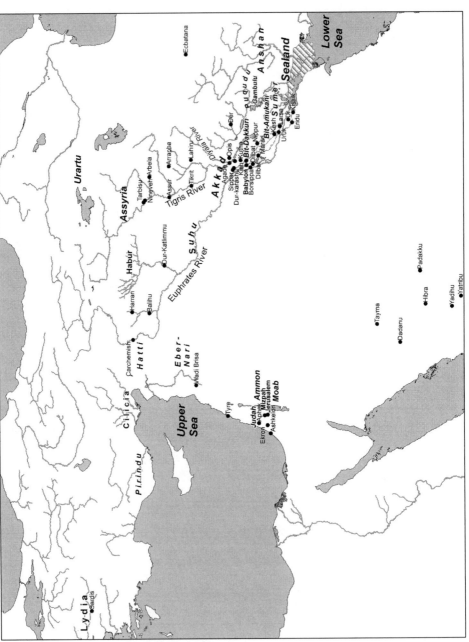

Map 9.1 The Babylonian Empire. Map Design: Stephen Batiuk, University of Toronto.

In their official inscriptions the Neo-Babylonian kings make few references to their Levantine dominions. The Etemenanki cylinder of Nebuchadnezzar provides the fullest description of the geographic reach of the empire:

> In order to build Etemenanki, I imposed upon them the corvée-basket: Ur, Uruk, Larsa, Eridu, Kullab, Nemed-[Laguda], Ugar-[Sin?], the entirety of [the lands of the Lower Sea], from top to bottom, Nippur, Isin, Larak, [Dilbat, Marad], Puqudu, Bit-[Dakkuri], Bit-Amukani, Bit-[Shilani], Bira[tu], Der, Agade, [Dur-Sharruku], Arrapha, Lahi[ru o o], the entirety of Ak[kad] and Assyria, the kings of E[ber-nari], the governors of Hatti, from the [Upper S]ea, to the [Lower S]ea, Su[mer and Akkad], Assyria, a[ll of them], the kings of far-away districts in the midst of the Upper Sea (i.e. the Mediterranean), the kings of far-away districts in the midst of the Lower Sea, the governors of Hatti (i.e. the Levant), Neberti-Purattu (i.e. Transeuphratene), to the sunset, over whom I exercise my rule by the word of my lord Marduk.[3]

The core of the empire is described in detail, with enumerations of its principal localities: first the Sealand (the lands of the Lower Sea) in the southernmost part of Iraq, then Babylonia proper (Akkad) and Assyria to the north. When the list moves west, regions are described in vague terms: Eber-nari ("Across the River"), Hatti (Levant), Neberti-Puratti (Transeuphratene) and especially the term "kings of faraway districts" reflect the hazy perception of those regions in the Babylonian perspective. The mention of both "governors" and "kings" being subjects of Nebuchadnezzar might reflect a dual system of provinces and vassal states after the Assyrian model, but we really lack data on the administration of those regions.

9.8 A Problematic Succession (562–556)

Nebuchadnezzar died in early October 562 and was succeeded by his son Amel-Marduk, whose reign lasted only two years (562–560). According to the Bible, in which his name appears under the form Evil-Merodach, he released the Judean king Jehoiakin from captivity (2 Kings 25:27–30). The Babylon Stele of Nabonidus describes him as incompetent. We find the same assessment in Berossus, who also claims that he was killed by his brother-in-law Neriglissar, who then seized power and reigned four years (560–556). The antecedents of Neriglissar (Nergal-sharru-usur) can be traced early in the reign of Nebuchadnezzar. He is almost certainly identical with the *simmagir* official Nergal-sharru-usur who appears in the *Hofkalender* of Nebuchadnezzar and was present at the second siege of Jerusalem in 587–586 (Jeremiah 39:3, Nergalsharezer *samgar*). In his inscriptions Neriglissar insists on his divine election to kingship, using the same rhetoric as Nabopolassar earlier; he was obviously self-conscious about starting a new royal line. He also claims to be the son of a "wise prince" named Bel-shumu-ishkun. This is probably the same Bel-shumu-ishkun who appears in the *Hofkalender* as sheikh of the Aramean tribe of Puqudu. On the basis of Berossus's testimony some have suggested that Neriglissar had married one of Nebuchadnezzar's daughters named Kasshaya. This is supported by a document from Uruk dated to the second decade of her father's reign which lists her contributions to the temple treasury alongside those of the king and of Bel-shumu-ishkun. Once in power Neriglissar married his own daughter Gigitu to the high priest of Ezida, the temple of the god Nabu in Borsippa. These data suggest a certain degree of fluidity across ethnic and social boundaries among the Babylonian upper strata. The empire continued its expansion. Chronicle 25 records that Neriglissar campaigned to Cilicia and stormed the kingdom of Pirindu, failed to capture its ruler Appuashu and during that same campaign even crossed the border of the kingdom of Lydia, the leading power in Asia Minor. Neriglissar died not long after his return to Babylon and was succeeded by his son Labashi-Marduk, who lost the throne after a reign which lasted only a few weeks.

9.9   Babylon's Twilight: The Reign of Nabonidus (555–539)

According to Berossus, Nabonidus took part in a conspiracy which removed Labashi-Marduk from the throne, after which the plotters agreed to confer the royal dignity on him. Nabonidus insists in a stele found at Babylon that he harbored no thought of becoming king. While one should regard such statements with suspicion, the real power behind the entire affair may well have been Nabonidus's son, the crown prince Bel-sharru-usur (the Biblical Belshazzar), who appears in documents dated to the reign of Neriglissar as court official and emerged as one of the beneficiaries of the coup d'état. Nabonidus claims in his inscriptions to be the son of one Nabu-balassu-iqbi, whom he calls a "wise prince," using the same language introduced by Neriglissar to refer to his father Bel-shumu-ishkun. Nothing further is known about Nabonidus's father, but we have more information about his mother Adad-guppi. Chronicle 26 contains a laconic entry that she died in the ninth year of her son's reign at Dur-Karashu near Sippar. A few years after her death Nabonidus erected at Harran in northern Syria a funerary stele in her honor which claims that she died a centenarian. It also discloses some details about her background. She probably originated from Harran and migrated to Babylon after Assyria's demise, served at the courts of Nabopolassar, Nebuchadnezzar, and Neriglissar and introduced her son to the latter two rulers. Unpublished texts from the storehouses of the royal palace at Babylon and dated to the reign of Nebuchadnezzar mention a "house(hold) of Nabu-na'id," perhaps identical with the future king. Thus, Nabonidus and his family must have been well acquainted with state affairs and court intrigues before his accession to the throne. Other documents from the early sixth century mention one Nabu-na'id invested with military responsibilities, but we cannot be certain that the same person is involved.

   More narrative sources have survived about the reign of Nabonidus than about any other king of the Neo-Babylonian dynasty. These include Chronicles 26 and 53, the latter ostensibly a piece of propaganda emanating from the royal chancery, and the Verse Account of Nabonidus, a pamphlet composed, if not at the behest, at least with the tacit approval of Cyrus after Babylon's downfall. Two other documents with negative views about Nabonidus are the Cyrus Cylinder and the Dynastic Prophecy. With the exception of the Cylinder these sources have survived only in manuscripts from the Achaemenid and Hellenistic periods. The royal inscriptions of Nabonidus also constitute an important source since they yield more historical and political data than those of his predecessors. One peculiarity ascribed to Nabonidus in some sources and corroborated by his own inscriptions is his devotion to the Mesopotamian moon god Sin. Harran was a major center for the cult of Sin and the fact that Nabonidus traced his familial roots there may explain his near obsessive devotion to that god, which came into full view not long after his rise to power. The main sanctuary of the god Sin in Babylonia lay in the ancient city of Ur. In the second year of his reign Nabonidus revived the institution of high priestess of the moon god in that city, although it had fallen into oblivion apparently since the end of the Second Dynasty of Isin. Nabonidus orchestrated an elaborate mise-en-scène to elevate his daughter to that office, waiting for a lunar eclipse which occurred, as astronomers could approximately predict, on the thirteenth day of the month Ululu in his second year (September 26, 554). According to an omen from the astrological compendium Enuma Anu Enlil, an eclipse of the moon occurring in that month signified that the moon god requested a high priestess: "If there is an eclipse of the moon in the month Ululu, (this means that) the (moon) god Sin requests a high-priestess." In conformity with the omen, Nabonidus renamed his daughter En-nigaldi-Nanna, a Sumerian name meaning "the high-priestess requested by the god Nanna" (Nanna is the Sumerian name of the moon god Sin). The name was modeled on the ancient Sumerian names of high priestesses of the god Nanna at Ur, the first incumbent having been En-hedu-anna "the high priestess fit for heaven," daughter of Sargon of Akkad. The consecration of En-nigaldi-Nanna is reported in Chronicle 53 and in a barrel-shaped cylinder of Nabonidus which conveys the antiquarian fervor of the period. Nabonidus even ordered excavations in Egipar, the residence of high-priestesses at Ur, where he allegedly discovered a stele of the Isin II king Nebuchadnezzar I, son of Ninurta-nadin-shumi, on which was depicted an image of the high priestess with her paraphernalia.

9.9.1 The Conquest of North Arabia

Other projects occupied Nabonidus during the initial phase of his reign, notably building work on the temple Ebabbar at Sippar and the fashioning of a new tiara for its patron deity the sun god Shamash. He also visited the southern cities of Kesh, Larsa, and Uruk, where a text records a number of decisions he made concerning the management of the Eanna temple. At the beginning of his third year, however, Nabonidus proceeded on a western campaign that eventually led him to northern Arabia (spring of 553). The Verse Account states that he proceeded directly to the oasis of Tayma, slew the local king, destroyed the flocks of the inhabitants, and established his residence there. Nabonidus claims in the

Harran Stele that he spent ten years in northern Arabia moving back and forth between Tayma, Dadanu, Padakku, Hibra, Yadihu, and Yatribu (modern Medina). Excavations at Tayma have revealed artifacts contemporary with the Babylonian occupation, including cuneiform tablets, a monumental stele with a poorly preserved inscription of Nabonidus, and graffiti in the local language mentioning the king as well as members of his retinue. A rock relief with another inscription of Nabonidus has also been identified at al-Hayit which confirms the identification of the site as ancient Padakku. Religious, commercial, and strategic motives have been invoked to explain the Arabian campaign. However, none of them accounts for Nabonidus's resolve to spend an entire decade there. His stay away from Babylon may reflect a rift between him and influential power groups in the capital. The Harran stele of Nabonidus alludes to internal political discord (Figure 9.3), a fact also noted in the anti-Nabonidus literature produced after 539. Chronicle 26, the Dynastic Prophecy, and the Verse Account also duly insist on the fact that the New Year Festival could not be performed during the king's absence. While Nabonidus resided in Tayma his son Bel-sharru-usur stepped in the role of regent, appearing alongside his father in accounts of royal offerings in temples. He is also seen performing a number of official duties. Building inscriptions, on the other hand, continued to be in Nabonidus's name exclusively. A few documents from Uruk record envoys traveling between Uruk and Tayma, some of them carrying the royal share of offerings from the Eanna temple, indicating that communication between the royal entourage and Babylonia had not been severed.

9.9.2   Geopolitical Upheaval

Nabonidus' campaigns in Arabia resulted in a considerable extension of Babylonian territory and influence. Parallel to these developments, however, a seismic geopolitical change was occurring in Iran and Anatolia. Chronicle 26 reports that Cyrus, the king of Anshan, overthrew his overlord the Median king Astyages in the sixth year of Nabonidus (550–549) and conquered his capital Ecbatana. The Medes had occupied the region of Harran since the city's capture and destruction in 610, when it had become the ultimate refuge of the last Assyrian monarch Ashur-uballit II. Nabonidus very much desired their removal, essential to carrying out his dream project to restore the Ehulhul of Harran, the temple of the moon god Sin, to its former glory. Such concerns are echoed in the Sippar Cylinder of Nabonidus (Figure 9.4).

> In the beginning of my everlasting reign they sent me a dream. The great lord Marduk, and Sin, the luminary of heaven and the netherworld, stood together. Marduk spoke with me: "Nabonidus, king of Babylon, carry bricks on your riding horse, build Ehulhul and cause the great lord Sin to establish his residence in its midst." Reverently I spoke to the Enlil of the gods, Marduk: "That temple

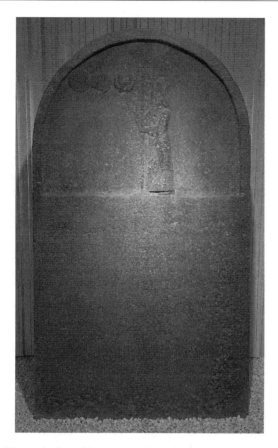

Figure 9.3   Nabonidus stele from Harran. In this stele set up at Harran to commemorate the rebuilding of the Ehulhul temple, Nabonidus alludes to his conflict with the priesthood of Babylonia and gives important details on his self-imposed exile in northern Arabia. The stele shows Nabonidus with the insignias of royalty paying homage to the symbols of the goddess Isthar (the planet Venus), the god Shamash (the sun), and the god Sin (the lunar crescent). The stele is preserved in the Şanlıurfa Museum in Turkey. *Source*: Klaus-Peter Simon: https://commons.wikimedia.org/wiki/File:UrfaMuseumNabnidstele.jpg (accessed April 10, 2017).

which you ordered (me) to build, the Mede surrounds it and his might is excessive." Marduk spoke with me: "The Mede whom you mentioned: he, his country and the kings who march at his side will be no more." At the beginning of the third year they aroused him: Cyrus, the king of Anshan, his second in rank, scattered the vast Median hordes with his small army. He captured Astyages, the king of the Medes, and took him to his country as captive. (Such was) the word of the great lord Marduk, and of Sin, the luminary of heaven and the underworld, whose command cannot be changed.[4]

Looking beyond the rhetoric of this dream report, one is probably not too far from the truth in assuming that Nabonidus had made an alliance with Cyrus and

Figure 9.4   Sippar Cylinder of Nabonidus. This building inscription discovered at Sippar commemorates the rebuilding of three temples, two in Sippar (the Ebabbar of the god Shamash and the Eulmash of the goddess Anunitu), and one in Harran (the Ehulhul of the god Sin). The cylinder tells about the rebellion of Cyrus against Astyages, the king of the Medes. It also mentions that inscriptions of Naram-Sin and Shagarakti-Shuriash were discovered during the work at Sippar, and Nabonidus offers dates for them that exaggerate their antiquity. The cylinder is preserved in the British Museum (BM 91109). Measurements: W: 22.86 × Diameter: 9.2 cm. *Source*: © The Trustees of the British Museum.

even prompted him to rebel against the Medes in the hope of becoming rid of them around Harran. The scheme initially paid off for the Babylonians, since Nabonidus was able to finish the rebuilding of Ehulhul by the time he returned to Babylon after ten years in Arabia. Meanwhile, however, Cyrus developed a more ambitious program and, not content with having unified Anshan, the Persians, and the Medes under his rule, turned his attention to Asia Minor where he defeated Croesus of Lydia, annexing his kingdom with its capital Sardis. According to Chronicle 26 these events unfolded at the beginning of the ninth year of Nabonidus (March to May 547):

> In the month of Nisannu, Cyrus, king of Persia, mustered his army and crossed the Tigris downstream from Arbela and, in the month of Ayaru, [march]ed on Ly[dia]. He put its king to death, seized its possessions, [and] set up his own garrison [there]. After that, the king and his garrison resided there.

It now seemed inevitable that a showdown would happen between Nabonidus and Cyrus, who now controlled an empire stretching from Asia Minor to the Persian Gulf.

9.9.3   The Last Days of Imperial Babylon

Nabonidus probably went back to Babylon in the middle of the thirteenth year of his reign, in the fall of 543. A turnover of officials at Uruk coincided with his return while Bel-sharru-usur ceased to appear in his capacity as regent, indicating that Nabonidus resumed fully the exercise of power. Inscriptions that are datable to the last few years of his reign ignore Marduk and give free rein to the expression of his fanatical devotion to the god Sin, now hailed as "lord of the gods of heaven and the netherworld" and "god of gods." Almost nothing is known about political and international events until Chronicle 26 resumes for his last regnal year. The Babylonians apparently expected a massive invasion in the summer of 539 since Nabonidus ordered the gathering of the main city gods in the capital to prevent their capture. Archival documents from Uruk provide interesting details on the arrangements made by the authorities of the Eanna temple at that time to send the statue of the goddess Isthar (the Lady-of-Uruk) to Babylon and provide for her cultic maintenance. Boatmen on hire took regular shipments of foodstuffs for offerings to the capital, where a priestly collegium in exile attended to the needs of their goddess. A letter from Uruk officials stationed in Babylon even quotes the king asking the high-priest of the Esagil temple: "How much of the property of the Lady-of-Uruk has come up to Babylon?" suggesting preparations for a siege. Persian troops invaded northeastern Babylonia in the month of Tashritu (September–October) and the only armed encounter recorded took place at Opis on the Tigris. On October 10 Sippar fell without a battle and Nabonidus fled. Two days later, on October 12, 539, Persian troops entered Babylon. Nabonidus tried to return to his capital, perhaps to organize resistance, but was captured there. The Dynastic Prophecy claims that Cyrus then removed Nabonidus to another country. Berossus corroborates this statement and specifies that Cyrus exiled him to Carmania (modern Kerman) in southern Iran.

NOTES

1. After Beaulieu 2000: 307.
2. After Beaulieu 2000: 308.
3. After Da Riva 2013b: 199.
4. After Beaulieu 2000: 311.

FURTHER READING

General surveys of the period are by Baker 2012 (archaeology), Jursa 2014 (history, society, economy), and Joannès 2004. Archival sources are reviewed by Jursa 2005, and royal inscriptions by Da Riva 2008. Select corpora of royal inscriptions are edited by Da Riva 2013a (Nabopolassar, Amel-Marduk, and Neriglissar), and Schaudig 2001

(Nabonidus); select translations in Beaulieu 2000. There is no recent edition of the inscriptions of Nebuchadnezzar; see however Da Riva 2012 for his inscriptions in Lebanon. Other important sources are edited by George 1992 (topographical descriptions of Babylon), Da Riva 2017 (historical literature on Nabopolassar), and Da Riva 2013b (*Hofkalender* of Nebuchadnezzar). The expansion in the Levant is discussed by Vanderhooft 2003; the reign of Nabonidus by Beaulieu 1989; the end of the empire by Beaulieu 1993 and Sandowicz 2015. Jursa et al 2010 discuss the economy of the period in depth; Beaulieu 2005 the building of palaces in Babylon; and Beaulieu 2013 the role of Chaldeans and Arameans. The question of the Hanging Gardens and their disputed existence is summarized by Finkel 1988, and treated more speculatively by Dalley 2013.

Baker, Heather D. 2012. "The Neo-Babylonian Empire." In Potts, Daniel (ed.), *A Companion to the Archaeology of the Ancient Near East*. Oxford: Wiley-Blackwell. 914–30.

Beaulieu, Paul-Alain. 1989. *The Reign of Nabonidus: King of Babylon (556–539 BC)*. New Haven and London: Yale University Press.

Beaulieu, Paul-Alain. 1993. "An Episode in the Fall of Babylon to the Persians." *Journal of Near Eastern Studies* 52: 241–61.

Beaulieu, Paul-Alain. 2000. "Neo-Babylonian Royal Inscriptions." In Hallo, William W., and Younger, K. Lawson (eds.), *The Context of Scripture*, vol. II. *Monumental Inscriptions from the Biblical World*. Leiden: Brill. 306–14.

Beaulieu, Paul-Alain. 2005. "Eanna's Contribution to the Building of the North Palace in Babylon," in Baker, Heather D., and Jursa, Michael (eds.), *Approaching the Babylonian Economy: Proceedings of the START Project Symposium Held in Vienna, 1–3 July 2004*. Münster: Ugarit-Verlag. 45–74.

Beaulieu, Paul-Alain. 2013. "Arameans, Chaldeans and Arabs in Late Babylonian Sources." In Berlejung, Angelika, and Streck, Michael (eds.), *Aramaeans, Chaldaeans, and Arabs in Babylonia and Palestine in the First Millennium B.C.* Wiesbaden; Harrassowitz. 31–55.

Dalley, Stephanie. 2013. *The Mystery of the Hanging Garden of Babylon*. Oxford: Oxford University Press.

Da Riva, Rocio. 2008. *The Neo-Babylonian Royal Inscriptions: An Introduction*. Münster: Ugarit-Verlag.

Da Riva, Rocio. 2012 *The Twin Inscriptions of Nebuchadnezzar at Brisa (Wadi esh-Sharbin, Lebanon): a Historical and Philological Study*. Horn: Austria.

Da Riva, Rocio. 2013a. *The Inscriptions of Nabopolassar, Amēl-Marduk and Neriglissar*. Berlin: De Gruyter.

Da Riva, Rocio. 2013b. "Nebuchadnezzar II's Prism (EK 7834): A New Edition." *Zeitschrift für Assyriologie und vorderasiatischen Archäologie* 103: 196–229.

Da Riva, Rocio. 2017. "The Figure of Nabopolassar in late Achaemenid and Hellenistic Historiographic Tradition: BM 34793 and CUA 90." *Journal of Near Eastern Studies* 76: 75–92.

Finkel, Irving. 1988. "The Hanging Gardens of Babylon." In Clayton, P., and Price, M. (eds.), *The Seven Wonders of the Ancient World*. London, Routledge. 38–58.

George, Andrew. 1992. *Babylonian Topographical Texts*. Louvain: Peeters.

Joannès, Francis. 2004. *The Age of Empires: Mesopotamia in the First Millennium BC*. Edinburgh University Press.

Jursa, Michael. 2005. *Neo-Babylonian Legal and Administrative Documents: Typology, Contents and Archives*. Münster: Ugarit Verlag.

Jursa, Michael. 2014. "The Neo-Babylonian Empire." In Gehler, N., and Rollinger, R. (eds.), *Imperien und Reiche in der Weltgeschichte*. Harrassowitz, Wiesbaden. 121–48.

Jursa, Michael et al. (eds.). 2010. *Aspects of the Economic History of Babylonia in the First Millennium BC: Economic Geography, Economic Mentalities, Agriculture, the Use of Money and the Problem of Economic Growth.* Münster: Ugarit-Verlag.

Sandowicz, Małgorzata. 2015. "More on the End of the Neo-Babylonian Empire." *Journal of Near Eastern Studies* 74: 197–210.

Schaudig, Hanspeter. 2001. *Die Inschriften Nabonids von Babylon und Kyros' der Großen.* Münster: Ugarit-Verlag.

Vanderhooft, David. 2003. "Babylonian Strategies of Imperial Control in the West: Royal Practice and Rhetoric." In Lipschits, Oded and Blenkinsopp, Joseph (eds.), *Judah and the Judeans in the Neo-Babylonian Period.* Winona Lake, IN: Eisenbrauns. 235–62.

10

Babylon under Foreign Rule

The fall of Babylon in 539 marks the end of the last native Mesopotamian state. Babylonia then became part of far-flung multinational empires ruled by foreign dynasties, first the Achaemenid Persians (538–331), then the Greco-Macedonian dynasties of the Argeads (330–305) and the Seleucids (304–141), and finally the Parthian Arsacid kings (from 141). Thus, after 539, Babylon has no independent political history, and this closing chapter will cover only the main trends and events affecting Babylonia. The city of Babylon itself retained some significance as a secondary residence of the Achaemenid court, and Alexander the Great briefly made it de facto capital of his empire until his death there in 323. Even the foundation of a rival capital at Seleucia-on-the-Tigris by Seleucus I a generation later did not signal the end of the city, as it continued to live on as religious and cultural center. With the demise of the native monarchy in 539 the city elites of Babylonia assumed the leadership of their civilization. Two abortive waves of rebellions in 522-521 and 484 resulted in the partial displacement of those city elites in favor of groups trusted by imperial authorities. The conquest of the Persian Empire by Alexander, culminating in his triumphal entrance into Babylon in 331, firmly anchored Babylonia in the emerging world of Hellenism. During the period of Seleucid rule Babylonian cities and their venerable institutions continued to thrive and even experienced some kind of revival. However, two decades of political instability and depredations in the middle of the second century, coinciding with the arrival of the Parthians, precipitated the demise of Babylonian civilization, which became extinct in the first two centuries of our era.

Table 10.1 lists Achaemenid kings recognized in Babylonian documents. It excludes those with ephemeral or contested rules in other parts of the Persian Empire. The four Babylonian pretenders of the years 522–521 and 484 have

A History of Babylon: 2200 BC–AD 75, First Edition. Paul-Alain Beaulieu.
© 2018 John Wiley & Sons Ltd. Published 2018 by John Wiley & Sons Ltd.

Table 10.1   The Achaemenid Period: Rulers recognized in Babylonia

Cyrus II	539–530
Cambyses II	530–522
Bardiya (Smerdis)	522
Darius I	522–486
Nebuchadnezzar III (Nidintu-Bel)	**522**
Nebuchadnezzar IV (Arakha)	**521**
Xerxes I	486–465
Bel-shimanni	**484**
Shamash-eriba	**484**
Artaxerxes I	465–424
Darius II	423–404
Artaxerxes II	404–358
Artaxerxes III	358–338
(Artaxerxes IV Arses)	338–336
Darius III	336–330

been included since they too were recognized in Babylonia. They are highlighted in bold characters. Artaxerxes IV was certainly recognized in Babylonia although no documentation from his reign has survived.

10.1   Cyrus Enters Babylon

The last document recognizing Nabonidus was drafted on October 13, one day after the capture of Babylon by the vanguard of the Persian army. Two days later (October 15, 539) the first transaction dated by the accession year of Cyrus appeared at Sippar. According to Chronicle 26 Cyrus made his formal entrance into Babylon two weeks later (October 29), decreed a state of peace for the city and returned to their cities the gods which had been brought to Babylon. One of the first concerns of Cyrus after his victory was to discredit Nabonidus, and this was accomplished within a Babylonian theological framework. According to the new rhetoric, Nabonidus had ruled contrary to the will of the gods, oppressed his subjects, committed sacrileges against shrines, and neglected the cult of Marduk. Even the gathering of divine images in Babylon prior to the conquest, a normal gesture designed to prevent their capture by invading armies, was turned on its head; Nabonidus had brought them to the capital as captives. In despair Marduk searched for a righteous king who could rule Babylon according to divine will, and he found Cyrus, allowing him to conquer his city easily, as the Cyrus Cylinder claims:

> The god Marduk, the great lord, who nurtures his people, saw with pleasure his (Cyrus') fine deeds and true heart, and ordered that he should go to Babylon. He had him take the road to Tintir (i.e. Babylon) and, like a friend and companion, he walked at his side. His vast troops whose number, like the water of the river, could

not be counted, were marching fully armed at his side. He had him enter without fighting or battle right into Shuanna (i.e. Babylon); he saved his city Babylon from hardship. He handed over to him Nabonidus, the king who did not worship him. All the people of Tintir, of all Sumer and Akkad, nobles and governors, bowed down before him and kissed his feet, rejoicing over his kingship and their faces shone. They blessed him sweetly and praised his name (as) a lord through whose help all were rescued from death and who saved them all from distress and hardship.[1]

Formally, the Cyrus Cylinder is a building inscription written in the Standard Babylonian literary language. It commemorates the repair of the defensive wall Imgur-Enlil at Babylon and adheres to Babylonian as well as Assyrian models; indeed, the find of an inscription of Ashurbanipal during repair of the wall is mentioned. But the inscription also assumes the character of a proclamation, heralding the installation of a new regime. The recent discovery in the British Museum of fragments of a tablet with the text of the Cylinder and a colophon naming the scribe who copied it, suggests that the text enjoyed wider circulation than most building inscriptions and may have been used as a tract of political propaganda. The Verse Account of Nabonidus, which shares a number of motifs with the Cylinder, certainly filled the same function. At the same time one must refrain from presentism and not overstate the nature of the Cylinder as the first "Charter of Human Rights," as has been done in the recent past for various political and cultural motives. Modern concepts of freedom are absent from the Cylinder, which does not address such concerns in any perceivable manner.

10.2   A Smooth Transition

The Cylinder claims that the transition to Persian rule ran smoothly. Before the conquest of Babylon, Cyrus is just called "king of Anshan" in the inscription. After the conquest this title is relegated to his forebears and Cyrus himself sports the full array of Babylonian royal titles: "I (am) Cyrus, king of the totality, great king, mighty king, king of Babylon, king of Sumer and Akkad, king of the four quarters." Already legitimized by divine election, he further insists that he belongs to an "eternal seed of kingship," a concept going back to Babylon's First Dynasty. Significantly, Cyrus did not continue the count of his regnal years since his accession as king of Anshan. Rather, he started from zero again as king of Babylon. Some uncertainty persisted initially in archival documents. A number of texts from north-central Babylonia contain a double dating to the first year of Cyrus as "king of the lands" and his son Cambyses as "king of Babylon." These belong to the year 538 and indicate that co-regency was one of the political solutions contemplated at first, but they are few in number. From his accession until his third year (539–536), Cyrus appears in fact with three different titles in date formulas: either "king of Babylon" (*shar Babili*), or "king of the lands" (*shar matati*), or a combination of both, "king of Babylon and the lands" (*shar Babili u matati*) or "king of Babylon, king of the lands" (*shar Babili shar matati*). However, by his fourth year Cyrus' title stabilized to "king of Babylon, king of the lands," which would remain in use in cuneiform documents until the beginning of the reign of Xerxes.

Other changes occurred in the fourth year of Cyrus. Nabu-ahhe-bullit, the "governor of the land" (*shakin mati*) who had been in office since Nabonidus, is no longer attested after 535 and the position seems in fact to have been abolished. In the fourth year we have the first evidence for a large territorial unit called "province of Babylon and Across-the-River" (*pihat Babili u eber nari*). The term Across-the-River, often translated as Transeuphratene, refers to the lands west of the Euphrates. Transeuphratene included most of the non-Mesopotamian territories formerly ruled by imperial Babylon. We know the names of two governors of Babylon and Across-the River: Gubaru (Gobryas), probably installed by Cyrus after his son Cambyses relinquished his position as co-regent; and Ushtanu, who appears in cuneiform documentation during the reign of Darius I. Therefore it appears that Cyrus envisaged the creation of a large province that would include the territories of the former Babylonian empire under the authority of a single governor. However, separate governors are also attested in the documentation for the province of Babylon and the province of Transeuphratene.

Cuneiform archives also provide evidence of an easy transition. In private archives we cannot find one case of an entrepreneur whose business ended or declined because of the political change. On the contrary, some families like the Egibi in Babylon saw their opportunities expand. The same continuity can be seen at the institutional level. The temple archives of Sippar, Uruk, and Borsippa show that the individuals in post under Nabonidus remained in office, and that these positions continued to be monopolized by the same urban elite families. Throughout the reigns of Cyrus, Cambyses, and Darius cities continued to be under the authority of governors (*shakin temi*) who were all Babylonian and stemmed mostly from the families who staffed the temples. The titles and the hierarchy of administrative posts in temples also remained the same at least until the beginning of the reign of Darius I for Uruk, and until the beginning of the reign of Xerxes for Sippar. However, rent farmers at Uruk and Sippar, who were royal appointees and depended on favors from the previous regime, did not fare as well as the urban elites. The rent farming system in fact fell out of favor temporarily under Cyrus to be revived during the reign of Cambyses.

The most apparent and immediate change marking the transition to Persian rule concerns the royal sponsorship of temples and building projects. Apart from the Cylinder, we have only two short inscriptions of Cyrus on bricks from Ur and Uruk. They give a brief royal titulature but do not refer to the rebuilding of a temple; more important, they are the only such inscriptions of a Persian ruler found in Babylonia. The fact that no one among Cyrus' successors emulated him in this respect is significant; the Persians considered themselves foreigners with no obligation to embrace Babylonian traditions. Providing for temples had been the main responsibility of Babylonian kings. All previous foreign dynasties, Amorites, Kassites, Chaldeans, and Assyrians supported temples and left royal inscriptions proclaiming these deeds. The withdrawal of Persians from that role constitutes a radical shift. For the first time in its history, Babylon could not assimilate foreigners into its cultural and symbolic world.

10.3   The Babylonian Pretenders of 522–521

The death of Cambyses in 522 ushered in a dynastic and political crisis known mainly from the rock relief inscription of Darius I at Bisitun and the Histories of Herodotus. According to Darius, whose version has often been dismissed by historians, Cambyses had murdered his own brother Smerdis and concealed the fact. In March 522 an imposter by the name of Gaumata, a Magian, rose against Cambyses and claimed to be that same Smerdis. Cambyses died in Syria on his way to suppress the rebellion. This enabled Gaumata to seize the throne. His reign began on March 11, 522 and lasted until September 29 when he was killed by Darius and his associates in his stronghold of Sikayauvati (modern Ziwiye) in Media, south of Lake Urmia. A number of cuneiform texts are dated to the reign of the false Smerdis, who appears in them under the name Bardiya or Barziya. After his elimination Darius ascended the throne. It seems clear that Darius did not belong to the lineage of Cyrus and Cambyses, who claimed descent from Teispis. Darius, who must be considered the real founder of the Achaemenid royal house, descended from Achaemenes but may have been distantly related to the Teispids, perhaps a collateral branch. Shortly after his accession an unprecedented wave of uprisings shook the very foundations of the Persian realm, affecting almost every province.

One of the first areas affected by the rebellions was Babylon, where a usurper named Nidintu-Bel arose in the fall of 522. Nidintu-Bel occupied the function of *zazakku*, a central taxation official, when he made his bid for the throne. He took the regnal name of Nebuchadnezzar (III), pretending to be a son of Nabonidus; he appears with the title of "king of Babylon" in cuneiform documents dated to his "accession year." The earliest such document is dated October 3, 522. Nidintu-Bel was defeated in two battles, first on December 13, 522 near the Tigris River, and finally on December 18, 522 at Zazannu near Sippar. He took refuge in Babylon, but Darius captured the city and killed him. The last cuneiform document from his reign is dated December 16, 522, and the earliest one acknowledging Darius I after this is dated December 22, 522. The winter and spring of the year 521 saw Darius busy suppressing other rebellions. In May of that year a new Babylonian pretender appeared: Arakha, son of Haldita, who also adopted the throne name of Nebuchadnezzar (IV). It seems that this new insurrectionist claimed to represent the same royal figure as Nebuchadnezzar III; he also posed as son of Nabonidus, and cuneiform documents that recognize him date transactions to his first year rather than his accession year, as if the reign of Nebuchadnezzar III had not ended a few months before. The only difference lies in his title, not simply "king of Babylon," but "king of Babylon and the lands." This hints at a bid for the whole empire rather than one for the mere independence of Babylonia; indeed, Arakha was not a Babylonian according to the Bisitun inscription, but an Armenian, and the name of his father is in fact Urartean. His reign lasted longer than that of his namesake owing to the fact that Darius was residing in Media and Persia at the time of the uprising. Arakha was not immediately recognized everywhere in Babylonia. His earliest document dates from May 17, 521. Until August 27, 521 various places in Babylonia continued to date by Darius. Documents from Uruk show that like Nabonidus two decades earlier, Arakha ordered the shipment of the image of the goddess Ishtar to Babylon to prevent its capture by the Persians. After November 3, 521, however, there are no more documents dated to the reign of Nebuchadnezzar IV, and by November 18 the goddess Ishtar had already returned to Uruk. Darius sent one of his courtiers, Intaphernes (Vindafarna), to Babylonia to suppress the rebellion. On 27 November 521 Arakha was defeated, taken prisoner and impaled in Babylon with 2,500 followers. On December 6, 521 cuneiform documents dated by the reign of Darius I resumed.

10.4   The Reforms of Darius I

The account of the rebellion at Bisitun is the earliest and longest Achaemenid royal inscription. The text was carved in Old Persian, Elamite, and Babylonian. A version in Aramaic was discovered on a papyrus at Elephantine in Egypt, suggesting that the inscription was meant, like the Cyrus Cylinder, as a proclamation. Aramaic and Elamite became the main languages of the Achaemenid administration, as amply evidenced by the archives discovered at Persepolis. The Old Persian script occurs for the first time at Bisitun and was probably created for the specific purpose of writing a version of that inscription in the Persian language. The inclusion of a Babylonian version reflects the importance of the former Babylonian empire as component of the Achaemenid realm. However, contrary to the Cyrus Cylinder, the text shows little continuity with royal inscriptions of the Babylonian empire in style, content, and language. The latter were in the Standard Babylonian literary language whereas the Babylonian language of Bisitun derives mainly from the Late Babylonian of contemporary letters and documents and is influenced by Persian. The Bisitun relief depicts Darius standing in triumph over Gaumata with the other defeated rebels standing bound before him (Figure 10.1). Its iconography is influenced by Mesopotamian antecedents, notably the victory stele of Naram-Sin, presumably in view at Susa at that time, and also especially by the rock relief of the Lullubian king Anu-banini at Sar-e Pol-e Zahab dating to the end of the third millennium. The connection with Naram-Sin runs deeper since the Bisitun inscription resurrects the literary motif of the Great Rebellion. Fragments of a stele showing Darius in triumph over the two Babylonian pretenders were also discovered at Babylon. They reveal the need for a strong reassertion of Achaemenid power. The rebellions took place less than two decades after the fall of Nabonidus, and the two pretenders claimed to be his son. The memory of the

Figure 10.1   Bisitun Inscription. After suppressing a wave of rebellions at the onset of his reign, Darius commemorated his victory on a giant rock relief at Bisitun which harked back to literary and iconographic models established during the Old Akkadian period two millennia earlier. The trilingual inscription (Old Persian, Elamite, Akkadian) is the longest royal inscription produced by an Achaemenid ruler. *Source*: Hara1603: https://commons.wikimedia. org/wiki/File:Bisotun_Iran_Relief_Achamenid_Period.JPG (accessed April 10, 2017).

previous regime and of a glorious imperial era, reflected in the throne name of Nebuchadnezzar adopted by the pretenders, was still fresh and certainly motivated the Babylonian phase of the uprisings.

Darius kept the title "king of Babylon and the lands" after suppressing the rebellions, but cuneiform sources show that the Persian administration became more interventionist. There is no interruption in archives except at Uruk where the Eanna temple documentation stops in the second year of Darius (520). However, we have stray texts after that until the end of his reign and unpublished private archives from Uruk which prove that no disruption took place in the activities of the temple. The apparent end of archival documentation must therefore be attributed to the fact that the documentation we have is a dead archive stored in a room or discarded in 520. Herodotus writes that Darius introduced a number of changes in the administration of the empire, notably that he imposed regular taxes in money to replace the extraction of tribute. The cuneiform evidence does not support such claim of massive transfers of monies from Babylonia to the imperial coffers. However, many new forms of taxation appear in the texts dated to Darius, taxes to be paid in kind, in the form of labor service or sometimes in cash. These forms of taxation already existed in the time of the Babylonian empire, the changes occurring under Darius representing more of an extension and intensification of the previous system rather than innovations. The increased tax burden, especially on urban families, may have prompted the second wave of rebellion against Persian rule in 484. We also see the creation of new posts designated by Persian words such as *ganzabara* "treasurer," *umarzanapata* or *uppadetu* "city administrator" and *databara* "judge." The latter probably refers to officials in charge of enforcing the king's law and decrees rather than traditional Babylonian law. Several references to these laws, called *datu sha sharri* "decree of the king" appear in texts dated to Darius. Significantly, the individuals who held the new offices were all Persians.

10.5 The Babylonian Pretenders of 484

Darius was succeeded by his son Xerxes in 486. In the course of his first full regnal year a new string of royal titles appeared in cuneiform documents: "Xerxes, king of Babylon, of the lands, of the Persians and of the land of Media." In his second year Babylonia experienced a second wave of rebellion. Although Greek writers such as Herodotus, Ctesias, and Arrian preserve memories of the episode, the most direct evidence comes from cuneiform documents. Four tablets are dated to the accession year of one Bel-shimanni, and thirteen to the accession year of one Shamash-eriba. The tablets cover three months (July–October) only. The chronology of the rebellions has long been debated but the accumulation of circumstantial evidence now shows that they both took place in the second year of Xerxes (484). The reign of the two pretenders partly overlapped; Bel-shimanni controlled the area south of Babylon, while Shamaseriba's power base was located initially in the north before he moved south and eliminated Bel-shimanni. The Persians reasserted their rule in October and harsh repressive measures apparently followed. Herodotus claims that Xerxes captured Babylon, abducted the cultic image from the Esagil temple and destroyed the ziggurat. Arrian reports that Xerxes suppressed a Babylonian uprising upon his return from Greece in 479 and as retaliation shut down the temple of Bel, that is, the Esagil. The date given by Arrian can no longer be correlated specifically with the uprising of Bel-shimanni or Shamash-eriba, but if he reports accurate information there may have been another round of agitation in 479 that is not reflected in cuneiform sources.

The alleged punitive measures against the Esagil and the cult of Marduk have sometimes been explained in light of the *daiva* (i.e. "demons") inscription of Xerxes, which states in rather vague terms that he eliminated the worship of demons in a subject country that rebelled at the beginning of his reign.

The identification of this rebel country as Babylonia is far from certain, and even if we accept it, the interpretation of the conflict as religious war seems difficult. However, the suppression of the rebellions had some impact on the organization of temples. Almost all cuneiform archives come to an end in the second year of Xerxes. This phenomenon affects twenty-five archives, private and institutional, concentrated mostly in Babylon, Borsippa, and Sippar. Some of these archives had accumulated since the seventh century, notably the archive of the Egibi family in Babylon and of the Ebabbar temple at Sippar. The end of so many archives at the same time, a phenomenon almost unparalleled in the history of Babylonia, cannot be ascribed to chance. The end of archives is limited largely to northern Babylonia, which had been the center of the rebellions, and it affected mostly urban elite families who held priestly offices in the temples. The logical conclusion is that they must have been the main supporters of the uprisings and were brutally eliminated after the Persians regained control. A parallel trend can be observed at Uruk, which as far as we know did not take part in the insurrection. Between the eighth and the early sixth centuries elite families from Babylon had migrated to Uruk, possibly encouraged by the monarchy. With them came an increased local devotion to the gods Marduk and Nabu, whose cultic symbols were introduced in the Eanna temple and paired with the goddesses Ishtar and Nanaya during the reign of Nebuchadnezzar II. These families controlled some of the most important prebendary offices in the Eanna temple. After the second year of Xerxes they completely disappeared from Uruk, leaving a more restricted group of deep-rooted Uruk families in charge of local cults. The Babylon families were probably expelled from Uruk as part of the retributive measures enacted by Xerxes, whose aim may have been to dismantle the remnants of the former Babylonian state, its religious institutions, elites, and territorial cohesion.

10.6   Babylonia in the Late Achaemenid Period

The archives which survived the crisis of 484, or appeared after that either come from cities that did not take part in the movement (Ur, Uruk, and Kutha) or belonged to businessmen tied to the Persian administration. Among the latter we find the archive of Belshunu (426–400) at Babylon, the Tattannu archive (ca. 505–402) at Borsippa, and the Murashu archive at Nippur (454–404). Belshunu was governor of the province of Babylon during the late fifth century and is probably identical with the satrap Belesys of Greek sources. The archive includes over a hundred tablets which deal essentially with agriculture; the agents of Belshunu leased and farmed out land mostly in the region of Babylon and Borsippa. Tattannu must likely be identified with Tattenai, the governor of Transeuphratene mentioned in the Book of Ezra. His activities and the dealings of his agents and descendants bear strong similarities to those of Belshunu, involving mostly agriculture and tax farming. The most extensive evidence for this type of business comes from the Murashu archive, which totals more than seven hundred tablets. The Murashus acted as intermediaries between cultivators and institutional landowners. They also extended credit to individuals, especially military colonists, holding land grants that were tied to various types of service and tax obligations. The archive thus provides abundant data on the system of military colonies under the late Achaemenids, although earlier interpretations which viewed these documents as witnesses to a new type of organization have been abandoned because of accumulating evidence that similar institutions existed in the time of the Babylonian empire. At some point the Murashu business ceased to be a family affair and went to one of their employees, a certain Enlil-supe-muhur, who seems to have been an agent for the Achaemenid prince Arsham. The fact that the largest cuneiform archives of the fifth century were generated by Achaemenid governors and princes or their subordinates probably reflects the increased influence of that class in the economic and institutional affairs of Babylonia.

At Uruk an important religious transformation happened in the wake of the events of 484. The god Anu, an old deity of Uruk and nominal head of the Mesopotamian pantheon of gods, was propelled to the summit of the local cultic hierarchy with his wife Antu, while Ishtar assumed a lesser position. In Uruk texts dated after Xerxes most individuals already have names honoring the god Anu, but the rise of the god really came to full fruition during the Seleucid period with the construction of two new temples, the Resh and Irigal, dedicated to the cult of Anu and Antu and their divine retinue. By that time devotion to Anu had become almost monolatric. The vast majority of personal names are formed with Anu, while the religious and scholarly traditions of the city had been reinvented to place the god at the very center of intellectual and cultic life. Contrary to the long prevailing view, however, the triumph of Anu was not sudden. The god had slowly risen in popularity during the sixth century, particularly among old Uruk families who tended more and more to adopt Anu names. The expulsion of northern Babylonian families from Uruk, who had been responsible for upholding the primacy of Marduk and Nabu, gave free reins to local families to promote Anu as counterweight to the dynastic gods of the former Babylonian monarchy. Persian authorities no doubt viewed this reform with approbation, since it favored the fragmentation of Babylonia and further undermined the power of the elites which had backed the rebellions of 484.

In the latter years of his reign Xerxes dropped the title "king of Babylon" and abandoned the four-fold titulature he had adopted after his accession. From that point on the title of all subsequent Achaemenid rulers in cuneiform documents became "king of the lands," and this practice continued with Macedonian dynasts until the Seleucids adopted the simple title of "king." The large province of Babylonia and Transeuphratene ceased to be attested with Xerxes, a possible sign of its dissolution. These changes may have reduced Babylon's status even further. After 400 cuneiform sources become very sparse until the end of the Achaemenid period, to the extent that nothing substantial can be said about events affecting Babylonia as well as the general conditions prevailing in the country.

10.7   Hellenistic Babylonia

Alexander the Great defeated the Persian king Darius III at the battle of Gaugamela on October 1, 331, and made his triumphal entrance into Babylon a few weeks later. The dates of these events are confirmed by the Astronomical Diaries. Alexander's victory was to alter the course of history in the Near East dramatically. For Babylonia it meant more than a change of rulers and dynasties (Table 10.2). Indeed, for the next two centuries the country became a province of the Hellenistic world, and continued to contribute to its culture even after the Parthian takeover in the middle of the second century.

Sources for Hellenistic Babylonia are varied. Whereas cuneiform historical texts dealing with the Achaemenids are almost non-existent, several Babylonian chronicles cover the Hellenistic era, although many of them are in a fragmentary state. Astronomical Diaries become much more numerous at the end of the fourth century and they contain a higher concentration of historical entries after the beginning of the second century. Cuneiform archives and libraries have yielded thousands of tablets and fragments, mostly from Babylon and Uruk. These archives begin in some cases under the last Persian kings to end at various points under Seleucid and Parthian rule. The most important collection is the library of the Esagil temple in Babylon, which includes the Diaries and many

Table 10.2   Macedonian Rulers recognized in Babylon

Argead Dynasty	
Alexander III the Great	331–323
Philip III Arrhidaeus	323–317/316
Alexander IV	316–305
Antigonus Monophtalmos (not as king)	316–311
Seleucid Dynasty	
Seleucus I Nicator	305–281
Antiochus I Soter	281–261
Antiochus II Theos	261–246
Seleucus II Callinicus	246–225
Seleucus III Soter	225–223
Antiochus III the Great	222–187
Seleucus IV Philopator	187–175
Antiochus IV Epiphanes	175–164
Antiochus V Eupator	164–162
Demetrius I Soter	162–150
Alexander I Balas	150–145
Demetrius II Nicator	145–141
Parthian rule	141–130
Antiochus VII Sidetes	130–129
Parthian rule	129–128
Hyspaosines of Charax	128–127
Parthian rule	from 127

texts related to astronomy and astrology. Babylon became a major center for astronomical research in that era, as well as a center for the production of historical texts. The late chronicles come from that archive and seem closely related to the Diaries in content and formulation. Groups of administrative and legal texts from the Esagil and its satellite temples begin with Artaxerxes III and continue with several breaks, sometimes only as a trickle, until the early part of the first century. Uruk has produced important scholarly libraries discovered in the Resh temple and the houses of priests and scholars; in addition, hundreds of well-preserved, beautifully written and sealed legal texts shed considerable light on the closely knit world of these priestly families, documenting their transactions in temple prebends, real estate, and slaves. Finally, Greek authors preserve some important information on the political history of the Seleucids, and these data occasionally shed light on events in Babylonia.

10.8   Alexander and his Successors in Babylon (331–311)

Arrian in his *Anabasis of Alexander* describes the conqueror's triumphal entrance into Babylon and the welcome extended by its inhabitants:

> He (Alexander) was already near Babylon, and was leading his force in battle order, when the Babylonians came to meet him in mass, with their priests and rulers, each section of the inhabitants bringing gifts and offering surrender of the city, the citadel and the treasure. On entering Babylon Alexander directed the Babylonians to rebuild the temples Xerxes destroyed, and especially the temple of Bel, whom the Babylonians honor more than any other god … At Babylon too he met the Chaldeans, and carried out all their recommendations on the Babylonian temples, and in particular sacrificed to Bel, according to their instructions.[2]

Arrian is generally regarded as the most reliable source on the life of Alexander. However, his claim that Alexander ordered the rebuilding of the temples destroyed by Xerxes must be handled critically. All evidence indicates that the temple of Bel (Esagil) was a prosperous institution when Alexander entered Babylon. Nevertheless, some cuneiform documents dated mostly to Alexander IV the son of Alexander, record donations of cash "to clear the debris of Esagil," suggesting that he may indeed have initiated repair work on the temple. One interesting aspect of Arrian's account is the encounter with the "Chaldeans," described as the leading priestly class in Babylon. This new meaning for the term Chaldean occurs for the first time in Herodotus, but its origin seems obscure. It is not attested even once in cuneiform sources. Perhaps the priestly classes of Babylon who lost control of the temples after the rebellions against Xerxes were replaced with families of Chaldean ancestry, but this cannot be substantiated. In the Hellenistic and Roman world the Chaldeans were a class of astrologers and soothsayers who traced their knowledge mostly to Babylonia. Indeed, in the latter part of the fourth century the Esagil temple had become an important center for scientific research. Lists recording the salaries of specialists employed by the temple mention fourteen astronomers, fifty lamentation singers, and over a hundred exorcists. Such concentration of knowledge among the Babylonian priestly classes earned the Chaldeans an enviable reputation in the Greek world. When Alexander came back to Babylon in 323 the Chaldeans warned him not to enter the city because of unfavorable omens. Alexander ignored the warning and died not long after. The exact date of his death is recorded in the Diaries as June 11, 323.

After Alexander's death a consensus emerged to grant the royal dignity jointly on Alexander's feeble-minded half-brother Philip III Arrhidaeus and the still unborn child of Alexander with his Persian wife Roxane, the future Alexander IV. Since Philip was unable to govern, the exercise of power passed to Alexander's generals, who fought bitterly among themselves to carve out zones of influence and eventually separate kingdoms. Chronographic documents such as the Ptolemaic Canon, the Uruk King List, the Saros Canon, and the King List of the Hellenistic Period slightly disagree on the tally of reigns for that period. Babylonian documents from the period 330–305 were first dated to the reign of Alexander the Great (330 to 324–323), his count of years beginning when he ascended the throne in Macedonia. Then they acknowledge Philip from 323 until 316. Philip was in fact murdered in Macedonia in the fall of 317 but one document probably from Babylon is dated one year later in his eighth year. This posthumous dating reflects the political instability of the period. The Saros Canon and the Uruk King List assign Philip a reign of six years only (323–322 to 318–317) and reckon the following six years as the hegemony of Antigonus Monophtalmos (317–316 to 312–311). The King List of the Hellenistic Period introduces further details, claiming that after Philip "there was no king in the country" for a period of at least one year (the full number is lost), during which period "Antigonus, the commander-in-chief of the army, controlled the land." The next entry states that "Alexander (IV), son of Alex(ander III, reigned until) the sixth year (of the Seleucid era)," the seventh year of the Seleucid era being the first regnal year of Seleucus I, the year 305. Babylonian documents recognize the regnal years of Alexander IV from 316–315 until 306–305 (his first to his eleventh year). However, between 315 and 311 his dates are used concurrently with those of Antigonus, who receives the title of "commander-in-chief of the army," not of king. The dates of Antigonus are attested from his third to his seventh years (315 to 311) since he claimed that his tenure started from the time of the death of Philip III in 317. After Antigonus lost control of Babylon to Seleucus, documents acknowledge again the regnal years of Alexander IV until 306–305, even though he was assassinated with his mother in Macedonia in 310. In 305 Seleucus assumed the title of king and the first cuneiform document acknowledging his reign is dated the following year (304–303). The document is dated to his eighth year since Seleucus chose to begin his reign retroactively in the year 311–310. The Uruk King List and the Saros Canon both recognize the year 311 as his first regnal year. Thus, 311 became the first year of the Seleucid era.

10.9   Babylon and Seleucia

Seleucus received Babylonia at the new division of spheres of influence which took place at Triparadisus in 320. In 315, however, relations between Seleucus and Antigonus soured rapidly and Seleucus took refuge with Ptolemy in Egypt. In the spring of 311, Seleucus departed for Mesopotamia with a group of followers and troops furnished by Ptolemy. In May 311 he entered Babylon and until 309 vied with Nicanor, Demetrius, and finally Antigonus for control of his satrapy. Diodorus of Sicily preserves a tradition that the Babylonians welcomed him with open arms:

> When he (Seleucus) pushed into Babylonia, most of the inhabitants came to meet him, and, declaring themselves on his side, promised to aid him as he saw fit; for, when he had been for four years satrap of that country, he had shown himself generous to all, winning the goodwill of the common people and long in advance securing men who would assist him if an opportunity should ever be given to him to make a bid for supreme power.[3]

This report of alleged Babylonian enthusiasm may be taken with a pinch of salt. Nevertheless, Diodorus' report coheres with other evidence that the Seleucids courted Babylonian sentiment. The Greek historian and diplomat Megasthenes, a contemporary of Seleucus, revived the figure of Nebuchadnezzar II as one of the great conquerors of world history, probably with the view to present him as model for Seleucus. Berossus also promoted Nebuchadnezzar as exemplum in his *Babyloniaka*, which he dedicated to Antiochus I, the son of Seleucus. The Diaries for the year 188–187 mention that Antiochus III, during a visit to the sanctuaries of Babylon, was shown a garment that had belonged to Nebuchadnezzar. Historical nostalgia for Babylon's imperial past is equally present in the Uruk Prophecy, which presents Nebuchadnezzar, without naming him directly, as a redeemer who will rise again to restore Uruk to its former glory. The text, preserved in a copy contemporary with the installation of Seleucid rule in Babylonia, may well reflect pro-Seleucid sentiments, harboring the hope that the new dynasty would make Babylon again the center of a mighty empire.

These hopes failed to materialize. Regardless of his favorable dispositions towards the Babylonians, Seleucus remained a foreigner and founded a capital city of his own at Seleucia on the Tigris River (see Map 10.1), corresponding to the modern site of Tell Umar some sixty kilometers north of Babylon and thirty kilometers south of Baghdad. The date of Seleucia's foundation is uncertain, probably between 305 and 301. It was intended to become the new capital city and royal residence since Babylonian sources refer to it as the "royal city" (*al sharruti*). However, Seleucia did not remain the sole Seleucid capital. After he annexed Syria and parts of Asia Minor upon defeating Antigonus at the battle of Ipsus in 301, Seleucus proceeded to create another capital named Antioch (modern Antakya) on the Orontes River in northern Levantine Syria. Antioch in fact became the main capital and royal residence of the Seleucid dynasty.

Map 10.1   Achaemenid and Hellenistic Babylonia. Map Design: Stephen Batiuk, University of Toronto.

However, this did not impede the development of Seleucia. Pausanias claims that Seleucus when he founded Seleucia brought colonists from Babylon, but spared Babylon's wall and the sanctuary of Bel, allowing the "Chaldeans" to live around it. Excavations at Tell Umar have uncovered a city with a typical Greek grid plan, but its material culture displays Babylonian elements as well, which might confirm Pausanias on the transfer of population from Babylon. The foundation of Seleucia hastened Babylon's decline. Seleucia became a large metropolis, competing with Alexandria in size and to some degree in cultural importance, while Babylon assumed the status of provincial center, cultivating its religious and cultural traditions but losing international significance. The contrast between the two cities reflects the paradox of Seleucid Babylonia, nerve center of an empire stretching from Syria to Bactria, but with its traditional culture increasingly an oddity in the cosmopolitan world of Hellenism.

10.10   An Age of Renewal

Within this new configuration, however, Babylonian civilization still continued to flourish. The Seleucids granted Babylonian cities some administrative autonomy. At Babylon local authority was exercised by the high priest of the Esagil temple, the *shatammu*, together with the assembly of the temple, the *kinishtu*, often also designated as "the Babylonians" (*Babilayu*). Enough administrative documentation has survived to make a list of *shatammu*s from the third to the first century, although with many gaps. The texts also provide evidence that the function was at times hereditary and held jointly by father and son (Table 10.3).

The institutions of the *shatammu* and assembly of Esagil long predated the advent of the Seleucids. Since no other governing establishment is mentioned in administrative and legal texts from Babylon or in the Diaries until the beginning of the second century, it seems that temple authorities in fact ruled the city up to that time, explaining statements by some Greek authors that Babylon had become inhabited mainly by priests ("Chaldeans"). Seleucid rulers sponsored the rebuilding of sanctuaries, a radical departure from the distant attitude of the Achaemenids. The Ruin of Esagil Chronicle, which dates probably from the year 292–291, describes the crown prince Antiochus removing the debris of the Esagil temple in Babylon with the help of his troops: "The son of the king, his [troop]s,

Table 10.3   The High Priests of Babylon under Seleucid and Parthian rule

Bel-kusurshu	285–284
Bel-ibni	266–261
Marduk-shumu-iddin	258–257
Bel-re'ushunu and Marduk-shumu-iddin	258–252
Nergal-teshe-etir and Bel-ibni	237–221
Nabu-mushetiq-udi	162–161
Marduk-zeru-ibni	138–137
Bel-lumur	127–97
Marduk-shumu-iddin	96–95
Bel-bullissu	93–87
Liblut and Akkudaya(?)	78–77

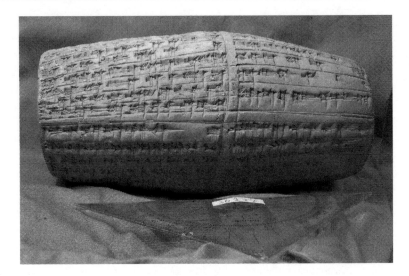

Figure 10.2   Antiochus Cylinder. This royal inscription is the last such artifact from Babylonia. It commemorates the rebuilding of the temple of the god Nabu in Borsippa. In spite of its Babylonian language and outward appearance it displays a number of features that are Greek. The cylinder is preserved in the British Museum (BM 36277). *Source*: Bert van der Spek: https://commons.wikimedia.org/wiki/File:Antiochus_Cylinder.jpg?uselang=fr (accessed April 7, 2017).

his wagons, and elephants removed the debris of Esagil." Work continued for a number of years since the Diaries for the year 274–273 state that in "that year a large number of bricks for the reconstruction of Esagil were molded above Babylon and below Babylon." A remarkable document from Borsippa, the Antiochus Cylinder, illustrates the direct involvement of the Seleucid king in these works a few years later (Figure 10.2). The Cylinder is the only royal inscription from Babylonia written in Akkadian cuneiform after the reign of Cyrus. The inscription claims that Antiochus I laid the first brick of Ezida, the temple of the god Nabu in Borsippa, on March 27, 268:

> Antiochus (I), great king, mighty king, king of the totality, king of Babylon, king of the lands, provider of Esagil and Ezida, foremost son of king Seleucus (I), the Macedonian, king of Babylon, I, when I decided to rebuild Esagil and Ezida, I molded bricks for Esagil and Ezida in the country of Syria with my pure hands (and) with fine oil, and I brought them to lay the foundations of Esagil and Ezida. On the twentieth day of the month Addaru in the forty-third year (of the Seleucid era), I laid the foundations of Ezida, the legitimate temple of Nabu, which is in Borsippa.[4]

The interest of Antiochus in the Ezida temple probably derived from his promotion of the Greek god Apollo as protector of the Seleucid dynasty. Apollo was identified with Nabu, the chief deity of Borsippa. The Cylinder offers clues hinting at this identification, as it repeats several times the epithet of Nabu as *apal* "heir (of the god Bel-Marduk)," *apal* being consonant with Apollo. Therefore the inscription does not reflect, as it has sometimes been claimed, a process of acculturation of the Seleucids as Babylonian rulers, but rather their willingness to meet the Babylonians halfway and select cultural spaces and artifacts through which they could present a native face to their subjects while maintaining their own ethnic identity. Indeed, if Antiochus claims traditional Babylonian titles, he insists on the Macedonian origin of his father and on Syria as the locus of his power, Antioch having become the new Seleucid capital.

All the same, Antiochus I and the other Seleucid kings of the third century demonstrated some genuine interest in Babylonia, a policy which enabled them to co-opt city and temple elites as their local representatives. Some documents allude to a donation of land, originally granted by Antiochus II to his wife and children and eventually passed on to the Babylonians, Borsippeans, and Kutheans, recalling earlier temple endowments such as the donation of Kurigalzu and showing Seleucid willingness to support Babylonian temples financially. At Uruk a building inscription dated to the year 244 informs us that the local governor (*shaknu*), a certain Anu-uballit of the Ahutu family, who had been conferred the honorary Greek name of Nikarchos by Antiochus II, claims to have built and completed the Resh, the temple of Anu and Antu. The inscription acknowledges the rule of Seleucus II but does not mention royal sponsorship of the project. However, the enormous size of the temples built at that time in Uruk suggests either a very wealthy community or some contribution from the state. One generation later, another scion of the Ahutu family named Anu-balassu-iqbi appears with the title of "chief of the officials of Uruk" (*rab sha resh ali sha Uruk*). He and his relatives occupied a number of important posts at Uruk. His son Anu-uballit, who bore also the Greek name Kephalon, succeeded his father in that same position. Stamped bricks have been found in the Resh temple with an inscription in his name dated to the year 202 in which he claims to have renovated the chapels of Anu and Antu in the Resh "for the life of Antiochus (III)." The commemoration being dated specifically to the second day of Nisannu (the first month), one wonders if the inscription and royal dedication were not intended to coincide with the New Year Festival at Uruk. During the Hellenistic period the celebrations of the New Year at Uruk had become almost a replica of the New Year Festival at Babylon, with the exception that the god Anu stood at the center of the celebrations. The ritual also prescribed royal participation, although such involvement had long become theoretical. However, the Diaries do record one instance where Antiochus III played a role in the New Year Festival at Babylon in the spring of 205, proceeding on the eighth day of the month Nisannu from the palace to the gate Kasikilla, the main entrance of the Esagil temple, and making offerings.

10.11 Hellenization of Babylonia

Seleucid recognition of Babylonian civilization found reciprocity among the Babylonians, who became gradually attracted to Greek language and culture. The earliest and most prominent case is Berossus, who was allegedly a priest of Bel in Babylon. The form Berossus probably reflects the Babylonian name Bel-re'ushunu "the god Bel is their shepherd." A *shatammu* of Esagil in the years 258–253 bore that very same name, although identification of this official with Berossus is debatable. The fact that Berossus wrote his *Babyloniaka* in Greek and dedicated them to Antiochus I on the occasion of his accession in 281 shows how much the world of Hellenism had penetrated the country half a century after Alexander's entrance into Babylon. While the *Babyloniaka* remain essentially Babylonian in their overall structure and thematic interests, there is still much in the surviving fragments which caters to Greek sensibility, such as the reinterpretation of Babylonian mythology under a Greek guise or the geographical and ethnographic introduction which has no clear parallel in cuneiform literature but fits the mood of the court culture of the Seleucids, where ethnographers were creating works that made the vast Seleucid realm intelligible to its rulers.

At the same time, cuneiform sources from the Seleucid era remain seemingly impervious to Greek influence. Loanwords are an important indicator of cultural influence. Cuneiform texts from that period, archival and scholarly, display a very small number of Greek loanwords, which significantly all belong to the administrative sphere. They reflect Greek realities imposed by the Seleucid administration and for which no Babylonian term existed. Not a single Greek word from the realm of thought is present. However, we must be wary not to overstate the significance of this fact. By that time the cuneiform corpus no longer reflected the culture of Babylonia, only the intellectual culture of the priestly class. With the exception of texts from the realm of astronomy, it largely consists of copies of traditional texts which antedate the Macedonian conquest. Even texts which are innovative still operate within the parameters set by cuneiform learning. The vernacular dialect of Babylonian, Late Babylonian, had almost certainly died out as spoken language during the Persian period, although it survived in an ossified form in legal and administrative documents and some scientific and scholarly texts as well. Certain cuneiform legal texts were even back-translations from Aramaic originals on parchments. The city elites of Babylonia had adopted Aramaic as everyday language, and they formed only a minority in Babylonia. Many other groups, Arameans, Jews, Persians, Arabs, Chaldeans, and increasingly, Greeks, lived alongside them without necessarily sharing their cultural heritage. However, the documentation written in these languages has perished, and only cuneiform has survived owing to the durability of clay tablets. One isolated and fragmentary text from Larsa dated to the year 225 mentions the "assembly of all officials of Larsa" (*kinishtu sha resh ali gabbi sha Larsaya*). The list of witnesses includes a surprisingly high number of Greek names, presumably all representatives of the Seleucid administration, suggesting that the local sanctuary, Ebabbar, was closely monitored by the royal administration, and probably in the Greek language.

One marker of Greek cultural influence is the spread of Greek personal names among native Babylonians. For most of the third century such names are few and were sometimes conferred by the Seleucid rulers as a mark of distinction upon local elites. By the end of the third century and the beginning of the second, however, we see members of the Uruk citizenry adopt Greek names in larger numbers apparently on a voluntarily basis, possibly to signal their ambition to partake in the political and administrative life of the Seleucid realm. The situation at Babylon is less clear because of the small number of archival texts from that period. A more serious turn in the progress of Hellenization occurred after the treaty of Apamea in 188 between Antiochus III and the Roman Republic. The Seleucids then lost control of Asia Minor and relinquished hegemony to Rome in the Eastern Mediterranean. At the same time the Parthians were threatening to take control of the Iranian plateau in its entirety. Pressed on two sides, the Seleucids turned on the defensive. Antiochus III and his successors Seleucus IV and Antiochus IV tried to consolidate their empire and reinforce its cohesion, notably with a new wave of foundation of Greek cities. It is amidst these efforts that some Babylonian cities received the status of Greek *poleis*, Uruk probably under Antiochus III or Seleucus IV, and Babylon under Antiochus III or IV. A Greek inscription from Babylon dated to the year 167–166 hails Antiochus IV as "savior of Asia" and "foun[der and benefactor] of the city." Greek institutions replaced Babylonian ones as conveyors of Seleucid power. The Diaries mention that now royal decrees were read before the governor of Babylon (*pahat Babili*) and the assembly of the *politai*, the Greek (and Hellenized) citizens, in the theater at Babylon, probably built in the early part of the second century. They were no longer transmitted to the *shatammu* and the assembly of the Esagil as before. The function of *pahat Babili* also constitutes an innovation of the second century and translated the Greek term *epistates*. The transformation of Babylonian cities into Greek *poleis* marginalized Babylonian temples even further. They became living remnants of an ancient culture, an object of benevolent curiosity, but as institutions increasingly irrelevant to the world of politics and administration.

10.12   Parthian Takeover

After the death of Antiochus IV in 164 the Seleucid kingdom entered a period of rapid decline from which it never recovered. A usurper named Timarchus, a former companion of Antiochus IV, arose in Media in 162 and ruled over Babylonia for about a year. According to the Greek historian Appian his regime proved so detestable to the Babylonians that when the legitimate king Demetrius I (161–150) defeated him he was acclaimed with the title of Soter, an epithet claimed earlier by Antiochus I:

> He (Demetrius) removed Heraclides from office and killed Timarchus, who rebelled and who had administered the government of Babylon badly in other respects. For this he received the surname of Soter (the Protector), which was first bestowed upon him by the Babylonians.[5]

In 153 Demetrius confronted another usurper, Alexander I Balas, but was not able to overcome him. Alexander reigned for five years (150–145) and eventually lost his throne to the son of Demetrius I, Demetrius II (145–138), who relinquished all Seleucid territories east of the Euphrates to the Parthian king

Mithridates I in 141. The Diaries for that year contain a long but damaged entry which seems to record the inauguration of the Arsacid (i.e. Parthian) dating era in Babylon in replacement of the Seleucid one. Other passages mention the entrance of important individuals, perhaps the Parthian king himself, into Seleucia and Babylon.

During the first decade of Parthian rule, from 141 to 130, Babylonia became a military frontier between Parthians and Seleucids. Meanwhile the fragmentation of power encouraged the rise of local potentates. Demetrius II confronted the Parthians again in Babylonian territory in 138 but was captured and brought to the Parthian court where he received due honors and even married a daughter of the king. In the same year (138–137) according to the Diaries Babylonia became the theater of further troubles with new actors entering the scene, namely the ruler of Elymais (i.e. Elam) and Hyspaosines, an official of Antiochus IV who established a separate kingdom in the former Sealand, ruling from his capital at Charax on the Persian Gulf. Parthian rule was challenged again by the Seleucid king Antiochus VII Sidetes who tried to reconquer the territories lost under Demetrius II and succeeded in capturing Babylon for about a year in 130–129. By the fall of 129, however, the Parthian king Phraates II had carried out his counter-offensive and was recognized in Babylon by November 129. This marked the end of Seleucid rule in the ancient city. The following year, however, Hyspaosines of Charax extended his power as far north as Babylon. A protocol drafted there records a judgment by the *shatammu* and assembly of Esagil for the appointment of two astronomers, both sons of one Itti-Marduk-balatu who was also an astronomer working for the temple. The protocol is dated May 30, 127 and recognizes Hyspaosines as king. Later in that year the Parthians recaptured Babylon since the Diaries acknowledge the rule of Phraates II in November 127.

10.13 Sic Transit

The reestablishment of Parthian rule after 127 did not go entirely unchallenged. Hyspaosines occurs in the Diaries until his death in 124 and the king of Elymais intervened in Babylonia as well. Starting in the year 126 the Diaries also mention frequent Arab raids against Babylon, sometimes also Borsippa. However, by the end of the second century Parthian rule appears to have become secure. The Arsacid kings established their imperial capital and winter residence at Ctesiphon, a suburb of Seleucia across from the Tigris River. The new metropolis became one of the largest cities in the world and functioned as the political hub of the Parthian and Sasanian empires until the Arab-Muslim conquest. Apart from one isolated legal text drafted at Uruk in the spring of the year 108, cuneiform sources now come from Babylon exclusively. The last administrative texts are dated between the years 94 and 92; they belong to the archive of a certain Rahimesu and deal with the management of temples. The Diaries continue until the year 60–59. Clay tablets with excerpts of traditional cuneiform texts transcribed into Greek letters probably belong to this era. Such texts indicate that, even as Babylonia became a province of the Parthian empire, knowledge of Greek continued to progress among the Babylonians. After all, the early Parthians kings boasted to be philhellenes. During the second and first centuries some Hellenized Babylonians participated fully in the wider intellectual and scientific community of the eastern Mediterranean world, even though the country was no longer ruled by Greco-Macedonian dynasts after 141. The best known case is the astronomer Seleucus of Babylon, also known as Seleucus of Seleucia and Seleucus the Chaldean. He lived in the mid-second century and became the main supporter of the heliocentric theory of the universe put forward by Aristarchus of Samos. During the Parthian era Greek had probably become the second language of Babylonian intellectuals alongside their native Aramaic.

After the middle of the first century BC cuneiform texts from Babylon are all astronomical, the last one being datable to the year AD 75, although arguments have been advanced that one isolated astronomical text from Uruk might be assigned to the year AD 79–80 but this is a moot point. Knowledge of cuneiform probably ceased around that time. It seems likely that excerpts of Babylonian scholarly and literary texts continued in Greek or Aramaic transcription, but these would have been written on parchment or papyrus and all disappeared. According to the testimony of Classical writers the site of Babylon had become deserted by the second century AD. After that the memory of Babylon was preserved mostly in the Bible and the works of Berossus, Herodotus, and a few others. In the sixth century of our era the Neo-Platonist philosopher Damascius, in his treatise on the First Principles, quoted accurately from the list of primeval gods appearing in the first tablet of Enuma elish, the Babylonian Epic of Creation, but this constitutes an exception. The world had to wait until modern excavations in Iraq and the decipherment of the cuneiform script to rediscover the lost history of Babylon.

NOTES

1. After Finkel 2013: 5–6.
2. After Brunt 1929, vol. 1: 275–7.
3. After Geer 1954: 79–81.
4. After Beaulieu 2014a: 22–3.
5. After White 1912: 195.

FURTHER READING

Archival sources are surveyed by Jursa 2005. Chronographic texts and the historical entries of astronomical diaries are conveniently assembled and edited by Del Monte 1997. The fragments of the *Babyloniaca* of Berossus are translated and discussed by Verbrugghe and Wickersham 1996. On the economy of the period see Pirngruber 2017; Boiy 2004 for the history of the city of Babylon; Clancier 2011 for Hellenistic Uruk; Monerie 2014 for the Hellenization of Babylonia; Clancier and Monerie 2014 for Babylonian temples.

Specific historical topics are treated by Jursa 2007 (transition from Babylonian to Persian Empire), Finkel 2012 (edition and discussion of the Cyrus Cylinder), Stolper 1989 (creation of the province of Babylon and Transeuphratene), Beaulieu 2014b (Babylonian revolts against Darius I), Waerzeggers 2003/2004 (Babylonian revolts against Xerxes), Stolper 1995 (the Belshunu archive), and Beaulieu 2014a (edition and discussion of the Antiochus Cylinder).

Beaulieu, Paul-Alain. 2014a. "Nabû and Apollo: the Two Faces of Seleucid Religious Policy." In Hoffmann, Friedhelm, and Schmidt, Karin Stella (eds.), *Orient und Okzident in hellenistischer Zeit*. Vaterstetten: Verlag Patrick Brose. 13–30.

Beaulieu, Paul-Alain. 2014b. "An Episode in the Reign of the Babylonian Pretender Nebuchadnezzar IV." In Henkelman, Wouter et al. (eds.). *Extraction and Control: Studies in Honor of Matthew W. Stolper*. Chicago: The Oriental Institute of the University of Chicago. 17–26.

Boyi, Tom. 2004. *Late Achaemenid and Hellenistic Babylon*. Leuven: Peeters.

Brunt, P. A. 1929. *History of Alexander and Indica*, 2 vols. Loeb Classical Library. Cambridge, MA: Harvard University Press.

Clancier, Philippe. 2011. "Cuneiform Culture's Last Guardians: The Old Urban Notability of Hellenistic Uruk." In Radner, Karen, and Robson, Eleonor (eds.), *The Oxford Handbook of Cuneiform Culture*. Oxford University Press. 752–73.

Clancier, Philippe, and Monerie, Julien. 2014. "Les sanctuaires babyloniens à l'époque hellénistique: Évolution d'un relais de pouvoir." *Topoi Orient-Occident* 19: 181–237.

Del Monte, Giuseppe. 1997. *Testi dalla Babilonia ellenistica. Vol. 1: Testi cronografici*. Pisa and Rome: Istituti Editoriali e Poligrafici Internazionali.

Finkel, Irving (ed.). 2013. *The Cyrus Cylinder: The King of Persia's Proclamation from Ancient Babylon*. London: I. B. Tauris.

Geer, Russel M. 1954. *Diodorus of Sicily vol. X*. Loeb Classical Library. Cambridge, MA: Harvard University Press.

Jursa, Michael. 2005. *Neo-Babylonian Legal and Administrative Documents: Typology, Contents and Archives*. Münster: Ugarit Verlag.

Jursa, Michael. 2007. "The Transition of Babylonia from the Neo-Babylonian Empire to Achaemenid Rule." In Crawford, Harriet (ed.), *Regime Change in the Ancient Near East and Egypt: From Sargon of Agade to Saddam Hussein*. Oxford University Press. 73–94.

Monerie, Julien. 2014. *D'Alexandre à Zoïlos. Dictionnaire prosopographique des porteurs de nom grec dans les sources cunéiformes*. Stuttgart: Franz Steiner Verlag.

Pirngruber, Reinhard. 2017. *The Economy of Late Achaemenid and Seleucid Babylonia*. Cambridge, UK: Cambridge University Press.

Stolper, Matthew Wolfgang. 1989. "The Governor of Babylon and Across-the-River in 486 B.C." *Journal of Near Eastern Studies* 48: 283–305.

Stolper, Matthew Wolfgang. 1995. "The Babylonian Enterprise of Belesys." *Pallas* 43: 217–38.

Verbrugghe, Gerald P., and Wickersham, John M. 1996. *Berossus and Manetho: Native Traditions in Ancient Mesopotamia and Egypt*. Ann Arbor: The University of Michigan Press.

Waerzeggers, Caroline. 2003/2004. "The Babylonian Revolts against Xerxes and the 'End of Archives'." *Archiv für Orientforschung* 50: 150–73.

White, Horace. 1912. *Appian: Roman History, Vol. II*. Loeb Classical Library. Cambridge, MA: Harvard University Press.

Appendix: Checklist of Chronicles

A number of ancient king lists and chronicles are mentioned in this book. The king lists are listed in Chapter 1, section 1.1.1.3.1. The chronicles are listed in the following Table A.1 (chronicles are also discussed in 1.1.1.3.3). The first column in the table gives the number of the chronicle according to the edition by J.-J. Glassner, *Mesopotamian Chronicles* (Atlanta: 2004), abbreviated as MC. The third column gives the edition of the same chronicle by A. K. Grayson, *Assyrian and Babylonian Chronicles* (Winona Lake, IN: 2000), abbreviated as ABC. In the second column one finds the name of each chronicle in Glassner's edition, with the other, conventional name for the same chronicle between parentheses (these names correspond usually to the ones found in Grayson's edition). Throughout this book I still refer to some chronographic documents edited by Glassner by their conventional names rather than by numbers. This is the case for SKL, the Sumerian King List (Glassner's Chronicle 1), the Dynastic Chronicle (Chronicle 3), the Tummal Chronicle (Chronicle 7), the Neo-Assyrian Canon of Eponyms (Chronicle 9), and the Synchronistic History (Chronicle 10). A preliminary edition of the Ruin of Esagil Chronicle, quoted in Chapter 10, section 10.10, can be found on the Livius Web Site (as Babylonian Chronicle of the Hellenistic Period 6): http://www.livius.org/cg-cm/chronicles/bchp-ruin_esagila/ruin_esagila_01.html.

Table A.1 Checklist of Chronicles

MC	Name of Chronicle in MC (conventional names in parenthesis)	Grayson
1	Chronicle of the Single Monarchy (Sumerian King List) = SKL	
3	The Babylonian Royal Chronicle (Dynastic Chronicle)	ABC 18
7	The Tummal Chronicle	
9	Eponym Chronicle – First Millennium (Neo-Assyrian Canon of Eponyms)	

A History of Babylon: 2200 BC–AD 75, First Edition. Paul-Alain Beaulieu.
© 2018 John Wiley & Sons Ltd. Published 2018 by John Wiley & Sons Ltd.

Table A.1   (Continued)

MC	Name of Chronicle in MC (conventional names in parenthesis)	Grayson
10	Synchronistic Chronicle (Synchronistic History)	ABC 21
14	Chronicle of Ashur-resha-ishi I (1132–1115)	
15	Chronicle of Tiglath-pileser I (1114–1076)	
16	From Nabonassar to Shamash-shumu-ukin (745–668)	ABC 1
18	Esarhaddon's Chronicle, Beginning of the Reign of Shamash-shumu-ukin (680–668) (Esarhaddon Chronicle)	ABC 14
19	From the end of Ashur-nadin-shumi to the Revolt of Shamash-shumu-ukin (694–652) and a Few Earlier Reigns (Shamash-shumu-ukin Chronicle)	ABC 15
20	Chronicle of the New Year's Festival (689–626) (Akitu Chronicle)	ABC 16
21	Chronicle of the First Years of Nabopolassar (626–623) (Early Years of Nabopolassar Chronicle)	ABC 2
22	Nabopolassar and the Fall of the Assyrian Empire (616–609) (Fall of Nineveh Chronicle)	ABC 3
23	Chronicle of Nabopolassar (608–606) (Late years of Nabopolassar Chronicle)	ABC 4
24	The Death of Nabopolassar and the First Years of Nebuchadnezzar II (605–595) (Early years of Nebuchadnezzar Chronicle)	ABC 5
25	Chronicle of the Third Year of Neriglissar (557) (Third year of Neriglissar Chronicle)	ABC 6
26	Chronicle of Nabonidus (556–539) (Nabonidus Chronicle)	ABC 7
40	Chronicle of Ancient Kings (Early Kings Chronicle)	ABC 20
45	Chronicle of the Kassite Kings (Chronicle P)	ABC 22
46	Chronicle of the Last Kassite Kings and the Kings of Isin (Walker Chronicle)	
47	Chronicle of the Kings of Babylon from the Second Isin Dynasty to the Assyrian Conquest (Eclectic Chronicle)	ABC 24
51	Religious Chronicle	ABC 17
52	Chronographic Document concerning Nabu-shuma-ishkun	
53	Chronographic Document concerning Nabonidus	

Bibliography

General short introductions on Babylon: André-Salvini 2001, Jursa 2004, Arnold 2004, and Bryce 2016. More in-depth histories are King 1915 (outdated), Saggs 1962 (includes extensive chapters on Babylonian civilization), and Oates 1979. Koldewey 1990 (1925) offers a synthesis of the pre-World War I German excavations which he directed; Unger 1931 is in the same vein but includes extensive textual material, although many of his identifications of topographical features have now been abandoned. In 2008 an important exhibition on Babylon was organized in Paris (Louvre), Berlin (Vorderasiatisches Museum), and London (British Museum); the catalogues include many important essays and abundant illustrations, and cover the history of Babylon as well as its afterlife as a myth (André-Salvini 2008, Finkel and Seymour 2008, Marzahn 2008, Schauerte 2008). Renger 1999, Leick 2007, and Cancik-Kirschbaum 2011 are important collections of articles on the city and on various aspects of the history and culture of Babylonia.

André-Salvini, Béatrice, 2001. *Babylone*. Paris: Presses Universitaires de France.
André-Salvini, Béatrice (ed.). 2008. *Babylone. Catalogue de l'exposition "Babylone" Paris, Musée du Louvre*. Paris: Hazan and Musée du Louvre.
Arnold, Bill T. 2004. *Who Were the Babylonians?* Atlanta: Society of Biblical Literature.
Bryce, Trevor, 2016. *Babylonia A Very Short Introduction*. Oxford: Oxford University Press.
Cancik-Kirschbaum, Eva, et al., (ed.) 2011. *Babylon: Wissenskultur in Orient und Okzident*. Topoi, Berlin Studies in the Ancient World, Vol. 1. Berlin: Walter de Gruyter.
Finkel, Irving L., and Seymour, Michael J. (eds.) 2008. *Babylon*. Oxford: Oxford University Press.
Jursa, Michael. 2004. *Die Babylonier. Geschichte – Gesellschaft – Kultur*. Munich: C. H. Beck.
King, Leonard W. 1915. *A History of Babylon from the Foundation of the Monarchy to the Persian Conquest*. London: Chatto and Windus.

A History of Babylon: 2200 BC–AD 75, First Edition. Paul-Alain Beaulieu.
© 2018 John Wiley & Sons Ltd. Published 2018 by John Wiley & Sons Ltd.

Koldewey, Robert. 1990. *Das wiedererstehende Babylon*. Leipzig: 1925; 5th rev. ed., Munich.

Leick, Gwendolyn (ed.) 2007. *The Babylonian World*. London: Routledge.

Marzahn, Joachim, et al. (eds.) 2008. *Babylon. Wahrheit*. Berlin: Staatliche Museen zu Berlin, and Munich: Hirmer Verlag.

Oates, Joan. 1979. *Babylon*. London: Thames and Hudson.

Renger, Johannes (ed.) 1999. *Babylon: Focus mesopotamischer Geschichte, Wiege früher Gelehrsamkeit, Mythos in der Moderne*. 2. Internationales Colloquium der DOG, Berlin, 1998. Saarbrücken: SDV.

Saggs, H. W. F. 1962. *The Greatness that was Babylon*. New York City: Hawthorn Books.

Schauerte, Günther, et al. (eds.) 2008. *Babylon. Mythos*. Berlin: Staatliche Museen zu Berlin, and Munich: Hirmer Verlag.

Unger, Eckard. 1931. *Babylon: Die Heilige Stadt nach der Beschreibung der Babylonier*. Berlin: Walter de Guryter.

Index

A History of Babylon: 2200 BC–AD 75, First Edition. Paul-Alain Beaulieu.
© 2018 John Wiley & Sons Ltd. Published 2018 by John Wiley & Sons Ltd.

Ptolemy (scientist), 2, 190
Ptolemy I, 20, 259
Pulu (= Tiglathpileser III), 197
Puqudu, 172, 215, 225, 237
Puzrish-Dagan, 55–58, 68
Puzur-Inshushinak, 53
Puzur-Ishtar, 225

Qal'at al-Bahrain, 132
Qatna, 80, 84
Qattara *see* Tell al-Rimah
Qedarites, 216–217
Quran, 163

Rab-bani (ancestor), 203
Rabbilu, 188
Ramses II, 144
Rapiqum, 75, 78–80, 166
Resh temple, 255, 257, 263
Rim-Anum, 100–103
Rim-Sin I, 72, 75–76, 78, 80, 82–84, 99
Rim-Sin II, 99–103, 108
Rimush, 45, 47, 49
Rome, 265
Roxane, 258
Royal Canal, 232
royal inscriptions, 8–9, 18 (as primary
  sources), 34 and 36 (earliest), 38, 42,
  53, 62, 76, 102–103, 105, 111, 113–114,
  132, 135, 137, 144–145, 152, 155, 163,
  171, 193, 199, 201, 206, 208, 210,
  212–213, 217, 220–221, 227, 229–232,
  237, 239–242, 247–249, 251, 253, 262
royal titles, 14, 24, 37, 41, 45, 48, 50–54,
  62–63, 67–68, 72, 75, 86, 122–123,
  127, 131, 135, 140–141, 144, 148, 155,
  158, 163, 179, 184, 186, 197, 201, 207,
  209, 212–213, 248–250, 252–253, 255,
  262–263, 265
Ruin of Esagil Chronicle, 261

Sabium, 67, 72–74, 119
Sabum, 102
Saggaratum, 106
Saggil-kinam-ubbib, 169
Sakikku, 169
Samaria, 198
Samarra culture, 29–30
Samharites, 116, 118

Samsi-Addu, 8, 64, 67, 77–79, 105, 144
Samsu-ditana, 67, 97, 111, 113, 117–119,
  122, 130, 164
Samsu-iluna, 9, 18, 47, 60, 67–68, 92–93,
  97–106, 108–111, 113–114, 119, 127,
  139, 145–146
Sa'muna, 206
Sardanapalus, 216
Sardis, 242
Sargon (of Agade), 9, 16, 41–42, 44–46,
  78, 102, 176, 178, 239
Sargon II (of Assyria), 172, 189, 194,
  198–201, 208, 227
Sargonic Dynasty, 15–16, 22, 77–78,
  102–103 (memory of)
Sargonic (Old Akkadian) period, 41–51
  passim, 251
Saros Canon, 190, 258
Saushtattar II, 142
schools, 18, 35, 53, 56, 62, 68, 87, 102,
  108–110, 119, 127, 130
scribes, 32–33, 56, 108, 183, 194, 222,
  227 *see also* literacy
Sealand (region, kingdom, province), 13
  (definition), 104, 108, 112, 114, 118,
  131, 135, 164, 169, 175–177, 186–187,
  193, 198, 201, 203–205, 209–210,
  214–215, 223, 237, 266
Sealand I *see* First Dynasty of the Sealand
Sealand II *see* Second Dynasty of the
  Sealand
secondary sources, 17–19 (definition)
Second Dynasty of Isin, 10, 12, 132, 134,
  151, 154–169 *passim*, 171–172,
  176–177, 179, 207, 239
Second Dynasty of the Sealand, 12,
  176–177
Seleucia-on-the-Tigris (Tell Umar), 246,
  259–261, 266–267
Seleucid Dynasty, 12, 14, 246, 255–267
  passim
Seleucid Era, 17, 20 (definition), 258
Seleucus I, 20, 246, 258–260, 262
Seleucus II, 11, 263
Seleucus IV, 265
Seleucus of Babylon, 267
Semiramis, 2–3
Semitic (languages and peoples), 4–5,
  43–44, 64, 167, 175

Made in United States
Orlando, FL
04 May 2024

46501003R00170